Mark Milbank
Scrambled Africa

Prime Chirume beef

Published by

LANTERN TOWER

An Imprint of Melrose Press Limited
St Thomas Place, Ely
Cambridgeshire
CB7 4GG, UK
www.melrosebooks.com

FIRST EDITION

Copyright © Mark Milbank 2010

The Author asserts his moral right to
be identified as the author of this work

ISBN 978 1 907040 75 7

Printed and bound in Great Britain by:
CPI Antony Rowe, Chippenham, Wiltshire

By Jack Milbank

AS THE YOUNGEST OF THREE BOYS BY some eight years, I always knew that there was a lot of 'life' lived by my family before I came on the scene. I was fascinated by our family history, and how we had come to live in a small farming community in Southern Africa. Between my parents' divorce when I was quite young and going to boarding school, I had a lot of unanswered questions. *Scrambled Africa*, I believe, provided an outlet for so many of the bottled-up feelings and experiences the older generation has been so incapable of showing.

I think we are getting better at expressing ourselves and this book is testament to that. I remember that, when my mum was killed, my older cousin, whom I love dearly, rang up and said, "Chin up, old chap."

This was typical of how we were brought up as children of colonials.

After years of being pestered to write a book about his life, my dad finally yielded at the age of seventy. I suppose by this time he felt he had accumulated enough material worthy of documentation. Having been involved in three wars and lived in four countries and in the volatile environment that Africa always seems to present, he has written a book that readers can use as a yardstick against which to measure their own life's experiences.

I now live in Australia like so many other ex-Zimbabweans, and I absolutely love it, but following the tragedy that has unfolded in Zimbabwe over the last decade and the complete transformation of my home country from 'the food bowl of Africa to the basket case', I really wanted the next generation of Milbanks to understand what a fascinating journey previous generations had been on for our kids to end up where they are now.

I am eternally grateful to my dad for wearing his heart on his sleeve and telling the world about his life. I can imagine it would be quite daunting to expose your life to be analyzed by thousands of strangers. Thanks too for giving me the opportunity to become an Australian and for instilling in me his fervent sense of adventure so evident in this book. I will always have a piece of my heart in Africa.

Despite all we have been through as a family I am grateful to Africa for providing us with such a colourful life and for developing the strength of character needed to face the challenges of the next seventy years. *Scrambled Africa* takes the reader on a real life journey through the changing face of the continent over the last seventy years. I hope it helps to give people a greater appreciation of how much the world has changed, and how far we have to go in bringing Africa to a civilized understanding of its place in the world.

Thanks

I HAD NEVER INTENDED TO WRITE A BOOK, and if I had known what was involved I do not think I would ever have started. But after my divorce I spent a lot of time with my youngest son, Spratt, and told him stories about my past. "You should write a book, Father," he said. So I did. He must therefore take much of the blame, but he has continued to encourage me and assist with the printing and marketing. However, the thing would never have got off the ground without the expertise and considerable patience of my one time brother-in-law, Richard Holme (aka Holmé), who undertook the unenviable task of putting my jumble of badly spelled stories and shocking grammar into the presentable book you now hold. Incorrect spelling of the names of people or of places is my fault alone. I must also record my thanks to Nikki for her patience while I monopolized the computer and to Sue for her continued encouragement and help.

I have mentioned the names of a lot of people in this book. Some I have been polite about, some I have been pretty rude about! I have consulted some and told them what I am saying but most I have not. To them I apologize if I have been too rude or inaccurate in what I say. This book is written largely from memory and is not meant to be a definitive account of the times I have lived through. It is just my story.

Dedication

Scrambled Africa is dedicated to my family.

ZIMBABWE FARMERS TRUST FUND

Many people have been very sympathetic towards the white farmers in Zimbabwe who were turfed off their farms during the purge earlier this century. A lot of thoroughly good, honest, hardworking farmers lost everything.

No one has been more supportive in England than George Campbell-Johnston of the Zimbabwe Farmers Trust Fund. His organization has helped many destitute families arriving penniless in England.

Nikki and I lost an awful lot as well but we were luckier than some.

I very much doubt that this book will make a huge amount of money, but for every one that is sold one GBP will go to this Trust as a thank-you to George for his help and a pittance towards the ongoing needs of these very worthy people.

Better buy the book for that reason alone!

Contents

Picture Section 1

Picture Section 2

Goodbye England, Hello Africa

N 1948, WHEN I WAS JUST TEN, my English parents decided to leave England where we had all been born, and head for the colonies to make a new life. 'We' consisted of my mother and father, two sisters – one older and one younger than me – myself and two dogs.

My father had fought in the war and my mother had brought up the family in very difficult circumstances. Life in England immediately after the war was not great, so the idea of moving to Africa held infinite appeal.

The journey out on the *Llangibby Castle* was pure heaven. The ship was full of young families like ours leaving cold, hungry, wet, war-ravaged England for a new life in the sun. Most of us were bound for Kenya and would be disembarking at Mombasa, while a few others were going on to Dar-es-Salaam to settle in Tanganyika. The first few days were unpleasant, as there was a biggish storm in the Bay of Biscay and I was predictably seasick, but as soon as we entered the Mediterranean things looked up. We stopped first at Marseilles, then at Genoa, and in both ports we stayed a couple of days and all went ashore. Life on board was great fun and all sorts of games and competitions were organized for the children; there was a swimming pool and a tuck shop and we had regular, very good meals. We ran riot and saw very little of our parents who were enjoying their own form of entertainment.

Soon we reached the entrance to the Suez Canal, preceded by Port Suez and Port Said. As the ship docked it was surrounded by a flotilla of little boats, all full of locals trying to sell everything under the sun. We called them 'fuzzy wuzzies', as many had long curly hair. They were the first coloured people we children had seen. Some were allowed on board to perform special tricks for a fee. These were the 'Gully-Gully' men who, amongst other things, put their hand containing an egg down our shirts and brought it out again holding a little live chicken. Some volunteered to dive off the top deck of the ship and others to swim underneath it. We urged Father to subscribe to these feats and when he and others did so we were able to witness these hitherto undreamed-of acts of daring.

It was very hot going through the canal and I was lying on my bunk with a fan going when my mother dragged me out on deck to see us travelling along the man-made canal which was considered one of the wonders of the modern world. I regret that I did not truly appreciate what I was seeing but when the Suez crisis hit the headlines eight years later I was able to visualize the whole thing better than most. Our last stop was at Aden and again we all went ashore; then a longish haul down the Horn of Africa brought us at last to our destination – Mombasa, the main trading port of the colony of Kenya.

We arrived on September 9, 1948, my eleventh birthday, and I was determined that a usually insignificant part of my body should be the first to touch our new country. Therefore I crouched at the end of the gangplank and touched the soil of Kenya with the little finger of my left hand! It was actually a concrete wharf, but it was thick with dust and after all that is really soil, isn't it?

We were met by my Great Aunt Betty and driven from Kilindini harbour on the island of Mombasa to the ferry, which would take us to the mainland at Likoni. The ferry was exciting, with a lot of sweaty natives crowded on board with our car, and a cranky old diesel engine chugged us across. The natives spoke a foreign language (Swahili, I learned later) and the local Europeans referred to them as 'wogs'. They deferred to us and there was no question as to who got off the ferry first – us.

We drove the short distance back up the creek we had just crossed, but on the mainland side, to where my great uncle had a small beach cottage. Here he greeted us – the legendary F O'B Wilson. He was a large avuncular man with a heavy chin and a pronounced limp from an old war wound. He appeared to be relaxed and jovial, and indeed was most of the time, but he was famous for a ferocious temper and his native name was 'Kitila', which means 'The One Who Beats' – a reference to his methods of correcting the wrongs perpetrated by his native workers.

Great Uncle Frank had come to Kenya in 1910 when it really was virgin Africa. He had fought in the First World War, returned to Kenya and then gone to England in search of a wife. He looked no further than his native North Yorkshire. Indeed, not beyond a few of the better-known families there, of whom it was said: 'Vauxs give you a holler, Peases give you a nod, Wilsons speak to Milbanks, Milbanks speak to God!' Betty was a Pease. She was also tough and had been a great help to Frank in getting the farm, called 'Kilima Kiu', into the shape it now was in 1948. She had also had four children, started an Arab horse stud and shot a lion from her veranda – amongst other things!

My father was to become one of his uncle's workers but was not a native so probably would not get beaten. However, I think he was a bit nervous; F O'B was a renowned taskmaster and did not suffer fools gladly. My father was not a fool but he had little farming experience and none at all under African conditions – he could not even speak the language.

We stayed in Mombasa for about a week while my father picked up a car that he had ordered and dealt with the immigration and customs formalities. Then, while he set off by road in the new car for Ulu, my mother and we children boarded the overnight Mombasa-Nairobi train. The two dogs went with Father.

This then was my introduction to Africa, which was to become home for the rest of my life. Until then life had not been too good, but it was about to take a radical turn for the better.

I am 71 now and will probably be a lot older (or dead) before you read this. I now live in Mugabe's Zimbabwe and was turfed off my farm, as were a lot of other farmers, some seven years ago. Since then I have not had a lot to do, have not had a lot of money, but have had plenty of time, so I started writing this. It is still OK living in Zimbabwe despite the current chaotic Government, and my wife Nikki and I have decided to stick it out, partly because we cannot afford to go anywhere else but also because we are still happy here. I have lived most of my life in Africa, first in Kenya, then South Africa and finally Rhodesia, later Zimbabwe-Rhodesia and then Zimbabwe. It has been an interesting life and a roller-coaster ride from the colonial days of Kenya and the Mau Mau rebellion, through apartheid South Africa, Rhodesia's UDI and bush war, to independence and relative prosperity and finally the purge of white farmers. If I haven't seen it all I have seen quite a bit of it. I hope you will find it interesting.

CHAPTER 1

Privilege and Pain

MY FATHER'S STATED OCCUPATION ON MY BIRTH certificate is one word only – Gentleman. This will tell you that I was lucky enough to be born into the upper bracket of English society. This did not mean that I was born into the upper bracket of English wealth though. My grandfather was well enough off, with a lovely estate in North Yorkshire, but my father was his third son so, in the way of the English custom of inheritance, got precious little. Soon after birth I was shown to my long widowed, aged great-grandmother, who gazed upon my naked, squirming body and said, "If my memory serves me right – a boy!"

My early life was apparently spent in Yorkshire but the family soon moved to Shropshire, where my father was involved in selling paint for some obscure reason: to make some money, I suppose. I have no recollection of him then, or of any paint sales, as the Second World War broke out when I was just two and I did not really get to know him until he returned in 1945, by which time I was eight.

My mother was around, of course, and so was my elder sister, Penel. A smaller version of Penel arrived in 1942 – the result of some army leave. I do remember Sue being born when I was four and a half, so that is probably my first recollection of anything of importance in this world.

Sue was born in Yorkshire as well, which means that we had moved back there from Shropshire. I think that my mother had a horrid time during the war. We had no home of our own and seemed to move around all over the place. She had three small children to look after – the two girls were very difficult but the other child a saint! – very little money, and a continual worry about my father, who seemed to have been in all the hotspots of the war, like the desert under Montgomery and the battle for Monte Cassino in Italy. Simple matters like food were a worry and I know that my mother used a little 28-bore shotgun to shoot rabbits to feed us all. Things like sweets were strictly rationed and we very rarely had any – perhaps one after lunch on a Sunday. The sweet tin was kept on top of a very high cupboard; we could see it but not reach it.

There was the odd children's party but, being very shy, I did not enjoy these at all, except for the jelly which was always a big feature of these gatherings. At one of these parties we were all given a piece of string when we arrived and had to follow this to its end. Attached to this was a small present for each child. Mine was a very small, lead airplane. It was really pretty awful and, being made of lead, never had any hope of getting airborne. I did not want it a bit, but when I picked it up one wing fell off. I was about to wander off and just leave it, when I suddenly realized that I could make some capital out of the breakage, so I held up the broken little airplane and howled. My mother rushed up and told me not to make such a fuss, but I waved the wretched broken thing about and howled louder. That attracted the attention of the hostess who bustled up full of sympathy and gave me a jar of honey instead! This was a rare treat, as such things were virtually unattainable in the war, so my mother promptly confiscated it and we all had to share it. But I had made a point!

When I was about six and still living at some house in North Yorkshire I was sent to a day school in Darlington run by a bunch of frustrated old spinsters who used to whack us with a long wooden spoon for any small crime. My friend in those days was Carolyn Wilson, the daughter of my father's first cousin, Gerry Wilson and his wife Ursie. She was almost exactly my age and we planned to get married, sooner rather than later. Later, would appear to be more appropriate though, as it still hasn't happened!

We did not have a lot of fun, but I do remember going to local point-to-point meetings. Despite these being invariably freezing cold and usually wet, they were often quite exciting. My mother would give us three sixpences each and we could go up to the bookies and back our fancies. There were usually six races, so if we lost on the first three that was it, no more money. This made us back the favourites to start with in the hope that at least one of them would win, which would give us enough money to back some outsiders in the last three races to make a killing. We never did, but we got to know the horses in our area and loved going out and standing by jumps in the country. I have loved steeplechasing ever since and I am sure it dates back to those days.

As we all know, the Second World War ended in 1945, first with the German surrender and then with the two atom bombs and the Japanese surrender. I was only seven at the time, but can remember it quite well. My mother took us all to church for a thanksgiving service. When the congregation started to recite The Lord's Prayer – 'Our Father, who art in Heaven, etc,' – I am said to have shouted out in my piping little treble, "Our father's coming home now!" This, it seems, reduced the entire church to happy laughter.

Our father was of course coming home, but not nearly as soon as we all hoped. It seemed there was a lot of 'clearing up' to do and my mother got quite frustrated at the time it all took. I hardly knew my father then. I had been much too young to remember him from before the war, and there had been just that one brief bit of leave in 1941 (when I imagine Sue was conceived), when I do just recall him.

Quite how it was decided which prep school I should go to, I do not know, but my father was still not home when my mother first took me to The Elms in Colwell near all those Malvern Hills. This was a pity; if my father had been around, I am sure I would have been saved a very nasty start to my school career. I am not really blaming my mother because she was not to know that little boys going as boarders to their prep school do not take cuddly, toy animals to put in their beds. I did not know either, but my father would have known that in those days it was just not done.

I took a toy penguin and fluffy little panda, and when the matron had unpacked my suitcase she put these on my pillow, in a large dormitory in which I was the only new boy. This simple action caused me untold misery for the whole of my first term, as I was teased unmercifully. The Elms was an old-fashioned privately owned preparatory school for boys only; co-ed schools were unheard of in those days. It was owned by the Singleton family. The old man, whom we called 'Ping', was the headmaster for my first term, before he handed over to his son Michael. The other brother, Sandy, was the current captain of Worcestershire County Cricket side. He later emigrated to Southern Rhodesia and I bumped into him again much later on when I went to Rhodesia and he was on the staff at Peterhouse School.

Sometime in the nineties Nikki and I were visiting England, and motoring round the West Country. I suddenly saw a sign to Colwell. On an impulse, we turned in and visited The Elms. A young master showed us round. In a junior dormitory every bed had a small, cuddly toy on the pillow! Such is the decline of empire! Or is the world a softer, kinder place now?

In 1945, most good young schoolmasters were still in the forces, so prep schools like The Elms had to make do with some pretty second-rate old creeps, who were clearly not capable of frightening any Germans but were allowed to take out their frustrations on small boys instead. We certainly had our fair share of them. Bullying was rife, and one was beaten by the headmaster for the most trifling of offences. I was a bit slow, at the age of eight, in mastering my irregular Latin verbs. The solution seemed to be that, if the Latin master could not get the answers in through my head, the headmaster should have a go at beating them into me from the other end. Neither actually worked, and both were painful experiences.

The only Latin I remember is: *Caesar ad sum iam forte, Pompey ad erat. Pompey sic in omnibus, Caesar in is at.* And even this is most certainly spelt entirely incorrectly.

Another favourite punishment meted out for any trivial offence was 'The Colwell Crouch'. This involved being made to squat on your haunches and then hop, frog-like, for any given distance. This form of torture has many other names, but none make it less painful. As you progressed through the school, so you moved to more senior dormitories. Each move heralded an initiation ceremony and one had to endure this on the first night of a new term. I remember some of the more sadistic tortures: your head was held down the loo while the chain was pulled; you had to swing along a high bar while everyone else flicked you with wet towels, and if you let go and fell off you had to start all over again; you had to push a drawing pin the length of the dormitory with your nose. Above all, I remember being cold. There was no sort of central heating, we only got a (fairly) hot bath once a week, none of the windows shut properly and it seemed to rain the entire time. I longed for the holidays and some form of escape.

To start with, my mother was still living on her own in a variety of rented or borrowed houses. I think we moved something like fourteen times from when I was born to the time we left for Kenya, so I was never quite sure where I would be going for the holidays. For the last eighteen months or so, after my father had returned from the war, we did live in one place, as he had bought a very small farm near the village of Cradley in Worcestershire. This was not too far from my school, but that did not make much difference as we were never allowed home for the night during term time and could only go out, very briefly, on three Sundays a term. Most of the time on these Sundays was spent eyeing the clock and dreading the hour when one had to be taken back.

We had one 'treat' a year, and this usually took the shape of the whole school being taken to Worcestershire County Cricket ground to watch Sandy Singleton captain the county side. A full day watching county cricket was initially not very inspiring for a small boy, but it did eventually instil in me a love of cricket which I retain to this day. When the 'invincible' Australian team started their tour of England at Worcester

5

in May, 1948, I persuaded my parents to take me there to watch and was rewarded by seeing the incomparable Don Bradman make a hundred.

Shortly after I arrived at The Elms, in 1945, there was great excitement, as it was rumoured that for pudding that day we were to have a fruit that had not been seen in England since before the war. Silence fell throughout the dining room as this delicacy was produced and soon I found myself eating my first ever banana!

It was sport that gradually made school more bearable. I discovered that I had been lucky enough to be born with a good eye for a ball and could also run reasonably fast. In a boys' prep school these attributes are a far bigger help than being good at Latin! My father had been, and to a certain extent still was, a very good rugger player. Before the war he played regularly for Wasps Rugby Football Club and at one time had a trial for England; he might well have won his cap had he not been injured in the game. Perhaps I inherited some of his ability, as by the time I was ten I found myself in the school first rugger fifteen and was even awarded my 'colours'. This, of course, did an enormous amount of good to my standing in the school and even the toy penguin and panda were finally forgotten.

I still got beaten fairly regularly, but then so did everybody else. Most days there was a short queue outside Micky Singleton's office and there would always be a small group of us peeping round corners to watch the recipients of Micky's attentions emerging from his office in varying degrees of distress. The first request to them would be for a sight of their 'trade mark', which was the blue and green bruises streaked across their bums. There has been much debate over the years concerning the administration of corporal punishment in schools and now, of course, you cannot so much as cuff a troublemaker across the ear. I would guess that almost to a man anyone who was beaten at school would say that it certainly did him no harm. Perhaps a more pertinent question should be... did it do him any good?

The winter of 1947 was one of the coldest on record in England and I can well remember country lanes in which the snow was level with the tops of the hedges. The River Tees in Yorkshire, near where my cousins the Wilsons lived, froze over and a horse and cart actually crossed on the ice from one side to the other. You can imagine what it was like at The Elms!

Before the war my father had wanted to go out to Kenya to join his uncle, Frank Wilson. However, first he got married and then the war intervened so he never went. Despite having bought the little farm at Cradley, he and my mother decided to go and have a look and the cold winter of '47 seemed a good time to go. They flew out in an ancient York aircraft, the full journey to Nairobi taking four days.

They were impressed by what they saw and came back with wonderful tales of wide-open spaces, wild animals, black servants and, above all, sunshine. It hardly needed we children's enthusiasm to help make up their minds to up sticks and go. Uncle Frank offered Father a job on his farm, the Cradley Farm was sold and a passage booked on the *Llangibby Castle* to take the five of us plus two dogs and all our worldly possessions (in a huge wooden crate) to Mombasa.

My last term at The Elms was that same summer and despite making the cricket first eleven and passing at least one Latin exam, I was not sad to bid it good riddance. We all assembled in London at the large Knightsbridge home of my mother's parents, Sir Richard and Lady Butler. It was an exciting time, the only blot being the fact that my little dog was being left behind. This was the Cairn Terrier that I had been given for my fifth birthday; it was called 'Rags', the same name as the dog my father had at the same age. I loved Rags dearly, the first of several dogs in my life, all of whom have had a very special place in my affections. My parents' two dogs – 'Buster', a Springer Spaniel, and 'Tara', an Alsatian – were coming in smart new kennels which would sit on deck. Why couldn't my little dog come as well? I was very upset.

I should make it very clear at this early stage that the then British Government wanted men like my father to go to the colonies. They wanted young men to go out and grow crops to feed a hungry Europe. They needed qualified engineers to open up mines to replenish stocks used up in the war and they badly needed people to occupy and develop their colonies. These colonies were populated by their indigenous populations, but the people had received scant education and knew nothing about running a country, so teachers, administrators, doctors and police were urgently required.

After fighting a bitter war for all of five years, many young men returning to civilian life in Britain became totally disillusioned by the boring reality of it all and longed for more adventure. The African colonies certainly promised this and there were plenty of applicants for all the jobs already mentioned. It was an exciting prospect.

After the First World War some would-be immigrants had been given land as a form of pension. For example, Major Herbert MacIlwaine, after serving with His Majesty's forces with distinction during that war, was encouraged to go and settle in the then Southern Rhodesia (now Zimbabwe). His fare out was paid and he was sold land some forty miles south-east of Salisbury (now Harare) on condition that he developed it for the good of the colony and British interests as a whole. This was land that the British had taken by force from the Mashona tribe some twenty years earlier, and now sold to Major Mac – 'sold', mind you. And who pocketed the money? The British Government, of course. Eighty years later, after three generations of MacIlwaines had given their working lives to the farm and developed a highly successful business, the farm was taken from them by force – no form of compensation was paid to them whatsoever, and now Maj, Mac's fifty-five-year-old grandson is an impoverished immigrant in New Zealand.

None of this concerned me at the time and I do not think that my parents gave any thought to the possible consequences of being white people living in a black man's country. The thought of the blacks ever actually ruling the country themselves was totally inconceivable.

CHAPTER 2

Kenya Schooldays

THE OVERNIGHT TRAIN JOURNEY FROM MOMBASA TO Ulu was almost unbearably exciting. We boarded at about five o'clock, so had just over an hour of daylight, during which time we gazed out of the window as the train slowly climbed out of the coastal plain. We had a compartment to ourselves – just my mother, Penel, Sue, and me. We passed groves of bananas, huge, swaying palm trees full of coconuts, native women in colourful clothes balancing impossible loads on their heads, goats, donkeys, monkeys and even the occasional camel. Cold, wet, war-torn England was five thousand miles away and it seemed like a million.

Darkness fell far too soon, but then there was a new excitement. A turbaned, whiskered old Indian knocked and entered our private compartment.

"Would we like to eat in the dining car now?" he asked, while he made up our beds. Yes, we would, and Sue and I tore off down the corridor of the rocking train to find this exciting dining car. Here a gleaming white tablecloth covered a small table with a bench seat on either side. There was a small bowl of flowers in the middle and a mass of silver-coloured cutlery, all bearing the stamp E.A.R. & H., which I was told stood for East African Railways and Harbours. A waiter in a long white gown, known as a 'kanzu', and wearing a tall red hat with a tassel on the top, called a 'fez', appeared and served us a very good three-course meal.

My mother had a glass of beer and we children some lemonade (no Coke in those days).

Returning to our compartment, we found that the back part of the seats had been lifted up on hinges to make bunks immediately above the original seats and so we had four beds, all with immaculate white sheets, blankets and pillows bearing the logo E.A.R. & H. on them. Curtains over the windows had been drawn and it was snug inside as the train thundered through the African night.

Competition for the top two bunks was heated and acrimonious but Penel and I prevailed. Sue was deemed to be too young and likely to fall out; a decision she accepted with poor grace! Sleep, of course, was impossible, but I suppose we must have drifted off, because in no time we were being shaken awake by the same old Indian who had made our beds and the train started slowing down as it entered a station.

This was Ulu. It was barely light outside and quite cold. I thought that Africa was meant to be hot and it had been hot at the coast. But now we were at nearly six thousand feet above sea level and it was pretty chilly in the early mornings. The train stopped and we stepped out on to a long dusty platform with a small central building – nothing much else. Ulu station was on the boundary of my Great Uncle Frank's farm and also served as a post office, so his address was, Wilson, Ulu, Kenya. That was quite enough.

Two figures emerged from out of the building – a tall, middle-aged lady with crinkly skin and an even taller, thickset man with a wide-brimmed hat covering steel-grey hair. The man was Robin Stanley, manager of the farm, and the lady was Dione Meddlecote, his assistant. They greeted us and we piled into two dusty old vehicles and were driven the twelve miles to the Wilsons' home, known as 'The Top House', as it was on top of a hill.

My father, driving the three hundred miles in the new car, arrived later that day.

* * *

Great Uncle Frank, my father's mother's younger brother, and my father's godfather, was something of a legend in Kenya, having been one of the very first settlers in the Machakos area. He had originally been in partnership with one Frank Joyce, and they had pegged out some forty thousand acres of bush and started developing it together. The first thing they tried was catching the wild ostriches, removing their feathers, and selling them to society ladies in England. The fashion changed and the First World War came along, so the venture was not a great moneyspinner. Instead they went in for milk, a rare commodity in Kenya in those days. However, a row developed over water found in some milk that was being sold, with each accusing the other of committing this heinous crime; also the question of their respective offspring's education became an issue as Uncle Frank had four children and Frank Joyce only one. The row was never resolved and the forty thousand acres split roughly in two, with a huge cleared swathe down the main hill ('Kilima', meaning hill) visible from the main road, denoting the divide. The two Franks never spoke to each other again and neither ever even stepped on to the other's portion of their once jointly-owned farm.

The splitting up of the farm was a tricky matter, so they called in a mutual friend to help. This was the father of Tony Seth-Smith who was later to become a friend of mine. Mr Seth-Smith senior agreed to act as 'referee' in the dispute on the condition that both parties agreed in advance to accept his decision. This they did and he then told one of the partners to divide the property as fairly as he possibly could, because the other partner would have the choice of which portion he wanted for himself.

"You halve, I choose," has been a solution to many domestic problems in our family to this day!

Both Franks went on to become highly respected members of the Kenya farming scene with both, at various times, holding important public positions. My great uncle, affectionately known by his initials,

F.O'B, was knighted by the King for his services to agriculture in Kenya. One up on Frank Joyce?

When we arrived, he was very involved in agricultural politics and spent a lot of each week in Nairobi, sixty miles and two-and-a-half hours away. This was why he needed a manager, and currently this was Robin Stanley. Robin was a very tough Anglo South African, who stood absolutely no nonsense at all from the local black labour. He had a nickname given him by these locals, as most people had, and it was 'Malaputa'. This was reputed to be so bad that no one knew what it actually meant! With Frank away so much, it fell to Robin to show my father the ropes, as it were.

My father had been a major in the war and had run the small dairy farm in England for a short time after that, but neither of these qualifications was very much help in running a huge setup like Kilima Kiu with a bunch of natives who spoke no English. 'Kilima Kiu' (known as 'KK') was primarily a dairy farm, producing some two thousand gallons of milk a day. The milk was pasteurized on the farm and sent by rail, every night, down to Mombasa.

One of the first things we all had to do was learn to speak Swahili. This is, in fact, a very easy language to learn, or, at least the 'upcountry' version is, as opposed to the proper Swahili as spoken by the tribe of that name at the coast. It must have been easy, because even I learned it quite quickly. Keen young civil servants coming out to Kenya for the first time by boat tended to try and learn the language on the way. They, of course, would learn the proper Swahili as taught in a book. This version is often barely understood on the upcountry farms. To ask for a cup of tea one would say, "Lete kikombe moja ya chai."

A young civil servant, keen to try out what he had learned when he arrived in Nairobi, said, "Ulete kikombe kimoja ki chai."

The waiter was heard to mutter, "Ki-rist!"

My mother also got involved, in that she worked in the farm office. In charge here was an old ally of Uncle Frank's, a dour Yorkshireman called

Stan Morgan. Stan had been in charge of the farm machinery and, to a certain extent, still was, but now spent a lot of his time in the office dealing with the extensive paperwork required in so large an enterprise. Apart from machines, Stan's big love was cricket, an interest he shared with his boss. My mother's job was to help him, but she was confused by the three trays on Stan's desk. The two labelled 'in' and 'out' were understandable but what, she enquired, was the one labelled 'lbw' for? "Let the buggers wait," growled Stan.

* * *

We stayed at the 'Top House' for a couple of months before moving to our own pad, which was a series of little bungalows known as 'The Bee Hives' on another nearby hill. It was an exciting time for a small boy of eleven. I had learnt to shoot in England and now my father let me have the use of his lovely little 28-bore shotgun; I spent most of my days wandering around anywhere within walking distance of our house shooting anything that moved! I teamed up with the child of one of the African foremen, who was about my age. He used to follow me round like a dog and carry anything I shot. It was a very early introduction to the master and servant relationship that was so prevalent in those colonial African days. I christened my new friend (servant?) 'Nugu', which means monkey. I was only eleven and had a bossy elder sister and was certainly not used to bossing anyone around, but Nugu accepted that I was boss and did everything I told him, without question. I rather enjoyed the experience. Nowadays one can call one's own child a little monkey, but to give this sort of name to one of the indigenous Africans would probably get you thrown into gaol.

Small children, known as 'totos', not much older than Nugu, were frequently employed in the kitchens of most households. There would, of course, be the cook, houseboy and possibly a maid of some sort as well, although it was mainly men who worked in the house then, but the 'kitchen toto' was an indispensable part of most kitchens. I suppose that

13

it was someone for everybody to blame, as the buck could certainly go no further. Aunt Betty, as I called her, omitting the 'great' bit, employed an extra toto specifically to remove the ticks from her dogs. She would give him an empty matchbox and he had to show her how many ticks he had collected at the end of each day; for these he would be paid one Kenya cent for each one. As there were a hundred Kenya cents in a shilling and twenty shillings in a pound, the toto stood little chance of getting very rich, even from the most tick-infested dog.

There were plenty of horses around and they would all be paraded in front of the house every morning for Aunt Betty to inspect. They would all have their temperatures taken to see if they might be developing the lethal horse-sickness virus. I remember being worried about the grooms, called syces. They all had bare feet and I wondered what would happen if a horse were to tread on their toes. I had ridden very little in England, but now I was introduced to an old, patient safety horse called Poppety and I began to appreciate the joys of riding round an African farm. I was also given a puppy – a small, black Spaniel, daughter of the Springer that my father had brought out from England. Life had certainly taken a dramatic upward turn, but there was a small cloud on the horizon – school.

Reasonably enough, my parents were keen to get me into a school as soon as possible. I had already missed one term with the journey out and settling in at 'KK', but now they found a last minute place for me in a boys' prep school in Nairobi and, reluctantly, I had to go. It was a full-time boarding school called Kenton College. I had been very unhappy at my English prep school, so the thought of starting all over again at a new one where I would not know anyone at all filled me with dread. To make it worse, no immediate place could be found for Penel, and Sue was too young to go to boarding school, so they both remained at home.

Kenton, by colonial standards, had some nice old buildings and was situated in some lovely grounds on the outskirts of Nairobi. It was run and owned by a fairly dodgy priest called 'Binky' Berks and had about seventy boys aged between eight and thirteen. I was eleven by then, so was just over halfway up the school. I was the only new boy the term that I arrived.

As far as I was concerned it was a much nicer school than The Elms, mainly, I think, because it was warm. My chief memories of school in England were of being either cold or wet or both practically all the time. I was ragged a bit for being a 'Pongo', which was local slang for an Englishman, but there was nothing like the bullying that there had been at The Elms. My limited sporting powers were immediately a big help and, after a few practice games, I found myself in the cricket first eleven. I had another most unusual triumph: I came top of my class at Latin! While my father was delighted about the cricket, the Latin bit worried him a lot! It need not have done. It was only because I had already done the Latin syllabus at The Elms and so was a jump ahead of everyone else in my class. As they caught up, I sank back to my more accustomed place in the subject, which was nearer the bottom, and my father could relax.

Quite quickly I made some very good friends, and two or three of these I count as my closest to this day. Perhaps it is necessary to say that all pupils at Kenton were white. While Kenya had no official apartheid policy, it was inconceivable that any blacks or even Indians should attend a European school. Whites in Kenya and, in most of the African colonies, were always referred to as 'Europeans', or at least that is how we referred to each other. What the Africans called us is another matter, but the Swahili word 'Mazungu' was probably the politest.

I remained at Kenton for two and a bit years. We were not allowed home for a single night during the term and could only be taken out once by our parents at half-term for the day. My parents would drive up from 'KK' and we would usually take a picnic lunch into the nearby Nairobi National Park. This was fun, as there was a lot of game there and I was enormously keen to learn all I could about the wonderful wildlife that was so plentiful in Kenya then.

A place was eventually found for Penel in a school, but for Sue, it was decided to import a governess from England. She would teach Sue at home, as well as a couple of other children of the same age who lived in the area. I have never quite understood this decision, but Pam Chamberlain, the twenty-two-year-old daughter of an English clergyman, was dispatched to Kenya by the same route as us and my father was told to meet her off the train at Ulu station.

"How will I know who she is?" he asked, "I have never met her."

My mother gently pointed out that it was unlikely there would be very many young English governesses arriving at Ulu station at six-thirty that morning! Pam remained with us for some five years, might have taught Sue something, fell in love with my father and ended up having a nervous breakdown, but remained a valued friend of the family. Sadly, she died recently and Sue was one of the last people to spend a bit of time with her.

She was a very naïve, young English girl then. Uncle Frank would frequently swim at lunchtime in a round sunken tank in the garden that served as a swimming pool. It was before the days of fancy chemicals and the water was always pretty murky so Uncle Frank would swim in the nude. Pam did not know this and had a habit of standing on the edge of the pool chatting, while Uncle Frank frantically trod water, getting more and more tired.

While school was OK, holidays were filled with excitement. On one of my first school holidays we went on safari – and I mean a proper safari. My father had never lived in Africa before, so, although he was a very accomplished birdshot, he had never shot any sort of African game, or knew anything about it. The rest of the family obviously knew even less. Nevertheless, we booked a hunting block in what is now the Maasai Mara National Park and set off in an ancient Jeep and a new Land Rover, which had been given to my mother by her parents. There were the five of us plus Pam and two of our workers – Buli, who was a sort of cook/houseboy and Wambua, who knew more about mechanics than all of us put together, which was not saying a lot!

It was undoubtedly the most exciting and fun holiday I have ever had. For two weeks we lived in a couple of tents and cooked over an open log fire. The only other person we saw in all that time was the local game warden called Lyn Temple-Boreham. He invited us down to his camp one day, shot a kongoni and tied it to the back of his Land Rover. This he dragged past a pride of lions, and as they came running after us he accelerated, and soon we had a whole pride chasing us. It was magical! There were lions all over the place. One evening I was getting a pot of hot water from the fire, which was only a few yards from the tents, when my mother suddenly said, quite quietly, "Mark, don't move, just stay where you are." Two lionesses were padding by between the fire and our tents.

Another day a herd of impala stampeded into our camp and one jumped right over the top of the main seven-foot high tent. They were followed by two lionesses – into the camp, not over the tent, that is! We were not licensed to shoot any dangerous game, but had an impressive list of plains game on our licence. I only had a .22 rifle, which was probably rather too small to shoot most antelope, but I did manage to get a number of the smaller ones such as steinbuck, duiker, Thompson's and even Grant's gazelle. My father had a .256 and with this shot zebra, wildebeest, kongoni, topi, eland and gazelle.

With all this shooting we had an unlimited supply of meat, so the two Africans with us, Buli and Wambua, could have as much as they liked. They had never known such plenty and gorged themselves until they literally could not walk. We tried to dry what we could not eat, but were not very good at it and made a poor fist of curing what we later learned was called biltong. The resulting smell of badly-cured meat attracted every hyena and jackal for miles round and most nights were accompanied by a cacophony of noise as they competed with Buli and Wambua for the choicer pieces. It was my first real introduction to African game and instilled in me a love of everything to do with the bush, a love that has never left me and which has given endless pleasure over many years.

My father did not stay long as manager of 'KK' but quite soon bought his own farm. This was a section of the farm owned by a crusty old colonel called Claud McWatt. McWatt kept the house and about five hundred acres, selling the remaining four thousand to my father. This portion contained precious little in the way of development, the biggest deficiency being no house. My parents had brought a lot of their furniture from England in a large, wooden pantechnicon and they initially lived in this, while we children shared a tent. Gradually, a three-room mud hut with a thatched roof was added, then the stables, a sort of office/store room/kitchen block and finally a very nice house built in a square with a quadrangle in the middle. All this was done with our own fairly basic farm labour.

* * *

Our first year on 'Momandu', as our new farm was called, was 1951 and this turned out to be one of the wettest ever on record, before or since. It was not the ideal time to be living in a mud hut and tent. I think my parents had a real battle getting the farm started. Milk was the main thing, and we tried to produce as much as we could; this was sold to 'Kilima Kiu' who pasteurized it and sold it on to Mombasa together with their own. 'Momandu' was almost totally undeveloped and in the first couple of years my father sank a couple of boreholes, which turned out to have very little water, built three largish dams, and did a lot of fencing and bush clearing.

I was only there during the school holidays and the financial problems of the farm were the last thing that concerned me. I had wonderful parents and they certainly never let any money worries filter down to us. Most of my time was spent shooting, while Penel and Sue were more involved with horses. I rode very little until my parents and other neighbours suddenly started a polo club in the middle of the Athi Plains. Polo is a rich man's sport and none of us had any money, but it was typical of the attitude of the then Kenyan settlers that this was in no way a reason for not doing things. I was thus introduced to this wonderful sport at a very early age. We were all incredibly bad, but that did not matter in the slightest; it was enormous fun.

At the end of the polo season we reckoned that the ponies had still not earned their keep, so we built a two-and-a-half mile point-to-point course and advertised for other horses to come and compete in a six-race meeting. Amazingly, we got horses from all over the country and held a very successful event. Not everybody wanted to jump the fences we had built, so they were allowed to go round, but this wasted a lot of time as we built a bit of a détour. The Jockey Club from Nairobi sent down a proper tote and the first of several Machakos point-to-points was an enormous success.

Aged fourteen, I rode in the children's race on a hot little horse that my mother had bought in a 'job lot' from a financially-embarrassed riding school. I had no control whatsoever and just let the horse go. He turned out to be very fast and we won easily. It was the best thing that could have happened to me from a riding point of view, as from then on riding – preferably at speed – competed with shooting as my main hobby. The horse was called 'Gunner' and was given to me, becoming the first horse or pony I had ever owned. Gunner steadfastly refused to play polo but I rode him in a number of races until I became too heavy. These races were all amateur, of course, and held in country districts like Molo, Limuru, and Nyeri.

All these places also boasted a pack of hounds, which hunted either reedbuck, jackals or a drag. One year we invited the Limuru pack, under the mastership of Robbie Barcroft, to come to our point-to-point meeting and organize a hunt on the Sunday after the meeting. We laid a drag over 'Momandu' and our dogs were horrified suddenly to find their space usurped by a large pack of hounds. There was so much real game around that the hunt was pretty chaotic, with hounds darting off in all directions after steinbuck, duiker, impala or even dik-dik, while Robbie got redder and redder in the face as he blew desperately on his horn.

Sue.was the keenest on riding of all of us and my parents bought another 'job lot' of young, locally bred, unbroken ponies from the Barclays at 'Menengai'. They were all related but no one really knew their breeding, although a bit of Somali would seem to have been one common denominator. We paid five pounds for the lot. Showjumping was a very popular sport in Nairobi, particularly amongst the young and Sue took this up in a big way. Within three years she came first, second and third in the national junior showjumping championship on three of these ponies. I remember overhearing one disgruntled Nairobi mother complaining to her husband saying, "It's easy for her, with her parents buying all those expensive ponies."

If ever ponies earned their keep, it was these. When Sue was not jumping on them, I was playing polo on them, and when neither of these things was happening they had to race as well! Best of the lot was the little grey mare called Lili Marlene, which I think was champion children's showjumper for three years running. But not far behind were Kelpie and Brandy Snap. As I say, we both played polo on all of them and I remember on one occasion riding Kelpie when he received a hard knock, and I felt I should change ponies in the middle of the chukka. I came galloping off, yelling "Brandy" at the top of my voice, wanting the groom to get Brandy Snap ready to change on to. My shout was misinterpreted by my headmaster, who happened to be watching the game.

Sue was riding Lili Marlene round the farm one day when, in the corner of the paddock, she came across a cheetah with cubs. Mother cheetah showed signs of aggression and Sue wanted to get out of her way, but was trapped in a corner surrounded by a four foot six inch barbed-wire fence. She took her jersey off, hung it on the fence and made Lili jump the fence where the jersey was, so that she knew there was wire. No problem!

Another time, she came across a baby giraffe that was only a few hours old and had been left lying in some long grass by its mother. Sue thought that it had been abandoned and set about trying to drive, and even lead, it home. The wobbly little giraffe was not the easiest of creatures to steer, but eventually Sue did get it back to the house. We raised this giraffe on cow's milk and had it for well over a year. There was always a herd of giraffe on the farm and we thought that the youngster would gravitate back to this herd as it grew up, as it was never restricted in any way. But, no, it seemed to prefer our company and, in particular, my mother's roses. It was very friendly and, as a result, highly dangerous. It would see one of us from some hundred yards away and, presumably thinking we had some goodies for it, would gallop flat out towards us with its huge, long, front legs windmilling around in front of it. It had grown to about fourteen feet by now and it was a terrifying sight seeing it coming. All the horses were scared stiff of it and so were we! I regret to say we eventually sold it to an animal dealer and it ended up in Chester Zoo in England. We visited it once and felt bitterly ashamed.

Another of Sue's pets was a bushbaby, and when eventually she was sent to Limuru Girls' School she took it with her. It lived down her shirt all day, but came alive in the dormitory at night. She fed it on scraps gleaned from the school dining room and for a whole term no member of staff knew that she had it.

We always seemed to have some sort of wild animal as a pet. I usually had a little buck of some sort – steinbuck, duiker or Tommy (Thompson's gazelle). Then there were mongooses, monkeys, a baby cheetah, and a crested crane called 'Derek', which used to perch on the ballcock which was supposed to stop the water tank from overflowing. This was on top of a high tower and, with precious water overflowing in all directions, it was impossible to persuade Derek to move.

When my father was in Nairobi one day, the herdboy came running up to the house to say that wild dogs were attacking the calves (by wild dogs I mean the Cape Hunting Dog or Painted Wolf). These lovely animals are one of the most endangered species in Africa now, but then I happily went out and shot several of them; I was an immediate hero in the eyes of the herdboy and, when he returned from Nairobi, my father.

It was during this time that I really started to get to know my father. He was quite a strict old-fashioned type but had an excellent sense of humour. Sue tested this to its limit once. As he was about to sit down for lunch, she pulled away the chair that he was about to sit on, resulting in him landing hard and very painfully on his coccyx. Sue's scream of mirth was quickly silenced when she saw my father's face.

We used to do a lot of shooting together, him with his 12-bore and me with a 28-bore that had originally been given to him by his father. Just the two of us and our dogs, my little black Spaniel called 'Bloomer' and his Springer, 'Buster'. We seldom shot a lot, as we did not start until the farm workers knocked off at five o'clock. Our quarry was partridges (really a small type of francolin), yellowneck (a larger type of francolin) and particularly guineafowl. The first two were comparatively easy to shoot, as they would sit tight in the long grass, enabling our dogs to flush them in front of us. Guineafowl run and only fly as a last resort so were much harder to shoot. After one very frustrating evening trying to catch up with the elusive birds, we were driving back home in an open jeep as dusk fell, when, on rounding a corner, there running down the middle of the road was a flock of some fifty guineafowl. The temptation was too much: we loaded quickly and fired both barrels at the bobbing heads of the birds. It was slaughter! We picked up seventeen dead guineafowl. My father was immediately mortified at what he had done and quickly explained to me that this sort of thing was not exactly sporting and added that I should not tell anyone how we had come to shoot so many birds. I didn't, and it was exciting to share a secret, albeit a slightly disgraceful one, with my father.

Another time one of the cattle herdboys came running up to the house to say that a leopard had been caught in a gin trap set for it. My father took his 12-bore loaded with SSG (or buckshot) to shoot it and I asked to come along as well. As we got close, we suddenly saw the leopard's head above some long grass. At the same time the leopard saw us and, with a ferocious growl, launched itself at us. The trap round its leg immediately jerked it back and my father had no difficulty dispatching it with a shot in the head. When we went up to it we discovered that the wretched leopard had eaten – and I mean eaten – its entire left foot beneath the trap and it was being held by just a slither of skin. If we had arrived on the scene five minutes later there would have been no leopard in the trap but a very angry, badly hurt leopard waiting in ambush for us.

With this sort of home life, going back to school was always a nightmare. My time at Kenton was drawing to a close and a decision had to be taken as to where I should go for my secondary education. There was no equivalent of an English public school in Kenya, just a government secondary school called the Prince of Wales and a brand new one called the Duke of York. Both were, of course, for whites only and there was nothing wrong with them. However, my mother thought that her little boy should be properly educated at an English public school – preferably Eton. Her little boy had other ideas! The thought of going back to England and another school there made me almost physically sick. I sought support from my father and, amongst other things, pointed out that Eton would cost him a lot of money and so would the airfares backwards and forwards, and a local government school would be virtually free. Luckily, he did not take a lot of persuading and my mother withdrew her case with good grace.

During my last term at Kenton we played hockey, a game I had not played in England. It was a big game in Kenya and, played on the hard, fast murram (a type of earthy gravel) pitches, was a lot of fun. I got into the Kenton first eleven and one of our games was against the Colts team of the new secondary school – the Duke of York. The buildings of this school were not ready for the first intake of boys so they were given temporary accommodation at Government House– no less! Our hockey match was not on a hard, fast murram pitch but on the very bumpy lawn, which was usually used to accommodate garden parties. The boys we were playing were slightly older than us and tended to hit the ball very hard. One clearance from their back rose like a rocket and hit me smack between the eyes. I dropped like a stone and was carried unconscious into Government House.

This experience did not prevent me from being enrolled to go to the Duke of York when I left Kenton. I was one of a batch of only the third intake to that school, so the oldest seniors were only, in fact, two years older than me at thirteen. The school had moved from Government House by now and was installed at its planned site along the Ngong road, some ten miles out of Nairobi. It did not have the tradition of Eton. It was a brand new school, but the staff had been carefully selected and already there was a good friendly atmosphere. The headmaster was called George James, nicknamed 'Pansy' for some reason that I never discovered. He was a very nice man and just what was needed to start a new school.

The holidays before I went to the Duke of York I was invited to join a bunch of Kenton friends on a fishing trip up Mount Kenya. I was not (and still am not) a great fisherman, but the idea seemed like fun and I accepted. It was all organized by the Hopcraft family and I imagine that I was asked because I was friendly with their son, David, or 'Dopey', as we called him. Fortunately, John Byng-Hall and John Clarke had been invited as well, because the fishing trip turned out to be a little more complex than just trying to catch some rainbow trout in the lovely mountain streams.

There were probably thirty or forty of us altogether – adults and boys – and we all slept in tents in a glade in the forest. Every morning a bugle would sound at six o'clock. On the first morning I assumed that this was to get us out of bed and ready for the day's excitements, so out I jumped. But no, we were not meant to get up at all but were meant to lie in bed for a further half hour and reflect on life, with particular emphasis on how we could please God during the coming day. This was OK I suppose, but I chafed a bit at not being allowed to get up and get on with the day. Worse was to follow though. Every evening, while sitting round a campfire, we were encouraged to stand up and tell everybody else what our thoughts had been during that 'quiet half hour'. The two Johns and I would sit together in miserable silence dreading being picked on. Most people did get up and have their say but, thankfully, we were never forced to. Nor were we asked on any more 'fishing trips'. It turned out that the Hopcraft and Barham families were big into the Moral Rearmament (MRA) movement and followers of the up-and-coming American evangelist, Billy Graham. They were looking for new recruits, but did not recruit us. Ken Barham went on to become head boy at the Duke of York before ending up as Bishop of Rwanda – his 'half hour' thoughts must have been purer than mine.

Several of my friends from Kenton went on with me to the Duke of York and I was delighted to discover that my main friend, John Byng-Hall, was in the same house as me. This was Lugard, named after an early British explorer in East Africa. There were only four houses at that stage, the others being Kirk, after another explorer, Delamere, after a very prominent early Kenyan settler, and Mitchell, after the current Governor of the colony, who had initially lent the school his house.

I never liked going back to school, but I must admit that, so long as I had to go, the 'Duke-o', as it became known, was not too bad. There were lovely extensive grounds, a big emphasis was put on sport and we were allowed quite a lot of freedom. Our housemaster was one Harry Hesketh, who was also the master in charge of cricket. Harry was a happy, laid-back soul, and when I eventually became captain of cricket he would invite me down to his house and pour me a glass of beer while we discussed the team.

CHAPTER 3

Duke-o

THERE WERE THREE STREAMS FOR EACH YEAR at the Duke of York: A, B and G (why G and not C, I never discovered). It took four years before you sat a Cambridge School Certificate exam and another two if you wanted to sit the higher version. This would mean six years at the school and as I was nearly thirteen when I first went it seemed a dauntingly long time. I was in the A stream, meaning that I was rated in the top third of that year intelligence-wise! Only just, I might add, as I was always near the bottom in the class of about twenty-five. My friend John Byng-Hall was so bright that he went straight into form 2A and came top of that. It is no coincidence that he went on to become a highly qualified doctor and a specialist in child and family therapy.

It was a good school, modelled on the English public school system and staffed by some excellent teachers, who had for the most part come out from England. Latin was high on the curriculum and we had a delightfully eccentric Latin master called Tom Evans, or 'Television' to us, as his initials were TLE. He wrote the school song – in Latin! We all had to learn to sing it and at speech day we all belted it out with great fervour. This both impressed and confused one new parent who, on emerging from the school hall, was heard to say, "That was a very impressive service, but why did they have to sing the school song in Swahili?"

Luckily, while not an academic I could more than hold my own at sport. At a boys' school this is an enormous advantage and, quite unfairly, the leading athletes or sportsmen in the school are the big heroes, while boys with equal or greater talents in other fields have to wait until later in life for these qualities to be recognized. This did not particularly worry me at the time though, and as the school was so new I was able to play in the first teams of most sports for two or even three years.

Our matches were invariably against men's club sides, as the only other school opponent was the Prince of Wales, which always provided the big game of the term. Once we took an athletics team to run against the all-African school called the Alliance High School. This was long before Kenyan runners became world famous distance runners, but we knew that they were pretty good. I fancied myself as a miler, so I and two others were pitted against three Africans running in bare feet. To be fair to us, I think they were considerably older than us, but we only saw them twice during the race – once at the start and again as they passed us on their fourth and last lap as we were just completing our third! They were all called 'Kip' something or other and at least one went on to win a gold medal at the Mexico Olympics. It was a salutary experience.

Cricket and rugger were important games but probably the most important was hockey. This was a game at which Kenya excelled, mainly because of the large Indian community, who were masters of the stick-work involved. I thoroughly enjoyed the game and in my last year was in the team which won the Craig Cup for the school. This was a prestigious competition open to all European clubs and the two main schools – us and the Prince of Wales. It was played on a knockout basis, so the final was a very big occasion, with the whole school transported to a stadium in the middle of Nairobi to cheer us on. My parents even drove up from the farm for the event. Our win was a huge boost to the new school and every member of the team received their 'colours'. Significantly, the competition was only open to European clubs. The best clubs were undoubtedly the Indian ones and our coach had been quite cunning in organizing matches for us against these before the start of the Craig Cup. The only way to beat an Indian side, who were mainly Sikhs, was to knock their turbans off. Sikhs never cut their hair and the long silky locks exposed by the removal of a turban rendered the player useless for some minutes until he could get it wound on again.

Our coach was called Brian Norman, or 'Bung-eye' to us, since he only had one eye. He was a very good player himself, despite this defect, and an excellent hockey coach. However, his main job at the school was to teach chemistry. If he was good at hockey, he was bad at chemistry – very bad. I was also very bad at chemistry and dreaded Monday mornings when we had a double chemistry period and invariably a written test on what we should have been swotting up over the weekend. This, I suspected, was to give Bung-eye time to collect his thoughts after the weekend. The fact that I had been helping his side win the ruddy Craig Cup and not learning about chemistry was no excuse. I was consistently last in the class and always failed the test. I think that it is why I still sleep badly on Sunday nights; subconsciously I am worrying about the chemistry test! I was really beyond help as far as chemistry was concerned, and certainly beyond Bung-eye's help, but John Byng was good at the subject and wanted to get better. He certainly was not going to do that thanks to Bung-eye. I had a study next door to Byng and during evening 'prep' it was a common occurrence to witness Bung-eye, with a hunted look on his face, hurrying into Byng's study. When I asked Byng what it was all about he told me that he was helping Bung-eye sort out something! Byng went on to get distinctions in chemistry – and every other subject and it was probably his help that enabled Bung-eye to keep his job.

Bung-eye had a very pretty wife and if he had a problem keeping his job he also had a problem keeping his wife. She was frequently disappearing with other men. This was, of course, great scandal for us boys. We were not meant to know about it but the mother of a boy in my dormitory was also on the staff. She was French and, as such, enjoyed this sort of thing, keeping her son fully informed as to its progress. He imparted this knowledge to us. I remember being taken out from school by my parents to attend the Royal Agricultural Show and filling them in on the latest gossip. Shortly after, we happened to bump into the headmaster, George James (Pansy) who was friendly with my parents. They stopped and chatted and jokingly my parents mentioned the Bung-eye scandal. Pansy was flabbergasted.

"How on earth do you know about that?" he exclaimed, "I have only just heard about it myself."

As at Kenton, we were never allowed out for the night but could be taken out by our parents for the day on three occasions during the term. However, in my last year, when I had reached the dizzy height of school prefect, I was allowed out any Sunday as long as I was back for chapel in the evening. This was great. John Byng-Hall was also allowed out, as well as a couple of other contemporaries: John Channer, with whom I shared a study, John Clarke and Michael Pitt-Moore, my main running rival. Mike had one enormous advantage, which made his friendship worth cultivating. He was the only son of a widowed, doting mother who had given him an ancient Land Rover, which he kept at school. Any Sunday when there was nothing else happening, the three Johns, Mike and I would pile into this vehicle and drive down to 'Momandu'. Here we would spend the day shooting. My parents were great and always laid on a big lunch with plenty of beer, and it was a wonderful way to spend our Sundays. Very sadly, Mike crashed his vehicle shortly after leaving school and killed himself.

My friend Bruce Rooken-Smith was made captain of rugger with me as vice-captain, so when Bruce badly injured himself early in the season I took over. My father, aged forty-three, was still playing rugger for Machakos and was captain of the club the same year as I was captaining the school. We had a match against Machakos, so I had the unusual experience of playing serious rugger against my father. We were both flank forwards so saw quite a lot of each other during the game. It was nail-biting stuff, but we just triumphed 18-17. What fun!

Mainly, though, I saw very little of my family during a school term. It was actually an embarrassment to have one's family around at school and on the odd occasion that my little sister turned up, on sports day for example, I would ignore her while with my contemporaries. I was actually very fond of her and we got on extremely well during the holidays. When my two older sons went to school in Rhodesia years later and young Jack was brought along, they used to scoop him up and take him to their dormitory and even in to supper with them. So much nicer and more natural.

All the time I was at the Duke of York, Kenya was suffering from the Mau Mau uprising. The Mau Mau were almost exclusively from the Kikuyu tribe. This tribe was the dominant one in Kenya and was based all round Nairobi and stretched up to Fort Hall, Nyeri and Nanyuki in one direction and to Limuru and the Kinankop in another. Mau Mau was probably one of the first of many African movements that set out to liberate themselves from the colonial yoke. Its avowed aims were to destroy Christianity and to murder or expel all Europeans from Kenya. There is no doubt that they obtained considerable support from Russia.

The whole ethos of the Mau Mau was to break down any kind of civilized standard or even tribal custom and to reduce members to mindless savages. To this end a series of seven oaths were devised, each one more degrading than the one before and all involving the maiming of animals and mutilation of human bodies. Having taken any of these oaths the participant was warned that if he disobeyed what was decided or if he assisted the whites, he would be castrated. His eyes would then be taken out and he would be held for seven days, then his head would be cut off and it would be seen if the clever whites could bring him back to life. Nor was this an idle threat. Many decent Kikuyu tried to resist taking these barbaric oaths but were forced to do so and therefore then bound by them with the threat hanging over them if they disobeyed any instructions.

Undoubted leader of the Kikuyu at this time and, by definition, the leader of Mau Mau was a teacher called Jomo Kenyatta. He was a well travelled and very well educated man. Certainly it was his wish to get most of the whites out of Kenya and to take control of the country himself, but it is doubtful if he wanted the situation to develop quite as it did. It is felt that he wanted a 'Day of The Long Knives' when all Kikuyu would rise up one night and slaughter their white employers. However, hotheads in the movement got impatient with waiting and started killing whites before any signal was given by Kenyatta. When this happened, Kenyatta and several other high-up members of the movement were arrested, put on trial and convicted on a number of fairly obscure counts, including being members of an unlawful society. They were sentenced to the maximum term that their crimes warranted, which was seven years' hard labour.

Down at Machakos we had the waKamba tribe, and they were not really involved in Mau Mau, so on the farm we were not directly affected to nearly the same extent as those farmers bordering on the Kikuyu reserves. A lot of my friends came into this category though and it was when staying with John Byng-Hall one holiday that I first heard about Mau Mau. His parents used to manage for Lord Delamere on 'Soysambu' but had recently bought their own farm right on the forest edge between Gilgil and Nakuru. All their labour was Kikuyu and John was very aware of the situation. His house had no sort of security fence, not even burglar bars on the windows. It would have been a cinch for anyone to get in. A lot of his neighbours were in a similar situation and it was a very frightening time for those isolated white farmers. All had help in the house and most counted these servants as loyal friends whom they had employed for many years. Often, they had helped them out financially in times of need and, similarly, these Kikuyu servants had helped bring up their employer's children and, in many cases, become genuinely fond of them. All this counted for nothing once they had actually taken an oath. So, when a gang came to the house where they were working and said that they had come to kill their white 'bwana', they meekly led them in.

In 1952 we went up to Nyeri to stay with friends for a horse show. They were two widows living on an isolated farm on the forest edge. 'Kitty' Hesselberger was probably sixty and her friend, 'Dot' Simpson, slightly younger. Shortly after we were there, the cook came into the sitting room with after-dinner coffee. He was followed by a Mau Mau gang wielding pangas. Kitty had a small pistol at her side and immediately shot the cook, while Dot shot one of the gang. Despite there being eight or ten in the gang, this scared them and they made a run for it. One tried to hide in the loo and Kitty shot him through the door while the rest disappeared into the night. The only sad part was that in the general fracas they had also shot their beloved boxer dog that was attacking one of the gang. It was a magnificent effort on the part of two elderly ladies and they were awarded the MBE by the new Queen.

Other people were not so lucky. Roger Ruck, whom we knew from polo, farmed on the Kinankop. One evening his groom called him out of the house saying that a horse was sick. Naïvely, Roger believed him and went out of the house to investigate. He was immediately set on by a gang and chopped to pieces with pangas. His wife, hearing the noise outside, also ran out carrying a shotgun but, before she could fire it, the gang caught and killed her too. They then went into the house and up to the bedroom of six-year-old Michael, where they butchered him as well.

Remembering stories like this, years later, one is staggered at how unprepared and badly equipped people were. Two decades later, in Rhodesia, I was on an isolated farm during the independence bush war and we were all fully armed, had security fences, radios and roving patrols. Admittedly this was a different sort of terrorism but the aim was just the same – to kill the white farmers. I suppose that back in the early 1950s people just did not believe that they were that unpopular and to quite what lengths the local African would go to obtain his independence.

I think it was the Ruck murder which precipitated a march by a lot of angry settlers on Government House, demanding that 'something be done' to stop this sort of atrocity. Something was done in that the colony remained in a state of Emergency for some seven years, British troops were deployed to help, all local white boys reaching the age of eighteen were called up for military service, and thousands of Kikuyu were sent back from where they were employed in Nairobi to their tribal areas or reserves, where they were incarcerated in so-called protected villages. When I eventually left school, I found myself in charge of one of these, but that was in the future.

We did take precautions at 'Momandu'. We locked the house at night and my father always had a gun handy. The local District Commissioner, Douglas Penwill, banned any Kikuyu from entering the Machakos district and I think that this probably helped stop the Mau Mau movement spreading to the waKamba. Our neighbour Dan Sauvage took the whole thing very seriously and said we should not drive around at night because of the danger of being ambushed. One day he was laying a new pipeline and had dug a ditch across the road to his house and put bushes round it as a warning that motorists should use a small détour that he had made. Ignoring his own advice, he returned from the club one night and on seeing bushes across the road thought he was being ambushed, so he accelerated and charged through, totally forgetting that it was he who had ordered a deep ditch dug across the road. He had a very hard time trying to account for the considerable damage to his vehicle.

At school, the elder boys took it in turns to act as sentries during the night. We did two-hour stints and it was fun because we got a sausage roll and cup of coffee when we went on duty. We were also allowed to sleep for a couple of hours after lunch, often missing some work. It must have been a worrying time for the staff though, as the school was quite isolated and there was a lot of bush in the grounds, but nothing really serious ever happened.

In fact, the main casualties were the parents, who regularly shot themselves with their own weapons. Most carried a pistol of some sort around with them, and not being too familiar with these things it was quite common for guns to go off unintentionally, so many serious injuries were self-inflicted.

I am not sure what my parents really thought about the Mau Mau and the long-term effect it would have on their lives. They had only been in Kenya for four years when it all started, had just bought their own farm and were very happy establishing a new life after the war. I certainly got the impression that most people thought it rather a nasty little glitch and that, with the help of Britain, it would soon be sorted out and the native would return to his subservient role. No one thought of selling up and leaving, as was the case later in Rhodesia when the terrorist war started there in earnest. Little did anyone realize that Mau Mau was just one of many nationalist movements throughout Africa which, in a very few years, would help to spell the end of the British Empire. I cannot say that the political future of the country concerned me too much, and it was not until I left school that I realized what a potentially big problem nationalism was.

In 1952 Princess Elizabeth and Prince Philip visited Kenya, and my cousin Richard Wilson acted as ADC to the Prince, as they had been together in the navy. The people of Kenya had given the royal couple a lovely little fishing lodge at Sagana, near Nyeri. It seemed a funny present to me – how often would they ever use it? Even then it was pretty dodgy to use it as the Mau Mau was just getting underway and the lodge was right on the edge of the Aberdare forest, which was full of Mau Mau. However, they did stay there and went on to the famous Tree Tops lodge. It was while they were there that they got the news that King George VI had died. We got the news at a hastily called school assembly, where Pansy James put on his most serious voice and announced that our King was dead. The royal couple hurried back to London and Richard Wilson was done out of the rest of an interesting experience.

The following year, 1953, my parents decided to visit England for the first time since they had left in 1948. My elder sister, Penel, was already there doing a children's nursing course in London. Sue and I were allowed to go along as well, even though it meant I had to miss a whole term from school. My parents had told Pansy that we were all going over for the Coronation and asked if it was OK by him if I went along. His reply was that, given the chance, no one should fail to see their Queen crowned, so I went.

* * *

No ship this time, but a fairly ancient Cloudmaster, a propeller-powered aeroplane. The flight took over twenty-four hours and included stops at

Entebbe, Khartoum and Rome. I arrived in a wet, cold London feeling like death, as we had to stack over Heathrow for nearly an hour before we could land and I was severely airsick.

We stayed in England for all of three months. Father had employed a manager on 'Momandu' and it was he who was 'holding the fort' while we were away. His name was Mike Ardagh.

The whole trip was actually a lot of fun as we did so much. We did go to the Coronation, and Penel and I sat all day in pouring rain in a stand just outside Buckingham Palace. To get there we had had to walk all the way from Hyde Park Corner, as no traffic was allowed closer than that. Our walk was much enlivened by excited newspapermen selling their papers, telling the story of Mount Everest being conquered for the first time.

We saw the whole procession leave for the Abbey, then a long wait, and they all came back again. The crowd cheered as they all went by (how do you cheer? Penel and I did not really know what to shout. Is it 'Hurray'? This sounds rather stupid if you go on saying it). The Queen and Prince Philip in that wonderful golden coach (which swayed around so much that it made the Queen quite queasy, we were told), followed by carriage after carriage of famous people – kings and queens of other countries, prime ministers, presidents, other members of the royal family, Winston Churchill, Field Marshal Montgomery, they were all there. I remember the huge, fat, laughing Queen of Tonga sitting in an open landau in the pouring rain with just one very small man sitting opposite her. It is said that when someone asked Noel Coward who he was, his laconic reply was, "probably her lunch".

When the whole procession was over, we were joined by my parents, who had been watching from the window of a nearby house, which also had the luxury of television so they were able to watch the actual Coronation service – and keep dry. We mingled with the rest of the crowd in front of the railings surrounding Buckingham Palace, waiting for the newly crowned Queen to come on to the balcony. When I say we mingled, we did not have much option. There was a huge crowd which stretched right back along The Mall and we were forced to remain in the middle of this until it dispersed. This was both frightening and exciting; it was like being in a tidal wave, because we just moved with the flow. The rain had stopped but everyone was pretty damp and there was a wonderful feeling of happiness and pride. There was a lot of noise, which of course, reached a climax of patriotic fervour when the Queen appeared. I had certainly never experienced anything like this before, nor have I since. It was a wonderful occasion and I was pleased to have been there – Pansy was right! It was just as well I did go, as there has not been another Coronation since.

We watched the Ashes Test match at Lord's and I saw my boyhood hero, Len Hutton, score 145, then Trevor Bailey and Willie Watson batting for nearly the whole of the last day to save the match. We watched from the box of 'Shrimp' Leveson-Gower (improbably pronounced 'Loosen-Gore', as only in England could it be) who was a distant cousin of the family. He was very big in the cricket world at that time, having been a national selector, president of Surrey for many years and recently knighted for his services to cricket. It was great to be in a box and not with the masses sitting on the grass, although that would have been fun as well; it is not allowed today. There was a bar where I could get lemonade and a continuous supply of delicious sandwiches – smoked salmon, cucumber, pâté and egg.

In the next-door box, on the second day, I suddenly spotted my old friend, the Queen of Tonga; she was tucking into a prawn cocktail – no sign of the little man though. Had she already eaten him? Or did she actually prefer prawn cocktails? If this were the case, 'Shrimp' Leveson-Gower had better watch out!

My father used to know London pretty well and he was much enjoying visiting some of his old haunts. One night he took us all (except Sue) to a 'revue'. One of the acts was a semi-naked girl with a tassel attached to each tit, which she could rotate in any direction, even different ways for each tit at the same time. I was fifteen and fascinated by this exhibition. I think my father got as much fun out of watching my reaction to all this as he did out of the act itself.

In early August we all went up to North Yorkshire to stay with my grandparents at the family home, 'Barningham'. The timing of this was no coincidence – the grouse-shooting season was about to start and 'Barningham' boasted its own lovely little grouse moor. These days, if you have that sort of thing, it would be leased out for a fat fee to rich foreigners, as indeed, the 'Barningham' moor is today. In those days, only family or very close friends were invited to shoot. I was family and it was virtually obligatory that I should shoot – not that I needed any urging. I had shot a lot in Kenya by then, but never at driven birds and certainly nothing like grouse, so my parents were a bit apprehensive as to how I would perform. Would the young colonial grandchild live up to the formidable family reputation? Formidable it was too. One of my ancestors still holds the world record for grouse shot in a single drive – one hundred and ninety in half an hour.

I was put in an outside butt and my mother was told to keep an eye on me – it would never do for the colonial grandson to shoot a beater, even by accident. Without doubt shooting driven grouse is the most exciting form of bird shooting. It is not easy, but the sight of a covey rising from the heather some half a mile away and flicking towards you low to the ground is a thrill hard to equal. The first covey that came my way was suddenly past me before I got off a shot, so fast were they going. I like to think that I did not disgrace myself that first day and managed to shoot a few, much to my mother's unconcealed delight, and my father's better-hidden relief. A grouse moor is a magical place when the sun is shining, but pretty gloomy when the wind blows and it is pouring with rain, but grouse remain the most sought after bird to shoot, mainly, I suppose, because they cannot be raised artificially like pheasants.

When my grandfather died, his son, my Uncle Mark, let the moor for fifteen years to pay off death duties. That was long ago and now the moor is still owned by the family, with Cousin Anthony depending largely on it to supplement the family coffers. 'Barningham' was, and still is, a wonderful place to wander around with a gun. There was no myxomatosis in those days and the place was alive with rabbits. I would go out most mornings that we stayed there and very soon shot as many as we could carry. When I say 'we', I mean Sue and me; she did not shoot, but was silly enough to help carry what I did. With all these exciting things going on, I was getting a very much better impression of England than what I remembered – it was not such a bad old place after all.

However, I was happy enough to return to Kenya when the time came, even if it did mean going back to school. In due course I took the Overseas Cambridge School Certificate (equivalent of today's 'O' level, I suppose), and got a reasonable pass, including a distinction in English, which is perhaps why I feel qualified to write all this drivel! A number of my friends left after taking this exam but I stayed on for another year to take some extra subsidiary subjects to try and get high enough grades to go to Cambridge. In reality, I should have stayed an extra two years and taken Higher School Certificate, but I was nearly eighteen by now and the thought of yet another year at school was too much.

A rather hearty friend of the family said that he could get me into his old college, Jesus, at Cambridge and he offered to write to them asking them to contact me. A little time after, I was at Nairobi races and he spotted me from the top of the stands. The other spectators were more than startled when he bellowed at me, "Have you heard from Jesus yet?" I never did, and no one else wanted me at Cambridge because the standard of my extra subjects was not good enough. So, at the end of 1955 I finally left school.

CHAPTER 4

KRTC

I DID NOT HAVE LONG TO SAVOUR MY newfound freedom after leaving school. While still there I had received my call-up papers for military training or National Service. The Mau Mau rebellion was still in full flow, there were several British regiments in the country, and any able-bodied Kenyan youth was immediately called up to serve for two years once he reached the age of eighteen.

We were called up to serve in the Kenya Regiment, as opposed to the King's African Rifles (KAR). The Kenya Regiment was at that time an all-white regiment affiliated to the Green Jackets. The KAR in those days had black, or native, troops with white officers. This led to some confusion when a girl, recently arrived from England, told her mother back in England that she wanted to marry a man who was serving with the KAR. "But, darling," the mother protested, "surely they are all black?"

"Oh no!" replied the girl, "only their privates are black."

I had barely recovered from the New Year's party for 1956 when I found myself on the back of an army lorry and being driven the one hundred miles from Nairobi to Nakuru and the Kenya Regiment Training Centre. With me on the back of the lorry were some thirty equally bewildered and apprehensive young men, some of whom I knew, as we had been at school together. Notable amongst these were John Byng-Hall, one of my closest friends, and Geoff (Duck) White, who had been in the Duke of York First Xl cricket team with me.

We had good reason to be apprehensive. Our rather privileged and comfortable colonial lifestyle was about to be rudely shattered. Tough non-commissioned training officers from the Brigade of Guards greeted us at the KRTC. We were divided into four squads of about thirty-five each. I imagine that it was all very like National Service in England or even Sandhurst, in that a lot of us were destined to be allocated jobs that would equate to those of commissioned officers, rather than just joining the ranks for a couple of years. Certainly we were put through our paces by this unique brand of instructor.

We were all young and fit, having just left school and not yet been exposed to the debauchery of young adult life. However, the army, in its great wisdom, was worried that such fit young men might be inclined to think more about fit young girls than the internal workings of a sub-machine gun. So, to combat such a terrible idea – it was widely rumoured – a substance known as bromide was put in our tea, and this was said to reduce substantially the sex drive normal in young male adults. We had no proof of this but it worried Bob Lake considerably. Bob was the assistant on our next-door farm at Machakos and had recently arrived from England, only to be called up to do his bit for Queen and country. Bob was older than us and had fallen in love with, and was engaged to be married to, a very pretty local girl. The wedding was to be immediately after the end of the course. The last thing Bob needed was bromide in his tea! He took the matter up with some vigour, starting with his sergeant, then to the CSM, the officer in charge of his squad, the commanding officer of KRTC. and finally the colonel of the regiment. I never discovered the result of all this, but Bob duly got married and his wife produced a son some nine months later.

I was in 3 squad, under the tender care of Sgt Humber of the Coldstream Guards and Sgt Hawkes of the King's Royal Rifle Corps. Overseeing all squads was Company Sergeant-Major (CSM) Stott of the Irish Guards. The expression usually used to recount one's first days at this sort of institution is that "our feet never touched the ground". I can do little better than repeat this. In a way, we were lucky to be coming straight from school and so were used to a certain amount of discipline. What the modern young man, having completed his gap year, would have thought of the sort of things we had to put up with, I shudder to think.

Sgt Humber had a dog called 'Cushie' and he would appear with this hound on his way back to his rooms from the Sergeants' Mess at about two in the morning, when he had apparently had a certain amount to drink. We were expected to leap out of bed and salute the ruddy dog.

We were issued with brand new, very stiff, black boots and within the first few days of getting them they had to look like glass, and I mean glass; you had to be able to see your face in them. The only way to achieve this was to burn them with a very hot iron to take out all the wrinkles, and then polish them for about fifty hours! The trick was to know someone who had been on the previous course and buy their boots. Highly polished boots were of no use on active service. We were also issued with a selection of ill-fitting uniforms. Half of these had to be made to fit really well, as our turnout was expected to be exemplary, while the other half we never used at all. The kit had to be folded so neatly that once that status was achieved we never dared unfold it, and it remained for the entire course on our wardrobe shelves, sitting in all its perfection just to pass the daily barrack room inspection.

Reveillé was sounded on a bugle every morning at 0530 and we had to be lined up in our squads, immaculately turned out, by 0555. Sgt Humber would then appear, also immaculately turned out but often a little red-eyed, and inspect us. This was a nerve-racking experience. He would walk very slowly along each row, stopping both in front and behind every recruit. We were expected to stare straight ahead and not move a muscle. If you were unlucky, the sergeant while standing behind you might bellow, "Am I hurting you?"

"No, sergeant" you would stammer.

"What did you say? I can't hear you."

So you would have to yell, "No sergeant," and he would yell back, "Well, I should be... I'm standing on your hair." This would mean that a five o'clock shadow had appeared somewhere below the line of your beret, and you were required to have yet another haircut or shave yet more exactly. Or he would stand in front of you and bellow,"Why have you come on parade naked?" This would mean he had detected a button not correctly done up.

This sort of heinous crime was punished either by being put 'on orders', which meant reporting to the commanding officer in your very brief off time and receiving some menial task to do in the precious time when you should have been polishing your boots, or by being told to run round the parade ground with your rifle held above your head. While you were doing this Sgt Humber would tell you to shout out repeatedly, "I'm a cunt!" upon which, he would think it hilariously funny to reply, "No, you're not, a cunt's useful and you are not!"

I need hardly add that the language of all the instructors was 'colourful' to say the least; the simplest of sentences could not be made without a varied selection of expletives. We were called every name under the sun, but the greatest insult of all was to be likened to a "bloody Grenadier". It seems that there is a certain rivalry within the Brigade of Guards.

Marching was the basis of these parades and it was essential to get it exactly right, but one poor little guy in our squad could NOT march in the accepted manner. When his right leg went forward, so did his right arm, and not back, as comes naturally to most people. This was the way he walked and it looked odd even then, so when it came to marching, he drove Sgt Humber almost literally to the point of insanity. If CSM Stott were to see Sgt Humber's squad marching off the parade ground with one member swinging his arms totally out of time with everybody else, it would be orders for Sgt Humber as well as the guy concerned. Sgt Humber referred to him as 'God', because he moved in a mysterious way. We quite enjoyed having 'God' in our squad because it took the pressure off us. He did sort of learn to march properly but it was always touch and go, so for the end of course passing-out parade when everything had to be just perfect, 'God' was told to report sick.

I talk a lot about Sgt Humber, with good reason – he ruled our lives. I think he was only about twenty-three, but this seemed old to us eighteen-year-olds. He was incredibly fit and incredibly strong. In full battle kit and carrying a rifle he could easily climb a twenty-foot rope using just his arms. On route marches he was often to be seen carrying two or three extra rifles belonging to the weaker members of our squad. He was cruiserweight boxing champion of the Brigade of Guards. He could also absorb an incredible amount of alcohol with no apparent effect next day. As I have mentioned, he was inordinately proud of his regiment, the Coldstream Guards, and held in utter contempt ALL other regiments, but in particular the Grenadiers. We thought, rather stupidly, that we would pull his leg over this.

Every Saturday afternoon we had 'off', that is to say we sat on our beds polishing our equipment. During the Emergency, as these times were called in Kenya, there was a forces' request programme broadcast over the local radio every Saturday afternoon and all members of the forces, including ourselves, listened in avidly just in case some misguided young girl sent one of us a request. We sort of longed to get one, but if one was sent the embarrassment was acute, as you were forced to listen to it and, worse still, the accompanying message, with all your grinning squad mates listening as well and watching you. Well, we thought we should send Sgt Humber a request. As I say, it was a stupid thing to do, particularly as we chose that great marching tune *'The British Grenadiers'* with love from his devoted 3 squad. We heard later that it was played in the Sergeants' Mess with everyone present and was particularly enjoyed by the sergeant from the Grenadiers.

Drill on Sundays was usually a fairly token exercise, followed by a church service. The Sunday after the broadcast, however, was one to remember. It went on for a full hour and not once did we stop for a stand easy. We were on our knees by the end and not once did Sgt Humber give the slightest hint of having heard our request.

Another unlikely fondness of his was cricket, and he turned out whenever he could for the local club, Rift Valley. One Sunday, the club was short of a player at the last minute and asked Sgt Humber to find a cricketer amongst his recruits to make up the numbers.

43

"Do any of you 'orrible shower think you can play cricket?" he asked during our last parade on the Saturday. No one breathed a word, as the last request had been for musicians and the couple of guys who had said they did know a bit about music found themselves loading the commanding officer's piano on to a removal van during their off time! However, someone sneaked on me and revealed to Sgt Humber that I had captained my school at cricket, so presumably could play a bit.

"You, Milbank, you 'orrible specimen, will come with me tomorrow and play cricket."

I had not at that stage been out of the camp for over a month and the thought of a day's cricket at the local club sounded good, even if I were to be under Sgt Humber's wing, as it were.

No sooner were we out of the camp and driving to the club than Sgt Humber's whole manner turned a dramatic somersault. He chatted animatedly about cricket, saying how much he loved the game and what fun it was playing in Kenya where the weather was always so good. He wanted to know what I did: was I a batsman or bowler? He lent me a pair of white trousers, and we arrived in great spirits at the ground, where he introduced me to my teammates. I had been an opening batsman at school, so the local captain asked me to open the innings. This I did and made 118! I had never made a century before. Sgt Humber, batting down the order, did not even get a bat and aided by a couple of wickets and a good catch from me, we ran out easy winners. I was the hero of the hour with Sgt Humber lavish in his praise. We had several drinks together and drove back to camp singing drinking songs, which he knew and which I was keen to learn. I was very pleased with my day's work: not only had I had a thoroughly enjoyable and successful day, but I had made great friends with the guy who had our future welfare entirely in his hands.

There was not a lot of time to get my boots quite up to scratch that evening, as we arrived back quite late and I was a little tiddly. But I was unconcerned. At tomorrow's inspection, Sgt Humber would overlook any small fault in my turnout, understanding that I had not had sufficient time to do it properly, having been his guest, as it were. He stood in front of me next morning at 0605 hours in the early morning cold.

"Where did you find those boots?" he yelled.

"They are mine," I said, and smiled at my erstwhile drinking friend. I thought he was going to explode!

"I don't give a shit whose bloody boots they are, they look as if they have been dragged out of a manure heap. Go and clean them now, then report on orders at four thirty, and take that fucking sloppy smile off your face."

From then on I was a marked man, and even 'God' got away with more than I did!

Halfway through the course there was a dance held at the mess and we were allowed three days' leave. It was dubbed 'The Intercourse Dance'. We were allowed, indeed encouraged, to invite young ladies up to Nakuru for this glamorous occasion. Not many came, mainly because very few of us knew any girls well enough to invite them to drive a hundred miles by themselves to this highly suspect event. The result was that 90% of us used the occasion to get smashed out of our minds on rum and coke. Perhaps the bromide had something to do with it.

We learned a lot in a very short time. Drill, it seemed, is the basis of all army training. We were taught to obey orders instinctively and quickly, and hardly a day went by when we did not have an hour or so of 'square bashing'. We learned other things as well though. Shooting was high on the list – reasonably enough, our ultimate job was to shoot people, wasn't it? There were many days spent on the range at Lion Hill firing at targets with ancient .303s or Bren guns; then we were introduced to the revolutionary new automatic rifle, the Belgian-made F.N., a weapon that I was to become all too familiar with many years hence, in the Rhodesian bush war. Later in the course we were introduced to the jungle lane and the assault course. Here we had to take snap shots at targets, figures which would suddenly pop up out of the bush while all the time a stream of bullets was being fired just over our heads to simulate real action. A bullet passing close over your head does not go 'bang'; all you hear is a crack as it goes through the sound barrier.

We learned about grenades and how to throw them. You pull out a pin, while still holding down the plunger which will detonate the grenade, then bowl it overarm in the general direction of the intended target. Depending upon the length of the fuse, it will then take between five and ten seconds to detonate. This gives you ample time to take cover yourself, usually by lying down behind a rise in the ground or in a trench, if you are lucky enough to be in one. Bowling a live grenade is a relatively straightforward procedure for anyone who is even moderately well co-ordinated. However, we have already seen that 'God' was not particularly well co-ordinated, so standing anywhere near him when it was his turn to bowl a grenade was a terrifying experience. He would frequently forget to let go, and the live grenade, far from landing far to our front, would end up coming back towards us. At least it taught us to move quickly.

All through the course we were being allocated points, both individually and as a squad, for practically everything we did.

Route marches in full kit were a big thing and here the emphasis was placed on finishing as a unit and not on individual brilliance; they were tough and tiring and it was during these that we began to appreciate how tough Sgt Humber was. He always marched with us and if a weaker member of the squad started to falter he would invariably carry that man's rifle for him; I remember him once carrying five. This built up good team spirit and we all really tried to be top squad. Sport also came into it and I managed to regain some favour with Sgt Humber by winning the cross-country. Remember, we were all 'whites' with no Kipsigis runners to show us up.

Most of all perhaps, we learned a bit about life. From a somewhat sheltered upbringing, we suddenly discovered that life could be a little rough, but it certainly did none of us any harm. There was more to follow, though. The KRTC. was just the training ground and at the end of the course we were deployed to put into practice some of the things we had learned, to the further confusion of the Mau Mau, who were still active in the country. Most of us joined the regiment proper and were posted to various areas of active combat, mainly round Mount Kenya and the Aberdares. Others were seconded to British regiments serving in Kenya at the time, to act as liaison officers. I however applied to join the Kikuyu Home Guard as a District Officer, and I was surprised and pleased to be selected for this challenging post.

The day of the passing-out parade loomed and we were given extra time 'off' in which to polish our boots and brasses to an even greater degree of perfection. Invitations were sent out to our parents, as well as to various dignitaries, to come and witness this momentous occasion. The result of the inter-squad competition was announced and, to Sgt Humber's undisguised delight and the confusion of his Grenadier colleague, we won. He took us all down to the NAAFI and bought us drinks.

My parents drove all the way up from Machakos and sat in the sun watching their little boy march off the square. The three of us then drove back home, myself for what I considered a well-earned week's leave.

47

CHAPTER 5

District Officer – Kikuyu Guard

THE WEEK'S LEAVE PASSED QUICKLY ENOUGH, AS my friend John Byng-Hall and I decided that the best thing to do with our newfound ability at shooting was to go and hunt some lions. A near neighbour of ours had a number of these eating his sheep and was only too pleased to let us have a go at them. It is, perhaps, a measure of our upbringing that, instead of hitting the bright lights of Nairobi after our tough three months, we elected to go and hunt lions. There were a couple of small snags. While both of us had done a lot of shooting, neither of us had ever shot a lion at that stage. The other problem was the rifle. My father had bought a lovely little .256 Männlicher Schonauer rifle, but, while this was an ideal weapon for plains game, it was hardly big enough for lion. We consoled ourselves with the knowledge that 'Karamoja' Bell used this calibre of rifle to shoot elephants. What we tended to ignore was that Mr Bell was not only highly experienced but a bit of a freak as well.

We spent five days in a small uncomfortable tent, eating tinned food and badly cooked impala meat. Probably fortunately, we saw neither hide nor hair of any lion. John then proceeded to the Kenya Regiment proper and I hitched a lift up to Fort Hall (now Muranga), some seventy miles north of Nairobi, situated in the foothills of the Aberdare mountain range, to take up my post as a District Officer Kikuyu Guard. The Aberdares and Mount Kenya were both pretty high, with Mount Kenya reaching over seventeen thousand feet and the Aberdares over twelve thousand.

Both were covered with thick equatorial forest and it was here that the remaining Mau Mau terrorists were making their last stand.

I call them terrorists, but now of course they are referred to as freedom fighters. Soon, in 1963, these very people would become the heroes of the newly independent Kenya, but now it was 1956; the worst of the reign of terror inspired by these gangsters was over and the gangs had taken refuge in the forests, only coming out to make sporadic raids, mainly for food. There were plenty of them left, though, and the country was still very much in a state of Emergency. Several companies of British troops were still in the colony and the Kenya Regiment was at full strength, as was the KAR. However, it had long since ceased to be a conventional war, if indeed it ever had been, and the days of Lancaster bombers dropping high explosives all over the forests, while pink-kneed English recruits tramped noisily through the undergrowth, were largely over, as both had proved totally ineffective. Much more subtle means were required to flush out the remaining and now very cunning gangsters, and to this end a concerted drive had been made to enlist the services of 'loyal' Kikuyu.

In the early days of the Emergency, in 1952 and even before, the Mau Mau had held total sway in the Kikuyu reserves. Virtually every adult Kikuyu had taken at least two of the seven oaths, oaths of increasing degree of revulsion, which bound them to total loyalty to the Mau Mau cause. The only way to combat this, in the eyes of the Kenya Government, assisted by the British Foreign Office, was to put all Kikuyu into protected villages; from these villages they could be more easily controlled and protected from the militant wing of the organization, who even then were basing themselves round the forest edge. It was these gangs who committed most of the well-documented atrocities against isolated white farming families, not to mention slaughtering thousands of their own tribesmen.

To guard these protected villages, local Kikuyu had to be recruited, given a very basic training and armed with ancient .303 rifles. Quite where their loyalties lay was the subject of some concern, particularly if they

49

were threatened by a large Mau Mau gang on a dark night. Therefore, to stiffen their resolve, a white officer was put in charge of them in each village. He had received basic military training, was also armed with an ancient .303 rifle and, because he was white, was assumed to be totally loyal to the Government. The fact that he was usually not much more than eighteen did not seem to matter.

In April 1956 at the Gikui protected village in the Kangema district of Fort Hall, I was that white officer. I had indeed received a basic military training, I was white and I was eighteen. Perhaps most importantly though, I was certainly totally loyal to the Government. I had not the slightest doubt that what I was doing was correct and that the terrorists were the scum of the earth and should be hunted down and killed. I did not hold the rest of the Kikuyu people in very high regard either. The fact that they had been forcibly removed from their homes and shambas (gardens) and all herded into protected villages was, in my opinion, their good luck, and it was quite right that they should be forced to do communal labour every day, to the mutual benefit of everybody.

Quite what qualified me to be lord and master of this lot is not clear but it certainly did not worry me. My command post was perched on a hilltop in the middle of the village. It was surrounded by a moat with earth sides and, driven into these sides were six-foot-long pointed sticks all facing outwards. Surmounting these was a ten-foot high barbed wire fence. There was one strong wooden gate, also ten feet high and covered in barbed wire, through which one could enter the post. The gate was locked and guarded at all times by a TPR (Tribal Police Reservist). A detail of some eight TPRs lived inside the post in communal quarters, while I lorded it in my own house. True, the house only had three rooms, was made of mud, wattle and thatch, and had an outside 'long drop' for a loo, but it was from here that I reigned supreme. I employed a cook, had an ancient short-wheelbase Land Rover plus driver, a camp bed and a small suitcase of clothes. Nothing much else.

Gikui was some seven and a half thousand feet above sea level on the lower slopes of the Aberdares, situated ten miles from the district headquarters of Kangema and thirty-five from Fort Hall. My nearest white neighbour was probably in Kangema, but there were others scattered throughout the area doing the same sort of thing as me. I had spent one night in Kangema on my way up and stayed with George Grimmett, the District Officer for the area and a permanent civil servant; he had given me a fairly sketchy briefing as to what my duties were. George was my boss and I was known as a District Officer Kikuyu Guard (DOKG).

My duties were pretty varied. As stated, I was in charge of a Gikui protected village and had to see that all able-bodied men and women reported for communal labour every morning. They were marched out of the village early under the watchful eyes of the TPRs and put to work on some project like clearing bush for a new road or building a spillway for a dam or terracing a cultivated area. The tools they were given were very basic and the work quite long and hard. I was not expected to spend all day watching them work, but was sometimes obliged to check back in the village to see that no one was shirking.

I had to co-operate with such security forces as were operating in my area from time to time. This was pretty frequently and usually involved helping to man ambushes on the forest edge, when I would take five or six of my TPRs and set an ambush on tracks coming out of the forest, tracks frequented by gangsters or, more likely, their supporters taking food in to them. A dawn-to-dusk curfew was enforced throughout the whole area, so everybody had to be back in his or her respective village by nightfall. This meant that anyone moving after dark could be shot. The rules were quite clear.

My third main job, if nothing else was happening, was to map the land in my area owned by known terrorists, and to submit the maps to some office in Nairobi, which would see to it that this bit of land was officially confiscated from the terrorist owner. I never did discover to whom it was given, nor, perhaps more to the point, who ended up with it after independence, a scant five years away.

Various branches of the security forces came my way. There was the Kenya Regiment of course, and I usually had some mates amongst

51

these, the KAR, some British regiments and, the most effective of all, the Special Forces. These last were wholly irregular and pretty much did their own thing. Amongst them were the very brave men who blackened their faces, joined up with Kikuyus who had been Mau Mau gangsters, and went into the forest pretending to be part of a friendly gang. We never knew when this lot would turn up; it was nearly always totally unannounced and we were obliged to drop everything and help them in any way we could. This often meant providing transport or laying ambushes for anyone that they might flush out of the forest. It often meant that at very short notice, I would suddenly find myself spending two or three nights in gross discomfort under a bush at nine thousand feet.

* * *

Interesting visitors were the British Regiments. At one stage a detachment from one such famous regiment was posted to Kangema to help out on some big 'push'. They were based at Gilgil, some sixty miles north of Nairobi, near Kenyatta Polo Club and within easy reach of some excellent duck shooting on Lake Naivasha – two activities in which the officers showed considerably more interest than in catching Mau Mau.

I had some sympathy with their somewhat detached attitude to our little war. After their heroics in the Crimea, the Boer War and two World Wars they now found themselves chasing a lot of ragged savages armed with guns made from pipes, with a bent nail on a bit of elastic as a firing pin!

A small party was sent to Kangema and duly arrived with a well-equipped range of tents: long ones for the men to sleep in; small square ones for each of the officers to sleep in; a large square one for the men to eat in and a very slightly smaller one, which would be the most important of all, the Officers' Mess.

There were three officers, all with double-barrelled names and two with titles as well. The officer in charge, Captain Sir Charles Montague-Smythe, was a regular soldier, while the other two were doing short-term commissions. All had considerable independent means and were in no way reliant on their army salary for their comfort.

I visited their mess two days after they arrived in Kangema, as I had been told they would be operating in my area. On entering the mess tent I could see the backs of two chairs crowned by a halo of smoke, and the points of two pairs of highly polished shoes at about the same height as the smoke. I coughed and shuffled my feet. No one moved. There was a slight rustling of imported newspapers. I advanced until I could see round the chairs and under the smoke haze. Two newspapers were lowered and two pairs of eyes glared at me from two very pink faces. No one spoke, so I thought I had better say something to get the show on the road, as it were. The conversation went something like this:

"Good evening, I am Mark Milbank. I'm the DOKG from Gikui, which is where you are coming tomorrow I believe."

"The what...?"

"DOKG, the District Officer Kikuyu Guard."

"Oh." This was followed by silence and the reraising of the newspapers.

I tried again. "I thought I would drop in to introduce myself, as we will be operating in the same area."

"Oh!"

"I see you are comfortably settled in, anyway."

"Ha!"

At this point a third individual entered from the back. He was slightly older than the others but no less pink. He wore a silk dressing-gown with a cravat at his throat and velvet slippers.

"Damn niggers, my bath water was cold again," he said to his two seated companions.

"Oh!"

"Who's this fellow?" he asked, ignoring me.

"A DOAT."

"Oh, what does he want?"

"Don't know."

"I say," he said, eventually turning to me, "be a good chap and state what you want, we are about to dine."

"Nothing important," I said and left.

I met this lot again when we all assembled for the joint operation, which was designed to flush out the leading Mau Mau 'general' of the time, Dedan Kimathi. It was six o'clock on a Thursday evening when we all met up on the forest edge, before moving into our positions under cover of darkness. George Grimmett, the District Officer from Kangema, was giving final instructions and the good captain, Montague-Smythe, was one of those meant to be listening to these instructions.

He affected an air of total boredom and at the end turned to his brother officers and drawled, "What time do you imagine this charade will end? I am due at the Muthaiga Club for lunch tomorrow; I have to finalise arrangements for my safari with Tony."

Muthaiga, as it was generally known by us, not the Muthaiga Club, was the club frequented by the settler community; my Great Uncle F O'B Wilson, had had a hand in the building of it and I was a member. Irrationally, I objected to this pompous oaf treating 'my' club as if it was his own, and this probably prompted me to blurt out, "The 'charade' ends when we catch all these buggers." Montague-Smythe turned and glared at me; "Oh!" he said.

As was not uncommon on these occasions, we spent a cold uncomfortable night at some nine thousand feet high in the Aberdares, seeing little and catching or shooting less. There was no sign of the gallant captain and his crew when we reassembled at the rendezvous point at nine o'clock next morning. No doubt he had hurried away to ensure he was not late for his lunch date.

Some two days after this, one of my scouts, Mwangi Kimau, who was stationed near the forest edge looking out for tracks of people entering or leaving the forest, told me that he had found a large dead buck and he wanted to go back and get some of the meat.

"That English Bwana shot a big buck and only took the horns," he said in Swahili, "so there is plenty of meat left for us."

As it was so high and cold the meat would probably still be OK I thought, so I decided to go with Mwangi and have a look.

Sure enough, about a mile into the forest on a disused track we encountered villagers armed with pangas carrying chunks of meat. There was very little left when we finally came up to the carcass, but minimal investigation revealed that the buck was a bongo, and a large male at that. The horns had been removed but the skin was more or less intact and the rich red colour with white lateral stripes made it quite obvious what it was. The bongo is very rare and could only be shot on a very special licence.

Had this bull been shot? If so, by whom? I got Mwangi to turn the skin over, and there just behind the shoulder were two very distinct small holes: bullet holes. Mwangi was correct. It was really none of my business, but when I happened to be in Kangema a couple of days later, I decided to wander round to the regimental mess. It was a Friday, so it was unsurprising that none of the officers was present. I wandered over towards the Sergeants' Mess and heard the sound of chopping coming from behind the tent. I peeped round the corner and there was an older man, stripped to the waist, chopping meat off an antelope skull topped by a magnificent set of bongo horns.

"Morning sorr, nice morning," he said, considerably more civil than his superiors.

"The best way to clean that," I said, "is to put it on top of an anthill. The ants will have it clean as a whistle in no time and save you a lot of work."

"Well I'll be damned, thank you sorr."

"Where did you get it?" I asked.

"Captain found the big deer dead in the forest, got the lads to carry this lot back."

"It is a bongo, which is an antelope."

"Is that so, sorr?"

"Where is the captain now?"

"Couldn't rightly say, sorr, took off in the jeep yesterday down the Fort Hall road and has not been back since."

"OK, thanks," I said and left.

Found it dead, had he? I really did not know what to do; it was nothing to do with me and, in fact, I was not above a bit of poaching myself, being a bloodthirsty young brute in those days. But a bongo! Shot by that pompous ass.

In the event, of course, I did nothing. We were very busy for the next few weeks in the final push to catch Kimathi. I saw little of the British contingent but they were still around. I was in one of the ambushes set to catch Kimathi, when he was shot and wounded, but I was not in the one he walked into. I do not think this is the reason, though, that Nairobi's main street is today named after him and not me. Kimathi was wounded and sent to hospital to recover, before being tried and hanged.

"Why did they bother to make him better first and then kill him?" asked my tribal policemen.

I found this question difficult to answer.

Soon after this George Grimmett was transferred and, as was the custom, threw a farewell party at his comparatively smart house in Kangema. All of us DOKGs were asked, as were members of the police, such members of the Kenya Regiment who happened to be around, other administrative staff and the officers of the British regiment, who were still stationed at Kangema. It happened to be a Wednesday, so they were back from the previous weekend's leave and had not yet gone on next weekend's!

I had long since given up trying to be civil to them and was enjoying the free booze and excellent snacks with my contemporaries, when I found myself standing just behind Montague-Smythe. He was talking in his loud superior voice to George.

"Picked up a set of bongo horns in the forest the other day. Want to take them home and hang them in the Hall, don't you know. No problem in doing that is there?"

"Well," said George, "bongo can only be shot on a very restricted licence."

"Found it dead, old boy."

"Even so, you should really hand them to the Game Department."

"Oh!" said the captain and turned away.

The party continued, the jokes got coarser; I got drunker and was one of the last to leave – long after the British officers. As I bade farewell to George, whom I had liked a lot during our time together, I blurted out, "That pompous, bloody Brit captain shot that bongo, you know."

"Thanks," said George, "Can you find me witnesses, besides yourself?"

"Plenty," I said.

"Good, I'll nail the bastard, leave it to me."

Before he finally left, I gave George the names of my contacts, including Mwangi, and forgot all about it.

Some two months later I was due some leave and opted to go home to my parents' farm near Machakos. To get there, I had to go through Nairobi, and while there I bought a newspaper. On thumbing through it, a small headline caught my eye.

BRITISH OFFICER IN COURT ON POACHING
CHARGE.

I quickly read the article:

> *Captain Sir Charles Montague-Smythe of a well-known British regiment, currently serving with that regiment in Kenya, yesterday pleaded 'not guilty' to a charge of shooting a bongo bull without a licence while stationed near Kangema in the Fort Hall district.*
>
> *However, three African witnesses, Mr Mwangi Kamau, Mr Stephen Chaguna and Mr John Waweru testified that they had been with Captain Montague-Smythe's patrol in the Aberdare forest when the animal had been shot and Mr Kamau had helped cut off the*

> *horns and give them to one of the captain's men to*
> *carry down the mountain. Captain Montague-Smythe*
> *was found guilty and severely reprimanded by the*
> *presiding magistrate, Mr Michael Fell.*
>
> *"This is an appalling example you have set when*
> *you are a visitor in our country and in a position of*
> *authority," he said, before fining him KSh.10,000, and*
> *banning him from ever holding a hunting licence in*
> *Kenya.*
>
> *Captain Montague-Smythe expressed regret, but*
> *pleaded to be allowed to hold a hunting licence as he*
> *had already booked and paid for a hunting safari with*
> *a prominent local professional hunter.*
>
> *"Under no circumstances – case closed,"*
> *concluded Mr. Fell.*

I drove the fifty miles to my parents' farm with a big grin on my face!

When I arrived, there was a strange Land Rover parked outside the front door, but I went straight to my own room, followed by my mother.

"Lovely to have you home, darling," she gushed, "You are looking so well. I am afraid we have got a visitor tonight. Uncle Tom wrote and said that the son of a great army friend of his was currently serving with a British regiment out here and would we be kind to him. Poor man, he has just had a horrid time in court on some trumped-up charge or other. Come and meet him, his name is Charles Montague-Smythe."

"Oh!" I said.

* * *

The catching of Dedan Kimathi was probably the highlight of my time as a DOKG. We were given thousands of leaflets bearing a photograph of Kimathi, handcuffed, and lying on a stretcher with his long matted hair tied up above his head. We were told to distribute these leaflets

throughout the whole area. I cannot remember the reaction of the villagers on receiving them, but certainly there was no mass rejoicing. I have
often wondered what they really thought. Dedan Kimathi was certainly
a bad man in our eyes. He had instigated and committed some heinous
crimes, but he was a Kikuyu and they were Kikuyu too. He was fighting
to get the whites out of his country, so if you or I had been a Kikuyu
which side would we have supported? These worries did not enter my
head as an eighteen-year-old; clearly we should all rejoice that this terrible man had been caught.

On visiting the Aberdare National Park fifty years later I was given a
tourist map of the whole area. A selected attraction was an old fig tree in
which Kimathi was supposed to 'post' messages to his men giving details
of security force movements. It was also interesting to note that he had
been posthumously promoted to 'Field Marshal'!

Kimathi was not, of course, the only 'general' out there in the
forests. General China was also caught, but he was let go again to try and
persuade his men to give up the fight and surrender to the security forces.
I do not think he did this at all; he was delighted to be set free and just
rejoined the gang, and certainly there was no mass surrender.

Stanley Mathengi was another big leader on the edge of our area.
It is reputed that he was once cornered by a small patrol and ran into a
native hut to hide. The patrol saw him enter the hut and proceeded to
spray it with automatic fire. After doing this for about five minutes they
assumed that anyone in the hut must be dead, so they moved in to recover
the body. What they had not realized was that Mr Mathengi had climbed
up into the roof of the hut and not been hit by any of the patrols' bullets,
which were all fired at head height or below, so when the men of the
patrol entered the hut, all looking at the ground for a corpse, Mathengi
opened fire at point blank range with his own automatic rifle.

Stanley Mathengi was never caught, nor did he emerge after independence as a hero, so we all thought he had died or been killed in the
forest. In 2002, some forty-five years after the Emergency in Kenya,
I was living in Zimbabwe, and driving into Harare one day I had the

car radio on. The BBC was reporting the fact that a very old Mau Mau general was finally returning to his native Kenya from Ethiopia, where he had been living ever since escaping there at the end of the Mau Mau rebellion – Stanley Mathengi!

It has been estimated that some 90% of Kikuyu took at least two Mau Mau oaths, and it was reasoned, probably correctly, that anyone who had taken such an oath could never really be himself again until he had renounced it in some way or other. So the government recruited 'tame' witch doctors to conduct cleansing ceremonies, to help so-called loyal Kikuyu to cast out the evil in them induced by the filthy oaths.

Those who had undergone these cleansing ceremonies and had gone on to help the government defeat the Mau Mau were issued with something called a 'Loyalty Certificate'. It was one of my responsibilities to hand out these certificates in my area. Again, they were not received with any untoward show of delight. I wonder what they were worth five years later at independence – certainly not a guaranteed place in the cabinet under Jomo Kenyatta, at that time off-stage and languishing in prison.

The Kikuyu is widely regarded as one of the cleverest and most industrious of all the tribes in Africa. The ones that I worked with in Kangema were certainly good guys. Quite what they thought of me I do not know. I was very young, but my word was law. Like most Africans they had a good sense of humour and nothing amused them more than an incident like someone careering down a hill on a bicycle with no brakes, falling off and preferably hurting himself really badly!

Towards the end of my time at Kangema my 'staff', such as it was, received a new member. This was a young man of about my own age called John Waweru. I did not recruit him and did not really want him; certainly I could not pay him a wage, but he hung around nonetheless, doing odd jobs like cleaning the Land Rover, chopping firewood or even repairing parts of the fence round my guard post.

He appeared to be better educated than his contemporaries, in that his English was quite good and I often saw him reading a book. He did not appear to have many friends and kept very much to himself. Whether or not he had taken any oaths I never found out; he claimed to have been away at school during all the main troubles and oath-taking in the Kangema area. At one stage a friend and I bought a horse, which I kept near my guard post. Some obscure legislation revealed that I could claim an allowance if I used the horse on official duty. So I did. I rode, rather than walked, to some of the remote 'shambas' that I had to map for confiscation from known terrorists, and claimed the allowance. With this money I was able to pay a groom, or syce, as we called them. John Waweru claimed that he had once helped look after horses, so I gave him a try. He did know a bit and, as the job was hardly demanding, this was enough and I employed him.

As I now saw more of him at close quarters, as it were, I got talking to him and asked where he had been to school, what his parents did and why he was not either a terrorist or in the Home Guard. It seems that his father had moved into Fort Hall and done well running a small shop, so well that he had been able to afford to send John away to school at the Alliance High School, which was probably the best African secondary school in the country, situated quite near Nairobi.

On leaving school John was at a loose end. With the country in turmoil, he had returned to Fort Hall, only to find that his father had closed the shop and moved back to his old home in Kangema. As all Kikuyu were then ordered to stay in their tribal areas, John had no option but to remain in Kangema. Something did not quite ring true and I probed further. Why did he have no friends and why did he not live with his parents in the village? Why was he so friendly to me?

All was soon revealed when one day he asked to be taken to the clinic in Kangema. He looked well enough, so I asked what he thought he was suffering from. This clearly embarrassed him and he tried to avoid answering, but, when I continued to probe, he suddenly not only told me the reason but also asked for my help.

It seemed that while he was away at school the time came for his age group to be circumcised. This is a very important ceremony in the life of a young Kikuyu, but also a very painful one and, to put it bluntly,

John Waweru had chickened out. At the end of one term, when he could easily have come home to Kangema and joined his age group in this initiation ceremony, he had opted to stay away with friends near Nairobi and missed the whole thing. Now that he was back home, he was pretty much ostracized by his one-time friends, who had undergone together the painful operation and were now considered men. John was not only considered to be not a man, but a coward to boot.

This was why he wanted to sneak off to the clinic and have the operation done as painlessly as possible, before declaring to his late mates that of course he had been circumcised and what was all the fuss about. I think he would not have got away with it, but it was certainly worth a try! I had some sympathy with him and took him to the clinic where the deed was done. I cannot say that it improved his social standing very much though. In Kikuyu tradition, the youths with whom you are circumcised become your circumcision brothers and this forms a very strong, lifelong bond. John Waweru had no such brothers.

The social life in Gikui village was not exactly stimulating. I turned nineteen in September of 1956 and was feeling fairly short of congenial company, female company in particular. I was therefore quite pleased to be transferred to Kangema village soon after my birthday. The need to have white officers stationed in remote areas was now not as acute as it had been and my invaluable services were required more in the headquarters of the area. Kangema was hardly the height of civilization, but at least there were other Europeans around and it was easier to get into Fort Hall – not that there were any girls there either! However, with so many fit young men around, there was some quite good sport available and Fort Hall fielded very respectable rugby and cricket sides. We called 'rugby' rugger in those days. I was a keen participant in both these sports and we occasionally took our team to play in Nairobi against club sides there. This was fun, involving a dash to Nairobi on Saturday morning in whatever private cars could be mustered, the game that afternoon, followed by a very drunken night on the tiles before slinking back to our bases on the Sunday. Some of us tried to set up dates with girls, but this was more to score points over one's mates if one succeeded in getting a date. It was not much fun for the wretched girl being surrounded by a lot of uncouth randy drunks, and often an embarrassment to oneself having to look after her in the face of mounting competition and the necessity of remaining reasonably sober oneself. I cannot say I had any notable successes at this time! I did not know many girls in Nairobi (or anywhere else, for that matter) – there were not many around in Kenya. 'Nice' girls tended to leave the country soon after school and go to Europe to be 'finished off', or detribalised, as we called it. However, I persuaded one to join me once. It was not a success and in no way helped to relieve my female-less existence.

I was possibly better at rugger than at picking up girls and was selected to play for Central Province one Sunday after one of our Saturday games. Sadly, I injured my right knee in the Saturday game, but was so keen to play on Sunday in my first representative match, that I strapped it up, took painkillers and played. The result was a knee that troubled me for many years, culminating in a big operation in 1994. How many others, like me, have had their lives blighted by rugger accidents in their youth, and by not paying enough attention to injuries that were thought to be insignificant?

CHAPTER 6

Kangema and Cape Town

KANGEMA WAS CERTAINLY MORE CIVILIZED THAN GIKUI. I had a proper house with running water, which I shared with an Englishman called Colin Hamilton-Day. Colin was in Kenya for what these days might be called his 'gap year'. He was out for a bit of fun and certainly had no interest at all in helping to solve the Mau Mau problem. I think that I did and so did my Kenya contemporaries, because Kenya was our home and we wanted to make a good life in the country. This could not happen with Mau Mau going on and we were keen to help put an end to it as soon as possible. We were fairly irresponsible, as one tends to be at that age, but we did do a fair day's work. We probably had more responsibility than our age or experience warranted though.

One of my new jobs in Kangema was to sign movement permits. No Kikuyu was allowed to go anywhere outside his own location without such a permit. Every day there was a stream of applicants outside my office – yes, I even had an office – and I had to assess if that person was a safe enough risk to be allowed out of his own area for whatever period of time. This gave me quite a lot of power as lots of people wanted to go to lots of other places.

Once I was offered money to let a fairly dodgy gentleman travel to Nairobi. I refused, not only the money but also permission for him to go, on principle. I do not think that it ever even entered my head to accept the money. I say this not because I am exceptional in any way at all but because it is indicative of how the country was run. A British civil servant, and when all is said and done that is what I then was, did not accept bribes and did not fiddle the books to enrich himself. It just was not done. I sometimes think of that today, when the British Empire is castigated for all its faults, yet one meekly pays a bribe as a matter of course to get the most trivial of things done in today's Africa.

I was an arrogant little bastard though. If, while I was driving around in my Land Rover, a Kikuyu on the side of the road failed to remove his hat to an officer of the administration, I would stop and confiscate that hat. This I nailed to the door of my office. The childish action was thoroughly approved of by my superiors. The native must be shown his place!

We DOKGs were largely drawn from the settler community in Kenya and, as such, considered ourselves superior beings to the permanent civil servants, who were recruited in England and posted to Kenya, or wherever else, for a four-year tour of duty before returning to England for 'home leave'. This we felt did not give them a real stake in the country. The Civil Service of course was headed by the Governor, at that time Evelyn Baring, and descended to the lowest of (white) Police Officers or District Officers. There was an ongoing rivalry between the settlers and the officials; indeed, the country's main sporting fixture was an annual cricket match between these two camps. This slight animosity manifested itself in our environment. I think that the police thought we were spoilt little privileged pricks, while we thought they were rather common.

This led to a few clashes, particularly at parties when the drink started to flow. Two of my friends, Pete Lucking and Nick Emery, were actually arrested and charged with causing malicious damage to a police post when, after a party at a remote post, they found the gate to the compound locked when they wanted to leave. Not wanting to disturb their host back in the house, they opened fire on the padlock, shattered it and drove off into the night. We considered this 'good form'; the police considered it a crime.

There were certainly plenty of 'characters' around. One of the job descriptions in the Emergency was that of a Field Intelligence Officer or FIO as we called them. This covered a multitude of sins. They were pretty much their own bosses and, as long as they brought in information concerning the whereabouts of terrorists, they were left to their own devices. They were usually slightly older than us and came from a variety of backgrounds.

In our area we had Ian Parker. Ian was considerably more interested in wild life than Mau Mau and was quite happy going off on his own into the Aberdare forest for days on end, often returning with some very nice trout, caught in the mountain streams, but also with very useful information regarding the movement of terrorist gangs. One day he was sitting quietly on the bank of a stream, fishing, when a terrorist suddenly appeared on the opposite bank and also started fishing. Ian, having his rifle at his side, slowly picked it up and shot the terrorist dead. The stream was too deep to cross so he just left him there and carried on fishing.

Ian Pritchard was largely responsible for the capture of Dedan Kimathi. At the end of the Emergency Ian retired to the coast and 'discovered' Turtle Bay at Watamu, near Malindi. It was he who, with a friend, built and started Ocean Sports, which was for many years a favourite place to stay at the coast for locals, and later, internationally well-known as well. Tragically, Ian broke his neck water-skiing in the bay soon after opening the resort and was paralysed from the neck down. Although confined to a wheelchair, he continued to run the place and even taught himself to paint, holding the brush in his mouth.

There was a continual coming and going of personnel, but as the administration got more and more on top of the terrorist situation so the more remote areas were not re-manned. Some of the first to be closed down were the two 'forts' deep in the forest at some nine-and-a-half thousand feet. These were heavily fortified wooden structures, permanently manned and serving as a base for security forces operating clandestinely in the forest. I used to go to both Fort Warwick and Fort Dunluce quite frequently. In many ways they were beautiful places with huge trees, dripping wet undergrowth and every chance of seeing rare game like the bongo, forest duiker, giant forest hog or Colobus monkeys. I have been rude about the British captain shooting a bongo, but I must confess to shooting some Colobus monkeys and having a blanket made out of their lovely skins.

The streams running off the Aberdares had been stocked with rainbow trout and before the Emergency the North and South Mathioya Rivers provided excellent fishing; a club was formed and a beautiful fishing camp built near Tuso, just below the forest edge. This was soon burned down by the Mau Mau and one of my last jobs in Kangema was to help recruit labour to build a new camp, in Kangema village. By 1957 fishermen were drifting back to the area and proper fly-fishing was being resumed. The security forces, I regret to say, had a rather quicker, if cruder, way of getting their supply of fish. A hand grenade tossed in to a pool produced a surprising amount of trout.

In 1996 I revisited Kangema with Nikki and stayed at a new fly-fishing camp built right on the banks of the South Mathioya, not far from the original camp at Tuso. It was a truly lovely, peaceful spot. We drove as far as we could up the old track towards Fort Warwick, but the track had become overgrown and was impassable. We got out and walked and were joined by an old local who remembered the Emergency well. I did not let on that I had been the arrogant young DO who used to confiscate people's hats. The protected villages had all long since been done away with and small huts and shambas were dotted haphazardly all over the place. I tried to find my old guard post at Gikui, but there was nothing there, just a hilltop with a few overgrown ditches.

Kangema itself was a revelation. There were hordes of people everywhere. A tarmac road headed off in the direction of Gikui, where in the old days, there had just been a track. My old office was still there, but it had been added to and there was a large parking lot surrounding it (no hats hanging on my office door!). People were friendly enough; indeed, as soon as one stopped the car was surrounded by a veritable swarm of individuals all wanting to sell something. The whole place was pretty scruffy though, with small stalls all selling vegetables or fruit alongside the road.

Were the people better off than in my day? Yes, probably. Then they were very much under the thumb of the government, particularly during the Emergency, and did not have a lot of freedom. Now they have the vote and have a government they themselves have elected, to set against the corruption that is now endemic in Kenya – and in all African countries.

My time doing National Service was finally up and I left Kangema. I was, however, still liable to be called up to do duty with the Kenya Regiment for two weeks every year for the next four years. Presumably this was just in case there was another uprising and my invaluable services might be required again to help put it down. In fact I only ever did one such stint and the Kenya Regiment ceased to exist a few years afterwards.

I had hoped to go to Cambridge University but, having only done one more year at school following school certificate, my grades were not good enough. So my father asked me what I wanted to do now that I had been released from my National Service. What I did not want to do was to go to England. Memories of my wartime upbringing, although now nine years old, were still too fresh; I had tasted the freedom and sunshine of Africa and so thought that I would like to see somewhere similar.

I agreed with my father that I should get out of Kenya and also, probably, Africa, to broaden my outlook on life in general. These days this sort of thing is referred to as a 'gap year', but then one very often went direct from school to university. I had already been out of school for eighteen months and had presumably grown up a bit thanks to the experience of chasing Mau Mau up and down the Aberdares, so I was more than ready for a bit more adventure. After that I was looking no further afield than returning to Kenya and helping Father run 'Momandu'. Macmillan had not yet made the fateful 'winds of change' speech, and with the apparent demise of the Mau Mau, I saw no reason why the life of a European farmer in Kenya should not continue for the foreseeable future. I think my family and most of our friends thought this too. Jomo

Kenyatta, now safely behind bars and serving seven years' hard labour, obviously did not!

* * *

I had always been interested in South America; it had an air of mystery and excitement about it which appealed, so in answer to my father's question I said I would like to go to Argentina for a bit and work on some of the huge cattle ranches, or estancias, as they were called. None of the family knew anything about Argentina or even how to get there, but a little chatter amongst friends revealed that there was a ranch near Laikipia in north Kenya that was owned by the Waldron family, who also had extensive farming interests in Argentina. Maurice Waldron, one of the brothers involved in the family business, spent a bit of time in Kenya and was in fact in the country in that May of 1957, so we arranged to meet him at Muthaiga Club in Nairobi. My mother told me to put on clean clothes before leaving the farm.

"But I am meant to be a farmer," I said.

"All right then, clean clothes, but make them a bit dirty."

Maurice Waldron was very pleasant and said he was sure his brothers in Argentina could fit me in somewhere as a 'cadet' – nothing military, mind you, but the equivalent of an Australian 'jackaroo'. He would write to them and let us know. My grandfather in Yorkshire was not impressed with this plan and was heard to remark, "You know what Denis is doing with that boy of his? Sending him off to Argentina! Knew a Mexican once – dreadful feller!"

I now had a bit of time on my hands and, it being the polo season, I was determined to play as much as I could. My mother, obviously impressed by my good clean clothes showing, bought me a new pony. The pony was called Damsel and was owned by Francis Erskine. Francis had distinguished himself in the Emergency by blackening his face and going into the forest as a pseudo gangster, accompanied only by genuine former Mau Mau, who had seen the error of their ways and chosen to help our side. They were meant to lead Francis to their old mates' hideout, and Francis would then radio this location back to his base. No one was quite sure what would actually happen when this lot, with Francis in tow, came up with a gang. Francis was awarded an MC for his bravery and, in my book, fully earned it.

Anyway, Francis was prepared to part with Damsel partly, I guessed later, because she was not very good at polo. It turned out that she had been trained by Amber May (née Hook) and was in fact an A-grade showjumper. This gave me ideas way above my station. My sister Sue was currently the leading junior showjumper in the country with her two lovely little ponies, Lili Marlene and Kelpie. I now had a senior A-grade showjumper and would show her a thing or two. Before I had played a chukka on Damsel I invited Sue to watch me pop round her practice fences, just to show her how it should be done. Damsel was very keen and I was very bad, so the net result was that we took the third fence by the roots. Damsel went head over heels and I shot over her head, putting out my right arm to break the fall and snapping my collarbone. Spencer Tryon, that great schooler of racehorses and polo ponies, happened to be staying at the time and was in the sitting room when I limped in supporting my right arm.

"Broken collar bone eh?" he said on seeing me, "nothing to it, I've broken mine nine times, just wire it up."

This was scant comfort. I was due to leave for Argentina in a couple of months, but there were three polo tournaments coming up before that, and the chances of me now playing in any of them was nil. I lent Damsel to Joey Harrison to jump at the big Nairobi show. She did better than me, in that she did not break anything except a lot of the fences. Then I had to watch Father trying to master a very hot Damsel on the polo field while I sulked on the side.

Time passed slowly, but finally it was time to fly to Cape Town to catch a cargo ship to Buenos Aires. I was given a farewell party at the Lobster Pot, Nairobi's best fish restaurant. My parents, my sister and brother-in-law, Penel and John, Sue, and Caroline Branson, a sort of current girl friend, made up the party. We moved on to the Equator Club after dinner. This was a well-known nightspot in those days, and it was here that my one-time army contemporary, Roger Whittaker, whom we knew as 'Hank', used to sing the song about Uhuru. 'Uhuru' was the Africans' call for an end to colonial rule, and meant 'freedom'. Hank's song, which eventually got him chucked out, ran something like this:

Uhuru, uhuru,
This is what we're going to do,
No more work,
No more tax,
We'll sit in the sun and just relax.

I don't think that Hank minded moving on, as he has since become very rich selling albums of his songs all over the world. Not this one though. I drank rather too much brandy, drove Caroline to her home in Langata, made a few amorous passes at her and drove back to my bed at Muthaiga Club.

I awoke feeling not too good, but aware that this was a big day for me. I was to spend the next eighteen months in Argentina. My father had said goodbye to me the night before and I did not see him that day – he drove back to the farm alone. So it was my mother, Penel, Sue and John who took me to the old Eastleigh Airport and put me on a plane for Johannesburg. Flying was a serious business in those days and you were expected to be properly dressed and wear a tie. There were no long-haul flights and my plane made a stop at Salisbury in Rhodesia before going on to Jo'burg. I was glad to be on my way and excited at the idea of what was ahead. My collarbone was mostly mended but not strong, and carrying heavy suitcases was a bad idea. My plane went no further than Jo'burg, so it meant spending the night there before flying on to Cape Town next morning.

When we landed in Cape Town some very ancient, distant cousins called Ken and Vivienne Cookson, who lived in a lovely house in the

Wynberg area, met me. I had heard a lot about South Africa but most of this had been good. Apartheid was not a word that I, or most people, had even heard of. Any discussion on South Africa revolved round the elevation to power of the Nationalist Party in the shape of the much-disliked Boers, or whether the Springboks could beat the All Blacks at rugger. The part of Cape Town where I found myself was still very much the preserve of the British South Africans and indeed most that I met were more British than South African or even than the British themselves.

That night I was taken to dinner at the Mount Nelson Hotel. There were nine of us in all and I was the youngest by sixty-one years – it was an eightieth birthday party!

Having been brought up in Kenya, where it was general for all ages to mix freely, made this less of an ordeal for a nineteen-year-old than it might have been for someone brought up in Britain. The food was excellent, and that helped – oysters, crayfish, fruit and cheese all from the area and served as fresh as could be.

I was to remain in the Cape for nearly two weeks. The ship I was due to sail on kept getting delayed and cousins Ken and Vivienne must have grown sick of the sight of me. To their eternal credit they never showed it and went out of their way to entertain me, taking me racing at Kenilworth, visiting Kirstenbosch Gardens and other endless flower gardens, to watch Pat Smythe competing at a local horse show and to numerous excellent little restaurants where I filled my face with more delicious seafood. I met no one of my own age, which was a pity, but walked for miles down wide leafy streets as far as Groote Schuur and the National Park given by Cecil Rhodes, which contained exotic animals that I had not seen before, like blesbok, bontebok and white-tailed gnu. I saw very few Africans and really one might have been in the upmarket suburb of a European city (except, perhaps for the white-tailed gnus). I revisited the Wynberg area forty years later and it was deemed unsafe to walk alone along these same streets. The whole area was built up, motorways tore through the lovely leafy suburb and thugs patrolled their patch ready to rob and beat up any idle stroller like me.

Finally my ship, the M.V. *Straat Malaka*, was ready to sail, and with muted sighs of relief I was deposited on board. It was a Dutch cargo ship with about four passengers. There was a very nice captain and friendly crew, large meals were served in the officers' dining room and booze cost virtually nothing. I was able to enjoy none of these pleasures for at least three days. I am an appalling sailor and, after just managing to appreciate the view leaving Cape Town harbour, lay groaning on my bunk as I was racked by seasickness. I was to be away for nearly two years, but that is another story.

CHAPTER 7

'Momandu'

EARLY IN 1959 I ARRIVED BACK IN Kenya, having taken another cargo boat as far as Mombasa and then catching a train up to Konza station, where my father met me. It was great to be back in Africa! On the surface everything seemed the same. The Emergency was over, Jomo Kenyatta was still in prison, the rains had been kind to us in Machakos and 'Momandu' was doing OK. But there was a nasty feeling simmering under the surface. The Emergency may have been over but I think everyone knew that the overall problem was far from settled. The black population wanted independence, and everyone also knew in their heart of hearts that they were going to get it sooner rather than later.

This led to a slightly false attitude to life – eat, drink and be merry, for tomorrow we may die. Farmers were not putting quite as much back into their farms as they used to. Certainly my father had never saved a penny in the years he had been on 'Momandu', as everything that could be spared had been ploughed back into the farm in the form of fencing, bush clearing, dams, boreholes, roads and better livestock. Now, although he was not 'milking' the land, there was not nearly as much long-term development going on.

He was still very busy and had hired a young European assistant called Brian Miller. I wondered a little bit where I would fit in to the scheme of things. This did not initially worry me as I was far too busy catching up with friends, playing polo, shooting big game and generally enjoying myself. Looking back now I wonder where the money came from. I had not saved anything from my jobs in Argentina and my parents had precious little to spare. I did help on the farm and was paid something, and this must have been enough for me to indulge in the rather exotic pastimes I mention.

Polo was probably my favourite pastime, then and in future years in other countries. Polo is often described as a game played by millionaires in a cloud of dust on the other side of the ground. Obviously this is not true of Kenya, but certainly in Europe or America it was and still is a very expensive sport. In those countries also it often has a certain social standing.

In Kenya in the early 1960s we played it on the horses that we rode round the farm for work. It was something to do over the weekend and a fun way to get together with our neighbours. There was no television in those days. We had a lot of fun and it did not matter at all that we were in fact pretty bad. We made a very dusty field on the edge of the Kapiti plains not too far from Konza station. Things like irrigation were unheard of and we just mowed the coarse plains grass, filled in the antbear holes – most of them – and marked out a full sized ground with whitewash.

To start with we did not have proper goal posts but just stuck a couple of sisal poles in the ground. Then a Nairobi team came to visit us and play a match. They were horrified by what they saw and where they had to play, but having survived the weekend each player donated a proper polo goalpost made of light plywood and covered in canvas. We painted them in our club colours of green and white. I think that this first team to visit Machakos Polo Club consisted of Ben Allen, Derek Erskine, Charles Markham and Peter Johnson. Having entertained these guests we were then obliged to travel to other clubs and pit our skills against them.

And so we went to Nairobi for the big annual New Year tournament. The only section that we were eligible to enter was the very lowest. This was a competition for teams with a maximum total handicap of six. Each team member was only allowed to use one pony and a match was played in conjunction with another one, in that you played one chukka then sat out and rested your pony while the other match played one chukka. The whole idea of this competition was to encourage young and penniless players, who perhaps only had one pony but wanted to play in a tournament. It was a great idea and was the brainchild of two old Indian Army colonels (of whom there were plenty in Kenya at that time) called Mervyn Ridley and Donald Ferguson. The competition became known as the 'Mugs' Mug' and was hugely popular. Not only was it a fun event, but also the prize for winning it was stunning. Each member of the team got a pure silver champagne goblet supported by three silver polo sticks, standing eight inches high. This lovely trophy was yours for keeps if you won so it was no great surprise that it was the most sought after trophy in Kenyan polo. The cost of these magnificent trophies had of course been borne by the two old colonels, but the fund was limited and it is perhaps fitting that it ran out the year before Kenya attained independence, as I am sure the two colonels would not have approved of the new government. The Mugs' Mug is still competed for annually in Kenya, but alas no solid silver trophy for the winner.

When we first competed for the trophy I think our total handicap was one, and we were soundly thrashed in the first round. The only person who had played any proper polo was Frank Howden and he it was who boasted the handicap of 1. The rest of us were 0 and only 0 because the idea of having minus ratings had not then been thought of. The rest of us were my father and Peter Leonard, a nearby farming friend, plus me. Most years we also entered the mixed tournament, which was for two men and two girls. Here, my father and I joined forces with my sister Sue and any spare girl who was brave enough to join our team. I think the first was Rose Powys (now Dyer) from North Kenya. Later John Shaw, who married my elder sister Penel and was quite a respectable player, boosted our men's team.

I have played a lot of polo since those days and reached a reasonable standard, playing some representative games with a handicap of 3, but I can honestly say that those early family games were the greatest fun I have ever had on the polo field. To go anywhere we had to walk the ponies fifteen miles across the Athi Plains to Konza station, passing vast herds of game on the way, and install them in a cattle truck and consign them to places like Molo or Nyeri. This would probably be on the Tuesday, and then we would follow by car early on the Friday, hoping to get there in time for our first match, which was usually that afternoon.

All clubs we visited, other than Nairobi, were in farming districts. Our ponies would be stabled at the ground and we would be put up by local farmers who were fellow polo players. Friday night there would be a dinner party at our host's home. Neighbours would be asked and very often it would be a dinner jacket and black tie occasion. Next morning there would often be a shoot laid on, either for birds or, if you were in North Kenya and anywhere near the Powyses, buffalo.

'Kisima Farm', which was and still is owned by the Powys family, stretched right up to the edge of the forest on the slopes of Mount Kenya. This was not a National Park in those days but it was full of game, and herds of buffalo and elephant would frequently cross the fence dividing the forest from the farming area. 'Kisima' grew wheat and a herd of buffalo could do a lot of damage to this crop in a single night, so it was both profitable and fun to entertain one's guests with a buffalo hunt. Tracking these magnificent animals through the dense undergrowth of equatorial forest was exciting and at times nerve-racking. The last thing you wanted to do was to wound one. Not only do you always want a clean kill, but also a wounded animal always has to be followed until you do kill it, and a wounded buffalo in thick bush is a formidable opponent. Slightly tamer but no less amusing shoots were held in the drier areas of the farm lower down the mountainside. Here were to be found flocks of guineafowl and francolin, and walking through the dry scrub with dogs and a shotgun was a wonderful way to spend a morning and in stark contrast to the thrill of the buffalo hunts. 'Kisima' and the adjoining farm, 'Ngare Ndare', also owned by the Powys family, provided an amazing contrast in scenery and climate in themselves, as they stretched from the forest edge at a height of over ten thousand feet above sea level right down to about four thousand feet.

On Saturday night there would always be a huge party held at the clubhouse. Finals, for those who could still stand, were on the Sunday morning, and after a large cold lunch washed down by pints of Pimms you would put the ponies back on a train and stagger off home, not getting there until after midnight. There may be better ways of spending a weekend, but offhand I cannot think of any. I met some wonderful people, and they remain friends to this day despite now being scattered all over the world. Many were great characters. As I have mentioned, there were then a large number of ex-Indian Army officers in Kenya. They had come to Kenya after India's independence in 1947 mainly because they were able to sustain the same sort of lifestyle that they had been used to. Most of them seemed to play polo and a lot had been pretty good. "Had been" was possibly the operative verb; most were over fifty and their glory days over. However, this did not stop them taking a very active part in the local polo scene.

Molo, situated at over eight thousand feet above sea level, was one of the colonels' strongholds. A tournament there would be fraught with the danger of offending one of many crusty old characters that regarded my generation as irresponsible Kenya 'cowboys'. Molo could easily raise a team consisting entirely of ageing colonels – Keighley, Sheppard, Knaggs and Broadfoot, to mention but four. They never did play as a team though, as they disapproved as much of each other (wrong regiment, old boy) as they did of us.

Any Molo team, though, had a fair sprinkling of them and their collective indignation reached a climax when my sister Sue was allowed to play in our team. It is comparatively common these days for women to play on equal terms in an otherwise all-male team, but then it was a clear sign that the empire had surely come to a very sticky end. Sue was not a particularly strong ball striker but was a more than capable strong rider, so in our match against Molo my father told her just to mark old Will Broadfoot, their ageing colonel who had been a 6 handicap. He had now slipped to a 3 but was still a very good, crafty player and at the level we were playing could totally dominate a game. That is, if he got a chance to hit the ball. He did not! Sue totally ignored the ball and spent the entire match riding old Will off, whether he was anywhere near the play or not. Always red in the face (what one could see under the sun cream that he used to cover himself in), Will slowly turned purple with rage and finally exploded in a series of expletives that would have done any of his company sergeant majors proud, and ended up by telling Sue to take her fucking stick out of his face. John Shaw, who had heard the exchange, immediately complained to the umpire, who insisted on Broadfoot apologizing. We won the game in a canter and to Will's eternal credit not only did he apologize most graciously but thereafter became an ardent admirer of Sue, referring to her as "my little tiger".

Another prominent character at Molo was Spencer Tryon. He was not a colonel or even a major, but, having served in the Boer War and First World War, had risen to the rank of captain. Spencer was a wonderful horseman and was for many years leading racehorse trainer in Kenya. In 1926 he bred, owned, trained and rode a horse called 'Restless' to win the Kenya Derby. He also played polo on tiny little Arab ponies, which made up for their lack of speed by being incredibly handy and quick on their feet. When I was sixteen and weighed considerably less than I did later, I spent school holidays with Spencer and his wife, Lillian. He tried to teach me something about polo and that most important part of the sport, schooling the ponies. As I was light, he also reckoned that he could teach me to ride his racehorses, particularly those that he ran in hurdle races. This was not because I was a potentially brilliant jockey but because I would do as I was told and could claim the 5lbs apprentice allowance. I rode in a few of these races for him at the very amusing amateur race meetings held at Limuru. I did not win any but did better than my friend Walter Raleigh Gilbert. He was mounted on a horse called 'Dusty Answer' owned by Vicky Jackman, but got run away with going down to the start and came thundering back past the stands before crashing into a tree and breaking the poor horse's neck. Walter returned to England and became a very well-known racing commentator under the name of Raleigh (pronounced Raw-ley) Gilbert. I imagine he was a better commentator than race rider, as he had not had a great racing career in Kenya.

Spencer used his grooms, or syces, as they were called in Kenya, to help train his ponies and those of visiting ponies sent to him for schooling. These syces also played in club chukkas at Molo Club and one or two became very good players. My father often maintained that they were as good as any of the top Europeans then playing in Kenya, so when an international side visited Kenya from South Africa I asked if any of Spencer's syces would be considered for the national side. My father was genuinely horrified at the idea and I remember saying, "What's the problem? It is their country as much as ours." This only made it worse and he accused me (jokingly) of being a follower of Fenner Brockway, the left-wing Labour MP currently crusading for black independence. I think my father's attitude was a fair reflection of the general feeling amongst whites in Kenya at that time.

Spencer's other great love was shooting birds over his Spaniels, and he and Lillian used to come down to Machakos to stay with us, as we had some very good francolin shooting on the farm. He was there when a mother cheetah and four large cubs started killing our calves. I was keen to go out and shoot them but Spencer, who in his youth had shot everything that moved, tried to persuade me not to. I am now getting on for the same age as Spencer was at that time and feel exactly the same way as he did. I could not bear to shoot a cheetah now, but I did then.

Spencer was a wiry little man who kept himself incredibly fit and was still riding in flat races at the age of eighty. One day, when he was riding back from a hard race, a well-meaning old lady of his acquaintance said to him, "Spencer, you really must stop doing this sort of thing at your age; one day it will kill you."

"Madam," he replied, "I sincerely hope it does; I can think of no better way to go."

Col 'Rhino' Fosdick represented the Colonels' brigade in Nairobi. He was still pretty good and played 'back' on huge horses while shouting instructions ('commands' would probably be a better word) to terrified beginners, who comprised most of Nairobi Polo Club at that time. All this was fine on the field of play, but his new wife tended to let him down a bit in the clubhouse. She was unable to refuse a drink and while she drank quite a lot of those given to her, others she hid behind curtains and in cupboards just in case she was not offered any more. On clearing up our clubhouse after one tournament we found half a dozen full glasses of Pimms hidden about the place.

Digby Tatham-Warter was another character. He was not a colonel but, like my father, a wartime major with a very distinguished record. It was he who led his company across the bridge at Arnhem 'armed' only with a tightly rolled umbrella, and he also organized the evacuation of resistance workers and 'evaders' from Nazi-occupied Holland, for which he was awarded a DSO. His friends said of him, "In battle we would follow Digby anywhere. Mind you, we might want to shoot him on the way back!"

He was probably the best polo player in Kenya at that time, being a 6 handicap. He captained the national team when Kenya had visits from Rhodesia and South Africa. He was always immaculately turned out in fawn-coloured britches and beautifully mounted on ponies that he schooled himself. He affected to be very pompous and if you let him get away with it he was. He had one really lovely pony called 'Vision' and at the start of one of the Test matches against South Africa he had his syce lead Vision on to the field of play in front of the grandstand. Digby, captain of the team, immaculate in every detail as usual, then approached, took hold of the reins, put his left foot in the stirrup and started to swing himself gracefully into the saddle, watched by an admiring crowd. The only trouble was that the stirrup leather was attached to the saddle by a bit of string, and as Digby's right leg was at its highest over Vision's back the string broke and Digby crashed on to his back in the dust. The resulting roar of laughter did little for Digby's temper or the long-term job prospects of the syce. When I got a bit better at polo,

I played a few representative games against the likes of Rhodesia under Digby's captaincy. It is a fact that some men are born to lead and some to follow. Digby was not a follower.

Not all the polo-playing characters were military men by any means. Derek Erskine was a grocer. He ran the biggest wholesale grocery business in Nairobi at that time – Erskine and Duncan. Derek was upper-class English, sported an enormous moustache, drove a Rolls-Royce and could not pronounce his 'r's'. He was also very left-wing for that era and incensed a lot of his friends by adopting a little Kikuyu boy during the Emergency at the same time as his son, Francis, was earning an MC for shooting slightly larger Kikuyu boys in the Aberdare forests. People sometimes asked Derek why he behaved quite like he did. He replied that it was good for business.

"I would be widing in my Wolls and someone would say, 'Who's that dweadful man?' and the weply would be, 'Oh! That's my gwocer,' and I would get another customer."

Derek loved his polo, but was not very good at it. He was inclined to charge down the ground, slightly out of control, yelling, "Out of my way, my ball", at the top of his voice and then miss it. "Sowwy," he would shout back over his shoulder. I am not quite sure what he did to deserve it, but Derek was eventually knighted for services to Kenya.

'Bwana' Begg had probably served in the war, but he boasted no military rank. He owned a large stretch of land near Gilgil in the Rift Valley, where he raised sheep and Boran cattle. A lot of the land was very flat, and 'Bwana' Begg, being a polo lover, created two of the best polo fields in the country and formed a club, which was called Kinyatta – modified to 'Manyatta' after independence in deference to the new president's name.

'Bwana' Begg had a lot of horses as well, and was most generous in lending them to all and sundry to further promote the game of polo. When I visited Kenya years later for Sue's wedding, he lent me two lovely ponies for the duration of my stay, thus enabling me to play in two tournaments. He also lent ponies to any member of the British Army who wanted to play polo while based at the nearby Gilgil barracks, made them honorary members of his club and generally entertained them right royally. In 1962 I was chosen to play in the Kenya polo trials to compete for a place in the team to play Rhodesia in their forthcoming visit. I had no chance of making the team, but numbers were required. The trials were held at Kinyatta and there not being much accommodation available, 'Bwana' Begg asked the nearby Officers' Mess if they would put up John Cullen and myself for the duration of the games. He no doubt figured that it would enable them in some small way to repay some of the hospitality that he had lavished on them. Imagine our surprise, therefore, when John and I were presented with a mess bill on the morning of our departure! I am afraid that Brits who visited Kenya (and later Rhodesia/Zimbabwe) got a bit of a reputation for this sort of behaviour. They were great at accepting hospitality but, particularly back in England, terrible at returning it.

Most of those mentioned were of course considerably older than me, but they were a fair sample of that generation then living in Kenya. I had plenty of friends of my own age who were characters in their own right. Most of them were sons of farmers. While by world standards it was cheap enough to play polo if you lived in Nairobi, it was infinitely cheaper to play if you lived on a farm and used the ponies for farm work. I think it is true to say that only the very best players kept ponies exclusively for polo.

One of these was Don Rooken-Smith. He had been at school with me but three years my senior. Don posed a serious challenge to the superiority of the colonel brigade and was much the best player of we youngsters, rising to the dizzy heights of a 6 handicap. His family farmed north of Nairobi near Kipkabus and both his brother, Bruce, and father, Hal, were good players. Don married Mary Foster who was also a very good player in her own right. Mary was very pretty, which surprised some people when they looked at her brothers Robo and Fuz. Both these two also played polo, when not duck shooting, so the two families could raise a couple of formidable polo teams. Robo and Fuz never married, but lived on in Kenya and had sufficient godchildren to make up for any lack of family of their own. Sadly, Robo died in 2006. Don and Mary live in Florida now and have four daughters. I saw them there in 2007 and we had long talks about those Kenya days. Don has an amazing memory and remembers all the ponies he used to ride and a lot of those ridden by others. He also had a wonderful collection of old photos.

I had been at school with the Powys brothers, who worked with their father on 'Kisima', so I often stayed with them. Hunting big game was Gilfred's passion and he was known to adopt some fairly unusual methods. Herds of zebra frequented part of the farm and Gilfred had a market for their skins so, rather than shoot them and damage the skin, he would gallop after them on his polo ponies and beat them over the head with a knobkerrie. Crude, yes, but difficult and exciting, both of which were essential requirements for Gilfred.

One afternoon he arrived rather late for his polo game, so he parked his Land Rover on the side of the ground, leaped out and on to his waiting pony, played a hard four chukkas and repaired to the bar. Sometime in the evening I went outside for a pee and noticed a godawful stink coming from his Land Rover. I went over to it and peered inside. There I saw three very dead lions. Gilfred had been out all night after them, as they had been killing his cattle. Having got them, he had chucked them into the back of the Landy and forgotten all about them. There were a lot of lions about in those days and they did a lot of damage to livestock. Gilfred told me that it was the custom in the area, that if you had a lion problem on your farm, you were honour bound to sort it out yourself and not enlist the help of neighbours such as the Murrays or Craigs. A bit macho? Well, yes.

One got very little sleep staying with the Powyses – that seemed to bore them. We would always be up by four-thirty and rarely in bed before eleven. One Sunday morning when I had been staying with Charlie, Gilfred, who had gone out the evening before on his own, had not returned by well after breakfast, so we mounted a bit of a search party. Before long we spotted his Land Rover parked beside a small

84

track and on getting nearer we could see a pair of legs sticking out from underneath. We feared the worst and thought that Gilfred had had one prang too many but on peering under the vehicle found him peacefully snoring and completely oblivious to the time. Perhaps he needed more sleep than he thought. Charlie was slightly the saner of the two, but it was he who came to a tragic end. He failed to unload his heavy rifle when putting it away one night after shooting meat for his labour's Christmas. In putting it away he banged it on the door of the safe and it discharged a high velocity bullet straight into his chest. It was a terrible loss to our age group, as Charlie had been very much a leader in the community. He got on very well with, and understood, the local Africans at a time when the whole political situation was pretty tense and cool heads were needed. He had recently married the lovely Joffa Long and had a small daughter.

Other friends of mine were the Fernandes family, who lived at Mweiga, near Nyeri, some hundred miles north of Nairobi. They were also farmers, headed by their father, Charles. I first met Bobby, the youngest of three brothers and a sister, in a children's point-to-point race at their local annual gymkhana when we were both teenagers. It was pouring with rain and both my sister Sue and I were entered in some of the races. My mother tried to dissuade us from starting, as the course was terribly wet and getting wetter and very slippery. I was due to ride a newish pony I had, called 'Gunner', while Sue was to ride her old patent safety, 'Punch'. I had not done a lot of riding at that stage of my life and was fairly keen to accept my mother's advice, particularly as I knew I would have no control whatsoever over Gunner once we got started. But Sue was keen to give it a go, so I could hardly chicken out.

There were probably ten other riders, including Bobby, who set off on a course of some one and a half miles over about a dozen fences. At the start Gunner shot off into the lead with me hanging on for dear life, closely followed by Sue on Punch. The two of us kicked up a continuous shower of mud into the faces of Bobby and the rest of them and we were never headed. Gunner was first, Punch second with Bobby a very muddy third. It was the start of a lifetime friendship. Bobby and I got up to a lot of mischief together over the next few years in Kenya. He wanted to marry Sue, followed us to South Africa when we eventually moved there, became my best man, and I his, when we both moved on to Rhodesia. He is now semi-retired in England, but I sometimes look at the little silver cup that Gunner won that day in 1952 and remember everything that has happened since. It was the first cup I ever won. A sideline to this story is that, if you look at Bobby today, you would be hard pressed to visualize him as a jockey.

Bobby's brother Eddie took over as manager on Kisima soon after Charlie's death and ran the place most efficiently for about thirty years. He and his wife, Bisto, remained in Kenya after independence and are still there. When he retired from 'Kisima', he became the first white man to buy back a commercial farm that had originally been owned by a white settler and then an indigenous black. The eldest brother, Micky, also remained in Kenya, on the farm owned by his in-laws, before finally retiring to England. I sometimes wonder why I did not remain in Kenya as they did. Kenya certainly had its ups and downs over the next forty or so years but Eddie, Micky and many others of my age lived very fulfilling lives there and had a lot of fun. It is ironic that, as I write this in 2009, my son Harry is happily farming in Kenya, having moved there some two years ago after being kicked off his farm in Zimbabwe by Mugabe's thugs.

The Fernandes's sister, Jane, was a much sought after young girl in the 1950s and Kenya manhood's pride was severely dented when Jane was 'stolen' by a visiting Rhodesian polo player called Eric Snook. She moved to his farm near Bindura in what was then Rhodesia and I saw a lot of them when I finally ended up there myself. When Eric died in 2003, Jane moved to Canada to be with her daughter, just another of the many good people who in their retirement left Zimbabwe because of Mugabe's ruinous anti-white policies.

In the mid fifties and early sixties Kenya had visits from two other polo-playing countries. South Africa was the first to send a team, and then Rhodesia came up twice. These visits were prolonged affairs and not a bit like the flying ones undertaken on an annual basis these days. A team of six would drive up (not with their ponies) and stay in the country for over a month, playing against most of the club sides, with three Test matches being included at regular intervals. In between the actual matches, the visiting players would experience the considerable hospitality extended by the Kenya players. This would include a lot of shooting, visits to Kenya's stunning coast, expeditions to various game parks and even a bit of farming.

I played against all these sides and made some very good contacts in both South Africa and Rhodesia, two countries in which I subsequently lived. The first South African side was captained by Craig Brown from Natal, and it included Abie Tren from Johannesburg, and Hugh Fraser and Cedric Bastard from East Griqualand. The Bastard family were well represented in Kenya and Cedric was a cousin of theirs. When Princess Elizabeth visited Kenya in 1952 and toured their farming area, all the families' children dressed alike and lined the road as she drove past. The Princess turned to her aide and asked who they all were.

"Oh!" was the reply. "They are all the little Bastard children."

"Really?" replied the Princess, "what a good idea to dress them all alike."

The reserve player in this South African team was Lawrence Slatter, whose brother's farm in Natal was later bought by my parents after both were killed in an air crash.

The Rhodesians were a bunch of cheerful, hard-drinking farmers – Rodney Morris, Ralph Townsend, Peter Haarhoff, Tim Riley, Eric Snook and Philip Duncan. I got to know them all well when I moved to Rhodesia in 1967. They were followed by a younger bunch that I played my last game of polo in Kenya against – David Meikle, Basil and Chris Kearns, John Browning and Henry Tuckey. David was older than me and I have not played polo for ten years, but he has just died at the age of eighty-two while practising to play in a tournament with his grandson. The British Army also sent out a team, and I was chosen to represent the Kenya Regiment in a match against them, with Don Rooken-Smith, Eddie Fernandes and John Chart. We got well beaten by a side consisting of Ronnie Ferguson, Patrick Beresford, Paul Withers and James Harman. While we all had a lot in common with the African teams from the south of us, we did not get on nearly so well with the 'Poms', who appeared to enjoy the company at Government House rather more than ours.

When in Nairobi a lot of the entertaining of these teams took place at Muthaiga Club. These could be wild affairs, and my brother-in-law's father, Sir Robert Shaw, had been attending these parties for many years. When deciding whether or not to marry his wife, Joan, he was found sitting on the roof of the club, tossing off the tiles and chanting, "She loves me, she loves me not..."

The club management always took a very relaxed view of this sort of behaviour. They calmly watched it all happen, totted up what it would cost to repair the damage caused, doubled this amount, and sent a bill to the perpetrators, who, by the time they got the bill were so ashamed of what they had done that they meekly paid it. This was a far better policy than having a row with members during the party – and much more profitable. Sir Robert was a notorious culprit and regularly got a bill. Once he got one when he had not even been at the party!

One year our whole family was in Nairobi for the annual New Year polo tournament, and of course the New Year's Eve dance. Sue was just about old enough both to attend the dance and to play in our mixed team in the polo tournament. At about 4:30am, when the party was beginning to wind down, Sue's beau decided that instead of going to bed it would be more fun to visit Nairobi National Park. This they duly did, accompanied by two others, one of whom was Bobby Fernandes. As dawn broke it occurred to them that maybe they should all go home and get some breakfast before attempting to play polo. Bobby was staying at the club and Sue at the house of friends where my parents were also staying, so they all went first to drop off Sue.

The 'beau' was driving, so it was left to Bobby to walk Sue up to the front door. The owners of the house had laid an ambush for her by putting a bucket of water over the front door. It didn't fall on Sue however but my father, who, on hearing a car approaching, had come storming down in his pyjamas to see if it was his daughter returning. Bobby was the comparatively innocent party but took the full brunt of my father's rage. He retreated before the blows from Father's polo whip only to discover that the 'beau' had driven off in terror, leaving Bobby stranded miles from his bed in a dinner jacket with dawn breaking. Having failed to catch Bobby, Father turned his wrath on Sue, and it soon became apparent that he was not in the least concerned about her virtue but far more about how terrible her polo was likely to be following a sleepless night!

Muthaiga survived independence and is still going strong. It is still patronized by those of the white community who remain in Kenya. There are of course black members as well, but when Nikki and I stayed there on a visit from Zimbabwe in 2006 we did not see any, and the place was full.

CHAPTER 8

England Again

BY THE EARLY 1960S THERE WAS MORE and more chat in Kenya about the possibility of the colony being granted independence from Britain and the blacks therefore running the country. No one was actually leaving yet, and having been back from my travels for over a year now I was very happy to continue farming on 'Momandu' with my father. However, his very pretty goddaughter, Viv Taylor, from England, had been staying with us on and off for the past few months and, despite her having a current beau back there, I had fallen in love with her. She had now returned to England and I was wondering what to do about it.

My eccentric grandmother Alice, Lady Butler, had also been staying with us on 'Momandu' for some three months, which was probably a couple of months longer than my father would have liked. It had not worried me, as I was often away, and when not away I found her an engaging old bird. Anyway, suddenly she said that she must return to London but was frightened of flying. Would I go with her if she paid my fare? Too right I would. Viv was there now and presumably back in the arms of her beloved, but I saw no reason why I should not try to prise her loose from them. I did stay with her at her parents' place near Oxford, and we went to Badminton Horse Trials together, but I was never in with a chance. We parted good friends and she named her eldest son Mark – small consolation.

My sister Sue was also in England at that time, at Hartwell House near Aylesbury, attending an institution called the House of Citizenship, which was run with a rod of iron by Richard Holme's cousin, Miss Dorothy Neville-Rolfe. The place was supposed to rub the rough edges off young colonial ladies like Sue, and make them into beings suitable for English society. They must have been quite good, because they were faced with quite a challenge in Sue and yet turned her out pretty well in the end – not that there was anything wrong with her before in my view.

During Sue's holidays we went together to Ireland and drove round in a Mini Minor that I had bought in England. This was fun, as we visited distant relatives scattered all over the south; we also made a pilgrimage to my mother's old family home in Carlow called 'Ballin Temple', which had been burned down in 'The Bad Times' of 1916 by Irish nationalists and never rebuilt. The Butler family still owned land there and had a delightful little cottage on the Slaney River, where we stayed.

From there we visited old family friends, the Rathdonalds, who lived nearby in Lisnavagh, a freezing, cold, old house standing in lovely grounds. The current Lady Rathdonald called herself Pamela Drew, perhaps because she was a pretty good artist and sold pictures of aeroplanes under that name. She was eccentric as well. She gave a dinner party for us and insisted that it was held in total darkness. This made eating difficult and conversation interesting, because you never knew who you were talking to. Pamela had a resident lover called Hugh Massey who had been in Kenya; she referred to him as 'Carruthers'. When we came to leave we could not find our Mini. It took a good half hour and a lot of mirth before we discovered that Carruthers and Pamela's son Ben had picked it up and carried it through the French windows into the schoolroom. Minis were very new in those days and they had never seen so small a car.

We also stayed with another very eccentric friend of the family, Aunt Obby to me, or to give her her full title the Countess Olive Fitzwilliam. She was not an aunt at all but was my godmother. I had never met her previously. She lived on a large, beautiful estate called 'Coollattin', which had an equally large and beautiful old house. Aunt Obby did not like daylight. She slept all day and only emerged in the evenings, when she drank large quantities of gin, and she insisted that her racehorse trainer came to talk to her about his charges at times like two o'clock in the morning. We stayed a couple of days but did not see a lot of her as we tended to be about in the daytime. Some years later she left me some money, but we were living in illegal Rhodesia at the time and her petty-minded lawyer, Macwatt, would not send it to me.

I liked Ireland. Most people seemed to be eccentric to a greater or lesser degree but very friendly and laid back. I think we were lucky with the weather because we got very little rain and this was unusual: it is not called 'the Emerald Isle' for nothing. We took the ferry back across to Liverpool with the Mini on board and sat up most of the night drinking with Ben Rathdonald. I am usually hopelessly seasick but on this occasion my intake of alcohol appeared to cancel out the queasiness.

* * *

I was now out of money, so I got a job on a farm in Sussex working for Mick Reed. Mick had dairy cattle and a pedigree Sussex herd amongst other things, but he was not then too interested in the day-to-day running of the two farms he owned. He was still very involved in flying and was a bit like Aunt Obby in that he was awake more at night than in the day. What little money I made and all the spare time I got was spent playing polo at Cowdray Park. A Kenyan friend, Peter Barclay, introduced me to the setup there, where you could hire ponies at thirty shillings per chukka and play in various low goal tournaments if considered good enough. The standard was not high and I made the grade in this regard all right.

Thirty shillings a chukka may not sound a lot, but I was not earning very much and so it was a lot to me, and I wanted to make the most of it. For one of my first tournaments I was teamed up with the legendary Indian high goal player, Rao Raja Hanut Singh. He was rated about 6 then (having at one time been 10), while I was a lowly 2. The result was that whenever I got anywhere near the ball, there would be a bellow of "leave it!" from behind me and I was expected to gallop on, waiting for a pass from Hanut which never came. I quickly worked out that I was getting very little value for my thirty bob, so I took the unprecedented step of ignoring Hanut's shouts and having a dip at the ball myself. I was not asked to play with him again.

I played in a few other tournaments, notably with a very pleasant ex-Indian Army colonel called Alec Harper. In one match we were confronted by the well-known comedian Jimmy Edwards, who rode a huge greyish-coloured horse, which was covered with black spots. This was not because it was a particularly good polo pony, but because it served to advertise his current TV programme, *Whacko*, which was about him being headmaster of a school and doling out black marks to pupils, resulting in them being whacked. Neither the programme nor Jimmy Edwards were particularly good.

Polo in England was not nearly as much fun as it was in Kenya. It was frequently cold and wet and a lot of people played it for the wrong reasons. They just wanted to be seen doing it and playing with celebrities like Jimmy Edwards. My uncle knew Lord Cowdray quite well and this resulted in my getting an invitation to dinner at the main house after one tournament. This required a dinner jacket and I did not possess one. I consulted my team captain, Alec Harper.

"I'll find you one," he said, and immediately borrowed one belonging to an Indian prince who was staying with him. Clad in this, I presented myself for dinner and was pleasantly surprised to have a very enjoyable evening.

Lord Cowdray was an excellent host and I ended the evening playing billiard fives against him. Here I felt I would have a considerable advantage, as he only had one arm. This disability certainly did not prevent him from playing polo though. Fortunately it was the left arm that he had lost, so on to the stump he had strapped a leather contraption with a hook on the end. With this, he could hold the reins and with a certain amount of difficulty control his pony. At billiard fives you badly need both arms and

I was at a loss as to know how unsporting I should be by sending the ball to his left side. I need not have worried though. Having sportingly played only on his right side I soon found myself five-love down, so I switched to the other side only to find that he was far too nimble for me and still won easily. I suspect it was something of a party piece of his to defeat young men at this game, but it was all a lot of fun.

I did sufficient work on Mick's farm to realize that farming in England was not for me. Although it was mid-summer and we were in the far south of the country, it always seemed to be wet, and usually cold. Huge Friesian dairy cows are not my favourite; they appeared to produce a never-ending stream of liquid shit in the dairy, and it was my job to clean it up.

I had a widowed cousin in London who was heavily involved in the 'deb' scene. Anxious mothers, with a daughter who was 'coming out' that season and who did not know enough eligible young men to invite to her party, would contact my cousin and get her to invite a selection of suitable young men to make up the numbers. My cousin thought that I would qualify as such a young man. Little did she know! The result was that I got a stream of very smart invitations from people I had never heard of. There were usually two for the same occasion, one for a dinner party and one for the actual dance.

Not having any nearby Indian princes, I had to invest in a dinner jacket and after evening milking I would drive miles down unknown lanes in my Mini to some very smart stately pile where the dinner party was to be held. I would arrive, usually late, smelling strongly of cow shit and be introduced to a stream of very smart strangers. They all knew each other and none of the young set – my age group – did any work. They were permanent partygoers, for the summer at any rate, attending dinners and dances at least three nights a week, with events like Lord's, Henley and Ascot, where they could nurse their hangovers during the day.

An excellent dinner would be followed by another long drive down more narrow lanes (no motorways in those days), after which we would arrive at an even more stately pile where the actual dance was to be held. It was probably well after ten o'clock by now. More introductions, and the crowd I had had dinner with and got to know slightly, disappeared into the throng to meet yet more of their friends. The band would strike up and I would look desperately round for someone to dance with. If I did manage to convince some naïve girl that she should partner me, she would spend most of the dance shouting over my shoulder at her friends and pay no attention at all to my fascinating stories about Mau Mau terrorists, African rhinos and Argentinian gauchos. I had been told that it was polite to dance with each female member of your dinner party. This became a problem because I often could not remember what they looked like and certainly could not remember their names, and by now they had all disappeared into the mass of decorative humanity milling around the huge house, and of course the garden if it was not raining.

Usually around about midnight some celebrity would be introduced to do a cabaret. Once it was the singer Sammy Davis junior, but he had lost his voice so he just stood there grinning. After that, dancing continued until dawn, when fried eggs and bacon would be served. Dawn was the time that I was meant to be milking the shitty cows and what with all the narrow lanes traversed at night, I had very little idea where I was or how to get back to them. I would arrive, still in my dinner jacket having had no sleep, do a quick change and off to the shit shovelling while others went to Lord's or Ascot.

* * *

A friend of mine doing the same sort of thing once woke up in a strange bed and needed a pee. He was sharing a room with another man, who had just come in and gone to sleep. Not wanting to wake him up by turning on the light, he got out of bed and felt his way towards the door. On the way he knocked over what he thought was a glass of water on the dressing table, and spilt it all over his hands. 'No problem, just water,' he thought as he continued to feel his way along the wall to the door, out into the corridor and eventually to the bathroom. Here he turned on the light, and he was horrified to discover that he had knocked over, not a glass of water, but an ink bottle (writing materials being frequently provided in large country houses at that time) and that his right hand was soaked in black ink. It gets light early in summer in the south of England, and having had a good wash and pee he started retracing his steps to his room. In the dim dawn light he was able to detect a clear line of black fingerprints all the way along the corridor and along the wall of the bedroom as far as the dressing table where a pool of ink had spilt all over his room-mate's wallet. He told me that as it was nearly time for him to leave anyway he got dressed and quietly left.

Some time later he happened to be passing the very house where he had disgraced himself with the ink. He had written to apologize but had had no acknowledgement, so he thought that he should do the decent thing and call to clear his name, as it were. He was shown to the sitting-room by an elderly butler who said that her ladyship was in the garden and that he would call her. Meanwhile, would he not like to sit down?

The butler indicated the sofa and he duly sat. It was a pretty uncomfortable, lumpy sofa, but he didn't dare move in case he upset something else. It was all of ten minutes before her ladyship, clearly annoyed at being dragged from her precious garden, came bustling in.

"Yes, yes, hello, who are you?" she said as he rose from the sofa and started to explain that he had been one of her less desirable houseguests. His explanations stuttered to a halt when he saw the expression on her face. She was not looking at him but where he had been sitting. Without a word she moved forward and picked up a very dead Pekinese puppy, the lump he had thought to be part of the sofa!

I never did anything quite as bad as that, but the whole 'deb' scene was not a great success for me and I asked my cousin to remove my name from her list of eligible young men. It was a pity really, as I am sure that most of my fellow guests were actually very nice people, and there were some very pretty girls – it was just that we moved in very different circles and I usually smelt of cow shit.

* * *

Mick was a good employer, overlooking some of my late returns from these escapades and paying me a bonus when I left in August. I was not quite ready to go back to Kenya so had made a plan to meet two of my old school friends who were at Cambridge, to do a tour of the Continent, ending up at the Rome Olympic Games. I sold my Mini and joined John Byng-Hall and John Clarke in Byng's little Morris Minor.

John Byng had had a horrible two years. After leaving school and doing his bit chasing Mau Mau, he had left Kenya by ship to take up his place at Cambridge University. Travelling through the Red Sea he had contracted polio. The ship's crew did not want to handle the problem so they put him ashore at an obscure Italian port. Luckily John had another school friend travelling with him as he was very sick and in no condition to fend for himself. His friend Peter got him into a fairly basic hospital and stayed with him for a bit, but John had a pretty grim time there before being transferred to England, where he spent a year recuperating. Few people ever get over polio completely and now John could only walk with the aid of crutches. He was not too good even with these and we had to take along a collapsible wheelchair strapped to the roof of the Morris Minor. He could drive though; the vehicle had been specially adapted so that he did not have to use his feet. This was OK for him but we had to learn to drive it when it was our turn to take the wheel.

Our first stop was Paris, where I found myself driving round the Arc de Triomphe without the use of my feet on any of the controls. I think I circled the thing five or six times before I could get the ruddy car into the right gear and right speed to get off the roundabout. A Kenyan friend in a prime area right next door to the Sorbonne University had lent us a flat. The only snag was that it was on the top floor of the building and had no lift. No problem for Clarke and me, but no way could Byng climb those stairs. There were eighty-four – I counted them – and we had to take it in turns carrying Byng up and down. We stayed a week in Paris and were pretty fit by the time we left. It was fun, and we did all the conventional things – the Louvre, the Eiffel Tower, Versailles etc – met up with some of the Sorbonne students, ate and drank very well. I was looking at photos of us in Paris the other day and was interested in our attire. Nowadays we would have worn a tee shirt, shorts and trainers. Then we wore proper walking shoes, long grey trousers, shirt with collar and tie, plus a blazer.

Leaving Paris, we drove south and stayed at youth hostels while exploring the chateau country, also numerous cathedrals, which were of particular interest to Byng but did less for Clarke and me. We encountered another problem at the hostels. All the loos were the French type that you had to squat over if you wanted to do anything serious. Byng could not squat, so our first call every morning was to a smart hotel in the nearest town. Here Clarke and I would pretend to try and book in while Byng went off in search of an English-type loo on which he could sit.

We hit the Mediterranean at Marseilles, then drove along the coast to northern Italy. Here Byng left us. He did not want to go to the Olympic Games and had arranged to meet another friend. He took the car and, very bravely, set off on his own. Clarke and I had one very small tent between us and our thumbs. We got lifts easily enough and arrived in Rome just as the Games were starting. We pitched our tent in a camping area and set off to investigate. Clarke had a couple of friends from Cambridge competing – Bruce Tulloch in the long distance events for England and the incomparable Herb Elliot in the 1,500 metres for Australia. Herb won this event in world record time. I knew some of the Kenya hockey team, having competed against them and having even had a trial to join them. They were highly rated in those days and, while not winning a medal, did very well. The team was all Kenyan Indians except for the goalkeeper who was a white. Black Kenyan runners had not yet made their mark on the international stage and there were none even competing.

We watched a lot of the athletics, buying tickets to get in at the gate. We also watched some of the boxing, which included seeing a slim youth of seventeen win a gold medal. His name was Cassius Clay. When it was all over we took a train back to London. I spent a few days there before flying back to Kenya.

CHAPTER 9

On the Kenya Plains

BACK FROM MY ABORTIVE TRIP TO ENGLAND, it was back to work on 'Momandu'. I talk a lot about polo, but there were, of course, plenty of other things happening as well. I did a bit of work on the farm and a very interesting time it was too. Kenya is a very fertile country with some wonderful soil; there is no frost except perhaps on the very highest farms at over eight thousand feet. There are two rainy seasons and as long as it does rain then you can grow nearly anything.

The main problem was that the rain was unreliable, and in those days very little irrigation was practised. The day of the huge centre-pivot irrigation scheme was far off. On 'Momandu' we produced milk as our main source of income, while also running a beef herd. We grew very little in the way of crops, due to the unreliable rain. The dairy cows were milked in the open with little or no supplementary feed, so they relied heavily on the natural grass. Our milk was collected every day by a lorry from my great uncle's farm, 'Kilima Kiu', some fifteen miles away. There, the milk was pasteurized and sent on to Mombasa by overnight train.

Our nearest shop was in Machakos village, twenty miles away. There was no such thing as a Farmers' Co-op in those days, so all farming supplies – such as wire, dip, cattle salt or any of the dozens of other things that are required on a farm – were bought from the local Indian dealer. He also supplied every type of household requirement, be it groceries, frying pans, booze or loo paper. In our case we used a certain Mr Maine and his son, Christian. These Indians were very shrewd businessmen; they knew that we had to buy from them, so they marked up the prices considerably, but they also allowed extended credit. Some farmers only paid their accounts once a year. We paid more regularly than this, but when Maine's bill arrived in the post my father always wore a very long face.

Maine had a rival in Machakos called Puri. Mr Puri supplied exactly the same things as Maine, so competition for our trade and that of the other farmers in the area was great. To ensure your custom Maine not only extended credit but also gave very generous Christmas presents to each member of the family – tobacco and bottles of whisky and wine for my father, boxes of chocolates, imported soap and scent for my mother and toys for the children. Puri, of course, did exactly the same for his customers so the trick was to change suppliers in early December. This way you got presents from Puri to keep your business and also from Maine in an attempt to get it back.

I do not think that any of us would ever have got rich farming on 'Momandu'. My father had had no formal training in agriculture and was not a particularly experienced farmer. He had run the small dairy farm in England after being demobbed in 1946, and had had two years on 'KK'. He worked hard at improving the farm by building dams and weirs in the sandy dongas, providing water for every paddock that was used. He did a lot of bush clearing and fencing, but at the end of each month there was not a lot of change from the milk cheque. What did remain was soon spent, as we lived pretty well.

Our farm labour did not live so well. We employed about thirty in all and they were all housed in mud huts on the farm, although the more senior staff did get slightly better accommodation, even running to electric light when we finally got a generator to provide light for the main house. Most of them had an ancestral home quite nearby in what we knew as the waKamba Reserve. Here they would have another mud hut where their parents and probably other relations all lived in a very basic fashion. There would certainly be no piped water anywhere near so of course, no indoor sanitation. They would probably not own the land where their house was, in that they would not have any sort of title deeds, but they would have the right to plant some crops nearby and run a few cattle, sheep or goats on some communal grazing. It did not amount to much, and, basic as our labour quarters were, they were certainly better than what they had 'at home'.

We employed three people in the house alone – a cook called Kimuyu, a houseboy called Buli and the inevitable 'kitchen toto', called Buto. My mother did a lot of the cooking herself though and once, when the cook was away, prepared dinner for a party we were having. Just before the guests arrived, Buli rushed into my father's dressing-room, shouting that the memsahib had gone mad – she was ironing the pudding! We did not have electricity, and my mother, wanting to make a crème brulé for pudding, had heated a flat iron and was pressing it on top of the creamy mix to make the lovely crisp surface so necessary in a good crème brulé.

Some of the larger farms had what they called 'squatter areas'. This was a part of the farm owned by the white settler that he chose to put aside purely for the use of his labour force. My Great Uncle F O'B Wilson, had such an area on his 24,000-acre farm, 'Kilima Kiu'. Here the labour could do much as they did in the reserve, but having this privilege were bound to work for the farm owner if and when he needed them.

The waKamba tribe who lived in the Reserve that bordered a lot of the Machakos farms were a cheerful lot, their main claim to fame being that they made good soldiers. The King's African Rifle regiments contained many waKamba tribesmen. When I was stationed at Fort Hall during the Emergency, the two sergeant-majors in charge of the Kikuyu tribal police were both waKamba.

The historical enemy of the waKamba was and probably still is the Maasai. In the 'old days', i.e. before the white man came along at the turn of the last century, the waKamba and Maasai were pretty much in a permanent state of war. The Maasai were very much the aggressors and their weekend sport was to raid the waKamba, kill the young men, rape the young women and steal as many cattle as they could. When the white settlers arrived, a line of farms some twenty-five miles deep and a couple of hundred long was pegged, separating these two tribes and allocating the land to the settlers. This was certainly not specially selected as the best land, as is so often claimed; it was much more of an administrative aid to keep the two warring tribes apart. Much the same thing was done in Southern Rhodesia to stop the Matabele raiding the Mashona.

'Momandu' marched with the waKamba Reserve on our north boundary for about five miles. We did not stretch as far as the Maasai Reserve which started with the Mombasa /Nairobi railway line. The waKamba Reserve was fairly densely populated, tended to be in more hilly country and contained very little game. The Maasai Reserve was totally different, being lovely open rolling plains, very sparsely populated and full of game. The Maasai were strictly nomadic and you never really knew where they were going to be. Very few of them condescended to work for the white man and nor were they really interested in politics.

Many books have been written about this picturesque tribe and I am not about to add much to that, except to say that I loved visiting the Maasai Reserve. In those days, you could take out a hunting licence for a few pounds, and I often used to do this, take a truck and a tent and camp there for a few days shooting a few zebra, wildebeest, kongoni, gazelle or eland. I would bring the meat back for our labour. I would usually meet a few Maasai and initially would offer them some meat, but as a tribe they did not eat much meat, preferring blood and milk. The waKamba were totally different and loved any meat except zebra. Tony Church, who still lives in Kenya and now runs a very successful riding safari business, often came with me.

On one occasion a friend of mine lost his way; seeing a Maasai moran dressed in all his red finery, standing on one leg and leaning on his spear as was their wont, he tried to ask him the best way to get back to Konza station. In those days a lot of Maasai did not even bother to learn Swahili, the lingua franca of the country, and he was in some doubt as to whether he could make himself understood. He rabbited on a bit in Swahili while the moran looked down his long, aquiline nose at him and said nothing. Finally my friend ground to a halt and the moran shifted legs before saying in perfect English, "If you want Konza station, old boy, just keep going on this road." My friend was staggered, and asked him how he came to speak such perfect English. "At Oxford, actually," he said, in blasé tones.

"So what the hell are you doing here, standing on one leg and covered in red mud?"

"Long vac., came back home to see the folks." It was an amazing encounter! It turned out he was the son of a local chief and was indeed at Oxford University.

Farms adjoining the Maasai Reserve tended to be large open stretches of country suitable only for ranching cattle. Most of these farms were still occupied by the original settlers or their descendants. Game had always been prolific in these areas and many of the first settlers had used this to their advantage, finding the exploitation of game more profitable than trying to work out how to stop commercial cattle from dying from one of the many tropical diseases prevalent in Kenya. Indeed, it was in the Machakos area that the idea of professional big game hunting first raised its head. The likes of Philip and Blaney Percival, Harold and Clifford Hill found conventional farming far too difficult and unprofitable. They had to shoot so many predators in order to protect their stock that it led to them beginning to invite friends to help them. For the more adventurous visitors this was a lot of fun and friends of friends started asking if they could also come and help – to shoot a lion, for example.

It is said that Harold Hill shot some hundred and thirty lions on his farm. I had lunch with him once and he showed me a series of photographs of a lion charging him. There were three frames, the first of a heavily maned lion bursting out of a thicket, the second of the lion in full charge and the third of the lion falling dead at the feet of the photographer. As a lion can cover a hundred yards somewhat faster than an Olympic gold medallist, I consider them truly remarkable photographs, bearing in mind that they were taken well before the Great War. Not only must the photographer have had a very steady hand, but he must also have had enormous faith in Harold.

Harold was a very keen cricketer and was one of the founders of Machakos Cricket Club. I played the odd game for Machakos and Harold, despite his age and failing eyesight, insisted on umpiring. This was a hazardous occupation for any visiting team. I remember my cousin, Richard Wilson, once as captain, winning the toss and asking Harold what he should do about choice of innings.

"You put them in, and I'll give them out," said Harold with a chuckle.

One of his earlier ventures was to try and raise chickens. No batteries in those days, just a few broody hens. He had one lovely clutch of some dozen eggs, well set under a good mother and just waiting to hatch when, on checking on them in their nest, he found not the broody hen but a python curled up there digesting the whole clutch. So angry was Harold that he shot the snake, cut it open, took the eggs out and reset them under the terrified mother hen. History does not relate if they ever actually hatched out.

I do not know who is credited with first charging a client for arranging a lion hunt, but the idea soon caught on and as early as 1909 President Theodore Roosevelt and his son Kermit were taken on a hunt on the Kapiti Plains by Philip Percival. I knew old Philip a bit as he was very much one of the characters in the area, as well as the Hill cousins. Blaney died before I was on the scene and was buried just behind my house on 'Momandu'.

Our next-door neighbour was old Ernest Button, living on a farm called 'Kalazoni'. I use the word 'old' a lot because these characters were old. Most had fought in the Boer War and moved up to Kenya soon after that conflict ended. Ernest certainly had, and married a little lady called Phyllis who had come out from England as a schoolteacher. They had two children, Anne and Tommy, who were only ten or so years older than me, as Ernest had married very late in life. If my father was not a progressive farmer, Ernest was positively archaic. Inevitably, Tommy was known as 'Tummy Button' and when caught picking his nose by his mother, was told to 'stop unpacking his trunk'. Phyllis was a constant source of embarrassment to old Ernest. Once, when a lot of his cattle died of East Coast Fever because he had not dipped them properly, Phyllis was heard telling the story in a loud voice at a big party, adding that it really did not matter as they were terribly overstocked anyway.

* * *

Kenya was very much the place to visit from England. The climate, particularly in the foul northern hemisphere months of January and February, was perfect, and of course there were wonderful game parks to visit. As a result, we had a fairly continuous stream of visitors, some of whom stayed a long time.

My grandmother, the slightly eccentric Lady Butler, once stayed for over three months. In her youth she travelled extensively with her father and later also with her husband, but latterly she did not move too far from her Knightsbridge flat and the convenient Harrods, her local shop. On her first visit to France, she is said to have been most impressed by the intelligence of the children there, saying to her father on her return, "Do you know, they are much more advanced than our children, even quite young ones speak very good French."

What she thought of the intelligence of our local African children I do not know, as they spoke a totally incomprehensible language quite well. On another of her travels, she was due to land at a French colonial island but wrote home saying that she was unable to do so because she did not have the correct French letters. Granny originally came from the American South and a troop of slaves used to look after her, as they had her ancestors, so I think she rated our locals not far above that category and just referred to them as 'Nig Nigs'.

My father's brother's wife Verena also stayed for a couple of months. She was also fairly eccentric and forgetful. Her husband, my Uncle Mark, was then Master of the Queen's Household, so she had to mind her p's and q's a bit. I can't remember if it was her or another equally eccentric aunt called Massie who, at a reception to meet the Queen, nipped into the loo just before entering the Queen's presence. Being in a bit of a rush, she grabbed the flat box containing Bronco lavatory paper, instead of her smart, small handbag, and was introduced to her monarch with a box of loo paper under one arm. Another time she arrived in her car at a very smart country house to spend the weekend. Parked outside the front door on the beautifully raked gravel, she was greeted by her host and hostess, followed by the butler. The aunt opened the boot and indicated her suitcase to him, then, with her hand still on the open boot, turned to speak to her host. The butler reached into the boot to remove the suitcase only to have aunty slam it shut while looking the other way and deep in conversation. The catch of the lock caught the butler squarely on the back of the head and laid him out cold, pumping an impressive stream of blood, which left a very nasty stain on the beautifully raked gravel.

My mother's elder sister Joan and her three children also stopped over with us on their way back from India, where her husband Nigel had held a high-powered job with Shell. Joan had led a somewhat sheltered life and was not very worldly-wise. Before she went out to India to get married, her father opened a bank account for her and explained that, instead of carrying money everywhere, she could write a cheque to pay for things. Joan thought this was marvellous and wrote a lot of cheques for a lot of things. So many in fact, that the bank manager had to call her in one day and ask how she intended to pay off the considerable overdraft that she had run up.

"Oh!" said Joan, "that's easy," and wrote him a cheque.

Joan loved animals but her husband, Nigel, hated them, so Joan had never had much to do with dogs; she perhaps did not understand them, never having owned any. My mother, on the other hand, loved her animals and dogs were her particular favourite. She had two or three of her own, my father had a couple and we children had one each, so there were plenty of canines around the house. This worried Joan a lot, and the situation became critical when all the bitches started coming into season at the same time. Joan got quite desperate, so, to give her a break, my mother took her up to Nairobi for the day and to lunch at the smart New Stanley Hotel. The waiter appeared with the menu, resplendent in white kanzu and red-tasselled hat. Joan surveyed the long menu, selected fish, and then wanted to choose some vegetables to go with it. None were detailed, it just said, 'Vegetables in season'. Joan had had enough.

"Even the bloody vegetables are in season in this damn country," she said, and stormed out of the dining-room.

My Great Aunt Betty Wilson, who had been in Kenya since just after the First World War, had an endless stream of visitors from England over the years. She was a tough old bird and regarded most of her anaemic guests from colder climes as being in urgent need of toughening up. After all it had been pretty tough when she had first arrived. Being related to us as well, many of them came on to us, a few miles down the road. Our house was some five miles from the main Mombasa/Nairobi road and we had a long straight drive leading up to it. Betty was in the habit of dropping those of her guests who were coming on to visit us at the end of this drive and telling them to walk up to our house. We could see most of the drive from our veranda and on several occasions had to rush down the drive to rescue some miserable sunburnt visitor lugging a heavy suitcase in the midday sun. When we complained to Betty that it was a bit inhospitable she would just snap back, "Nonsense, very good for them."

Once she had a newly married couple from England to stay, who were honeymooning in Kenya. On the evening of their arrival, bride and groom were strolling through Betty's rose garden. The groom gallantly stooped to pluck a lovely red rose for his beloved but found Kenya roses somewhat tougher than English ones, and in trying to break it off pricked his finger quite badly on a thorn. He returned to the house sucking the wound and Betty dabbed on some mercurochrome solution (her sovereign remedy for all such ills) and a strip of plaster. When the happy couple appeared for breakfast next morning, the assembled company were amazed to hear Betty greet the groom with the salutation, "Good morning to you, and how's your prick today?"

All these people were delightful and we enjoyed having them immensely; also it was a great excuse to take them on safari and visit some of the wonderful places which were so near at hand.

* * *

The closest game park to us was Amboseli National Park, situated on a dry lake near the Tanganyika border at the foot of Mount Kilimanjaro. It was (and still is, I think) a wonderful little park. There were no fancy lodges in those days, just a few little bandas, with very basic cooking facilities where one cooked one's own food. There was no electricity or fridge. Amboseli was only about three hours' drive from us and whenever we had visitors we went there. After lunch my parents and the older guests would usually have bit of a zizz, but my sister Sue and I would not want to miss a minute of seeing the wonderful selection of game on offer, so would take the car and do our own private little game drive.

I well remember that on one occasion we came back with shattered nerves. Round practically every corner we had had to slam on the brakes and skid through the thick dust, which is a feature of Amboseli, to avoid hitting a rhino having a dust bath in the middle of the road. We were sick of the sight of rhino by then, and now, fifty years later, you open a bottle of champagne if you manage to see just one.

Young English girls came out to Kenya to spend a few months growing up, or perhaps to get away from an undesirable romance. The two Ackroyd sisters from Yorkshire, Vicky and Jan, arrived and based themselves with the Fernandes family. They were known as 'the imported fillies'. Then of course there had been Viv, my father's goddaughter. Soon after her arrival, Eddie Fernandes, Simon Fletcher and myself took her, Vicky and Jan down to the coast, where we rented a holiday cottage at Malindi for four or five days. It was four or five days that might have changed my life, for I fell in love with Viv. She came back to 'Momandu' and was based with us for about four months. We did a lot together, including winning a polo tournament at Molo and going on a memorable safari to Samburu National Park in the NFD (Northern Frontier District) in my old Ford Zephyr, the 'Blue Peril'. Sadly, my courtship was in vain, for Viv was secretly engaged to marry Nick Ansell, the son of blind Col. Mike Ansell of showjumping fame. They married soon after she left Kenya, but the few months we had together remain a very special part of my memories of Kenya.

* * *

In October 1960 my parents went on holiday to the coast, and I was left in charge of 'Momandu'. This was the first time I had been in charge on my own and I was determined to make a success of the job, but things did not go at all well. First the borehole pump broke down at what was a dry time of year when we were very short of water, then two large fat oxen were stolen and a couple of days were wasted trying to help the police track them. Then, one night, just after I had gone to sleep, there was a frantic knocking on the front door, a lot of shouting and dogs barking. I stumbled out, still half asleep, to find the superintendent from Machakos police standing there. I thought he had come about the stolen oxen and was surprised that so senior an officer should come himself at such a late hour on such a comparatively minor issue.

I knew him slightly and he did not mince his words. "Mark," he said, "John Shaw has just been killed in a car smash."

John was my sister Penel's husband and father of their three very young children. On these occasions you do not immediately register the full implications of what has been said. I asked a few inconsequential questions and was told that John had been driving back from Nairobi in his Land Rover with a heavy mower in the back when he had had a head-on crash with a lorry on the main road near Lukenya. He had been killed instantly.

The policeman found a glass of brandy for me and suggested that I drive over to 'Bondoni', the Shaws' Farm, to be with my sister. This I did, and I found her in the sitting room with her in-laws, old Sir Robert and Lady Shaw. What do you say? I just went up to Penel and put my arms round her. The old Shaws were too stunned to do anything very much so I had to take over all funeral arrangements. The Machakos farming area had no telephones then, so it was very difficult to get word around and, most important of all, I had to try and contact my parents at the coast. I did not even know exactly where they were staying. I drove the fifteen miles to Konza station early next morning and sent off a series of telegrams to places at the coast where I thought they might be. Then I went on to Nairobi, where I had to undergo the grisly business of officially identifying the broken body lying in the morgue. I bought a coffin and drove him back to Machakos. My parents received one of my telegrams and arrived in a state of shock and exhaustion just in time for the funeral at Machakos Anglican church. The whole of the farming community and several people from Nairobi turned up for the simple service, after which we drove Penel and the three children back to 'Momandu', where they moved in with us while some plans for their future were thrashed out. There was no money in the family at all. In fact John had recently cashed in his life insurance policy to pay off some debts. Penel eventually left and went to live in England, where family and friends rallied round financially, but she was in for a very tough few years.

Kenya was very much in a state of flux at that time with independence looming and we farmers uncertain of our future. The short rains, due in November that year, failed badly and we were all feeling the crunch. I was getting more and more involved on the farm without really knowing quite where we were headed. It was a very worrying time, and really that was the beginning of the end of our time in Kenya.

The one really bright spot that I remember was the New Year polo tournament in Nairobi. John had been a stalwart of our little team so it was with some hesitation that we entered the famous Mugs' Mug tournament. Bob Lake joined us in the team of my father, myself and

Peter Leonard. The funds were running out, so it was the last year that we would be playing for the famous silver champagne goblet trophies, and a replica would be presented to each player in the winning team. We battled our way through to the final, where we met a team which contained my old mate Bobby Fernandes. In an emotional game we won 2-1 and the 'Mug', which now sits on my mantelpiece in Zimbabwe, is one of my most treasured possessions, as it symbolizes for me all the fun that I had in Kenya in those days.

* * *

Politics was a topic which was discussed more and more. Joan Shaw, John's mother, was a Member of Parliament, so we got quite a bit of inside information as to what was going on. Even then there were black MPs, who up to then had been very ineffective as there were so few of them, and the white majority could quickly quash any suggestions they made. However suddenly they were becoming much more vocal, and even travelling abroad in search of support for their drive towards independence.

One of the most influential, and indeed a very able MP, was a Kikuyu called Tom Mboya. He was being widely tipped as the future Prime Minister of a newly independent Kenya; this was before Jomo Kenyatta was released from gaol. On one of Mboya's sorties overseas he received an honorary doctorate from some obscure university. On his return to Kenya he resumed his seat in the House and Sir Charles Markham, our local MP, rose to congratulate him.

"I would like to congratulate Mr Tom Mboya on the recent doctorate he has just received," he said, and added, "We had a Tom once, and it was much better after it had been doctored!"

Alas, it did not do Mboya much good; he was perceived as far too great a threat to Kenyatta and later gunned down in broad daylight on the streets of Nairobi.

* * *

The Emergency was long over, but the British Army still sent out companies from a variety of regiments, either to help train a future Kenyan
Army or for their own training in semi-desert or tropical conditions. The
Coldstream Guards had done their bit fighting the Mau Mau and now
they were back again, and who should be with them, doing his National
Service, but my cousin Anthony Milbank. I had no brother, was more
than happy with two lovely sisters, but Anthony was as close to being a
brother as I ever got. He was a bit younger than me and we did not meet
that often, but we had a lot of interests in common and, perhaps more
importantly, had the same rather warped sense of humour. He was based
at Gilgil with his regiment, but as in the past they appeared to have a
lot of time off, and a great deal of his time was spent with us. Shooting
ranked high on our list of priorities and we were able to do a lot of this on
'Momandu'. My father arranged a big shoot one day when he was staying
and invited two or three neighbours round. He also co-opted some of the
farm labour to act as beaters for the shoot, at which we planned to flight
the duck off our big dam.

Anthony was given a place in some thick reeds, and I happened to be
next to him. A few duck came over us and we may even have hit some,
but then suddenly the two crowned cranes which my father had raised
from chicks and released on the dam came lumbering over Anthony's
head. Crowned cranes are probably the most spectacular bird in Kenya
and strictly protected. Anthony did not know this. To him they looked
like a pair of rather exotic African geese and he was delighted when he
managed to shoot them both with a right and left. Luckily I had seen it
happen and was able to rush over to him and help hide the corpses deep in
the reeds. We did not tell Father until years later when his only comment
was, "I often wondered where they had got to."

Anthony had another claim to fame as far as duck are concerned.
Living as he did in St James's Palace in London he was within sight of
Green Park with all its ponds and waterfowl. One night when his father
was away he had a party for his London mates and for a small bet said

that if they would act as beaters he would shoot a duck by moonlight in the park. They duly drove the duck over his head while he stood in the Mall, and he did shoot a mallard as it flew over.

Another bet was that he could not reach a speed of 100mph in the Mall between Buckingham Palace and Admiralty Arch in a friend's new Bentley Continental. Obviously this was not possible during the day, but three o'clock in the morning appeared to be a time of little traffic, so this is when the challenge took place. Ant did get up to 100 and was not booked for speeding. However a friend of his, trying to emulate the feat in an E-type Jag, was not so lucky. Some hundred and fifty yards short of the Arch the speedometer just touched the ton and the friend was slowing down and about to congratulate himself when he was overtaken by a policeman on a motorcycle. What speed the policeman was going I do not know, but he was able to get well ahead of the Jag and flag him down. Trouble!

The friend was nothing if not quickwitted. He stepped out of the Jaguar and walked towards the fuming policeman, shaking his head and with a wry grin on his face.

"My God," he said, "that was the finest bit of motor-bike riding I have ever seen. What type of bike is it? What acceleration! And what skill – you must ride professionally."

The policeman, who was reaching for his notebook, then got involved in an animated discussion with the Jag driver on the attributes of motor bikes in general and his skill in riding them in particular. They parted the best of friends.

Anthony and I did a couple of memorable hunting safaris together, which instilled in him a love of Africa, and through the years he has returned on several occasions with his wife Bea and family, when we have explored some of the more exotic areas of this lovely continent.

I still saw quite a lot of Bobby Fernandes, but he had now moved up to Uganda, as he was worried about the future of farming in Kenya and what market there would be for the family farm if they all decided to leave. It was his father Charles who was partly instrumental in getting the British Government to pay out the Kenya settlers in pounds sterling if and when their farms were redistributed to local black Kenyans. I do not think that the British were too keen to do this, but the settlers had in their ranks some fairly influential British subjects who were members of the aristocracy, and Charles motivated them into putting pressure on the authorities so that 'proper' money was made available. My parents certainly took advantage of this, and when they finally decided to leave Kenya in 1963 'Momandu' was sold to a local waKamba co-operative and the British Government paid them out in pounds. All this is in stark contrast to the end of my farming days in Africa, when my family and I were forcibly evicted by Mugabe in 2002, and to this day have not received one penny in compensation in Zimbabwe money or any other currency. It is a fitting coincidence that Bobby Fernandes is now trying to do, through his own company Agric Africa, exactly what his father did in Kenya forty years earlier – trying to get the British Government to honour their commitment to the community that they originally encouraged to populate their colonies. I fear Bobby may have a harder road to travel.

CHAPTER 10

Athi-Tiva

THE SHORT RAINS AT THE END OF 1960 had been very poor in the Machakos area, so we eagerly awaited the onset of the long rains in March, 1961. To be fair, they were not too bad and we were all beginning to think that perhaps we had a decent season in front of us when disaster struck.

Just as the rains ended and there was lovely short green grass everywhere, the whole area suffered a plague of armyworm. Everybody knows about locusts and how they devour everything in sight, but few people know about armyworm, which do exactly the same thing. Perhaps not exactly the same as they do not climb trees and eat all the foliage as locusts do, but they sweep through the fresh new grazing like a bush fire.

An armyworm hatches from an egg and starts life as a very small black and yellow caterpillar. Over the period of a very few days it grows into quite a fat large caterpillar, and this is because during those few days it never stops eating. I remember looking at a big slope of short green grass, which had a line down the middle. On one side it was fresh and green, on the other it was brown and bare. You could not actually see the line moving, but look away for half an hour and then look back and it had moved perhaps a yard. In the short period of a couple of weeks practically all the lovely new grazing had disappeared and, as it was now the end of the rains, there was no chance of it growing again until the advent of the short rains in eight months.

Cattle were already thin and in poor condition following the long dry period leading up to the rain and now they would undoubtedly die of starvation. The armyworm plague affected the whole of the Machakos area and extended into the Maasai reserve over the Mombasa/Nairobi railway line. This was predominantly a hunting area and populated by large numbers of plains game, particularly zebra, eland and the gazelles – Thompson's and Grant's. The armyworm had eaten all their grazing as well, so they crossed the railway line and came on to our farms looking for any grass they could find. Obviously, the armyworm had missed the odd patch here and there and these small areas were worth more than gold dust. The starving cattle were suddenly invaded by hundreds of starving zebra. I had never seen a zebra on 'Momandu', but one morning there were suddenly about a hundred.

We applied for Government help. They did not know what to do, but applied the old formula – when in doubt send in the army. The army came and, forming a line several miles long, tried to drive out the game. Starving animals will not stay where there is nothing to eat, and as soon as the army went to bed that night the animals came straight back again. Shoot them! OK we did, my friend and neighbour, Bob Lake, and I; we went out one day and shot a hundred zebra. It was slaughter, with rapidly rotting carcasses littering the countryside. Zebra meat is very yellow, sickly and most unpalatable; even the locals, who love meat, would not eat it and the few predators around were soon gorged to repletion, so the meat just rotted – and stank. How it stank! We tried to skin everything we shot, but it was a massive, time-consuming task and it was not possible to cure the skins properly, because there were so many. We became sick of the slaughter and it was not making the slightest difference anyway.

At the end of one particularly heavy day's shooting, we realized we had shot the mother of a very small foal. It was standing forlornly beside its dead mother, and so, illogically, we picked it up and took it home. My mother and I sat up a lot of the night trying to feed it. Next day the cook asked me why I spent all day shooting zebra and then sat up all night to keep one alive.

The whole area faced ruin. A meeting was called at the local club and a lot of grim-faced farmers attended. What could be done? Farming representatives from other areas were also there and some offered grazing in their areas – for a fee. These offers were, in fact, quickly snapped up, but at the end of the day there were still some seven thousand head with nowhere to go and nothing to eat if they stayed where they were. It was then that the government veterinary officer from Kitui spoke up. Kitui is a small town some sixty miles northeast of Machakos. There were no European farms in the area as it was deep in what was then the waKamba Reserve. The area was large and ran southeast towards the coast, encompassing the Yatta plateau and ending on the edge of the Tsavo East National Park. The top part of the area was inhabited by waKamba tribesmen, but as it dropped in altitude towards Tsavo, it became drier and, what was much more serious, it was infested with the dreaded tsetse fly, thus preventing the keeping of any domestic livestock. Therefore nobody lived there and it was designated as a hunting area. A very good hunting area it was too, with large herds of buffalo, elephant, plains game and even quite a lot of black rhino. Officially the area was called B2 Yatta Controlled Hunting Block and was about a quarter of a million acres.

What the government vet had to say was interesting. He said that the area between the Athi and Tiva Rivers, which included the Yatta plateau, had in parts recently been cleared of a certain amount of bush, and the number of tsetse flies had been thus considerably reduced in those areas. Also, a new but not yet fully tested vaccine was available that might prevent cattle dying of trypanosomiasis from tsetse fly bites. 'Trips' causes sleeping sickness in humans and is usually fatal to cattle, and the bottom line was whether or not cattle could survive in areas where there was tsetse fly. This Athi-Tiva grazing scheme, as it was called, was intended for the settlement of more waKamba if it was proved that cattle could survive there, but so far they had been very reluctant to take up the challenge. The government was therefore prepared to offer this area to the Machakos farmers for their cattle for a fee if they were prepared, in effect, to be guinea pigs.

There was a little discussion, but it soon became abundantly clear that there was no option, so the offer was accepted. Someone had to go with the cattle, together with the herdsmen, to supervise and put in place a huge number of things necessary for the introduction of domestic cattle to a virgin area. Things had to be constructed: bomas for them to sleep in; places for them to drink water; some form of dip. Tsetse flies were not the only problem; ticks had to be controlled as well. Roads had to be made, accommodation for the herdsmen had to be constructed, and so on and so on. My friend and neighbour, Bob Lake, and myself were chosen for this task, mainly, I suspect, because we were both young and knew something about ranching cattle in remote areas. It was an exciting challenge and I was delighted to have been chosen.

There was little time for any planning or reconnaissance of the area – hungry cattle need feeding – so the very next morning Bob and I set off down the Nairobi/Mombasa road in his battered old Land Rover, followed by a five-ton lorry owned by a farmer called Jock Stanley, which contained tents, tools and about twenty labourers from various farmers. We drove as far as the little dorp of Kibwezi, which was the railway station where cattle would be railed to from our local station, Konza. From there they would have to walk some forty miles to the bottom end of the grazing scheme.

Bob and I turned off the main road at Kibwezi and headed into the bush on a rough dirt track. Our first objective was to decide where cattle, walking from the station, would spend their first night on the road so we dropped off some guys so they could build a boma for them to sleep in. There were no fences of any sort, so the cattle, used to running free in a fenced paddock at home, would have to be restrained to stop them trying to run back to Konza. Also, it soon became apparent that there was quite a lot of game, including lions, in the area.

We left the labour, with some food, at two separate places, telling them to make a large boma out of thorn trees. They would have to sleep there in the open or in the boma if they wanted. No one seemed to mind this, and all were apparently enjoying the adventure, especially as we promised to bring back some nyama (meat) on our return.

We, ourselves, drove on to the bottom of the designated area, which was a little native village called Ikutha. Here, the colonial government had built two small rondavels, which were reserved for the area's administrators when touring the area – which they did perhaps twice a year. One rondavel was labelled, 'PC (for Provincial Commissioner) Southern Province', and the other, 'DC (District Commissioner) Kitui'. Both houses had a small enclosure some ten yards away, which on inspection contained toilet facilities. These were pretty basic in that one enclosure had nothing there at all except a deep hole, while the other, that of the DC, had the refinement of an orange box with the middle plank removed, sited over the hole. The PC who far outranks the DC apparently had to squat.

Speaking of loos (as one does) there were two types built in Kenya in public places, one for Europeans, which was the conventional sit-down job with a proper seat, and the other, deemed suitable for Asians and Africans, which was just a hole in the ground. At the Nakuru Agricultural Show, there were steps leading down to the public toilet facilities, at the bottom of which was a large notice advising patrons that to the right was 'the European type' and to the left, 'the Asian type'. All very helpful. After a late night party at the show one year, some wit had hung a large white china chamber pot between these two notices bearing the legend, 'Proto type'.

But enough about loos! We unloaded our limited luggage in this desirable accommodation and drove on up a very rough track into the area said to be the grazing scheme. It was a beautiful bit of country. Soon the wooded area, which was dominant along the road from Kibwezi, gave way to some lovely open plains and what looked like some pretty good grazing. There was plenty of game about and I had no trouble in shooting a kongoni (Coke's hartebeest) for the pot and to make good our promise to the labour gang. We returned to our camp soon after dark to find the local chief waiting to see us.

He was a fiery little man called Matuku who readily accepted beer, which we had deemed a top priority in our hasty packing. Chief Matuku told us we were mad to think of bringing cattle to this area as they would surely all die. There was much sickness, too many lions and no water. He enlarged on this theme at some length while considerably reducing our limited stock of beer, until we eventually had to drive him home.

Very soon cattle started arriving at Kibwezi station, from where they had to start the long walk of thirty-seven miles, first to Ikutha and then on into the scheme. Some were already much too weak to attempt it and we were lent lorries by the veterinary department to transport them. Some, cows with calves at foot, were so weak that they had to be lifted on to the lorry and then lifted off again at the other end. Not all of these got any further than that; they just lay down and died. The young stock was OK though, and we soon had a continuous stream of cattle in herds of two or three hundred trudging down the Kibwezi/Ikutha road. The vet. dept. lent us one of their men, Richard Skeels, to supervise the unloading of each batch as it arrived early in the morning from Konza; he bore the title of Livestock Officer (LO for short). I would then drive down the road checking on each batch and deciding how far it should walk that day.

One day I got all the way to Kibwezi before I could locate the new batch for that day. They had not even been unloaded and were still in the railway truck. And where was LO Skeels? He was high in the branches of a fever tree, clearly agitated and gesticulating wildly towards an area behind the still loaded trucks. On peering round, I discovered the cause for his alarm; there was a large herd of elephants quietly munching the stationmaster's bananas. Skeels himself had been woken up in the night when attacked by a column of siafu, or safari ants, and had rushed outside straight into the herd of elephants.

We had plenty of other alarms while the five thousand head of cattle undertook this journey. Water was one of the main problems. There was plenty in the Athi River, which was about halfway, but on reaching

Ikutha, which stood on the banks of the Tiva River, at the end of the first leg, we had a problem. The Tiva was dry and we had to dig down some three or four feet through the sand to reach water. Five thousand thirsty cattle at the end of a thirty-seven mile hike drink an awful lot of water. We had to do a lot of digging, hiring labour from the nearby village to do it.

The cattle, on arriving at the Tiva River, would smell the water and all make a run for it. They would arrive at the edge of the three-foot hole, with its little pool of water in the bottom, charge down, and in doing so fill the hole with sand again. We had to stop the approaching herd some two miles short of the river and bring them along in small batches of twenty or thirty. Even so, it was a very difficult undertaking and we were forced to ring the newly dug water hole with thorns, leaving one small entrance so that we could regulate the passage of the thirsty animals.

One evening we got a report of lions in the area of one of our bomas, so Bob and I drove down to investigate. There had been lions around, but there was not a lot we could do about it, except stiffen the resolve of the herders with promises of more meat. We then set off 'home' just as dusk was falling. We had covered perhaps half of the twenty-five mile return journey when Bob's ancient Land Rover spluttered to a stop. Neither of us were great mechanics, but it soon became clear that it was an electrical fault and that we would not be able to fix it where we were. What to do? Either spend a very uncomfortable night in the open vehicle, or walk the twelve miles back to our base in Ikutha. We walked. It took a long time, there was a lot of game about (lions?) and we only had one shotgun between us. Beer has seldom tasted so good, when we eventually made it back to our base at about midnight.

On another occasion, when I went to Kibwezi to meet the cattle, I called in at the local Indian duka for a few provisions and found the proprietor – a funny little man with long beard and huge turban – in a state of great agitation. A consignment of seafood had been unloaded off the overnight train from Mombasa, destined for an upmarket safari camp in the area. Doubtless it was intended for the palates of some wealthy

American hunters, but the local hunter in charge of the group had not pitched up. The Indian duka wallah only had a very small paraffin fridge, and the precious seafood was in grave danger of going bad. Very sportingly, I agreed to take it off him for a fraction of its worth, and that night Bob and I dined like kings off oysters, prawns and crayfish.

Bob soon moved on to the grazing scheme proper to try and establish a sort of headquarters, to make some sort of dipping arrangements, and of course to search for the all-important water. For water we had to use the same method as at Ikutha, as the grazing area was near the Tiva River and not the Athi; also, the Yatta plateau prevented us getting to the Athi for water. Dipping was a serious problem. By the time the cattle got to their destination they had been on the road for all of a week, walking through tick-infested country, and they were covered in ticks. A huge, long race was constructed out of the local timber, and as the herds arrived they had to walk through this race, where they were individually hand sprayed by men with knapsack sprays – all five thousand head. There was no hard bottom to the race, just earth, so it very quickly became a gigantic quagmire.

The men were not at all experienced at using these sprays, so they frequently sprayed each other instead of the cattle. I well remember receiving a full squirt of Coopertox dip straight in the face from one of Bob's herders. I think it was a genuine mistake, but I had had a minor row with him a couple of days before over a missing calf. Then, each herd had to be allocated a grazing area, bomas had to be constructed for them to sleep in, and regular trips to the river for water arranged. Chaos reigned. The African herdboys had walked the eighty-odd miles with the cattle and had no accommodation at all when they finally arrived, so they were tired and not too happy. Every evening when I returned from my trips into Kibwezi I would go out and shoot something, as the one thing that would keep the herders moderately happy was a regular supply of meat.

We had a wide selection of labour of different tribes employed by different bosses. They now found themselves in very uncomfortable circumstances, all lumped together under the rule of two young guys whom they did not know. Some were old, favoured employees of very experienced cattle farmers; others were youngsters who had been hastily employed just to do this job. There was a certain amount of dissension in their ranks and a strike looked imminent. The men from Dick Percival's farm were the main 'stirrers'. We called them all together one evening and Bob put it to them that this was a difficult situation for all of us, and that if any of us wanted a job left at the end of it we all had to put up with a bit of discomfort and get on with it. The ringleaders of the possible revolt were told to stand under one tree and those who wanted to continue working for us were told to stand under another tree; we then walked away. We returned after about half an hour to find most people under the 'other' tree (and breathed a sigh of relief). These we called together and told to go back to their cattle and get on with the job. The others we ignored. Some time later they pitched up at our tents asking, "What about us?"

Bob was very firm and said, "As you do not want to work for us you are free to go home, goodbye."

We had no more trouble after that. It had been a risky call – the year was 1961 and independence was only just round the corner.

One evening when I was returning with two dead kongoni in the back of the stripped-down Land Rover, a jackal suddenly jumped out in front of the vehicle. My Border Collie, Later, always travelled with me and stood with his front feet on the dashboard peering out down the road ahead. As soon as the jackal appeared, he shot over the front of the vehicle in pursuit. I slammed on the brakes but still hit him. Stopping as quickly as I could, I rushed back up the road to see what damage I had done. I could not find him. It was very nearly dark by now and I was twenty miles from base. I searched the whole area calling and calling, but found nothing. Eventually I had to leave and I drove back very upset. Later was a special dog and my constant companion. I had got him before going to England and had 'lent' him to my close friend, John Clarke. While I was away, John became very fond of him and was reluctant to give him back. He did bring him, at last, in the back of his truck to a party at our club, and at about ten o'clock that night told me that he was there. Now Later was a wonderful guard dog and would never let anyone near a car that he was in, so John said, "If you can get him out of the truck you can have him back."

I had not seen Later for some eighteen months, so John reckoned he was on to a pretty good thing.

I approached his truck, parked near the club in the dark. Immediately there was a crescendo of barking interspersed with ferocious growling. I walked nearer – to hysterical barking.

"Later Loo," I called, softly. Less barking. "Later Loo," I called again. Silence. I walked to the back of the truck and opened it. Later jumped out, wagging his tail, and jumped all over me.

"OK," said John, "he's yours!" To this day, John, who now lives in Florida, has a dog named Later. Later was a special dog and now he was lost.

Next morning I had to go back down the road to Kibwezi, the opposite direction to where I had lost my dog, but I was back there that evening, twenty miles from my base. I found the exact spot where Later had jumped off the front of the Land Rover after the jackal and scoured the area calling until it was dark. No sign. I spent a very unhappy two days mourning the loss of my companion. Then, when I was having a cup of coffee outside my hut at about ten thirty, having returned from the inevitable Kibwezi run, who should limp in but Later Loo! He showed little emotion, just a wag of the tail and, with red tongue lolling, threw himself down at my feet. He had lost weight and was quite badly scraped all down one side but nothing appeared to be broken. Why had he disappeared when I first went back to look for him immediately after it had happened? Collies are very sensitive dogs and I can only think that he assumed I was very cross with him for jumping out after the jackal and had deliberately hit him with the vehicle, so he had run off into the bush, being hurt both in body and feelings. He was pretty stiff and sore for a few days but was soon his old self and ready for more adventures, which were not long in coming.

Shortly after this the last of the five thousand cattle arrived and my job at Ikutha was over, so I moved up to join Bob at his newly established headquarters in the centre of the grazing area. We each had a tent, which was pitched some five hundred yards from the hastily constructed cattle yards, where pandemonium continued to reign. No sooner had we managed to dip all the five thousand head than the first ones were due to be dipped again; one has to do it once a week in this sort of place.

Meanwhile, we had got hold of some of the farmers' builders and were hurriedly trying to build proper spray races. This, of course, meant getting hold of some proper building material. Cement and piping had to be brought in, but we made cement blocks on the spot with cement and the local sand and stone. Water had to be piped and pumped to these sites, so mobile diesel pumps had to be bought and installed in the Tiva River at places where we had dug for water. Rough roads had to be made, as there was just the one dirt track that ran the full length of the scheme, otherwise we just could not get about.

The cattle were now quite scattered, as the grazing anywhere near the handling facilities had been totally flattened. Bomas, and some sort of accommodation for the herders, had to be constructed near where the various herds of cattle had been allocated grazing. Bob and I only had one ancient Land Rover and a Peugeot saloon car between us. We were up at five-thirty every morning and collapsed into bed soon after it got dark in the evening.

* * *

The owners of the cattle had tactfully kept away while we tried to instil some sort of order into the whole project, but they were understandably most anxious as to what was happening to their precious cattle – cattle that in many cases represented their life savings. Gradually they started driving down to have a look for themselves. There were twelve separate owners in all. We knew them all quite well, of course, but the first to arrive was someone we did not really know.

Air Commodore Beisiegel had only very recently moved into the area, having retired from the Royal Air Force and bought a farm near Konza station. He had sunk his pension into a herd of Boran cattle, about which, having never farmed before, he knew very little, but about which he cared a lot. Yes, he had served in the British air force, not the German, as his name and, as we were to discover, his manner might suggest. He was known as 'Bike' and had innumerable books and pamphlets on how cattle should be managed. The books and pamphlets were excellent and cattle certainly should be managed as dictated in their pages. Unfortunately though, this was just not possible under the conditions in which we found ourselves – Bike thought it should be. He would arrive and immediately expect either Bob or me to drop what we were doing and take him on a conducted tour of all his animals. If he spotted a cow with a sore eye, for example, he would demand that it be taken to the crush for treatment. It would not matter that the crush was five miles away and certainly full of other people's cattle being dipped. Or a calf might not be looking too good, so Bike would want some special food given to it. It made things very tricky; we were in our early twenties and Bike was a retired 'war hero'. I regret to say that after a couple of these visits we detailed a lookout to warn us if Bike's vehicle was approaching. With this warning we made ourselves scarce, which was not too difficult. We salved our consciences by assuring ourselves that we gave Bike's cattle just as much personal attention as those of everybody else. This was perfectly true but it was precious little.

Other owners came as well. They had all been ranching cattle in Kenya for quite a long time and fully appreciated the problems we were facing. Many made very helpful suggestions and were generous in donating or lending equipment or personnel to help us. Who was our boss? Everybody wanted a say in how the whole complicated operation was conducted, and all had a very strong vested interest, but we could not take orders from twelve different people – including Bike. A committee was formed and Dennis Wilson, my cousin from 'Kilima Kiu', was elected chairman, so he, in effect, was our boss. Certainly he and his committee dictated overall policy and negotiated with the government over terms of the lease for the area, etc., but they were so far away that the week by week running of the setup was left very much to Bob and me. Bob was in fact senior to me and this meant that he had to do all the accounts and keep the records of what everyone's cattle and employees were up to. This suited me fine as I was left to do most of the legwork.

Another visitor we had was the man in charge of the very efficient Kenya Meat Commission. He wanted to see if he was going to get any nice fat cattle out of this little venture. His name was Peter King and he was a bit of a high flyer. Bob and I were both on hand to show him round and assess if anything would be fat enough to sell to the Commission in a few months' time. This would entail a full day driving round all the scattered herds. We prepared to set off in Bob's battered old Land Rover and mentioned lunch.

"Don't worry," said Peter, "I've brought something for us all, I know how difficult it is for you two youngsters out here to get supplies."

We drove for miles, saw a lot of cattle, got very thirsty and hungry, and finally stopped on the banks of the Tiva River for Peter's much anticipated lunch. He opened a large hamper and produced a bottle of Beefeater gin, some very expensive pâté de fois gras and some small, dry cheese biscuits – nothing else! Nor did he ever take any of our cattle to his ruddy meat commission.

* * *

Cattle did get sick, they did die; some went missing, some were in such bad nick that they never got over the long move. Most found it difficult adjusting to the régime of being kept in a boma all night, all found the watering facilities inadequate; but most of them survived and if they had stayed at home they would surely have died. It was all fascinating work and a great challenge that I thoroughly enjoyed.

The cattle were soon quite widely dispersed, and I moved from the headquarter area to a new site some twenty miles away, where I started supervising the laying of a pipeline from the Tiva River, construction of a new road and the building of another spray race and cattle-handling facilities. I pitched my tent on top of a small hill with a wonderful view over much of the grazing scheme and in particular a lovely valley, which we had christened 'Tit Hill Valley', in deference to the cone-shaped little hill at one end of it shaped like a maiden's breast. There were not many maidens around Athi-Tiva, but as far as we could recall, that was more or less the shape.

I lived in this small one-roomed tent for some nine months. I had an old cook called Mwangi, who lived in a little grass hut just behind my tent, and every evening he lit a fire, around which I sat with my two dogs, Later and Bloomer, a Spaniel. Fresh food was a bit of a problem, being so far away from any shop, and so I relied heavily on what I shot. The labour had their posho – maize meal – and I would have a bit of that for breakfast followed by some grilled buck's liver and sometimes an egg. Coffee was essential, and it was no problem as it did not go off. Lunch would be a roast leg of something and dinner invariably a bird – guinea-fowl or francolin. Vegetables were very difficult, except potatoes, which I love, so I did not do too badly. I kept a crate of beer and probably had a bottle a night, but there was no fridge or ice of any kind, which possibly accounts for my preference for warm beer to this day. Also, there was no form of communication with the outside world at all. There was no telephone of course, and the two-way radio system that Bob and I had tried to set up so that we could speak to each other never worked. I had no form of security at all, sleeping always in an open tent with no one for miles except the old cook. I had a loaded rifle near at hand at all times and a shotgun not far away. It was a lonely life in many ways but I have seldom been more content than at Athi-Tiva.

Bob and I would meet occasionally and go off looking for new grazing areas. This was always an adventure. Bob's Land Rover was not the most reliable vehicle in the world and one evening, far from our camp, the ruddy thing suddenly boiled. We were nowhere near the river, so we emptied our water bottles into the radiator. This worked for a bit but then it boiled again. There was only one thing for it and that was to pee into the radiator. I regret to say that we did not produce very much between us as we were pretty hot and dry ourselves, but we did manage to limp back to camp.

The shooting was superb. I have mentioned that the whole area was a designated hunting block and from time to time a hunting party would come and hunt in the area. Invariably they would come and see me to ask what game I had seen. I had always seen a lot and sometimes I would help them – sometimes not. I soon came to look on the area as my own private hunting preserve and resented intruders. Part of our agreement allowed us to shoot for the pot, but my attitude was a bit cheeky, especially as the hunters were paying good money for the privilege of hunting in the area. Most were foreign clients accompanied by a local professional hunter.

Their main quarry would be buffalo, elephant, lion, leopard and plains game. It used to include black rhino, but they had been taken off the licence because even then in 1961 it was realised that these special animals were already in danger. There were plenty of them about though, and a day would seldom go by without me seeing one or more. In fact they caused quite a lot of problems, disrupting the cattle movements and chasing the herdsmen. I regret to say that we even had to shoot one. Poaching of them was rife. One day I took the Land Rover and drove cross-country all day looking for more suitable grazing, and in that time I counted the remains of no fewer than ten dead rhinos. No wonder there are none left there now. Often the rhino were wounded and we had numerous scares from them. On one occasion it would seem we had pitched our tents on a path frequently used by one particular resident of the area. This did not please or bother him, as, on encountering our tent, he just went straight through it, scattering it and a lot of the contents to the four winds.

One of the professional hunters who occasionally came our way was an old school friend of mine called Tony Seth-Smith. He told me that there was one particularly big elephant which was sometimes seen in the area where I was camped, and he asked if I would keep an eye out for it and let him know if I or my men saw it. Well, we did see it. One of my herders came in and said that a huge elephant with teeth 'like this', and he stretched his arms as wide as he could, had come down to drink at the Tiva the previous evening. I immediately shot off with him to see if it was still around, and sure enough we soon found him, all alone and dozing under a tree. He was huge and the tusks much the largest I had ever seen. There was no doubt that this was the elephant Tony had in mind. I needed an excuse to go to Kibwezi, some sixty miles away, to get some more rations, so I drove straight on in and sent a telegram to Tony saying that his elephant was here and he had better come quickly.

Tony did not get my telegram for three weeks, as he was out with a client in Tanganyika. However, some ten days later the same herds-man who had originally spotted the monster came and told me that the elephant had been shot. An Indian hunter with very little experience, who owned a music shop in Nairobi, had obtained an elephant licence and been allocated this area in which to hunt. He had never shot an elephant before, but he shot this one. It proved to be a Kenya record with tusks weighing 173lbs and 168lbs – as far as I can remember.

If the big game and plains game shooting was good, the bird shooting was even better. There were flocks of guineafowl everywhere and quantities of red-necked francolin in all the vleis and along the riverbanks. I used to wander round with a shotgun virtually every evening as I relied on these birds for my food. These walks were highly entertaining. It was usually just my two dogs and me. We would walk along the banks of the Tiva River from about half past five until dark, armed only with a 12-bore shotgun. I would have probably a dozen or so shots at birds and, very often, one or two in the air to scare off rhino or buffalo. Later fancied himself as a rhino dog and would chase them. Quite what he would have done if he had ever caught one I do not know.

John Clarke came to visit me and we put aside a full afternoon to shoot birds. He had brought a couple of the non-feathered variety with him and they acted as beaters, so we were having an excellent afternoon, when we suddenly bumped into the inevitable rhino. We happened to be in very open country and it almost immediately became apparent that this was a very angry rhino. All rhino appear to be angry and tend to rush around with their heads in the air looking for something to vent their anger on, but they usually push off without causing any trouble. This one, though, had every reason to be angry; it had a huge, gaping sore on its left shoulder, almost certainly caused by a waKamba poisoned arrow.

I hope we did not smell like a waKamba poacher, but the rhino did not seem to care. We were humans and a human was at the root of his immediate problem, namely a very sore shoulder, so he was intent on revenge. I am not sure a rhino actually thinks like this, but it does not really matter; it was a very cross rhino and we were in its immediate line of attack. I do not know if I smelled more like a waKamba poacher than John, but perhaps I did, because the rhino made a beeline straight for me. I was right in the open with Later at my side. There was one small thorn tree some thirty yards away, so I fired my shotgun just in front of the rhino, which made no difference at all, and beat it for the tree.

I would never have made it as rhinos run quite fast. I, too, could run quite fast in those days and it is very true that fear lends wings to your feet. I was terrified, but even the wings were clearly not enough and I had a big problem. Then Later took a hand, or paw, rather. He had chased a lot of rhino and now one was chasing him – or so he thought – and he was incensed. I was painfully under the impression that it was after me. Whatever, Later turned and went for the rhino. Not a fair contest, Later weighing perhaps thirty pounds and the rhino a couple of tons, but the mere presence of this furious black and white bundle of rage distracted the rhino to such an extent that he switched his attentions to Later and away from me.

Collies are very agile dogs and Later had no problem avoiding the cumbersome lunges made by the rhino. I am certain that I would not have been nearly so agile and was delighted to have the chance now of reaching the comparative safety of the thorn tree. Gratefully, I swung up into its branches and was just in time to watch the rhino abandon its futile efforts to nail Later and concentrate on getting John instead.

John still claims that I commandeered the only tree in the area at his expense and left him with nothing. This is of course rubbish – it is hardly the time for niceties when being chased by an enraged black rhino – so even if I had thought of offering the tree to John, as my guest, I would never have done so. As it was he had to be pretty nimble, and I quite admired his turn of speed as he dived into a small donga, the rhino thundering past with Later now chasing it and marking up a psychological victory. We laugh a lot about it now and Later grew in favour for the part he had taken in the adventure, but it was quite scary at the time. The girls had had a grandstand view of the whole thing, seated as they were on top of Tit Hill.

Shortly after this I was walking along the banks of the Tiva River, when a waterbuck suddenly dashed out of the bush, slithered down the bank and turned at bay in one of the waterholes we had dug for the cattle. It was closely followed by a pack of screaming native dogs (we called them 'kaffir dogs' in those days) and not far behind them were four waKamba poachers armed with spears and bows with poisoned arrows, exactly the sort of people who had wounded our rhino. What should I do? I did not think they had seen me yet and my first concern was for my own dogs. If they joined the fray they would very soon meet a sticky end at the hands (jaws, actually) of the battle-hardened native dogs, so I quickly grabbed them.

I could have slipped away unnoticed but, with the memory of the rhino chase fresh in my mind, I wanted to do something. I could hardly approach them saying, "I say, you chaps, this sort of thing is not quite on you know, you are under arrest."

At best, I think they would have ignored me, at worst, shot me. Instead, I shot a couple of their dogs. The waterbuck escaped and the poachers and I stood looking at each other across the dry, sandy riverbed. It was a stand off. I had a gun, but was alone and far from my vehicle. They were four and had poisoned arrows. We stood like this for what seemed like an age but was probably only about thirty seconds, and then they suddenly turned and disappeared into the bush. I hastened them on their way with a couple of shots over their heads and made tracks for my vehicle, trying not to look over my shoulder all the time.

In recent times in Kenya and many other parts of Africa, poachers such as these can be shot if caught in the act, as these were. This, admittedly, is supposed to be done by registered government game scouts. I was hardly that, but I had been very tempted to shoot them when I thought of the quantity of dead and wounded rhinos that I regularly encountered.

The whole question of what is poaching in Africa is a very tricky one. From time immemorial the locals have killed game for food, which I reckon was fair enough. There used to be plenty of game and not too many locals, who, in any case, were not armed with sophisticated weapons. Then the white man appeared and started shooting everything in sight – not for food, but for fun and profit. Suddenly they realized that they were killing off everything and had to preserve some, or game would become extinct (too late for the quagga). So they declared certain areas 'National Parks', where nothing could be shot. Other areas were designated hunting blocks, and here animals could be shot, but strictly on a licence sold by the government. Money derived from these sales went back to the government to pay for more game scouts to see that their laws were obeyed.

But what about the poor locals who lived either in the hunting blocks or on the fringe of the new National Parks? They were allowed to shoot or kill nothing, yet they received no monetary recompense for the denial of a traditional and historical source of food. Daily, they would see rich tourists enjoying watching or shooting 'their' game, while they went hungry. They were told that they must not interfere with these tourists, as they brought in valuable foreign currency, which was vital to the country. Vital to the government, perhaps, but how much of it ever filtered down to the wretched local? Nothing – so it is little wonder that they poached.

I could quite understand and sympathize with them poaching for food, but killing rhino for their horns was quite another matter. These were professional killers, hired by dealers in the city who had a market to export the horns to the East as an aphrodisiac or to the Yemen to make dagger handles for the young bloods. It is this trade that has virtually eliminated the wild rhino population from the whole of Africa today, and that was just really taking hold in 1961. The poachers took most of the risk and reaped little of the lucrative rewards. It was easy to hire the poachers and just pay them for every horn they produced. If they got caught or shot, there were plenty more to take their place.

In the 1990s in Zimbabwe, black rhino were virtually extinct in the wild and neighbours of ours were breeding them in captivity. They had to be locked up at night and have an armed guard on them twenty-four hours a day – and still they got shot by poachers, both the rhino and the armed guard, so profitable was this trade in rhino horn. It was in Zimbabwe also in the 1980s that the plight of the locals living on the periphery of tourist areas was realized and some action taken. A scheme known as 'Camp Fire' was set up, in which the locals became actively involved in the preservation of their game and were paid a percentage of the money realized from every animal shot in that area. It worked very well until all such projects crumbled and disappeared amidst the political chaos that wrecked a wonderful country in the early 2000s.

It may not appear so, but all this time I was paying some attention to the cattle as well. In fact we were making some fairly dramatic inroads into developing the whole area. By now we had a reasonable road system, so we could get about much more easily. Huge thorn bomas had been constructed and sited throughout the best grazing areas. Water was now being pumped by diesel motors from the Tiva and piped to water tanks often several miles away from the river. This water was contained and stored in what we called 'turkey nest' tanks, which were tanks of up to 50,000 litres made entirely of mud, tightly compressed by tractors driving along the walls after dumping a load of soil. These tanks were used not only for watering the cattle out of troughs fed by gravity from them but also to supply water to the two spray races that we now had operational, thus eliminating most of the dreaded hand-spraying.

Some fairly basic cattle-handling facilities had also been built, so at least some of Bike's sick cattle could be treated. All this cost a lot of money, but we were helped in paying for it all by government on condition that we left everything behind when we left. This we did when the time came to leave, and to my mind it proved that cattle could be kept in the Athi-Tiva area. Would the waKamba take advantage of this?

I went back to Athi-Tiva for a look in September 1963, when I was in Kenya for my sister's wedding. The roads were still OK, but all the pumps were missing, the spray races broken and there were no cattle in sight. We shot a lot of birds but did not see much other game. In 1996 I again visited Athi-Tiva with Nikki, when we drove up from Zimbabwe. It nearly made me cry. The whole area had been completely taken over by the waKamba. There were little 'shambas'everywhere, horrible euphorbia fences down every road, people all over the place and not a wild animal or bird anywhere in sight. The place was totally unrecognizable. It was all originally planned for waKamba resettlement and this is what had happened but, thank goodness, I had seen it as God made it.

Meanwhile in the rest of the country, nationalist politics was raising its ugly head. Mau Mau had been squashed but certainly not African Nationalism. The British Prime Minister, Harold Macmillan, had made his fateful 'Wind of Change' speech in Cape Town and the breeze was picking up in Kenya. During the Emergency we had thought that we had seen the last of Jomo Kenyatta when he was locked up in 1952, and now we were horrified to hear that he had been released in August 1961. I was at Athi-Tiva with little contact with the outside world, but my parents were getting increasingly concerned, and like a lot of people wondering if their future lay in an independent Kenya.

My father was worried about me burying my head in the bush of Athi-Tiva. The farm was suffering a severe setback financially as a result of the droughts and armyworm, so he would not be able to offer me much of a job once the Athi-Tiva saga was over. He had just been to England to see his old mother (my grandmother) in Yorkshire and, while passing through London, had contacted an old friend, who ran a pedigree live-stock export business, and asked what the prospects were of my getting a job there. Apparently there was an opening; my father came to visit me in my tent and we chatted about it.

The outcome was that I decided to give it a go. I was twenty-four by now and had no qualifications except for quite a lot of experience in a variety of fields. Africa was certainly at a watershed and maybe my future lay elsewhere. It was now November and the short rains were just starting. I had a chat with Bob, who reckoned that he could manage on his own for the next few weeks, after which there would hopefully be sufficient grass for the cattle to return to the Machakos farming area.

I pulled down my tent and packed it and my few belongings into my battered old Peugeot car. My old cook, Mwangi, climbed in plus the two dogs and we drove up the full length of the grazing scheme via Bob's camp and on up the Yatta plateau, heading for Kitui, as I had decided to take the northern exit route rather than go via Kibwezi. It was about three o'clock when I said goodbye to Bob and it was pouring with rain. The three-hour drive to Kitui took six hours and we were lucky to get across a couple of dongas, because they came down in flood as we were crossing them. If I had stayed one more day I do not think I would have got out until Christmas – Bob certainly did not. The short rains in November/December were some of the heaviest on record.

I had very little time back on the farm with my parents, as a seat on a plane for London had already been booked. My father was to take me to the airport, and we set off, again in pouring rain. We got as far as Athi River (the town, that is, situated on the same Athi that formed the boundary of the grazing scheme). Here there was a high-level bridge on a tarmac road over the river, but the swirling waters of the Athi were several feet over this. There was no possibility of crossing by that bridge. My flight was due to leave in about four hours and it was still pouring down. We drove back to the little Indian duka in the town and miraculously found a telephone that worked. Even more miraculously, we got through to Bobby Fernandes, who then worked in Nairobi, and I asked him to drive down and meet us on the other side of the railway bridge. This bridge was considerably higher than the road bridge and my father helped me carry my suitcases over to Bobby's car on the other side. Bobby then drove me to Embakasi airport just in time to catch my flight for London. It was a dramatic farewell to Africa and I did not then know when or even if I would ever return.

In many ways I consider Kenya as 'home'. Although I lived there for only fourteen years, they were my formative years. Perhaps I did not see the best of Kenya, I do not know. The early years of the 1900s must have been very exciting – the time when Uncle Frank arrived. But one tends to dwell on the romantic side and forget the fact that there were no roads, no electricity and very poor medical facilities. It was tough, and a lot of people died or went broke, but you only remember the survivors.

What about the 'Happy Valley' days just before the Second World War? Everything worked a bit better then, one could get about more easily in those funny old Ford cars and safaris were the big thing, with game of every description in all directions. Farming was perhaps a little easier but I do not think many people made much money – they were too busy having fun after the great depression.

'My' era was next – immediately after the Second World War. In many ways we saw the best of Kenya. It was easy to get around, farming was better organized, there was an efficient administration and the country was still totally unspoilt, in that there were still wonderful wild areas where one could hunt or just disappear into the wilderness. Certainly I saw the end of Kenya as it was. The Mau Mau cast a long shadow over the country. Books have been written saying that this uprising – comparatively small though it was – presaged the end of Empire and that excessive methods were used to try and prolong the inevitable.

I do not think this is true. American writers pontificating fifty years after the event cannot fail to read things totally out of context.

Kenya has now been independent for well over forty years. It has had its ups and downs, but broadly speaking it can consider itself one of the very few comparative success stories in the sorry saga of Africa's independence from colonial rule. It will always have a very special place in my memories.

*Above: My grandparents: Sir
     Frederick and Lady Milbank
     with Sir Richard and Lady
     Butler*
*Right: My parents' wedding in
     1934*

Above left: MRM aged two
Above: MRM aged five, with
Carolyn Wilson and
'Rags'
Below: Maize planting on
Momandu: My father,
sister and Sarah Blunt

Top: Sister Sue with her three 'expensive' ponies
Above: Dam construction on Momandu

*Top: Machakos Polo Team, Peter Leonard, MRM, John Shaw, Denis Milbank
 [my father]*
Above: Duke of York school prefects 1955, 'Pansy' James headmaster

Top: *Duke of York Craig Cup winning team 1955. Coach – 'Bung-eye', MRM back row 3rd from right*
Above: My staff at Gikui, Kangema

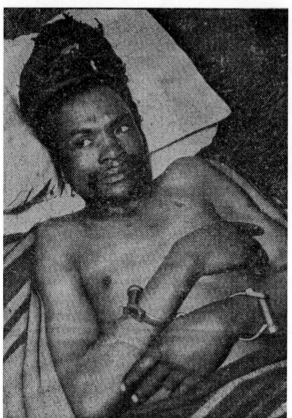

Left: We had to distribute this pamphlet depicting the captured Dedan Kimathi to everyone in our area

Below: Kikuyu Reserve with the Aberdares in background

Top: My mother at Lobo Lodge, Serengeti National Park, early 1970s
Above: Rival rugger captains: my father for Machakos and MRM for Duke of
*   York School*

*Top: School friends at Momandu – Mike Pitt-Moore, MRM, John Byng-Hall,
    Penel, John Channer, my father*
Above: My sister Sue, with tame giraffe

Top: Gertie & calf in Amboseli National Park, Kenya – early 1960s
Above: Baby elephants playing at being big elephants

Top: Which of these is the white rhino?   None – they are all black rhinos!
Above: Watering thirsty cattle in the dry Tiva River

*Left: Spraying
5,000 cattle
by hand
Below: Athi Tiva
– turkey
nest water
tank under
construction,
supervised
by Later*

Left: Bob Lake
& MRM
at Athi
Tiva
camp
Below: John
Clarke
& John
Byng-
Hall
bid each
other
farewell
on the
road to
Rome,
1960

Top: Buffalo Springs, NFD, Kenya early 1960s, Viv Taylor and Sarah Wilson
Above: Sue and Tony's wedding at Kilima Kiu, Kenya

Top: Sitting room at Scorror, home of Rick and Midge Holme, entertaining American client, Tom Moore
Above: Kudu bull – Chirume Game Park

Top: Chirume
Above: Fran, Robert and Harry outside Chirume during Bush War

Top: *Bush war transport*
Above: *Breakfast on the Sitatunga, Okavango Delta, Botswana*

CHAPTER 11

British Livestock Export

SO, ON A COLD NOVEMBER MORNING I arrived in London straight from the African bush, where I had spent the previous nine months in a tent, living off what I had shot. Most of that time I had worn nothing much more than a pair of khaki shorts and sandals. A sheath knife was always tucked into my belt and a floppy sun hat completed my attire. Now, I was expected to wear a suit and tie at the very least and for starters anyway would be living at St James's Palace.

I had made the decision to leave Kenya and have another look at England with some reluctance, but now that I had made the move I was determined to 'give it a full go'; if it did not work out I was still young and single so could always go back to Africa.

At the airport I was met by my Aunt Verena. She was the wife of my father's eldest brother, Mark, my namesake and godfather and also at that time Master of the Queen's Household; an important job for which he was shortly to be knighted. He was already Sir Mark Milbank by virtue of his being the eldest son and inheriting the family baronetcy, so the knighthood made no difference to what he was called, but it did add a few more letters after his name to go with a wartime MC and one or two other things. He could have been a formidable and rather frightening figure but was in fact a charming man, and I was very fond of him. He used to say that his main job was to see that the Queen got cottage pie occasionally; a dish of which she was very fond but never got at the frequent banquets she had to attend. I think the Queen was very lucky to have him as her right-hand man. She probably realized this and so gave him a knighthood.

Uncle Mark lived in a grace-and-favour flat in St James's Palace, just down the road from Buckingham Palace, and this is where I was initially based when I arrived in London. It was quite a contrast from my tent. Another uncle, my mother's eldest brother, was no less distinguished. He was Col Sir Thomas Butler DSO etc., and was also a godfather. He was then Resident Governor of the Tower of London and actually lived in the Tower. So, I had two quite useful addresses. When at St James's I slept in a spare room on the top floor of the Palace, but when at the Tower I got Anne Boleyn's old bedroom, where she was incarcerated before losing her head.

An additional advantage of staying at St James's was that there was often a very pretty 'au pair' girl around, usually from Sweden, Denmark or France, and there had not been many of these at Athi-Tiva. They were in England to learn the language and I was keen to help. Unfortunately, my cousin Anthony was also in residence and, being the son of the household as it were, held a bit of an edge in this department.

Despite this slight clash of interest Anthony became and remains a very great friend. It was he who tried to introduce me to London society. He thought that I would be a bit of a novelty; after all, in my short life I had chased Mau Mau up and down the Aberdares, chased sheep all over Patagonia and been chased by rhino at Athi-Tiva. This was a good deal more than most of his contemporaries had done, but for a lot of this time I had lived alone and developed few social graces, so, after some polite oohs! and aahs! at some of my more fanciful stories, they tended to lose interest in me and revert to more pressing topics, like what hairdresser to go to or where they were going over the weekend. Most of them were nice enough, I suppose, but very much the upper-class English set who can be pretty offhand if they so choose. National Service for the young men had recently been abolished and in my opinion it would have done a lot of them a power of good. I could not help thinking of my encounter with those British Army officers during the Emergency in Kenya.

I did have a potential job lined up, as well as more permanent if less prestigious accommodation, sharing a flat with some Kenyan friends. The job was with a small company called British Livestock Exports, or BLE, as they were known. I went to their offices in Clifford Street and was interviewed by two of the directors, Gilbert Barling and Neil Stanford. It would appear that I impressed them a little more than I had Anthony's friends, because they offered me the job, and on December 1, 1962, I started work; I also moved into a flat in 83 Gloucester Place, sharing with Richard Holme and John Yeldham. Richard was at that time engaged to my sister Sue.

Monday morning saw me report at my new office, where I was briefed on my duties. The company specialized in taking foreign buyers round the stud farms of England, Wales and Scotland to select pedigree livestock for export to their country. The British Isles is one of the prime countries in the world for pedigree livestock, and there was a wonderful selection available, ranging from Aberdeen Angus bulls in Scotland and Romney Marsh sheep in Kent to Landrace pigs in Cambridgeshire, and much, much more besides.

Initially I was the 'leg man', in that it was I who met the visiting clients at the airport, installed them in their hotel and then took them round a predetermined selection of stud farms, where they could choose what they wanted to buy. Being pedigree stock, everything was sold in guineas, and we, the company, kept the shilling and paid the breeder in pounds.

I was not too bad at finding my way round the African bush, but now I had to learn my way round London, pretty speedily – followed by the rest of the British Isles. My hours were long and often extended into the evening, when the clients required entertaining. One of the top musicals in the West End at that time was the enchanting *My Fair Lady* with Rex Harrison and Julie Andrews. All visiting clients wanted to see this, so, as the directors had already seen it many times with previous clients, it became my job to take the new ones. I saw the show twenty-one times and can still remember most of the words of all the songs.

Initially I was a bit at sea in a smart West End office, and I had to be tactfully told the correct way to answer the telephone.

"You say, 'Milbank speaking' not 'Mr Milbank here'," I was told – and how to pronounce words like Harwich.

"Not 'HarWick', but 'Harritch'."

My attire was the subject of some concern as well, but Clifford Street joins Savile Row and our offices were just above those of the very upmarket tailors, Anderson and Shepherd, so I was forced to spend some of my hard-earned savings on a decent suit.

It was a fascinating job, and it took me all over England and Scotland, as well as a few places in Wales. More than that, when the animals had been selected, bought and paid for, they had to be transported to their new homes. Being fairly valuable, they needed an expert attendant to look after them on their journey. Suddenly, I became an expert attendant as well as a London guide. Most of the stuff was flown in cargo aeroplanes, and in a few short months I found myself escorting Jersey calves to Frankfurt, South Down sheep to Lisbon, a stallion to Los Angeles and Landrace pigs to Rome.

* * *

Then the Jordanian Government was given a herd of fully-grown Friesland cows, together with a bull. For this little lot we hired an ancient Globemaster with four propellers and a crew of five fairly dubious characters, who did not seem to mind their plane being full of farting, shitting, noisy cattle. I was designated 'expert attendant' but felt that I needed some help to deal with this larger than usual consignment. We were due to fly out to Amman on a Friday evening, unload the cattle on Saturday morning, pick up a return load of vegetables to offset the cost of the flight, and be back in London by Sunday evening.

I thought that Anthony could possibly tear himself away from the London debs for a couple of nights to come with me. He was supposed to be working in a Merchant Bank in the City, but even there his valuable presence would not be missed, as everything was due to happen over a weekend. He readily agreed to come, and for good measure we also enlisted the services of my flatmate's cousin, Charlie Yeldham, who worked at Lloyds in the City. Charlie arrived for duty straight from that office and was still dressed in pinstriped suit, shirt with stiff collar and studs, bowler hat and tightly rolled umbrella.

We loaded the cattle at Gatwick airport, and as they were a gift from the British Government to Jordan there were several 'dignitaries' to see us off. These included the boss of BLE, whom I had not previously met – Col Douglas Kennedy – who had been away at his ranch in Canada until then.

The loading, with an efficient ramp leading into the aircraft, was no real problem, and we took off in pretty good order, flying through the night to Amman. Here we landed and were met by many more dignitaries. There was a lot of handshaking and peering into the plane at the precious cargo. I was very much man of the moment and tried to pretend that the animals were a gift from me personally. I ordered Anthony and Charlie about outrageously, with much waving of my arms and curt orders to see to the cattle's water, etc.

All this was fine, but it suddenly dawned on us that there was no ramp anywhere to be seen, and with the belly of the plane some fifteen feet off the ground, we wondered how the cattle were expected to get off. The Jordanian Government had not thought of that. Perhaps they expected well-mannered British cattle to walk down a set of passenger steps.

I put the problem to the Minister of Agriculture; he referred it to his Permanent Secretary, who passed the question to the Under-Secretary. From here, the Chief Veterinary Officer was consulted. He referred it to the local Animal Health Inspector, who said that it was a transport problem and referred it to the Permanent Under-Secretary for Transport. It seemed that he had no jurisdiction over stationary aircraft, so he enlisted the help of the Airport Manager, who said that only the welfare of passengers was his concern and called for his Cargo Manager. He was on leave, so the Deputy Manager was summoned.

Time was passing, it was getting very hot and the buck was showing no sign of finding a stopping place. The cattle were getting thirsty and restive. Most of the dignitaries had hurried away in case they were made to do something, so there was no point in my shouting at Anthony and Charlie any more. The crew of the aircraft were not any help either. They had sloped off to the nearest bar, reasoning that it was their job to deliver the cargo and not unload it, so they had done their bit.

My Jordanian is not very good – never was – so communication with the remaining officials was a problem. It had been all right with the dignitaries when a bit of Pidgin English and much mutual backslapping had sufficed, but now we had to solve a real problem. From our vantage point high up on the plane, we spotted some construction work in progress on the edge of the airport, the dominant feature of which was a large crane. I am not sure quite whose idea it was, so I am prepared to take the credit, but someone suggested that a crane was what was needed to lift the cattle out and on to the ground.

It was a good idea, but trying to get it across to the dwindling group of officials and then persuading them to do something about it, took another two hours. However, by mid-morning we had commandeered the crane, rigged up a sort of sling and were ready to ease the first cow on to it. A fully-grown Friesland cow weighs well over half a ton, and if it does not want to go somewhere it is not easy to make it go. The first cow did not want to step into space on the off-chance that its fifteen-foot fall would be arrested by a flimsy looking bit of sacking. The combined pushing power of Anthony, Charlie and me made very little difference.

We enlisted the help of the crane driver, made him come closer, wrapped the sling round the cow while it was still in the aeroplane, and tied it on to her with a rope. We then signalled to the driver to move slowly away, thus wrenching the protesting cow into space. To the accompaniment of bellows of protest she was then lowered on to Jordanian soil. There were twenty-three more cows and one bull, all of whom had to undergo the same treatment, so it was after nine o'clock that evening before they had all been safely offloaded. We were exhausted. I had no voice left, Anthony had a black eye, and Charlie's pinstriped suit would never grace the City again.

We repaired to the nearest hotel, and I regret to say we got uproariously drunk on some filthy aniseed-flavoured local plonk. Next day was Sunday, and after staggering out of bed with crashing hangovers, we sought our unhelpful crew to ascertain when we would take off for home.

We were told that we would leave Amman just before lunch and would not be flying direct to London but via Cairo, to pick up the return load of vegetables. Anthony and Charlie exchanged anxious looks, worried about when they would get to London. The flight to Cairo was uneventful and we dozed, trying to rid our heads of aniseed fumes. On landing at Cairo airport there was an alarming smell of burning, and the aeroplane eventually came to a halt immersed in a cloud of smoke. We did not need the urging of the crew to get the hell out of it quickly, and we landed on Egyptian soil in an untidy heap and took off at a rate of knots.

The plane did not burst into flames, but clearly some serious damage had been done and it was in no fit state to fly that day. It was not in a fit state to fly the following day either, or the day after, or for the whole of that week! This did not worry me unduly. I was on company business and therefore on expense account. It did worry Anthony and Charlie considerably, because not only were they not on any expense account but they were due back in their respective offices on the Monday morning. This all happened in the early '60s when communications between Cairo and London were not perhaps what they are today. They sent telegrams to their bosses saying that they had been delayed in the country – a not unusual occurrence – but the excuse wore thinner and thinner as Monday became Tuesday and then Wednesday, until the whole week had gone with these mysterious telegrams from Cairo coming in and still no sign of their valued employees.

We spent our first night in the Nile Hilton, and very nice it was too, but a serious lack of funds dictated a fairly speedy move to cheaper accommodation. This we found on the other side of the Nile, and it was pretty grotty. However the week passed pleasantly enough, with visits to the Pyramids and the Sphinx. The only drawback to these visits was the swarms of young Egyptian children who besieged us as we stepped out of our taxi, trying to sell us anything from an ice cream to their sister. At one stage, Charlie could take no more of this and took to his heels screaming, flapping his hands at the attendant kids the way one does at a swarm of flies.

Eventually, after over a week in Cairo, the old aeroplane was pronounced cured and we were flown back to London. I demanded a couple of days off after my ordeal on behalf of the company. Anthony's and Charlie's companies demanded a bit of work out of them. A week later we read in the newspaper that our very aeroplane had crashed in the Alps, killing the entire crew.

* * *

Shortly after this, I flew with a stallion to Los Angeles. This was in a regular cargo plane where the stallion and I had a small portion partitioned off to ourselves, him in a crate and me on my feet. Shortly before take-off the American pilot paid us a visit. He handed me a weapon that looked like a sawn-off shotgun but was in fact a humane killer.

"If this son of a bitch gives any trouble, shoot the mother-fucker," was his encouraging greeting.

As someone had paid several thousand pounds for this highly pedigreed racehorse, I felt I would get a fairly cool reception if it were dead on arrival. But I could see the pilot's point; an hysterical stallion going bananas at thirty thousand feet over the Atlantic was not a happy thought.

Fortunately there was no trouble, and on arrival in Los Angeles I was able to hand over a living stallion. I was referred to as the 'jockey' (or 'jaackey' in Californian) by the new owners. Quite what weight they thought English racehorses had to carry I do not know, as I am over six feet and weighed a good hundred and seventy pounds in those days.

I then had a few days to spend there and visited Disney World, which was quite new then, also Jack Dempsey's bar, where I met the great boxer, and other bars on the Sunset Strip. It was my first visit to America and I liked what I saw, an opinion which was reinforced in later years when I spent a lot of time in that great country.

For most of the latter months of the summer of 1963 I was in charge of a delegation of Russian buyers who were purchasing a shipload of pedigree British livestock. Predominant amongst this consignment were: Aberdeen Angus, Hereford and Shorthorn bulls; Romney Marsh, Border Leicester and Suffolk rams. A whole shipload took a lot of finding, but it was fun driving round the remoter parts of Scotland seeking out some of the smaller breeders. Some of these only had one or two bulls to sell and the conclusion of a deal was a solemn occasion, particularly as their treasured animal was being exported to Russia, of all places. As the deal was finally agreed an unmarked bottle of colourless fluid would be produced and a generous portion poured into small glasses. When we all had a full glass (including me) the health of the bull was proposed, and we tossed back the contents of the glass. I dare say the Russians were used to doing this sort of thing with vodka, but even they gagged a bit when this lot hit the back of their throat. It was of course very good, single malt whisky. Whisky in its pure form is colourless. The colour is added, when it is to be sold commercially, to stop people thinking it is gin or vodka. What barbarian could ever do that?

Luckily we were seldom able to buy more than two or three bulls in a morning; otherwise the driver might have had some difficulty at the end of the day finding any farm at all. As it was, there would be another two or three in the afternoon and we would all be quite merry by the time we found the hotel for the night. I quickly learned to appreciate good whisky, but I could never afterwards buy what I had drunk, as I never knew what it was called. I do not think that stuff was ever sold on the open market.

Eventually the shipload was complete, and all the animals were transported to Hull, to be loaded on to a ship for onward transport to some remote Russian port. I was on hand to help load them, and I entertained hopes of being sent to Russia with them as one of the expert attendants. However, even I was not expert enough, as the Russians insisted on fully qualified vets travelling with this valuable consignment. It was the height of the Cold War and I was sad to miss out on a chance to visit Russia, particularly as I had become quite friendly with the three buyers, a couple of whom spoke average English. We had drunk a lot of whisky together and I had looked forward to repeating the exercise with vodka.

* * *

It was a long drive back from Hull before the days of motorways, and I was tired as I hit the outskirts of London after loading the ship. Dusk was just falling and I was looking forward to a few days off. I took a short cut down a wide-open road near Camden Town and was suddenly slammed into by a van hitting me at right angles just behind the driver's seat. My car, a Ford Zephyr, careered across the road and smashed into a line of parked vehicles. I climbed out very shaken, a bit bruised but otherwise unhurt. The van that had hit me was in a much worse state, and the driver and his companion were lying in the middle of the road. A crowd gathered and police were called, followed by an ambulance, which took away the two injured occupants. I was interviewed by the police and finally rang up Neil Stanford and asked him to come and take me back to my flat. I spent a very unhappy night, and next morning rang up the hospital where I knew the two injured men had been taken. I had to wait a long time on the line before eventually a male voice told me solemnly that the driver of the van had just died and the passenger was still in a critical condition.

What had I done? I had killed an innocent person. Certainly, I was very sorry for this, but to be totally honest my first reaction was fear for myself. Had it been my fault? I was tired certainly, but there was no suggestion of drink – there had been no whisky that day. How had the crash occurred? I was sure that I had been on the major road and had not been going fast. I was not expected in the office that day, so I went back to the site of the crash and walked down the stretch of road on which I had been driving immediately before I was hit by the van. There was the intersection from which the van had emerged and then, horror of horrors, I saw it. A signpost saying, 'HALT AT MAJOR ROAD AHEAD'.

No way had I halted, I had not even slowed down. I had not even seen the sign. The driver of the van had had right of way. It was all my fault. A cold, clammy feeling came over me. What would happen now? I returned to the flat feeling numb. I did not have long to wait to see what the next move would be; that very evening the frontdoor bell rang, and when I opened it a policeman was standing there looking grim. Was I Mark Richard Milbank, he asked? Yes, I was. In that case, I was being charged with causing death by dangerous driving and would appear in court on a given date. He left me with an impressive array of legal looking papers, copies of which I had had to sign and return to him.

"This is a very serious charge, be sure to turn up," was his parting remark.

I rang my Uncle Mark at the Palace. No, I was not hoping for a royal pardon but I was seeking the name of a good lawyer. This I got in the form of Mervyn Griffiths-Jones, QC, who was currently much in the news as he was very involved in the case concerning Christine Keeler and the then Minister of War, John Profumo.

My first court appearance was a very brief affair, as that court was too small to hear so serious a case. I was told that the case would be heard in the Old Bailey early in January the following year. It was then September.

There followed a pretty miserable four months. I had only one meeting with Mr Griffiths-Jones, but several with a nice young South African lawyer who was his underling. We revisited the scene of the crash, and he took photos of the stretch of road showing how difficult it was to see the rather small 'major road' sign. I told BLE everything that had happened, and they were very supportive. I wanted to contact the family of the man I had killed but my lawyers advised me not to as this could imply that I was accepting responsibility for his death. It turned out that he was in fact an illegal Greek immigrant whose family spoke virtually no English. I never did speak to them and have always felt a bit guilty that I did not.

It was an unhappy time for other reasons as well. My parents had finally decided to sell Momandu and leave Kenya for South Africa. Kenya was now independent and Jomo Kenyatta its new President. My parents and other farmers in the Machakos district were made an offer by the British Government to buy them out and be paid in British pounds. This was too good an offer to refuse and most accepted. 'Momandu' was sold and the whole area turned into a co-operative enterprise for the local waKamba tribe. I was too worried about my own problems to be any help or support to them, but I was upset. 'Momandu' had been our childhood home, and we had all been very happy there. Not wanting to burden my parents with more worries, I did not tell them of my own problems. This was stupid, because inevitably they heard from another source, and this worried them more.

January arrived, cold, wet and gloomy as only January can be in England. It matched my mood. On the sixth, I duly appeared at the Old Bailey. Mervyn Griffith-Jones was there to represent me, together with the young South African, and Anthony also turned up to lend his support. Evidence was heard from the prosecution and the defence and me. At lunchtime I was locked in a cell under the courtroom and given something to eat. I was not happy. What if I were sent to prison? The day ended with no verdict and I had to reappear the next day. Anthony took me out to dinner.

Proceedings were brief the next morning. I was found guilty of causing death by dangerous driving, fined one hundred pounds and banned from driving for three years. But I was not going to prison. The nightmare was over and a huge load lifted from my whole being. BLE paid my legal fees and I managed to scrape up the hundred pounds. Previously, BLE had offered me a wage increase and the promise of a directorship in a year or so. This would of course mean my staying permanently in England, and I had pretty much made up my mind that

I would do this. 'Momandu' was gone and Kenya was now run by the thugs that I had spent eighteen months fighting. Col Douglas Kennedy, the boss of BLE, cornered me at the annual bull sale in Hereford. As far as he was concerned, I was now of little use to the company. My main job had been driving clients around and now I would be unable to do this for the next three years. He put it all very nicely, and he emphasized what a good job I had done in the eighteen months I had worked for his company, but the message was clear: I was sacked.

I continued working for another couple of months and then got the job of looking after five bulls that were to travel on a ship to South Africa. I would be their expert attendant. I was going back to South Africa to visit my parents and then decide what I wanted to do. I was not unhappy about the idea.

CHAPTER 12

South Africa

THE JOURNEY OUT BY SHIP DOWN THE west coast of Africa was comfortable and relaxing. My duties were not onerous, consisting of feeding the bulls twice a day, grooming them a bit, and leading them on a halter up and down the deck for a bit of exercise most days.

When joining the ship I had expected to be housed with the crew, as after all I was just the animal attendant, and you cannot get much lower than that. However, after loading them I was introduced to the Chief Officer, and after chatting for a bit he said, "Lucky we had a chat. I was going to put you with the crew, but of course there is a cabin available on the upper deck." So I got a smart cabin all to myself. I wondered why. I would not have minded being with the crew a bit and indeed made good friends with them. It seemed the old British class system appeared to be alive and well, although I never had a plummy English accent.

As I left England the Macmillan Government was in turmoil. Mr Profumo had been caught sleeping with Christine Keeler, who was also sleeping with a Russian diplomat. Profumo made a 'personal statement' in the House of Commons denying that he had done this, but soon afterwards he had to admit that he had lied. His main crime was lying to 'the House', not lying with Miss Keeler, it seems. Obviously he had to resign, and my cousin James Ramsden took over as Minister of War. Profumo died in 2006, aged ninety-one. James is still alive but no one remembers him, while everybody remembers Profumo – such is notoriety!

We made one stop on the way, spending a couple of days at Las Palmas in the Canary Islands, then on to Cape Town, where I unloaded two bulls destined to travel by train all the way up to the Black family, who farmed in the Mazoe valley of Rhodesia.

Then it was on round the Cape to Durban, where I was met by Mr and Mrs. Quinton Smith and their daughter Jill, who took delivery of the remaining Hereford bulls and transported them to their farm near Johannesburg.

My job done, I telephoned my parents, who were now farming near Balgowan in the Natal Midlands, and they drove the eighty miles to Durban to pick me up. I had last seen my father when crossing the flooded Athi River in Kenya on my way to the airport some eighteen months previously, when he was still farming on 'Momandu'. A lot of water had passed under the bridge since then.

As independence approached for Kenya a lot of the old time settlers decided to leave. It was still very much a novelty for an ex-colony to be ruled by its indigenous Africans and most people were fairly apprehensive about the outcome. In Kenya we had seen at first-hand what happened when the Congo got independence from Belgium. Total chaos reigned and many of the resident Belgians were killed in appalling ways. The owner of a hotel near the Ugandan border, whom we knew slightly, had been put in his own oven and cooked.

I do not know what the British Government had planned to do about its citizens in its African colonies. It had encouraged them to go there, and indeed in some cases had given them land there as a thank you for fighting in two world wars. What now? Were these people to be abandoned to their fate in this new and very uncertain situation? The British Government had however done something; my parents had taken advantage of an offer from them to sell 'Momandu' and be paid out in pounds sterling. Most of our neighbours had had similar offers and virtually the whole area was acquired for resettlement of the waKamba people. All this took some time, but eventually only two people continued to farm in the area: David Stanley is still there, Peter Leonard died a few years ago.

My parents did not get a lot. The Athi-Tiva venture, while saving a lot of cattle from starvation, had been a very costly exercise, and after paying off existing debts there was not much left over to start again in South Africa. They had driven down to have a look and been taken under the wing of George Forder, who was head of the estate agents Tucker, Egeland and Forder, based in Estcourt in Natal.

*   *   *

My parents knew very few people in Natal, but they said that they had helped entertain a South African polo team that had toured Kenya some years previously. They mentioned Lawrence Slatter, and George told them that there had recently been a tragic air crash, in which a number of people from the Natal Midlands, on a charter flight to England, had been killed. One of those was Lawrence, together with his brother Mark and Mark's wife, Anne. Mark had recently bought a farm near Curry's Post in the Natal Midlands, having moved from the family home near Greytown. Mark was now dead and the farm was up for sale, so my parents went to look at it. Mark and Lawrence's parents were understandably in a state of shock. Amongst other things they were landed with Mark and Anne's three very young children and did not want any protracted negotiations over the farm, but just to get rid of it and have one less worry. The result was that my parents got the farm on very favourable terms, which, with a lot of credit, they could just afford.

'Newstead' was not a great farm, but was in a very nice area. It was also over two thousand acres, which was big for that area, and the new National highway joining Johannesburg and Durban was under construction right through the middle of it. So from that point of view it was a good buy. The Natal Midlands was not like Kenya at all. It was not good land, being steep and rocky, but it was also quite wet, and trees grew well, so timber – gum and pine – was one of the main crops on 'Newstead'. Not everybody farmed for a living; it was pleasant and cool, being situated at about four thousand feet, so several business tycoons from Jo'burg had bought smallholdings in the area, to which they either intended to retire or had already retired.

Our next-door neighbour was 'Punch' Barlow, a charming man whose father had founded a company dealing in caterpillar tractors. Punch had taken over the business and expanded it considerably to become Barlow International; he lived in Jo'burg but also owned 'Bosch Hoek', which boasted its own golf course and polo field. On a smallholding right in the middle of 'Newstead's' two thousand acres lived Ken and Ruth Pennington. He was a retired schoolmaster from nearby Michaelhouse School, where he had been very much 'Mr Chips', having devoted his life to it. He also had a unique collection of butterflies. Further down the road was John Voelcker, formerly a very high-powered Jo'burg businessman, with a deep interest in ornithology, and founder of the John Voelcker Bird Book Fund which sponsored the lovely and definitive seventh edition of *Roberts Birds of Southern Africa*. Also there was Gillespie Armstrong, who owned huge sugar estates north of Durban. So in a lot of ways my parents were out of their income bracket. They had nothing left after buying the farm and now had to make it pay.

It was to 'Newstead' that I was taken, and at first sight I was impressed. It was an old house with lovely yellowwood floors, situated in an extensive garden with a lovely view. Apart from timber, which was a very long-term crop, the main income would be from plums, as there was a large orchard boasting the early ripening Methley plum, which had been perfected on the property by previous owners of the farm – the Methley family.

I was happy to be out of London and back on a farm. The pleasure of this was much enhanced by the fact that there was a polo club nearby at Lions River, and despite the financial constraints my father had bought a couple of ponies and had started playing. I was taken to the club the weekend after I arrived. I had not been on a horse for some two years, but I was lent ponies by the club members and played six fast chukkas. I could hardly stand at the end of this but had thoroughly enjoyed it and apparently acquitted myself all right; ponies were comparatively cheap and plentiful and I was lent a couple for the season that was just starting. This was a wonderful introduction to the area and I very soon made good friends with my club mates. Early winter is a lovely time in Natal, after the rains have stopped and before it is cold. The sun shone, I was back on a farm, making friends and playing polo. Life was looking up after a fairly dodgy time in England. If my parents wanted me, I decided I would stay. They did want me. My father was over fifty and there was plenty to do on the place.

My mother was never happy in South Africa, though. In no way was she a snob but she was just not on the same wavelength as the South African women. It was then (and to a large extent still is) a very male-dominated society. If we went out for a meal, women were not allowed into the bar; they would sit in an anteroom, waiting while the men had a drink before the meal. A woman could not open a bank account in her own name without her husband's permission. At parties, all the men would congregate in one corner and talk about rugby, while the women would be left on their own. My mother hated all this. She was asked to come to tea by her neighbours shortly after arriving, and duly pitched up at about four o'clock in the afternoon, only to discover that 'tea' means eleven o'clock in the morning.

The language was also a problem. My parents did not speak Afrikaans, but even the way English was spoken made understanding difficult. Another neighbour asked if she could borrow a 'pin'. My mother searched in her handbag and produced a safety pin, thinking that this was what was wanted.

"No, no, a PIN."

It turned out that she wanted to borrow a PEN. 'Shame' was a much used word. If your husband died they all said 'shame'. If you gave birth to a beautiful baby, they still said 'shame'. It was all very confusing.

Names were difficult too. How did you pronounce Geldenhuis or Van Wyk? An ex-Kenyan friend of my mother introduced a mutual neighbour to her as Mrs du Toit (pronounced 'toy').

"No, no," said the lady, "Not du Toit – it's de Kok" (pronounced 'cock').

"Ah," said my mother's friend. "Sorry, but I knew it was something to play with."

This sort of joke did not go down well; Afrikaners often seemed to be confused by the more subtle English sense of humour.

It was all a bit confusing for my father and me as well. We had left Kenya because it was about to be taken over by the blacks. We had come to South Africa instead, presumably because it was still ruled by whites. Apartheid was at its virulent height; Nelson Mandela had just been arrested and the Nationalist Party (the Nats) was firmly in control. This party was composed mainly of the Afrikaners, Boers against whom members of our family had fought; some being killed in the Anglo-Boer War a mere sixty years before. But, as we had now come to their country, should we not support the Nat government?

* * *

Natal was very English and most of our new friends were English-speaking and of English descent – albeit a long time ago in most cases. They still basically disliked and distrusted the Nationalist government. There were of course plenty of Afrikaners in Natal. I had an early encounter that showed me that the Boer War was not yet over. My father had bought some sheep and these now needed shearing, so I was given the job of organizing this. I scouted around and soon discovered a person who had a gang and who did shearing on contract. He agreed to come on a set day and I went to meet him when he arrived. He was a youngish Afrikaner, who immediately started gabbling away to me in Afrikaans. Clearly I could not understand a word, so he switched very reluctantly into bad English. Shearing got under way, and, knowing a bit about the job from my Argentine experiences, I drew his attention to the odd thing that I did not like. I spoke directly to him as the supervisor and not to the shearers themselves.

As we were about to finish, I asked him if he would like to come to the house for a cup of tea. He indicated that he would, but as we approached the house our maid came running out to say that I was wanted urgently on the telephone. I ran on ahead, telling him to follow. When I had finished my call I looked round for him, but he was nowhere to be seen. I returned to the sheep, and there he was sitting on a log with his back to me. I asked him if he did not want the tea, upon which he spun round and started swearing at me in Afrikaans. I assume he was swearing, but then the whole language actually sounds like a succession of swear words! Eventually he switched to bad English, and it seemed that I was a patronizing, know-all little 'Pom', who expected him to follow me when I clicked my fingers at him like a little dog. Perhaps he should roll on his back and let me tickle his tummy! And I thought I was being hospitable.

The incident actually upset me quite a lot. Were these the sort of people I had come to live amongst? Was I a know-all, patronizing little 'Pom'? There were no Afrikaners at the polo club, but one member had lived a lot of his life in the Orange Free State, which was about as Afrikaans as you can get. His groom irritated him one morning and without hesitation he took the groom behind the clubhouse and set about him with his polo stick. I was not used to that sort of behaviour. South Africa had a reputation of being fairly intolerant towards its locals and this appeared to bear it out. We had been pretty rough during the Emergency in Kenya but then we had been at war. We had not thrashed our grooms with polo sticks.

We were not the only recently arrived ex-Kenyans around, and we had to be careful not to join that band who were continually comparing South Africa – unfavourably – with Kenya. They would preface most remarks with, "When we were in Kenya, we did such and such."

This quite reasonably irritated the locals, who would be tempted to reply, "Well, why the hell didn't you stay in Kenya, if it was so bloody marvellous!"

Ex-Kenyans came to be known as 'when-we's', not only in South Africa but in Australia and New Zealand as well. We did not want to become 'when-we's', so we tried to adjust to our new environment.

Natal is a lovely province, stretching as it does from the Indian Ocean in the east, inland to the timber belt round Karkloof and to Curry's Post, then on further west to some of the old battlefields of the Boer War at the turn of the century. Sixty years before, names like Ladysmith, Colenso and Spion Kop reverberated throughout England; General Buller's mighty British Expeditionary Force was taking a hammering from a bunch of tough Boers armed mainly with ancient muskets. Ancient they may have been, but the Boers were all wonderful shots, and shooting from the heights of Colenso across the Tugela River they were able to pick off the British officers in their bright scarlet uniforms at will. It was the carnage of the Boer War that eventually led to the introduction and development of camouflage.

Ladysmith, named after the Spanish wife of General Sir Harry Smith, one of the first administrators in the area, was an interesting town to visit. It is surrounded by a number of small hills and it was from these hills that the Boers commanded a view, not only of the whole town, but of all the approaches to it as well, so that they were able to enforce the famous siege which reduced the inhabitants of the town to eating their dogs and horses.

Rawdon's Hotel was a popular meeting place between us and Ladysmith and they had a wonderful cartoon on a tile in the gents' loo. It was a painting of a fat, regal looking lady wearing a tiara and strings of pearls, with a contented smile on her face, sitting on a loo. Underneath it a caption read, 'The Relief of Lady Smith'.

Spion Kop was not far away either. This was a slightly higher hill than the others. The British thought that if they could take command of this hill, they would have a clear view of the town of Ladysmith and so might be able to do something about lifting the embarrassing siege. I visited Spion Kop, climbed to the top, and tried to locate Ladysmith. It was miles away and you could not even see the place. Yet the battle of

Spion Kop was the bloodiest and most fiercely fought of all that took place in the Boer War. For twenty-four hours the two sides clashed on the very summit of the little hill, exchanging point-blank fire and even engaging in hand-to-hand combat. Hundreds were killed on both sides, and as dusk fell both sides thought they had lost and withdrew down the hill. It was only the following dawn that a young Boer girl, venturing up the hill again to see if she could locate a missing husband, found the top of the hill to be totally deserted of any living being – just mounds of corpses.

This battle has gone down in history as one of the most pointless ever fought. The British general – Buller – had not himself gone near the place. He had sat comfortably on the south side of the Tugela River, which runs along the foot of the hill, viewing proceedings through a telescope while refreshing himself with smoked salmon sandwiches and champagne.

The sites of these infamous battles are well preserved, and those really interested in ancient battles can be conducted on guided tours. Shortly after my arrival in Natal the sixtieth anniversary of Spion Kop was celebrated. A large photograph of surviving participants in the battle appeared on the front page of the *Natal Witness* newspaper. It showed some fifty old men from both sides of the conflict – mostly Boers but some English as well. Were they now all friends I wondered? Not really. A lot of bitterness was created at the end of the war as a result of the British – who, by then, were winning – rounding up Boer families to stop them feeding commandos still in the field. These women and children were concentrated into various camps, which were strictly under the control of the British Army. They thus became known as concentration camps, spawning a term that was to become universal in future conflicts.

Food was hard to come by and sanitation poor, so a lot of children died in the camps when disease became a problem. Women also died, and all emerged at the end in pretty poor nick. This gave rise to the theory banded about by the Boers that the filthy English had fed ground-up glass to their captured families. I do not believe for one moment that this was true, but hygiene was certainly bad and better care could probably have been taken of these wretched people. However the myth persists, and when my sister Sue's daughter Fiona visited us in Rhodesia some years later she was courted by a charming young Afrikaner boy. The romance was going well until the boy took Fiona to meet his parents. The old father lost no time in accusing Fiona of having ancestors who had fed crushed glass to his people. The romance died a quick death.

There is no doubt that British South Africans and Afrikaners were still stepping pretty cautiously round each other at the time I arrived in South Africa. Natal was predominantly British South African, and Tommy Bedford, one of the first non-Afrikaners to captain the Springbok rugby team, once famously referred to Natal as 'The Last Outpost of the British Empire'. South Africa was different from Kenya though, in many ways. Kenya had also been very British and as such it was really 'not on' to talk about your personal finances. In South Africa it was done quite openly and money matters were widely discussed. My father could not really handle this, but I found it quite refreshing. South Africa was a very rich country and there were plenty of rich, well-established people about. There was plenty to learn.

Our labour on the farm was all Zulu. I had read about the Zulu nation and admired their leaders like Chaka and Cetewayo, who had slaughtered a large part of the British expeditionary force in the Zulu wars of the previous century. I was expecting to find a proud, upstanding, warlike tribe. Instead they turned out to be a scruffy, drunken, downtrodden bunch of wasters. Goodness, how they drank! Our waKamba in Kenya had been bad enough but they would at least be moderately sober when they turned up for work on a Monday morning. This lot was invariably late and always very hung over, if not still drunk. They spoke virtually no English, so I found myself having to learn Zulu. If Afrikaans is difficult, Zulu is impossible. You don't speak most of the time; it is all a series of clicks. Fights were commonplace, particularly when they had been drinking over the weekend.

* * *

One Monday morning our tractor driver was sitting by himself when I went out at six o'clock to tell the labour what they would be doing that day. I thought he was just more hung over than usual, so I left him until last, but when I approached him he just remained sitting and pointed to his chest. Just below his right collarbone I could see a thin metal rod protruding from the skin. In my best Zulu I asked him how deep it was. He did not say anything but just pointed to his back, and there, also protruding from the skin, was the other end of the metal rod! It was the spoke from a bicycle wheel and had been stuck right through him.

We had a lot of trouble with the labour. All of them lived on the farm and had their own cattle. The farm was only just over two thousand acres, and they were taking up a lot of the best parts of it. My father told them they had to get rid of their cattle, as he wanted the grazing for his own cattle. This was not popular. Mark Slatter had planted a lot of new pine and gum plantations and these were now two or three feet high. Between each young tree there was a lot of grass – green in the summer, but dry as tinder in the rainless winter months. Suddenly we started getting fires in these plantations; they had fireguards round the outside, but the fires were almost impossible to put out once started within the plantation. This was particularly so as most of them seemed to start at night.

The blame was always put on a road construction gang who were camped on the farm, building the new National highway. I was not too sure though, and I only antagonized the road gang when I started accusing them. Someone suggested that I go and see a witch doctor. A witch doctor! How could he help and where did one find him? My friend told me of one near Weenen in the north of Natal. Weenen apparently means 'weeping' in Afrikaans, and it is said to be where the Afrikaner womenfolk were waiting for their men to return from negotiations with the Zulu Chief, Dingane. When the men did not return, because Dingane had bumped them all off, they all sat around crying, thus giving the name to the place. I went to Weenen to find the witch doctor. I went alone and had not told him I was coming (he was not on the telephone). With some difficulty I located him, and in a mixture of English and very bad Zulu related the story of the fires. I made no mention of our trouble with the labour or our insistence on their removing the cattle. He listened in silence, then, when I had finished, asked a few questions. He then did what witch doctors are meant to do – throw a few bones and bits of dried skin around. He asked more questions, and then he proclaimed that all the trouble stemmed from our telling the labour to remove their cattle. He would not say that the labour had actually started the fires themselves, despite my pressing him on this issue. Finally I paid him fifty rand and left. How had he known about the problem with the cattle? Weenen was a good hundred miles from our farm and I had told none of the labour where I was going. It was all a bit spooky.

We did not back down completely on the cattle issue, but we did tone down our demands by putting aside a small area of the farm specifically for their use. The fires did not stop completely either though, and we had a pretty disastrous first year with five or six good plantations burned.

Plums were the other main crop so, with the approach of spring in November, we eagerly awaited their ripening and sale to the fruit markets of Durban. They were looking good and we had just started reaping, when one lunchtime, a storm started brewing, and by the time it had ended half an hour later there was no more plum crop. Hail had completely wiped out the crop. It was a devastating blow. We were hard pushed financially and my parents were very depressed.

* * *

However there was some good news. My sister Sue became engaged to an ex-British Army officer whom she met when he was serving in Kenya. Sue still lived in Kenya and was working as a matron at Pembroke House preparatory school for boys near Gilgil. The wedding would be held in Kenya, so it gave my parents – particularly my mother – an excuse to go back to Kenya. It would not help the finances of course – rather the reverse – but it did cheer them up a bit.

Sue's future husband was called Tony Pelly. He was a skinny looking guy with a very big nose and a Pommy accent, and not a bit the sort of person one thought Sue would marry. It is only a slight exaggeration to say that all the remaining bachelors in Kenya were after Sue's hand in marriage and they were collectively appalled at her deciding to marry this 'bloody Pom'. I had never met him and tended to agree with them. Now, over forty years down the line, I am prepared to admit that I was very wrong.

My parents returned to Kenya and I also flew in for the wedding. This took place on 'Kilima Kiu' at the house of our cousins, the Wilsons, who were still farming there at that time. There can be few nicer settings for a wedding than an African garden and this was no exception. My father proudly gave Sue away; my mother revelled in the occasion and was delighted to be back amongst her old friends. I was an usher and was also very happy catching up with a number of my friends who were still in Kenya. It was a marvellous occasion.

Sue's main bridesmaid was her old schoolfriend Fran Holme, who had been an on-off girlfriend of mine for some years. Fran was a very pretty girl and a lot of fun. It was her brother Richard with whom I had shared a flat when I worked in London. He had been engaged to Sue for a short time and was still very fond of her, so there were some fairly complex relationships involved. I had seen quite a lot of Fran when I was in London, as she was then working as a nanny for a young couple in Wimbledon, so I was very pleased to meet up with her again. After the wedding, which started in the morning, a bunch of us, including Fran and John Clarke, drove the fifty miles to Nairobi and took over part of the dining-room of Muthaiga Club. Here we continued the celebrations in traditional manner.

Next morning John and I, plus Fran and a girl friend of his, set off for Athi-Tiva, my old stamping ground. We took very little with us – just a tent, basic food and drink, a shotgun each and a lot of ammo. It was only a couple of years since I had left so I was interested to see what was happening there. Not much was the answer. All our cattle had left a long time ago but the waKamba had not moved in at all. Indeed the two spray races so painstakingly erected by Bob, our gang, and me lay abandoned and unused. The water tanks were empty and the roads overgrown. This did not worry us one bit then as we had come to shoot and the shooting was still terrific. Game was still plentiful as well so we had a wonderful three days. We had to stop shooting birds quite soon as we had so many that we could not stop them going bad in the heat before taking them back to Nairobi. Those we did take back arrived in fairly dubious condition and I do not think that Fran's long-suffering boss appreciated them all being offloaded in her office.

I had a lot more fun during my brief visit back to Kenya. David Begg, that wonderful old character who ran the Kinyatta Polo Club near Gilgil, lent me a couple of ponies and I played in two polo tournaments at North Kenya and Nanyuki. I persuaded Fran to come to these tournaments with me and it was the start of her becoming hooked on polo. I was also beginning to hope that she was becoming hooked on me. Between these two tournaments I went on safari up to Marsabit in the Northern Frontier District with Mike Ardagh, who had for some years worked for my father on 'Momandu'. In those days one travelled quite freely with a gun and we did a lot of bird shooting anywhere that was not in a national park. The two weeks passed very quickly, and I departed wondering why I had ever left Kenya in the first place. Of course independence was just round the corner and still no one knew quite what was going to happen then. I returned to Natal not quite sure that I had done the right thing but perhaps my blossoming romance with Fran had something to do with that.

CHAPTER 13

Sport in Natal

NATAL WAS GOOD FUN THOUGH. MY PARENTS never really returned after Sue's wedding, and they handed 'Newstead' over to me to run while they got jobs in Kenya. This was probably a good idea. I enjoyed the challenge of running the farm on my own, and they both thoroughly enjoyed being back in Kenya and taking rich Americans out on safari; they had accepted work with the luxury tour operators, Abercrombie and Kent.

One sad note though was that my big sister Penel came out on holiday and, thinking that South Africa was a much better place to bring up her young family than England, decided to come and join us. This was excellent news but no sooner had she arrived than our parents moved back to Kenya. This initially upset Penel quite a lot, but she soon got over it and revelled in the sun and freedom of Natal after a pretty miserable few years in England. Initially she lived in the main house at 'Newstead', where of course I was also living. This gave me an early taste of sharing a house with a very young and boisterous family. Penel was great though, and it gave me a chance to get to know her better after her early marriage. She also acted as a very efficient housekeeper and it was fun having the children around. Then Penel caught me dosing myself on Sanatogen, a much advertised cure for strained nerves! Shortly afterwards she moved out to a little rented cottage nearby.

If farming was not easy, life in general was pretty good. Natal is a lovely province, and in the mid-sixties we white farmers were a pretty privileged lot. We might not have had much money but there was plenty around. I became very friendly with Brian Stanistreet. Brian was the resident manager of 'Bosch Hoek', Punch Barlow's luxurious country retreat. Punch lived in Jo'burg most of the time and only came down to 'Bosch Hoek' for about six weeks a year. For the rest of the time Brian ruled supreme. 'Bosch Hoek' boasted its own polo field, a private nine-hole golf course, a couple of lakes stocked with fish and complete with motor boats and water-skiing equipment, extensive lawns, stables for twenty horses, a tennis court and a full-sized billiard table in the main house. All this had to be looked after in Punch's absence and this meant using it, so very generously I offered to help Brian do just this!

Brian was a very keen polo player and was a member of the then top club in South Africa – Mooi River. I had joined the adjacent Lions River Club. Living right next door it was easy to ride over to 'Bosch Hoek' in the evenings with my ponies and practise my polo with Brian; then a groom would take the ponies back to 'Newstead' and I would stay on for a game of snooker and supper, often supplemented by some of Punch's red wine if he had happened to leave a few half-empty bottles on his previous visit. Chateauneuf du Pape appeared to be one of his favourites and I fully approved of his choice. Often, after a bottle or two, Brian, red-faced and with a lock of hair falling less than soberly forward, would launch into the *Lays of Ancient Rome*, striding up and down and reciting wholly from memory the story of Horatius and the Bridge, complete with theatrical gestures and arbitrary but wholly plausible accents.

This may sound a fairly exotic kind of lifestyle for someone arriving in a new country with no money, and I suppose it was. I never gave money much thought. There always seemed to be just enough, but I certainly never saved any. Ponies could be bought ridiculously cheaply. A lot of the local Zulu labour owned horses, which were basically the tough little Basuto strain. Cross these with a thoroughbred stallion and you get the perfect polo pony. The first pony I bought cost me twenty rand (about ten pounds); she was about three years old and just broken. I called her Dusky and I played top division polo on her that same season.

She must have been tough, because I went on playing her for the next seven seasons as well.

I was incredibly lucky with my polo, and it was a great introduction to Natal society and a lot of very nice people. Polo then was strictly amateur, but of quite a high standard. Mooi River boasted a top side with a total handicap of 24, their star being 'Pip' Davies who played off a 7 handicap. Lions River's best side rated 19 and our top player was the incomparable Ian de Gersigny, who was a 6. Soon after my arrival I played a few chukkas on borrowed ponies at the club and was planning to go and watch the annual Natal Championships to be held at nearby Richmond Polo Club. We had entered four teams in the various divisions, with our best side in the open division, where they would compete against the likes of Mooi River, Noodsberg, Kwambonambi and Gingindhlovo. Beautiful names. Gingindhlovu was Zulu for 'the place of the big elephant' – the said big elephant being Chaka – but was locally known as 'Gin, gin, I love you'.

The day before the five-day tournament was due to start, one of our best players, Mick Kimber, had a serious car crash and was unable to take his place in our top team. Other good players were committed to the teams playing in the lower divisions, so Ian de Gersigny took the very unwise decision of asking me to play in Mick's place on Mick's ponies. I was delighted, of course, but highly nervous; this would be 20-goal polo and the highest standard at which I had ever played was about 15, and that not very often. Also I was to ride ponies that I had never ridden before – it was a daunting prospect.

In the event it was enormous fun. Not only were my teammates – Ian, David Kimber and Duncan Mackenzie – very understanding and helpful, but so were the opposition players, setting an example of sportsmanship and love of the game which was to be a feature of all the polo I played in South Africa. Our first game was against Mooi River, no less. Pip Davies, Keir Hall, Peter Brown and David Henderson were the reigning South African champions, and not even Brian Stanistreet could get into that team. An interesting character in the team was Peter Brown. Unlike most

of us, who if not actually supporting the apartheid Nationalist government were quite happy to go along with it, Peter actively opposed it. For
doing this he had been placed under house arrest and was not allowed
to hold any sort of meeting. He had received special permission to play
polo but was not allowed to talk to us. I found myself marking him and
he talked a lot – not about the iniquities of the ruling party but about the
finer points of the game. Despite being my opponent he went out of his
way to tell me what I should be doing. At the end of the game we all rode
off to the pony lines and then made our way to the bar, while Peter had to
ride to the other side of the ground and go home like a good boy. It was
my first real insight into the thinking of the regime that I had decided I
should support, and I did not like it.

We ended up winning the handicap section of our division, not the
Open but a major triumph nonetheless, and it came with a nice tankard to
put beside my Mugs' Mug.

Ian de Gersigny was a wonderful character; he was married to Ros,
the sister of the Slatter brothers who had owned 'Newstead', so we had
got to know him outside polo, as he was involved in handing the farm
over to my parents. Ian was one of those incredibly gifted sportsmen
that one comes across from time to time. He played cricket, hockey and
polo for Natal (and polo for South Africa), was a brilliant tennis player
and single figure golfer. If he had taken any of these sports remotely
seriously, I am sure he could have gone to the very top. But he did not.
Ian was a party man, the centre of all après polo activities and a brilliant
mimic. Standing on the bar of many a clubhouse, he would be called on
to imitate various players, and with his crooked smile and wicked wit he
would give a cruelly accurate depiction of each player's less desirable
characteristics. It was all done with such humour though that no one ever
took offence – indeed one longed to have one's name called out and be
taken off by Ian. He was brilliant, and if sport had not been his thing he
could have made a fortune as a comedian. When not playing he was the
main commentator on games and here again his quick wit would enliven
the most boring of games.

I was lucky in playing in a lot of tournaments with Ian. Unlike many talented sportsmen, he fully understood the deficiencies of lesser mortals and was generous in his help and advice. In that first season in Natal he gave me one of his best ponies on permanent loan and lent me others when we were playing together. He was very competitive and always wanted to win, but once the game was over there were never any recriminations. We won the Zululand Open in a team with Buddy Chaplin and Harry ('Dagga') Tully; Buddy was Ian's brother-in-law and a big polo star in his own right. Quite how we achieved this win is a mystery, as it was held at Kwambonambi, in Zululand, and hosted by very rich and hospitable sugar farmers, who would not let us go to bed until dawn. Brian Stanistreet had lent me his best pony, Wheatsheaf, and I had two of Ian's, together with Dusky and another complete beginner of my own, but I was very pushed for ponies. When we suddenly had to play an extra chukka because we were tied with our hosts at the end of normal time, typically Ian lent me another pony, and we went on to win. What fun it all was.

Speaking of Harry Tully reminds me of a little story about him. About a year earlier he had got married, and at his bachelor party he was ceremoniously debagged and his balls painted purple with gentian violet. This is very hard to remove – particularly from sensitive areas. Nine months after the wedding, his wife produced twin girls. We christened them – Gentian and Violet.

I have played with a lot of very nice, very good players in my polo playing days but I can safely say that none was more fun to play with than Ian de Gersigny. He proposed our health at our wedding in Richmond but was killed shortly after, driving back from a polo party. One seldom sees grown men openly crying, but most of the hundreds at his funeral were doing just that.

I was lucky to get so much high goal polo to start with in Natal. Gradually I built up a bit of a string of my own and found my more rightful place in the Lions River B team, where I had a lot of fun playing with the likes of the Mackenzie brothers, Robert Smith, Mike Le Sueur and Travers Lister. All of these were farmers, as were ninety per cent of the other polo players in Natal. Transvaal was a different story, and a lot of their players were businessmen from Johannesburg. These were usually very rich and very ambitious. They were often not particularly good horsemen and provided a ready market for well-schooled ponies from Natal. I supplemented my very limited income by palming off some fairly poorly schooled ponies on them.

I went to Jo'burg once to play. I was selected to represent the Natal junior side at the inter-provincial championships held at Inanda Country Club. 'Junior' meant sort of under-25. We played against Transvaal (now Gauteng), East Griqualand and Orange Free State. Inanda was very much the smart place to go and be seen in those days; it was also incredibly cold in midwinter, being situated at over six thousand feet. I stayed with a very rich local businessman called Ronnie Herzog. It was said that the fittings on his baths were gold. I cannot vouch for this but certainly they were gold in colour. He was an excellent host though and looked after us very well during the four days of the tournament. We did not win, being just pipped by Transvaal. On the last day I played for East Griqualand as well as for Natal, substituting for David Walker who was injured. I thus played twelve fast championship chukkas running and much appreciated a hot bath that night in Ronnie's tub – gold taps or not!

Regular Inanda players were the fabled Goodman brothers, Allan and Derek. I had heard all about them and they had been written into songs by Jeremy Taylor. Their father was said to have made a lot of money on the stock exchange in Jo'burg and introduced his twin sons into polo at an early stage to 'meet the right people'. They showed much more aptitude at meeting these people and playing polo than they did in working for dad. They were flamboyant characters and pretty good polo players. Both got a little bored with Jo'burg, where the standard of polo was not that high, and opted to come and play in Natal. Derek joined Mooi River and Allan came to us at Lions River. Both were enormous assets – they were good players, tremendous fun and very nice people.

187

Allan still lived in Jo'burg but would stable his ponies with the Kimbers and drive the three hundred miles every weekend during the season.

He had a charming wife called Jorna, plus some five or six children. Jorna did not usually come down on these weekends, but once, having been given a new very fast little sports car, she decided to nip down and surprise Allan. Now the speed limit on South African roads at that time was a fairly generous 120kms per hour; however this was not nearly enough for Jorna and her smart new car, so going through the Free State on those lovely flat highways she wound it up to 160. Inevitably there was a speed trap and she was flagged down. "Lady," said the Afrikaner constable, "you was sommer going too fast – 140 kilometres per hour."

"I was not!" said Jorna, incensed, "I was doing 160 at least!"

There were many characters playing polo in those days, as I am sure there still are today. The difference then was that it was all totally amateur, and certainly in Natal there was no social standing attached to playing polo. It was all very like the polo I had played in Kenya, albeit without the ex-Indian Army colonels, but to a much higher standard.

Polo was played in the winter months throughout South Africa, months in which it virtually never rained. It meant that a lot of grounds that did not have irrigation got very dry, hard and dusty. The South African Open, which was pretty much the last tournament of the season, was usually played at Kokstad in September. Kokstad is in East Griqualand and pretty high, bleak and cold in September, so when the centenary of this tournament loomed it was decided to hold it at Richmond in Natal. The much sought-after trophy for winning the Open was called the Beresford Cup, and an English team, captained by Lord Patrick Beresford, had been invited to take part. The main reason for this was that the cup had been originally presented to the South African Polo Association by one of Lord Patrick's ancestors. Other members of his team were his brother Tyrone Waterford, also from Ireland, Ronnie Ferguson from England and Wyndham Lacey from Argentina; this was a team with a total handicap of 19 – somewhat below the best South Africa could muster but much on a par with the club sides they were likely to meet.

They arrived in Jo'burg and were met by the association's president, who happened to be Punch Barlow. After one practice game at Inanda they were scheduled to come to Natal for a series of matches culminating in the SA Championships at Richmond. Punch telephoned Brian Stanistreet and told him to drive up to Jo'burg and collect them because they would be based at 'Bosch Hoek' during their stay in Natal. Brian asked me to drive one of Punch's smart cars while he drove the other, and off we went to collect the team. I ended up driving Patrick and Tyrone down.

I think Brian asked me to accompany him because he felt that, with my English background, I would perhaps be more at ease chatting to these British aristocrats than would a local South African. In this he was totally wrong. I found them both almost impossible to chatter to during the long drive; they affected to be totally disinterested in anything that I tried to tell them and would usually reply with a bored, "Oh!"

I was sharply reminded of the British Army officers at Fort Hall! Perhaps I am or was then a very boring person, but I had got on very well with the South Africans I had met, who could not have been friendlier. I had met and played against Patrick and Ronnie Ferguson in Kenya a few years before but it seemed that counted for nothing. It was only when one of them twigged that my uncle was Master of the Queen's Household that they condescended to treat me as a human being. I think I preferred the sheep-shearing guy! If they were insufferable snobs, it did not stop them from playing good polo though. When Wyndham Lacey was injured and the very good young Transvaal player, Robin Wilson, took his place, they duly won the Beresford Cup.

Robin was the son of Peter Wilson who was senior partner in the stockbroking firm, Wilson and Mansfield, for whom Robin also worked. When my parents left Kenya they had invested what spare cash they had with this firm, and these funds were intended to help pay off the very large mortgage we had on 'Newstead'. However, one of the firm's clerks called Chwiden had perfected a monster fiddle, and my parents as well as a lot of others lost a very large part of their savings as the firm went under. This did not seem to have affected the lifestyle of the senior partners though, and I admit to feeling some resentment seeing Robin arrive in Richmond in a brand-new Mercedes, together with a lorry containing eight top polo ponies. His bloody firm had lost most of my parents' money, why should he not suffer a bit?

* * *

The polo season ended in about September, before the hoped-for summer rains, which usually fell from October onwards. This was quite a busy time on the farm, getting crops in the ground for the new season – not that we grew many annual crops on 'Newstead', relying more on fruit and timber. From a sporting point of view, October heralded the start of the local cricket season, and I joined Howick Cricket Club, which played in the very competitive Natal Country Districts league. First class cricket was played in the main towns of Durban and Pietermaritzburg, but many older very good players, not wanting to continue playing at this level, chose to play in our league. The result was regular matches between all the small towns or villages in Natal.

The captain, organizer, selector and chairman of the Howick team was a major character. His name was Tim Scott. He was not much good at cricket, claiming that he used to be a fast bowler but that a shoulder injury had cut short a promising career, and he now masqueraded as an opening batsman, his principal claim to fame being that he usually managed to run out his opening partner – the local doctor, who was a decent opening batsman. Tim was the son of a clergyman and had been sent to Natal from England under mysterious circumstances at the age of seventeen to run a small, family dairy farm on the edge of Howick village.

Tim was more English than the most dyed-in-the-wool Englishman, affected a very plummy accent and had three passions in life – cricket, girls and knowing the right people. The somewhat staid South Africans did not know what to make of him, but despite the undiluted bullshit that poured out of him he was an incredibly good organizer, and his sheer enthusiasm for life meant that you had to like him.

We formed a natural friendship fairly quickly, and I had a lot of fun playing cricket for Howick and later for Tim's own invitation club, the Grasshoppers. I would often drive the seventeen miles into Howick on the Saturday night, have a bit of a party, spend the night at Tim's house and be on the spot for cricket next morning.

Our team consisted mainly of bachelors and we were a fairly irresponsible lot, taking our cue from the leader. We did have a few decent cricketers though, and we managed to hold our own in the league, without ever threatening to win it. I made a few reasonable scores, took some wickets, and was pleased to be selected for the Natal Country Districts team to play other Country Districts in an annual festival in Pietermaritzburg. This lasted a full week, and we played against some very good players who were way above my class. Some had represented South Africa and were only a bit past their prime, so my cricketing career did not progress any further than that.

Tim was great at organizing tours, and I went with his team up to Johannesburg on a couple of occasions, when we played against local club sides in the daytime and followed Tim on an unrelenting search for 'skirt' at night. We achieved limited success in both departments. Jo'burg was pretty much what it is now, a huge sprawling metropolis containing every possible financial group. We tended to move amongst the very rich and privileged, playing our matches at places like the Johannesburg Country Club where the beautiful little cricket field had a huge tree at square leg. Pimms was served under other trees at lunchtime and the only blacks or coloureds in sight were clad in smart waiters' uniforms and came bearing the said Pimms to their lords and masters.

At night we would often venture into the seedy nightclubs in Hillbrow. The clubs were all run by whites. While there were certainly more blacks around, the area was still white dominated, even if these whites were a little off colour, and these so called 'poor whites' lived in squalid little flats crammed into what was often called the most densely populated suburb in the southern hemisphere.

Scott's Grasshoppers were all members by invitation only and were chosen more because he enjoyed their company than strictly on cricketing ability. This said, Scott made a point of getting to know good cricketers, so we had a fair sprinkling of them in our ranks as well.

When the last MCC (later called just plain 'England', which makes more sense) team visited South Africa in 1964/5, before all sporting tours stopped in protest against apartheid, Scott was at his most active. Mike Smith of Warwickshire, who had just succeeded Ted Dexter, captained the England team. When they came to Durban to play Natal, Scott was there with invitations to come water-skiing at Midmar dam on their Sunday off and to attend a braaivleis on the Saturday night; he also offered to entertain team members who were not playing in that match together with their camp followers, who in some cases included wives. Some of the wives were young and pretty, so Scott was at one stroke combining his three passions – cricket, important people and pretty girls.

Scott was a very good host and a lot of his invitations were accepted. I was raked in to help. I remember a dinner party at Rawdon's Hotel near Nottingham Road, where we entertained Mike Smith, Ken Barrington, Fred Titmus and Jim Parkes after a day on Midmar dam, but, as far as Tim was concerned, the 'Big Fish' was still missing. Ted Dexter had not yet arrived because he was standing for parliament. Finally he did arrive, and this coincided with the team's return to Natal for the Test match – and, what was more exciting, his pretty wife accompanied him.

I hatched a plan. Late one evening I rang Scott up from the farm. I put on my plummiest voice and pretended to be Ted Dexter. I said that I had heard from my teammates that Scott was very good at entertaining wives who were bored with the cricket and, that as 'my' wife really did not care for cricket all that much, would he look after her for a couple of days during the Test match?

Scott was almost incoherent with excitement – of course he could, what was she particularly interested in? Where should they meet? What days were most suitable? Couldn't Ted himself come along as well once the Test was over, etc, etc? After my initial spiel, I had to do very little talking, but just to agree to some of his many suggestions and set a time and place to meet. The 'place' was in Durban and this was much too far away for me, so I never went to the rendezvous – Scott did though! He vows to this day that he was not taken in and was going to Durban anyway, but I know otherwise.

One of the best experiences I had with Scott was a cricket tour to England and Holland. As usual this was impeccably organized, with a tight itinerary including eighteen matches against very good club sides. There were sixteen players in our touring party so it meant a lot of pretty concentrated cricket.

We started in Holland, and the first match was against the top Dutch club side; we won this quite easily. The next game was against a team consisting of a selection of coaches from all the Dutch clubs. We had no idea what sort of standard this would be, but we envisaged a few ageing English pros well past their 'sell by' date. How wrong we were. The coaches were all West Indians, young players from the Caribbean who were only just not good enough to make the national side, and who were earning a few bucks and getting a bit more experience coaching in Holland. One of them indeed was said to be a very young Curtly Ambrose – destined to become one of the world's finest fast bowlers with over four hundred Test wickets to his credit.

Remember we were all from apartheid South Africa, where playing against or with any black man was strictly forbidden. Now a team of eleven of them confronted us. I do not think that this worried any of us in the very least, but what did worry us was their ability. Most West Indians aspire to be fast bowlers and these guys were no exception. I do not think they were trying to take it out on us because we were white South Africans, it was just the way they were, but they all bowled very, very fast on a hard bouncy pitch. I was scheduled to bat at number eight, and when my turn came with our team in deep trouble, I was immensely heartened to note that the bowler about to bowl at me only had a run up of two paces, so he must be a spinner. He stood about six foot eight and his arms reached his knees and I had not noticed that the wicketkeeper was standing about thirty yards back – for a spinner!

The guy came in to bowl – there was a whirr of black arms, and the next thing I knew the wicketkeeper was throwing the ball back to him. The next ball hit me on the unprotected thigh and I have a dent there to this day. The next one I snicked for four over slips' heads and the following one I was out – thankfully!

We lost the match comprehensively but much enjoyed chatting to the young West Indians over several very good Dutch lagers. Later we toured Amsterdam's Canal Street. Several of our younger players had never been out of strait-laced South Africa before and their eyes were out on stalks.

For those of you who have not visited Canal Street in Amsterdam at night, it is or was then probably the most blatant exhibition of overt prostitution in the world. Pretty, scantily clad girls of every colour sat in shop windows, and you could view them like any other piece of merchandise. If you fancied this merchandise you could descend some steps and enter the room where it was. Curtains were discreetly drawn, blocking the view from the street and business would commence – or so I am told. Quite a day for the innocent young Natalians – eleven nice blacks to play cricket against, and now naked white women openly soliciting for sex!

We moved from Holland to London, and a game against a Hurlingham side captained by my old flatmate, John Yeldham. No blacks or prostitutes here, just a lunch between innings, a lunch which lasted for a couple of hours, during which we did full justice to a bottle of port and some fine cigars. I made fifty after that, so perhaps it is to be recommended.

There were many other enjoyable matches, played on some of the loveliest grounds in England. Mike Smith returned Scott's hospitality and entertained us royally in Warwickshire. We then went up to my family's home county of Yorkshire and played a couple of games in York. One was against the Yorkshire Gentlemen, captained by my first cousin, David Milbank. I was keen to do well and was indeed batting nicely and had forty-odd, when David moved himself to deep mid-on. I hit the very next ball straight down his throat.

One of our last games was against the Duchess of Norfolk's X1 at the stunningly beautiful Arundel ground. The duke had recently managed Ted Dexter's England side in Australia and was a very keen cricket lover. He also had several pretty daughters, so Scott was on the alert. However he should have taken note of the warning which the duke is alleged to have sent to the team in the form of a memorandum, when these daughters came out to Australia to join him. It is said to have read, 'My daughters will be visiting me shortly and will attend some matches and social functions. Please note that, while enjoying a party, they neither drink nor smoke. Norfolk.' The duchess's side contained a number of ex-England players, and it was a closely contested match which finally ended in a tie. This being the case, we all swapped ties, and I now have a very smart silk tie with the letter 'N' scattered all over it. Some ex-England player (Billy Griffith, I think) has mine, with one large grasshopper on it.

The tour ended with a match against Devon, played on a ground near Exeter University. Here we experienced our first and only disruption, from demonstrators against apartheid. A bunch of long-haired dirty youths, who turned out to be university students, hung about outside the ground waving placards. We went up and chatted to them and invited them to a drink at the local pub after the game. They duly pitched up – we were paying, after all – and they turned out to be very decent people, but pathetically naive.

While a lot of us agreed that apartheid was not a very nice thing, they really had no idea of the reasons for it or how the problem could realistically be solved. I am afraid that this is so often the case in this sort of demonstration, but no one should be prevented from saying what they think.

"I disagree with what you say, but will defend to the death your right to say it."

Hear, hear! Who said that? I forget, but how true it is.

* * *

Meanwhile, back on the ranch... at 'Newstead' things were not going particularly well, financially. My parents still owned the place and were keen to get some sort of dividend out of it; also I had to take my salary out of the farm and the farm was not making enough money. Matters were complicated when I suddenly decided to get married.

Fran, whom I had last seen in Kenya over Sue's wedding, had since then become engaged to an American when she visited her birthplace in Jamaica. It seemed that this did not work out, and she suddenly appeared in South Africa to stay with her parents, Rick and Midge Holme, who were farming just the other side of Pietermaritzburg from me. I went to see her. I had been introduced to a lot of perfectly nice South African girls in Natal – mainly by Scott – but had never formed any sort of liaison with any of them. We were on different wavelengths completely and the two or three girlfriends that I had had since coming to Natal were all ex-Kenyan girls. Now, an old favourite had arrived on my doorstep.

She was perhaps a bit on the rebound from her American boyfriend, but I was delighted to be reunited with a soulmate. Since I had last seen her she had had a serious motor accident and had been in a hospital in Kenya for some weeks. She had always been a temperamental and fiery character, and I think that this accident had done more damage to her than I or anyone realized. She suffered serious bouts of depression and could be very moody. But she was still very pretty and a lot of fun most of the time. She appeared to be glad to see me and within a month we became engaged. We were not engaged for very long and got married in September 1966 at Richmond church with the reception at the Polo Club. Bobby Fernandes was my best man; Richard Holme, Fran's brother and an ex-flatmate of mine, and Tim Scott were groomsmen. Fran's sister,

Bobs, and Catherine Lee were bridesmaids, and Penel's two little daughters, Jane and Anne, flower girls. Rick Holme gave Fran away and Ian de Gersigny proposed our health. My parents flew down from Kenya for the occasion, which was also attended by a few old friends from Kenya and new ones from South Africa.

After the reception we drove in pouring rain to the brand new Umhlanga Rocks Hotel, just north of Durban, for our first night, and immediately bumped into a lot of my Zululand polo mates, who had been watching a rugger match in Durban. Next day we flew to Windhoek in the then South West Africa, and thence to the Etosha Pan National Park for our honeymoon. We joined a group of other people and travelled in a large bus round the park. Accommodation at the lodges was not that great and we usually had to share a banda, where the wall dividing the two bedrooms only went halfway to the roof – also the beds squeaked! It was not a wild success.

Back at 'Newstead' we tried to adjust to married life – never easy. Fran had never lived in South Africa and had many of the same problems that my mother had about the attitude of locals to women. She had no real friends in the area and even her parents soon upped sticks and moved to Rhodesia. I was involved in sport as my recreation and she was expected to provide cakes and scones for teatime at the various events I took part in. She did not take kindly to this. She then became pregnant (or 'fell' pregnant, as the locals called it) but soon after had a miscarriage. Married life was not all roses.

Financial problems on the farm did not help, so drastic steps had to be taken. 'Newstead' was not a good farm. It was all on two steep hills and these hills had been burned every year for as long as anyone could remember. The result was very poor soil of minimal depth-covering rocks. However the place was valuable because of its situation. The Natal Midlands was a popular area with a nice climate, near good schools, and only an hour or so from the coast. More and more businessmen from Johannesburg were buying smallholdings, building smart houses and retiring there. It would make much more sense to sell the land for good money rather than trying to squeeze a living out of it.

I put it to my parents and they were keen on the idea. They were happy back in Kenya, had no wish to return to Natal and could do with the money. The plan was to divide 'Newstead' into eight and sell off individual blocks of about two hundred and fifty acres each. I would be allowed to retain the block on which the homestead stood as my own. This was by way of payment for what I had done on 'Newstead' for the past four years (I had never drawn much salary) and a sort of inheritance to get me started on my own. It was very generous of my parents, with whom I always had a very good relationship, but I think quite fair. They had not wanted to deal with 'Newstead'.

I set about getting the place sub-divided and this all happened quite easily and efficiently, so that quite soon I had seven blocks of land to sell. They were on offer at about twenty-five thousand rands each, depending on desirability, accessibility and location. This was a hell of a lot more money than we would ever have made out of 'Newstead' in a lifetime. The sales went well, and in no time three or four were sold and my parents had some much-needed cash to invest. We sold one plot to Mike Hoare of Congo mercenary fame.

Soon after our wedding, Rick and Midge, of whom I was very fond, had sold their farm near Richmond and moved up to Rhodesia, where they had bought a large farm, 'Scorror Estate', near Marandellas in Mashonaland East, taking advantage of very cheap land following the declaration of UDI (Unilateral Declaration of Independence) by Ian Smith and his Rhodesian Front government. Now, they invited Fran and me to drive up and see them.

It is a very pleasant drive up the Great North Road, through the battlefields of northern Natal – Colenso, Ladysmith, Elandslaagte – into Transvaal, then Northern Transvaal, through Pietersburg to Louis Trichardt and the Soutspansberg mountain range. We stopped there for the night, in a little pub called the Mountain Inn (it is still there), then on the next day to the border crossing at Beit Bridge over the Limpopo

River (which was dirty brown and not grey-green and greasy at all, as Mr Kipling insisted). Very clean and very efficient border posts on both sides of the river. Both posts were manned entirely by whites, so we were through in no time and drove on through Matabeleland, following the route of Rhodes's original pioneers as far as Fort Victoria.

Here we visited the Zimbabwe Ruins, as they were called then, spent the night in Fort Vic, and drove on the following day to the Holmes' Farm near Wedza. I had passed through Rhodesia very briefly on my way to Argentina some years before, but otherwise this was my first visit to that country. I liked what I saw.

CHAPTER 14

Rhodesia

WHEN WE FIRST WENT TO RHODESIA, IT was shortly after they had declared UDI. That is to say that, in the eyes of the Rhodesian Government headed by the redoubtable Ian Smith, Rhodesia was now an independent country, just like its neighbours, Zambia and Malawi, formerly Northern Rhodesia and Nyasaland. In the eyes of the rest of the world, Rhodesia was now an illegal régime and heavy sanctions were imposed.

Rhodesia maintained that the country had been effectively independent since the 1920s, when they opted not to be included in the newly formed Union of South Africa. They had black members of Parliament and there was a qualified vote for anyone who could reach a certain standard of civilization, so why should full independence not be granted to them officially, as it had to their erstwhile partners in the recent Federation, Zambia and Malawi? Britain maintained that no full independence could be granted until there was one-man one-vote. This would inevitably signal the end of the current Rhodesian Front government, and this being unacceptable to both the government and the white electorate, Mr Smith and his government decided to go it alone.

However Rhodesia did have some allies, and these were pretty crucial ones, as they were its immediate neighbours to the south and to the east, each providing a gateway to the sea. Mozambique was also known as Portuguese East Africa. The Salazar government in Portugal was keen to hang on to its colonies, and so it supported Smith in exchange for much needed revenue, derived from the use of the port of Beira and the rail and road link to Umtali. South Africa was at the height of its loathed apartheid era and was only too keen to have a white-dominated state on as many borders as possible.

The overall result was that there was a wonderful esprit de corps in Rhodesia. People felt that with the support of South Africa and Portugal they could wave two fingers at the rest of the world in general and at Britain's Prime Minister, Harold Wilson, in particular. And to a certain extent they could and did. Not all whites approved of what Smith had done, and probably very few blacks did, but as hardly any blacks actually had a say they were largely immaterial. There was some initial uncertainty and as a result property prices dropped, as did agricultural land prices, and several farms came on the market.

I had a fairly superficial knowledge of the intricacies involved. I was unhappy about Kenya being run by the people whom I used to chase in the Aberdares, but I did not really like what I saw in South Africa. Perhaps Rhodesia would be a good compromise, and I was excited at the prospect of visiting my in-laws on their new farm there.

Natal had been pleasant enough, and I had had a lot of fun there, but it was not 'Africa' as I remembered and wanted it. The Holmes' Farm in Rhodesia was much more to my liking – eight thousand acres of lovely open country, rivers, dams, bush, game birds and even a certain amount of game, such as kudu, reedbuck, steinbuck, duiker, etc. The climate was perfect and all the business about UDI did not seem to have filtered down to the farm labour, who were a cheerful bunch, very unlike the surly Zulus from Natal.

Fran and I thoroughly enjoyed our ten-day visit and on our return did a few sums. Property prices in the Natal Midlands were booming at the time and we calculated that if we sold the small part of 'Newstead' that my parents had given me we would have enough money to make a down payment on a farm in Rhodesia. With this idea in mind we put our bit of 'Newstead' on the market, and almost immediately found a buyer in Murray Armstrong, a polo-playing friend and part of a large, wealthy

Natal family. I then drove up to Rhodesia again alone to see what there was on offer.

There was not that much, to be honest, and in the short time I had available I did not find anything that I wanted to buy with the limited funds I had to spend. However in the Wedza area, not far from the Holmes' Farm there was a five thousand acre undeveloped cattle ranch which could be leased. On my last day I went to have a look at this. It was owned by an old Greek who spoke no English, so negotiations were tricky. Other Wedza farmers pitched up to have a look at the place while I was there and were clearly keen to take it over, so I took a gamble and said that I would definitely like to lease the place for two years, with an option to purchase at an agreed price at the end of this period. All this had to be tied up legally, so I delayed my return and got a proper agreement drawn up by a Marandellas solicitor, a Mr Phear. The old Greek, who was called Paliuras, duly signed and I drove back to Natal in triumph.

I had had very little opportunity to look round the farm that I was now committed to. It was called 'Chirume' and was a sub-division of a larger farm, half of which was being retained by the old Greek's son, Jim. I reckoned that the two years of leasing would give me time to have a proper look round for something that I might want to buy. Meanwhile we would pack up in Natal and move to Rhodesia.

Fran was well pleased with the idea, partly because she was not getting on too well with my polo friends and was generally fairly anti-South Africa. So we prepared to move as soon as possible We bought a young Hereford bull to take up with us in a railway truck, which would also take my three polo ponies – Dusky, Terry and Quick Step. One of our better Zulu workers called Zaiega agreed to travel with them. Then we hired a removals lorry and packed all our worldly goods into it and told the driver to proceed to 'Chirume Farm', Wedza, Rhodesia.

Fran's brother Richard was also moving to Rhodesia to join his parents, so, as he had pranged his car – again – he agreed to come with us and share the driving of our two vehicles, which were a Peugeot truck and a brand new Mercedes 200D. The Mercedes was bought with some of the proceeds of the sale of our bit of 'Newstead', with the excuse that we would need reliable transport in our new country and diesel would be easier to get than petrol, on account of the sanctions that had been imposed on the import of fuel.

Our three dogs came with us as well – my old, faithful Border Collie, Later, of rhino fame, Fran's little Peke, Poo Chow, who was blind after a losing battle with an Alsatian, and a highly neurotic Afghan hound called Porsena. Richard was a bit of a lover of the good things in life, and fearing that Rhodesia would not be able to provide him with his favourite cigarettes – Sullivan Powell cigarettes from Burlington Arcade – he had a large pack sent out before leaving. These we put on the floor by the back seat of our smart new Merc.

Fran and I started off in the Merc with Richard driving the truck. We had barely done a hundred miles when there was the most God-awful stink in our car, and we discovered that Later had shat all over Richard's cigarettes and most of the back of the car as well, so that was not a great start!

We got through the border on the first day and spent the night at the little motel on the Bubye River called 'The Lion and Elephant', which is still a favourite night stop for travellers on that road. Next day we arrived at 'Scorror Estate', the Holmes' Farm in Wedza. Fran and I stayed there for a week, driving the twenty miles over to 'Chirume' every day. The furniture van from South Africa duly arrived with all our stuff and we started making our new home habitable. It was an exciting time and on my thirtieth birthday, September 9, 1967, we moved into 'Chirume'. This was to remain my home for the next thirty-five years, before Nikki (not Fran by now) and I were forcibly removed by Mugabe's thugs on October 3, 2002. But this was a long time in the future and much was to happen during those thirty-five years.

'Chirume' was not a particularly good farm from a cropping point of view. It was very broken country with mainly poor soils. The previous owners – Paliuras and before him Col Price – had grown tobacco, but it was best suited to cattle ranching and this is why I had leased it. Tobacco was the main crop in Wedza though, and despite the sanctions imposed on its sale was Rhodesia's most valuable crop. Most other farmers in Wedza grew it, but I never did, concentrating instead entirely on cattle.

One of my first moves was to acquaint myself with our immediate neighbour, who lived some three miles away. His signboard at the end of our road had been interesting – it bore the unusual legend 'Cpl Hill, Leap Year Farm', and had two corporal's stripes beside it.

Mike and Jean Hill were very welcoming and very helpful in putting us right on a number of things, and I soon learned why he, and everybody else, called him Cpl Hill. He had left school early and enlisted in the Rhodesian Army to go and help Britain fight the war. He was in fact under-age but managed to wangle his way in, and he fought long and hard, ending up at Monte Cassino in Italy (where both my father and Nikki's also served) and gaining promotion to the rank of corporal.

After the war he borrowed as much money as he could and bought the farm next to 'Chirume'. Several other ex-army new settlers had also bought farms in the Wedza area at the same time and a review of the smart new signboards at the end of the roads leading to their farms revealed that most had achieved some sort of military rank of distinction. Many indeed had been in India as permanent soldiers and viewed farming in Rhodesia as a nice form of retirement. Colonels and majors were commonplace and there was even the odd general and naval commander, not to mention a lord and a couple of sirs. Mike Hill had fought hard for his rank and saw no reason why he should not put it on his signboard as well. By the time I got there, some twenty-two years after the war, most of the colonels and all the others had gone under, but the corporal remained and was prospering.

Rhodesia was often referred to as the Sergeants' Mess, while Kenya was known as the Officers' Mess. I suppose that there was some truth in that. A lot of the Kenyan settlers came from upper-class English families and some were 'remittance men', their upper-class families in England paying them a handsome allowance to stay away to avoid embarrassment. Nevertheless, everyone in Kenya spoke of England as 'home'. The

Civil Service came out to the colony for a three or four-year stint, and then returned to England for leave before a new posting, not necessarily even back to Kenya. In Rhodesia the Civil Service was recruited locally, and if they went anywhere for their leave it was to South Africa. Most of the settlers in the 1960s had been born in Rhodesia and in a lot of cases so had their parents and grandparents. If they had roots anywhere else, it was again more likely to be in South Africa than in England.

After buying their farm with borrowed money from the Land Bank, they would first build a set of barns to cure their tobacco while living in a shack or mud hut nearby. The result was that there were very few decent farmhouses in those days, just enlarged shacks with no view at all. In Kenya the proud owner of a new farm would first build a fancy house for his lady wife, followed by some stables, and then possibly some farm buildings. There was much more likely to be some family capital in the background for the new Kenyan farmer, whereas a lot of Rhodesian farmers started with nothing. They would work for an established tobacco farmer just for their keep for a couple of years, so as to learn how to grow tobacco. Then they would go on to a bonus system and after six or seven years might have saved enough money to put a down payment on their own bit of land. Many of my neighbours had started in this very way and were extremely capable farmers.

I think it is correct to say that Wedza had more than its fair share of the officer class, and Cpl Hill would not in any way have been exceptional in many other areas. Also of course, there were a lot of purely Afrikaner communities – many more than there had been in Kenya, where the Afrikaners who had come to Kenya tended to settle in one area round Eldoret, or 64 as it was known, from the fact that it had grown round the post office, which was on 'Farm 64'. 'Farm 64' itself had been called that because it was sixty four miles from the railhead at Kibigori.

The Boer War may have ended some sixty years previously, but the two communities, one Afrikaner and the other of British extraction, did not mix a lot. It was not until the independence bush war of the Seventies and then the land grab of early 2000, that the two lots really came together to unite against a common enemy. When I arrived in Wedza, there was a very strong small Afrikaner community not far from Chirume, in an area we referred to as 'Dutchman's Corner'. These people never came to the club, had a different church and did not join our agricultural discussion groups. We hardly knew them then, but by the time we were all kicked out in 2002 we were all very good friends.

One of the most rabid anti-British Afrikaners in the area was Rudi Erasmus. He farmed at the very bottom, or south, of the area, on three farms bordering the Save River. The local police force in those days was known as the British South Africa Police (BSAP) and was without any doubt the finest police force in Africa. As the name suggests, the officers at least were drawn mainly from British stock, so Rudi would have nothing to do with them. However one day he had serious problems with his labour and was forced to ask for their help.

A young fresh-faced officer, recently out of depot, arrived on Rudi's RMG ranch and presented himself to Rudi, enquiring what the problem was. Rudi stood on the steps of his veranda and took one look at this clearly British youngster. It was too much for him and, without mentioning the problem that needed sorting out, he launched into a virulent tirade against all things British, and virtually accused the young man's grandparents of poisoning his ancestors in concentration camps at the end of the Boer War. The young policeman stood silently listening to this slander, then, when Rudi finally drew breath, stepped forward, removed his Sam Browne belt and threw it on the ground.

"OK," Mr Erasmus," he said, "now I am no longer a police officer, please repeat what you have just said."

The young man was large, strong and extremely fit, Rudi was well past his prime. He backed down and with a sickly smile detailed the problem over which he needed help.

We did not get away to a very good start on 'Chirume' when 1967 proved to be the driest year on record, and the hoped-for rain in October/ November just did not materialize, so all the cattle we had bought – mostly on borrowed money – got thinner and thinner, rather than fatter and fatter. Then our neighbour, Jim Paliuras, from whose father we had bought half of the original 'Chirume', failed to honour an agreement to fence the boundary where the farm had been split in two. Also he continued to use my cattle dip but failed to pay the agreed fee. All this was worrying. The last thing I wanted was to have a row with my neighbour immediately after arriving in a new area. But I was short of cash and needed to be paid for the dip, and I desperately wanted the grazing that I could not use because there was no fence. I would drive over to talk to him, but he was seldom there, as he appeared to prefer big-game hunting to farming. Eventually I had to sue him, and he then paid up and erected the fence without the matter going to court. But it was a bad start having to do that to a neighbour.

Apart from him and the corporal our other neighbours were Col John Prentice and Mr Maurice Hawkes. John Prentice was one of the few remaining colonels and owned a lovely farm called 'Leeds'. He was a charming man with a distinguished war record and a limp to prove it, and he also had a very pleasant wife called Pam, who was definitely still living in the era of the Indian Raj. When visiting them in mid-afternoon, you were directed to the summerhouse at the bottom of an extensive garden, where a uniformed waiter in a white pyjama suit and red fez would serve you with cucumber sandwiches and hot buttered scones topped with strawberry jam, accompanied by China tea. Maurice Hawkes was a different kettle of fish altogether. He owned the lovely 'Collace Farm' and raised pedigree Polled Herefords. He had no time for the colonels and referred to Col Prentice as Mr Prentice. He was a very efficient farmer, but God finally got the better of him and he sold up, moved to Kariba and communed with the Almighty – in a very loud voice. We stayed in the house next door to him once, and we were woken up at midnight by his shouts of supplication, as he stood bare-chested and with arms outflung, begging for intervention in some cause or other.

Shortly after our arrival, the railway truck containing the three ponies, the Hereford bull and Zaiega arrived at Marandellas station in very good order. Jock Stanley, an old friend from Kenya now farming just outside Marandellas, lent us his lorry to take them all the thirty-two miles back to 'Chirume'. Zaiega stayed with us for a couple of weeks before we dispatched him back to Natal.

* * *

As I was only leasing the farm, I had a bit of capital to buy cattle, so having settled ourselves in I ventured out to the Headlands cattle sale, in search of some suitable animals. Headlands sale in those days was a festive occasion, one to which the whole community would turn out, whether they were selling or buying cattle or not. There would be a well-patronized bar and lunch served by the local ladies from noon until the sale ended, often as late as three o'clock. The whole occasion was overseen and orchestrated by the auctioneer who was responsible for the sale – namely 'Binks' Holland, ably assisted by George Brown. Binks lived in Umtali, where he and his father before him had been selling cattle and virtually anything else for as long as anyone could remember.

I approached Binks before the sale started and introduced myself. This was accomplished with some difficulty as Binks was seemingly permanently surrounded by a laughing, jostling crowd of farmers, already with beers in their hands. However, having fought my way through this lot, Binks could not have been nicer, and he offered to co-operate in every way in my cattle buying – as long as I paid! It was followed by a huge laugh and slap on the back. So started an association with J S Holland & Son which lasted for the rest of my farming days. Often I could not pay but was frequently offered generous credit terms.

I did buy one pen of steers that day, but competition was fierce. All the talk was about sanctions and what effect they were having on the farming industry. The main worry was tobacco. Traditionally this was sold every year between May and September by open auction in Salisbury. Buyers from the world's leading tobacco companies came to bid, and the tobacco auctions were quite a tourist attraction in their own right. With the advent of sanctions no buyers were allowed to come and the auctions closed. Tobacco was still sold though, but some fairly cunning, undercover deals had to be struck to achieve this. The result was that the price to the farmer of flue-cured tobacco dropped considerably, and a lot of smaller growers in marginal areas could no longer afford to grow the crop; they therefore diversified into other things, the most popular of which was cattle. So I had not chosen a great time to start my buying.

* * *

Binks Holland was just one of the auctioneers who sold cattle, and not the biggest. The biggest firm was undoubtedly H Shapiro & Co.; they were based in Harare and conducted our local sale at Marandellas, as well as in many other locations. They had started selling cattle in 1907. Mr Shapiro's daughter had married one Robbie Isaacson, and it was he who now ran the show. He was getting on a bit though and no longer did the actual auctioneering, which was left to the redoubtable 'Scotty' Macdonald, while Robbie prowled round the stands offering advice and handing out invoices to successful bidders. I had to make my number with Robbie, and I doubt if it were possible for anyone to be more different from Binks. No 'hail fellow, well met' here, just a hardnosed request as to how I intended to make my purchases pay. Fair enough. H Shapiro & Co later became the Cattle Co-op, and then CC Sales, and I still do business with them. They were always very helpful and often gave me extended credit, although the inability to repay this sometimes required some painful sessions in Robbie's grotty little office in Speke Avenue.

'Chirume' was nearly five thousand acres, so to stock it fully I needed some five to six hundred head, depending on the size of the animals. My limited capital certainly did not run to this, so I was forced to seek additional finance, and this was readily available through an excellent scheme run by the quasi-government organisation known as the Cold Storage Commission, the CSC. This was in fact the organisation that slaughtered cattle and provided meat for all the local butchers, as well as conducting a thriving export industry. Rhodesian beef had attained a reputation for the very best quality worldwide.

To ensure a continual supply of good beef, the CSC was prepared to lend money to farmers to buy cattle, on condition that these same cattle ended up with them for slaughter when they were fat. Their standards were high: they would only finance cattle of high quality; the farmer had to be visited and his cattle facilities and personal reputation scrutinized, and finally the cattle in question when bought were branded with the CSC brand and booked in for slaughter up to two years later, when, if the farmer was any good, they should be ready, or 'finished' to export standard. Once the cattle had been bought, they were inspected once a year, and a very convincing explanation was required for any shortfall in numbers. Two, or even three percent, was acceptable – cattle do die, even in the best of circles – but anything much more and you were unlikely to get another loan. It was of course strictly forbidden to sell cattle that had been financed by the CSC on the open market or privately. All open market sales were attended by a CSC inspector to prevent just this possibility.

However it was possible to sell to unscrupulous local butchers, and a somewhat suspect neighbour of mine, who shall remain nameless, did this at a time when he was very pushed for cash. He was a big customer of the CSC and had some four hundred of their cattle on hand. The dreaded annual inspection loomed and he knew he only had about three hundred and fifty animals that he could show the inspector, so he hatched a plan. He knew the inspector quite well and invited him to lunch, saying he would have all the cattle rounded up and driven past for him to count straight afterwards. Lunch was a prolonged affair enhanced by a certain amount of beer followed by some fairly rough local wine, so it was nearly three o'clock before they staggered out to view the cattle.

"You just sit here on this kopje and my guys will drive them past you," said my friend. So the inspector, feeling a bit drowsy by now, was glad to do just that. The three hundred and fifty head were religiously driven past very slowly, and then the first fifty were hurried round the back of the kopje and driven past again at the tail end of the original lot. A satisfied inspector was able to record having counted four hundred animals as well as having had a very good lunch.

Inevitably my friend was found out in the end, as you could not get away with much. The CSC was a very efficient organization in those days under the expert guidance of Nick Spoel. All through the period of sanctions in Rhodesia, beef continued to be exported, and the national herd grew and prospered.

Soon after independence some small-scale indigenous farmers were allowed the facility of CSC finance. Millions of dollars were lent to them, standards dropped, cattle were not inspected, and the custodians of these cattle quite blatantly sold them to local butchers whenever they needed cash. In many cases, when the required date arrived for them to deliver the animals to the abattoir as stipulated on their agreement, there were no cattle left at all. The result was that the once highly efficient CSC went broke, and there were no cattle to honour lucrative export contracts. This was just one of many tragedies brought about by lending money for reasons other than strictly business considerations. What I am saying is that the recipients of this finance were lent the money because Rhodesia was now Zimbabwe, and they were black farmers who believed that they should have the benefits that their erstwhile white Rhodesian counterparts had had, quite regardless of whether or not they had any 'track record' in raising quality cattle or even the facilities to do so.

I used the CSC for years, and it was very largely thanks to them that I was able to build up a viable herd of cattle. I am not saying I was a brilliant cattle farmer and I had many tricky moments when the likes of Grenville Tapson came to do the annual inspection, but I was able to repay all my loans – eventually.

There were other finance organizations that followed the CSC in providing money for cattle, and the first one of these was a co-operative that one was required to join. I was always out for any finance that I could get my hands on and was one of the first members of the newly formed Cattle Co-op under the management of Bob Graham. This outfit also flourished and was more lenient in what the finance was for, in that the cattle did not have to end up in their abattoir, mainly because they did not have one. They worked well in conjunction with the CSC as did other, more short-lived organizations like Bowmakers and Viking. I think I borrowed money from them all at one time or another.

* * *

Cattle are essentially a long-term business, and one does not have a regular income, so despite having five or six hundred cattle running round 'Chirume' I had no money. Quite the opposite – I had a lot of expenses. Cattle had to be fed and dipped, labour had to be paid and we had to live. More borrowed money was required. This necessitated visits to the Land Bank and to my commercial bank, the then Standard Bank of South Africa (now Standard Chartered). Both were reasonably co-operative, and after filling in endless forms and committing myself to repay untold amounts of money we were able to exist. Not a lot more than that though. Once, just after I had negotiated an overdraft with a new bank manager, I wrote a cheque for a small short-wave radio, which I gave to Fran for her birthday. The cheque bounced, and when I asked the bank manager why, he said that the overdraft facility was for agricultural purposes only. I pointed out that if I could not supply my wife with a few amusements, we would not remain on an isolated farm very long and therefore would have no need of his 'agricultural purposes only' loan. Mr Gomes never bothered to come and have a look at what we were doing, but other bank managers after him were more helpful and did take the trouble to come – that is until the war hotted up, when no one came.

I suppose I was lent all this money because I was young, white and reasonably qualified – at any rate on the practical side, if short on univer-sity degrees – at a time when Rhodesia desperately wanted anyone like me stupid enough to want to take the gamble of trying to farm under the threat of increased sanctions and a highly suspect security and political situation. It was certainly a challenging time. We were not on the mains electricity but had an ancient old Lister engine, which we cranked up every evening to give us light. Water came from a nearby stream and another old engine had to pump this up to the house. The telephone was on a party line, and each number had to be called with a series of long or short rings on the line, done by turning a handle vigorously for a long or very short time to indicate the last two digits of your number. Our number was 2331, so anyone wanting to ring us had to do three long rings and one short one (dah dah dah dit). This was sometimes hard to recognize, but you got used to it. So unfortunately did everybody else. One got to know everybody's ring, and it was not uncommon for half the party line to be listening in if there was a bit of scandal in the air.

Our nearest shop was thirty-five miles away in Marandellas, and food was difficult to keep fresh with no electricity. There was quite a bit of game on the farm, and I delighted in unpacking my 12-bore shotgun and putting it to good use on Swainson's francolin and guineafowl. My dog Later was back in his element. We had game animals as well, in the shape of steinbuck, duiker, reedbuck and the beautiful greater kudu. We also had baboons, monkeys, jackal, all manner of mongoose, crocodiles in the Chirume River, and even some hippo once.

* * *

I had brought my polo ponies up from Natal, so I felt obliged to play polo. This was not easy; the nearest club was Bromley, some sixty miles away. I had no means of transporting my ponies and in any case wanted them on the farm to ride. I did give it a go though for a couple of seasons, and during the polo season – May to September – stabled them with an old Kenyan friend who lived near Bromley. This was none other than one of the 'Molo Colonels' – Ted Maberly. Ted was a fiery little man with a bristly moustache, which he frequently brushed up with the back of his hand. He always wore a blue spotted cravat and highly polished shoes and talked very fast. Sadly he did not survive very long in Rhodesia, as he was run over and killed on the main Salisbury road.

The Bromley Polo Club was on the farm of Bob Draper, who was a very strong player himself, having represented Rhodesia off a 5 handicap. His wife, 'Doubles', was a leading racehorse trainer, so Bob had a regular supply of good ex-racehorses to turn into polo ponies. (How does a race 'horse' suddenly become a polo 'pony', I wonder?). During the second season that I played there, Doubles looked after my ponies.

We played once a week, and would drive the sixty miles on Sunday mornings, play about six chukkas, have lunch with fellow players who lived nearby and drive back again. So one only saw the ponies once a week, and it was not very satisfactory. It was also expensive and you must remember that we had no money. It was fun though, and it enabled us to make a lot of new friends and to get around the country when there were tournaments at other clubs. I played 'A' or 'B' division usually, with Pat Curry, Bill Collett, Bruce Campbell, Philip Duncan, John MacIlwaine or young Doug Stanley – Jock's son from Kenya. Pat and his wife Joan were our frequent hosts for lunch, as his house was next to the ground, and they lived up to their name by producing some wonderful curry lunches, washed down with quantities of Pimms.

One year we got to the final of the Carnival Cup, which was Rhodesia's premier polo event and the country's oldest sporting trophy. The old Salisbury polo ground had been given to the club by Cecil Rhodes and was situated bang next door to the Prime Minister's house on North Avenue. The day we played in that final Ian Smith wandered across from his house and the teams were introduced to him. It was the first time I had seen this controversial character.

"Nice to have you Kenya guys with us," he said as I was introduced to him.

This polo field is now Mugabe's private helicopter pad and the whole place fenced off with razor wire, while little men armed to the teeth with AK rifles patrol the perimeter and shoot you if you dare to stop or, God forbid, try to take a photograph. Is this what Cecil Rhodes wanted? But was it his to give in the first place? What had he paid for this bit of land and to whom?

The standard of polo in Rhodesia, at that time and indeed for many years to come, was very high. There only were about a hundred players, but there happened to be some exceptional talent at the top. The Kemple brothers – Mike and 'Packet' – the Hensman brothers – Gary and Rory – Dave Meikle and Basil Kearns were all rated at 6 or 7 goals and vied for a place in the national team. Polo was one of the very few sports at which Rhodesia could take on the full might of South Africa and win.

In the early seventies a high handicap Argentinean side visited South Africa to play a series of Test matches. It was far from Argentina's best side, but it did contain the legendary Juan-Carlos Harriott, rated at the maximum of 10 goals and much the best player in the world then, or perhaps ever. Having thrashed South Africa, this team came on to Salisbury to play one game against Rhodesia, mainly I think because the Hensman family had promised them some good big-game hunting in the Zambezi Valley.

Now we in Rhodesia reckoned we were better than South Africa, and we thought that we could perhaps give our illustrious opponents a very good game and perhaps even beat them, as they would after all be on borrowed ponies. A huge crowd turned up at the North Avenue ground, and after due pageantry the match got under way. Sure enough, Rhodesia opened the scoring, and after five minutes the score was Rhodesia 1 Argentina 0. Ah, ha! We all thought. Rhodesia did score another goal, but not until the end of the sixth chukka, by which time Argentina had scored 19! They were in a totally different class, but what a joy to watch.

As mentioned, they had of course to be mounted on local ponies, so with typical Rhodesian generosity most of the country's top players sent in their best ponies to form a pool from which the Argentinian players could choose the six or eight ponies they would require for the match. Peter Haaroff, who farmed a long way off near Mangula, sent his lorry in with five of his lovely ponies. As there was still room in the lorry he put in an extra youngster that had never played, but which could be used perhaps as an umpire's pony. Harriott was given the choice of Peter's ponies, amongst others, and not knowing anything about any of them started mounting Peter's youngster.

"No, no," said the groom, "Not that one."

Harriott spoke little English and just shrugged, saying, "I try."

Out of the twenty or so ponies he had to choose from, this youngster was his number one choice and he played it brilliantly in the test match. Peter's always-reddish face went even redder!

At the end of my second season with Bromley I decided to give up polo, for the time being at any rate. I sold Quick Step to Clive Style from the Lowveld and took Dusky and Terry back to the farm, where I put them in foal to a stallion owned by one of the Afrikaners from 'Dutchman's Corner', who went by the very English name of John Smith.

* * *

Returning from polo in Harare one Sunday evening in July 1968, we were invited over for drinks with the Prentices. On our way back to 'Chirume' from 'Leeds' to get some supper at home, Fran suddenly said, "I think you should keep going, back to Harare."

This I did, and we just made it to the Lady Chancellor Hospital in time for Robert Frederick Milbank to be born, the first Milbank of a new generation. It is not a unique experience to have a son and heir, it has happened before, and will doubtless happen again, but when it happens to you there can be few more exciting occasions in one's life. I was over the moon. It was late by the time I left the hospital, having seen my son, and I needed a bed as I was not driving home. I went to the old Meikle's Hotel and told them my problem – and the reason for it. Not only did they give me a bed, free of charge, but they sent up a plate of sandwiches and a bottle of whisky as well with congratulations and the compliments of the management. That's what I call good PR.

Fran and Robert did not remain in hospital for long. Fran's parents had suggested that we take a trained nurse back to 'Chirume' with us, and they selected and paid for a wonderful old bird who had overseen the early days of half the Rhodesian farmers. Her name was Sister Ballance – she may have had other names but, if anyone knew them, they were never used. She had just turned eighty. It was the best thing possible; she took complete charge, not only of the mother and child but of the whole household as well, and given half a chance would I am sure have run the farm. She stayed with us for a couple of weeks and was sorely missed when she departed.

* * *

On the farming front one thing became immediately apparent – the standard was very high. Rhodesian farmers then and right up to the time when Mr Mugabe saw fit to get rid of them all, were almost certainly the best in Africa. Nearly all had been to some form of agricultural college after leaving school. It might be Cirencester, Sealhayne, Wye or Lackham in England, Armadale or Gatton in Australia, Massey in New Zealand, Cedara in South Africa or one of the excellent local ones, Gwebi for agriculture in general, or Blackfordby, which specialized in tobacco.

Once you were on your farm, there was an excellent extension service known as CONEX (Conservation and Extension Services), and what was probably the best tobacco research station in the world at Kutsaga. Each area had a very active Farmers' Association, which, apart from monthly meetings, held field days and discussion groups throughout the year. Each area was divided into Intensive Conservation Areas (ICAs), and elected committee members from these organizations encouraged good farming practices to prevent things like erosion, overstocking, cutting down of indigenous timber and to ensure the burning of fireguards. In addition there was a very active veterinary department, which did regular spot checks on your cattle to see you were dipping properly, and issued movement permits for any stock you wanted to move.

In Wedza, and in other areas as far as I know, small groups of mainly young farmers got together one afternoon and evening a week, on one another's farms, to discuss mutual problems and share new ideas. In Wedza this was called Wedza Agricultural Discussion Society (WADS). There was absolutely no rivalry or competition; everybody went out of their way to help their neighbours, be it just with helpful advice or with the loan of equipment.

Added to this, there were numerous agriculture-related companies, which sent out representatives to advise farmers on what to buy in the way of fertilizer, crop chemicals, cattle dips or a multitude of other farming requirements. For those not near a railway station (most people), the Railway Motor Service (RMS) sent a lorry round the farms twice a week, delivering anything you wanted from town, be it fencing wire, asbestos roofing, cattle dip, fertilizer, crates of beer or your mail. All these things were just offloaded on the side of the road, and there they stayed until you went to pick them up. Nothing was ever stolen.

Contrary to popular belief, Rhodesia is not a particularly good or fertile agricultural country. It has poor soils, which suit tobacco, so with cheap labour for this very labour-intensive crop and expert management for a very difficult crop to grow well, tobacco became a vast money-spinner and contributed enormously to the country's foreign currency earnings. Tobacco was so profitable that many farmers did little else. Rainfall has always been erratic, so most progressive farmers spent a lot of money putting in dams and sophisticated irrigation systems. One of the great tragedies of Zimbabwe today is to have all these dams brimful of water but not being used for anything, while the government blames crop failures on drought. Zimbabwe is perfectly capable of feeding itself and of producing a surplus for export, as it showed only thirty years ago. Rhodesia certainly never starved when there were real sanctions imposed on all forms of trade with the rest of the world.

Most of this was in the future, as we set about trying to make the grade on 'Chirume'. Money was extremely short, and we stretched our credit facilities at the local Marandellas Farmers' Co-op to the absolute limit. Fran went in to Marandellas one day to buy some urgently needed bits and pieces at the Co-op and, knowing we were probably at our credit limit, asked how she should pay. I told her to give them a cheque.

"What, for everything?" she asked.

"Yes," I said, and she proceeded to write out a cheque for everything that we owed them, going back for three months. No way did we have that amount of money in the bank, so, as soon as Fran got back and I discovered what she had done, I tore back into Marandellas, burst into the credit controller's office and grabbed the cheque back from him. This did not go down at all well; he hit the roof and said my account would be closed and demanded immediate payment of my account in full. We did not part the best of friends. However it seems that I was not the only farmer giving him trouble and the next day he had a nervous breakdown. A week later my bank manager had a stroke and my doctor committed suicide – was I doing something that upset them all?

Perhaps I was not entirely to blame; the general manager of the Co-op, a charming man called 'Robbie' Roberts, drove all the way out to 'Chirume' one lunchtime and apologized for Mr Trimmer's (the credit controller) behaviour, and said that I could be reinstated as a member if I wanted.

"What about all the money I owe?" I asked.

"Just sign a stop-order with the CSC asking them to send us sufficient funds to cover what you owe, when your cattle are slaughtered," was his reply.

This was of course what all the tobacco farmers did, only with tobacco not cattle. Most of them would have huge loans with the Land Bank (later the Agricultural Finance Corporation or AFC) to enable them to grow the very expensive crop. Whoever sold their crop for them first paid off the lender of the money, then the farmer got the balance. If there was not enough to cover the loan – trouble!

All this time there was much talk and speculation about what was going to happen about UDI. Certainly amongst the farming community Ian Smith had the support of 90% of the whites, and he was regarded very much as a hero. Harold Wilson was the Labour Prime Minister in England

and was widely loathed. Many were the car stickers saying things like, 'I hate Harold'. Negotiations to settle the dispute were ongoing and followed with much interest. Smith and his senior ministers were invited to meet Wilson and his team on the British ship, HMS *Tiger* and later on HMS *Fearless*. I believe that at one of these meetings they did come to an agreement, but Smith insisted on talking to his full Cabinet back in Salisbury before signing anything. This consisted of such hardliners as P K Van der Byl and Desmond Lardner-Burke. They rejected the proposals and nothing was settled. We, the white farmers, were not privy to all this at the time, but Smith kept us in the picture as much as he could, and there were regular elections when we could have chucked out his party, the Rhodesian Front, if we had wanted to. Not enough did. Our local MP was David Smith (there were at least five Smiths in the Cabinet alone), who was Minister of Agriculture. He had come out from Scotland as a lad with no money at all, but had prospered mightily through good farming practices and hard work. He was a very good, shrewd man. I think we all wanted a settlement; we were basically British and did not really like being 'at war' with the old country, but we pretended not to give a damn and got on with breaking as many sanctions as possible with the help of South Africa and Mozambique.

* * *

Early in 1970 our little family was increased by the addition of Henry Mark Milbank. We always intended to call him Harry, but stupidly thought that he had to be christened Henry. He was named after a previous Harry Milbank, who had the dubious distinction of having been the last professional duellist to shoot a man in a duel in England. Having been banned from duelling in England, he went on plying his trade in France, until the inevitable happened and he got shot himself. His lovely duelling pistols are still kept at Barningham, and our Harry was allowed to hold them on his first visit there.

Sister Ballance, now well into her eighties, was hired again, and life on 'Chirume' became that little bit more complicated with two children to deal with. Very shortly after Harry's birth, my sister Penel, who was now working in a hotel in East Griqualand, rang up to say she was planning to get married again. I was delighted. It was now about ten years since John had been killed in Kenya, and after those very tough first few years, Penel had had quite a 'fling' in Natal, enjoying some of the sort of fun that she had been denied when getting married so young. Who was she marrying? I wanted to know. It was not any of the many suitors that had pursued her when I was around, but the part-owner of the motel where she was working and long time boss of Stockowners in Kokstad – a guy called Bob 'Huffie' Mills. I had never met him, so I said that Fran and I and the very small Harry would come down for the wedding.

Huffie had been married before, and his ex-wife was still around, so the wedding was a low-key affair. On the morning of the day I bought a bottle of champagne and took it to the local squash court, where I challenged Huffie to a game and then shared the bottle with him. I think we both enjoyed the game, the bottle and, more importantly, each other. After that just the three of us repaired to the Magistrates' Court and the deed was done.

CHAPTER 15

Abercrombie South

AFTER A COUPLE OF YEARS IT BECAME apparent that just doing cattle on five thousand acres was not going to make us a lot of money, so we would have to do something else as well. Our lease on the farm was expiring and we had to decide whether or not to exercise our option and buy the place. We did look at other places, and we actually held an option to buy a farm called 'Vureneme' in the Umvukwes area.

At this time my good friend John Clarke, from Kenya, pitched up and was looking for a farm to buy; I passed the option to buy 'Vureneme' on to him and decided to keep 'Chirume'. This, of course, necessitated a visit to the Land Bank and application for a long-term loan to pay off old Paliuras. Interest rates in those days were only about 6%, but I would still have to pay a hefty whack every six months. I paid thirty-five thousand Rhodesian dollars for 'Chirume', but the rate of exchange in those days was £1 = Rh$1, so in effect I had paid the equivalent of thirty-five thousand pounds.

The cattle were doing OK, and with a bit of trading to supplement a young breeding herd we were just about keeping our heads above water, but more money was needed. 'Chirume' was not a crop farm and I was not a crop man, so I had no intention of trying tobacco or even maize. Some other plan had to be made.

My parents, when they left South Africa and returned to Kenya, had done a variety of jobs to supplement their meagre income, like buying native cattle for the Kenya Meat Commission and sorting out abandoned farms for the government, but suddenly the opportunity arose to get involved with a small up-and-coming tour operator called Abercrombie and Kent, which was specializing in luxury camping safaris for upmarket Americans. The brains behind the new company were crusty old Col John Kent and his attractive wife, Valerie. Their idea was that you should not have to go on a shooting safari to enjoy camping in great comfort in the East African bush. Until then, photographic tourists had stayed at one or more of the very comfortable lodges scattered throughout the game-viewing areas of the country, but the idea of camping in the bush, just so long as one's comfort was ensured, soon caught on as being much more fun and rugged.

Obviously you could not send these tourists off on their own, so a pretty sophisticated courier had to take them in a smart four-wheel-drive vehicle to camps which had been set up by experienced staff in advance of their arrival. Col Kent recruited both my father and my mother to be two of his couriers.

My parents loved it and were very good at it. They wrote to me and asked if there was any similar sort of safari run in Rhodesia, and if not why did I not start one. Col Kent had a son called Geoff, and I had been at school with him. He had just left the British Army and was getting involved in his parents' business. He agreed to come down to Rhodesia and meet me to discuss the possible expansion of Abercrombie and Kent (A&K) into Rhodesia and the surrounding countries of Botswana, Mozambique and Malawi.

I drove up to Victoria Falls one day in 1970 and met Geoff there after he had been in nearby Botswana. As I say, I had been at school with Geoff but he had been my junior and I had not known him well, so it was a surprise to meet this bundle of energy and charm which greeted me at the old Victoria Falls Hotel. Geoff was dynamite! Ideas just poured out of him, and we were soon discussing ways of getting A&K off the ground in

Rhodesia. He had by now very much taken over the running of A&K in Kenya from his father, and his enthusiasm and total commitment to the job was infectious.

He had some very firm ideas on how a fledgling tour-operating company should be run.

"Anyone can start up a safari company," he said, "call it 'Rhino Safaris' or whatever, build a smart camp, buy some smart 4x4s and wait for the clients to come flocking in – they won't come because they have never heard of you, and, if by chance they have, there is a choice of a hundred and one other such setups. The most instances of young companies going broke are boutiques and tour operators."

Geoff and I inspected Victoria Falls, then drove to Wankie National Park and finally back to 'Chirume'. He seldom stopped talking and put it to me straight that if I were to start up a branch of A&K in Rhodesia this is how it would be done.

I would run the company from home – no fancy offices. I would use my own Mercedes car, getting it licensed as a Public Service Vehicle. If other vehicles were required they would be hired on the condition that we could put an A&K sticker on the side (thus pretending it was ours). We had a magnetic sticker made and slapped this on the side of any vehicle we hired. This worked fine until it got brushed off a Land Rover bashing its way through the bush, revealing the name of the true owner underneath. We would not camp initially, as Rhodesia did not lend itself to extended camping safaris to quite the same extent as East Africa. Instead, we would go to the excellent little camps that were just starting up. Menus would be typed out with the A&K logo on the top (again, implying that it was our camp), and we would use high-class local couriers to give a very professional and personal service. We would invite our clients back to selected private houses, to get a real feel for the country. We would not advertise locally, as we were not catering for the local market. Finally, all our energy, and as much money as we could spare would go on promoting our product where it would sell best – in America.

Soon after Geoff's visit I went up to Kenya and stayed with him in Nairobi, going into the A&K office every day. He had by now eased his parents out, and he was running the company himself with the help of his lovely wife Andrea, and a dedicated, hard-working staff headed by a bright young Kikuyu called Sammy Mwara. I spent a couple of weeks in Kenya, met some of Geoff's clients, visited a few camps and generally got the idea of how things worked. It was all very professional and stimulating.

Before I returned home we had decided to give it a go in Rhodesia. The first thing to agree on was what to call the company. The name 'Abercrombie and Kent' was becoming quite well-known and it was based in Kenya, an African country which refused to recognize the illegal Rhodesia. We felt it would be tactless to use the same name but wanted some sort of similarity. There never was anybody called Abercrombie even remotely connected with A&K, but the upmarket safari outfitters in New York were called Abercrombie and Fitch, and most travelling Americans associated this name with quality travel in Africa; also 'Ab' at the start of a word guaranteed a spot at the top of any index, so we wanted to use that word, and we finally decided on Abercrombie South Safaris.

Geoff's father-in-law, Cecil Joss, was a high-powered businessman in Johannesburg, being in charge of Munich Reinsurance, but as he was coming to the end of his contract he was keen to get involved in something else, so he agreed to start up a branch of Abercrombie South in South Africa. Both South Africa and Rhodesia at that time were highly unpopular in Kenya, so Geoff did not want his name to appear on our notepaper; consequently the directors of Abercrombie South Safaris (Rhodesia) Private Limited were: myself as managing director, Fran, and Cecil Joss. Geoff was good at getting the girls involved, and Fran said she was impressed by being married to a 'managing director' (despite the fact that he had not yet managed or directed anything). The very personal type of tour operating that was A&K's big selling point in their early days needed the very active co-operation of the boss man's wife. Andrea helped Geoff a lot and Fran was a big help to me when we started up.

In the sixties and seventies, A&K did not use agents at all; they dealt directly with the clients who were coming on safari with them, much in the same way that hunters deal directly with their professional hunter. Obviously this is much the best way of running a really sophisticated safari. One writes directly to the client early in the planning stages of his safari and finds out what things he particularly likes. Has he been to Africa before? Is he interested in birds, native tribes or old ruins? Does he want time at the coast? Does he like walking in the bush? Does he mind getting up early or doing late night game drives? What are his favourite drinks or food? One could go on and on; by the time he arrived, you had a pretty good idea of exactly what your client wanted.

Also, not using an agent meant it was cheaper for the client and more profitable for the tour operator, as no commission had to be built into the overall cost. The downside was that it was a lot of time-consuming hard work and it was relatively hard to get a regular volume of clients. A lot of the promotion was by word of mouth, and Geoff would go to the States at least twice a year to meet old clients, to be introduced to their friends, whom he would hope to persuade to come on safari with him. 'With him' was another snag. Geoff was a charmer, and clients meeting him through friends in America would expect him to be their courier when they came on safari in Kenya.

Geoff was a very busy man however, and he could not possibly take on safari all the clients that he had chatted up in America. He got round it, partly, by inviting them all to a cocktail party at his house the night they arrived. Here he would introduce them to the person who would be their courier for the duration of their stay. It nearly always worked, and the clients would often become lifelong friends of these couriers. So much so that many couriers thought they were God's gift to American tourists and immediately left Geoff's employ to start up their own companies – little realizing the enormous amount of work that is necessary to get clients into the country in the first place. Geoff, of course, was well aware of this and made his couriers sign forms saying they would not 'nick' his clients – or clients' friends. But there was not a lot he could do if they did. Tour operating is a very cut-throat business, with many grey areas.

All this I had to learn, quite apart from getting the best rates possible from all the hotels and lodges we would be using. When you pick up a brochure extolling the virtues of a certain place, it will usually have a loose bit of paper inside detailing their charges; this is known as 'the rack rate'. This is indeed what you will pay if you book directly with them. If an agent books you into the same place you will still pay this price, but the place in question will not get the full amount, as it will have to pay the agent something. Quite how much this something is depends on how good, well-known, honest, persuasive or desirable that particular agent is. As the new local boss man of Abercrombie South Safaris, I had to go round all the best places trying to persuade them that we were all of these good things. With no local track record they were understandably dubious.

Big outfits like the Southern Sun group would only give a decent rate if we promised to use their hotels in all the destinations we planned to visit. As they owned the old Victoria Falls Hotel, which was a 'must visit' in our area, we were more or less obliged to use their hotels or lodges if we took our clients to places like Wankie National Park or Salisbury. Smaller, private camp or lodge owners were usually happy to give us pretty good rates, as they were just starting up and were glad to get any clients at all, and much valued the exposure to overseas clients – particularly Americans. I well remember visiting Rob Fynn when he was just starting 'Kazangula Safaris' on the Matusadona mainland and Jeff Stutchbury's 'Camera Africa' on Spurwing Island. Going round all these places and deciding which were the best, and therefore the ones we would use, was a lot of fun, but it was also quite expensive. Geoff Kent never introduced any working capital into our fledgling company, only providing the knowhow and, initially at any rate, the all-important clients. He did also send down from Kenya an old, but good, Toyota Land Cruiser, which, being 4-wheel drive, was a very useful addition to my Mercedes Benz 220D.

To get Americans to come to Rhodesia in the early '70s was not easy. The American State Department branded Rhodesia an unsafe destination; there was no US Embassy here, very few airlines flew in, and no travel agent knew anything about the place. The only way that Geoff could get anyone to come here was to write personally to valued old clients who loved Africa, and tell them that Rhodesia was in fact God's own country. Not that Abercrombie South only covered Rhodesia. We operated into Mozambique, but they were tarred with the same colonial brush as us and were in fact already engaged in an independence war. We also went into Botswana, which was an independent state, but it was so heavily reliant on South Africa for virtually everything that it unhappily accepted the existence of them and us. I also reconnoitred these two countries and found some marvellous and totally unspoilt places, like the Okavango Delta, the Savuti Channel and Chobe National Park in Botswana, and the fabulous Gorongoza in Mozambique, as well as the wonderful Mozambique coast.

* * *

One of the best recces was to the Okavango. I had heard that an old Rhodesian friend, Tim Liversedge, had built a remarkable houseboat, in which he planned to travel the full length of the Okavango Delta from Shakawe in the north right down to Chief's Island. It was very much the sort of thing we wanted to offer our clients, so I planned to go and have a look. This coincided with Tim wanting to do his maiden voyage, which would be something of a trial, so he agreed to give me a special price if I could make up a boatload. I immediately telephoned Cousin Anthony in England and told him to get here quick, as this was likely to be the safari of a lifetime. He took very little persuading and agreed to come, together with his newish wife, Bea, and five others – Christopher and Olivia Stuart-Smith, Patrick and Jenny Scott plus Bernard Dewe-Matthews, a bachelor. So with Fran and me this made nine of us, which was in fact more than a boatload.

We drove from 'Chirume' to Bulawayo in the Land Cruiser and a Volkswagen minibus, and on through the border post near Plumtree to Francistown in Botswana, where we spent the night. The next day we drove up the long dusty road, skirted the great Magadigadi saltpans and arrived in Maun that evening. We were carrying shotguns with us and on the way had a very amusing little shoot of sand grouse coming in to drink at a roadside gravel pit. We also drove down the road to Tsoe for a few miles and saw vast herds of zebra and the magnificent gemsbok.

We overnighted at Croc Camp, and next morning boarded two small planes and flew up to Shakawe, having a magnificent overview of the whole delta on the way. We were met by Tim and June Liversedge and driven to the river where our boat, the *Sitatunga*, was moored. As there were so many of us there was another boat as well, the *African Queen*, which would act as a sort of backup, provide sleeping accommodation for Bernard, and carry extra provisions. It was under the command of a roughish diamond called Mike Smith. The *Sitatunga* was a unique construction – designed and built by Tim, with all the material brought overland some one thousand miles, via South West Africa (Namibia). It was three storeys high, with sleeping cabins at water level, living area in the middle and a wonderful open deck on the top.

The banks of the Okavango River are covered with high papyrus reeds, so in a conventional low motorboat one can see no further than the wall of papyrus. From the *Sitatunga's* deck one could see over these reeds and often spy dry land containing game and, lower down in the delta area, isolated islands. It was a magnificent way to travel, and as we could carry plenty of fuel and sleep on board, we were able to keep going into the very depths of the swamp and to visit areas that quite possibly no one had ever been to before. Small boats could only go so far and then they would have to turn round, as there was nowhere to camp and they could not carry enough fuel anyway.

Apart from the *African Queen*, we also towed two small boats with outboard motors behind us. The *Sitatunga* was quite slow, so every day we would leave it chugging along and go shooting off in the little boats, fishing and exploring, only returning for meals, and of course for the night. It was absolute magic! We had a new unexplored world all to ourselves. The water of the Okavango, sifted through hundreds of miles of sand, is so pure that you can put it in a car battery. It was gin clear all the way. Fishing was superb; tiger fish were the main quarry but there were also plenty of bream. We had our shotguns with us, and when we got further into the delta and encountered a few islands we went ashore and had some amusing little forays against guineafowl and francolin.

There was not a lot of game to be seen, as the reeds were so thick, but we did see the very rare sitatunga antelope which inhabits these swampy places, as well as red lechwe, hippo and crocodiles. Bird life though was excellent, with wonderful colonies of carmine bee-eaters wherever we encountered the tall earth banks in which they build their nests. Other species of water birds were also common – spurwing geese, knobnose duck, teal, pigmy geese, purple gallinule, and jacanas, to mention just a few.

We lived in luxury. Tim and June were marvellous hosts and they had a staff of two Africans, one a cook closely supervised by June, and the other a general 'dogsbody'. The boat boasted every conceivable type of drink, which was all included in the price, the food was excellent with fresh fish always on the menu, and the company great. We ran a 'book' on how many fish we would catch each day and the winning score was usually around fifty. This was mostly tiger fish, caught on a spinner; they were not big, but lean, fit river fish, and they gave a great fight played on a light line.

It took us the best part of a week to get to the bottom end of the delta, then we had to turn round and go all the way back against the current. This was quite hard work. There is very little current in the delta itself, but higher up in the 'pan handle' it is pretty strong. There are frequent hairpin bends, and it required enormous skill by Tim to negotiate these against the current. The *Sitatunga* was a big, very unwieldy craft. When we finally made it back to Shakawe and semi-civilization, it was a bit of a shock, as we had lived in our own little magic world for over two weeks.

We had a hell of a party on the final night, and an abiding memory is of Mike Smith, sitting in the branches of a huge tree, with the moon behind him, belting out Harry Belafonte's classic, *Day-O!*

We flew back to Maun, picked up our transport and started the drive home, stopping on the way for a night under the stars at Nxai Pan. We also shot a lot of guineafowl on the way, and on arrival at the new Monomatapa Hotel in Salisbury asked if they could deal with them.

"Certainly, sir," was the reply from the young and attractive girl at reception. "Are they alive or dead?"

It had indeed been a memorable safari, and it ranks high in, if not at the top of, the many adventures that I have been lucky enough to take part in. I took American clients on the *Sitatunga* with Tim on two occasions, and both times it was a resounding success. On these occasions we did not come back upstream on the boat but flew out of the newly constructed strip at the bottom of the delta. Tim would then take the boat back to be ready for the next trip. The life of the *Sitatunga* doing these unique trips was very short. After only a couple of seasons, Tim had a disagreement with his main sponsor, and when it was not resolved he walked away from the boat, leaving it at the bottom end of the delta. No one else had the slightest idea how to drive it back to Shakawe, so it remained at a lodge called Xugana and was used for sunset cruises round a lagoon, until it eventually caught fire. What a waste! But thank goodness I was able to experience this unique craft being used for its proper purpose. There has never been another.

* * *

It was time for the clients to start flocking in, and I had to find some couriers. I would take some myself, but, as Fran and I were Abercrombie South and we also had a farm to run, there really had to be someone at 'home base' to sort out any problems and welcome new clients – as well as deal with sick mombies. Most of the safaris that we organized in those days were for two or three weeks, and they involved two or three different countries, so any courier would be away for some time. We lived on 'Chirume', where we only got post twice a week and relied on a party line telephone, which only sometimes worked – hardly the most efficient way of running a sophisticated safari company.

My idea for couriers was to recruit local farmers. Most of them knew far more about Rhodesia than I did, having lived in the country all their lives, and many of them took their annual holiday as a hunting safari in the Zambezi Valley, so were very knowledgeable about the fauna and flora of the area; also they were very nice people. Geoff visited us again before loosing any of his clients on us, and I invited a selection of these farmers round for lunch to be addressed by Geoff on the duties of a courier. Probably more out of interest than anything else they all came – Norman Travers, Nigel Thornycroft, David Hamilton, Mike Jackson and Gerry von Memerty. Geoff is a brilliant speaker and soon had them all absolutely sold on the idea.

As any tourist coming to our area had to visit Victoria Falls, we decided to recruit a local who lived there to meet and entertain our clients at the Falls before sending them on. To this end we got Bernice Sharp to do the job for us. We did not have a sufficient volume of clients to warrant employing her full-time and exclusively for us, so she did freelance work for other companies as well, but when our clients arrived she wore an Abercrombie South badge and devoted her whole time to their wellbeing.

From July 1970 onwards we started corresponding with an old client of Geoff's, Senator Warren Brown from Idaho. His wife Jane did most of the corresponding while he, presumably, did his Senator bit. They had already been to Kenya and Tanzania – and loved it – so were keen to see more of Africa. I planned a fairly conservative two and a half week safari with us in Rhodesia and Mozambique, before they flew on to revisit Kenya. They would fly into Salisbury from Johannesburg, having flown from America. In Jo'burg Cecil Joss had looked after them for a few days and taken them down a gold mine, among other things.

They were bringing two friends with them and would arrive in Salisbury one evening. Fran and I drove into town and arranged a small welcoming dinner at Meikle's Hotel, but the appointed courier for the safari would meet them at Salisbury airport. The appointed courier was Nigel Thornycroft. Nigel was the quintessential colonial Englishman. Born and educated in England, he had gone to Cambridge University, from which base he had shot during most of the winter months and played cricket most days during the summer. When the war came he had joined up – naturally – but been captured quite early and spent most of his war in and out of various prisoner of war camps. 'In' because that is where the Germans put him, 'out' because he did not like being there; he was one of the comparatively few escapers who got away, but he was recaptured later. He and his wife Corona came to Rhodesia shortly after the war and bought a farm near 'Chirume'. Here, he grew some pretty good tobacco when he was not hunting in the Zambezi Valley, pursuing guineafowl or playing cricket. When the word 'eccentric' was invented, they probably had Nigel in mind. He could have fitted into Kenya every bit as well as, or even better than, in Rhodesia.

Many of my friends, hearing that I was employing Nigel for such a responsible job and knowing him better than I, said that I was crazy. Nigel, they maintained, was totally charming, but he would be driven mad by four Yanks in a car with him for over two weeks. The whole safari would end in tears. I was very nervous. It was our first safari and I was desperate for it to go well. I spent an hour with Nigel telling him all I knew about Americans on safari in general and the Warren Browns in particular, which was not a lot.

"Swot up on facts and figures about the country," I urged, "they always want to know things like that."

Fran and I waited nervously in the lobby of Meikle's Hotel, and in due course our white Mercedes with Nigel at the wheel drew up, and out got Warren and Jane Brown, together with their friends Innis and Opal Johnson. They were all roaring with laughter. It seems that as they set off from the airport, Warren, wanting to break the ice, asked Nigel what the population of Salisbury was. Despite my little lecture, Nigel did not have the slightest idea, so, putting his thumb and index finger about an inch apart, he said, "I've no idea, but the telephone directory is about that thick."

This well and truly broke the ice – Warren didn't really give a damn about the population of Salisbury, and from there on they all got on like a house on fire.

The safari was an outstanding success and they booked to come on a return visit the following year – on condition that Nigel was their courier. They did come on a second safari, and shortly after that Nigel and Corona visited them in Idaho. We charged them a lot of money for their safari here and for Nigel's services in particular, but when Nigel went there he did not have to put his hand in his pocket once – he and Corona were royally entertained. Also, when I visited Hawaii, Warren happened to be on the next-door island of Maui and, learning that I was around, sent his private plane to pick me up so that I could spend the day with them. They were truly delightful people and we could not have had better to get our business off to a great start.

All our couriers were in action early on. Norman Travers took the Leuthold family fishing off the Mozambique coast for marlin and on Kariba for tiger fish. David Hamilton had the Prescotts in Wankie and on Kariba. Ben Norton, whom I had got to know through polo, was also recruited as a courier, and he took our precious Mercedes up to Kariba to meet the Robertsons, who were flying in there from Victoria Falls, before visiting Bumi Hills and then driving down to Gorongoza with Ben. On the way up to Kariba in the dark, a herd of cattle jumped off a bank on the side of the road and squashed the Merc very flat. Miraculously, Ben survived, hired another car, slapped on the Abercrombie sticker and proceeded with the safari as if nothing had happened. The Mercedes was never quite the same again though.

Our first problem arose when Gerry von Memerty took the Sidenfadens down to Mozambique. Gerry was a very keen hunter and so, it turned out, was Sid Sidenfaden. His wife, who had the unlikely name of Oral, was not, so they had come to Africa on a photographic safari. Gerry and Sid chatted a lot about hunting though, and Gerry enlarged on his views on how best to shoot the 'Big Five'. The only way to get a leopard, he said, was to bait it. Some days later, two small children dragging a goat behind them ran across the road in front of Gerry and caused him to slam on the brakes. As he swerved and drove past, he turned to Sid and said, "Leopard bait."

Oral, sitting in the back, had not seen the goat and assumed that Gerry was referring to the children. She said nothing then, but I got the most vitriolic letters from her, and Sid, asking how I could possibly employ someone who was prepared to bait his leopard traps with live African children. They did not come on a return safari, nor did Gerry visit them in America.

Gerry did better with an English couple called Horden. They were on honeymoon and went with Gerry to Gorongoza, amongst other places. Gorongoza was famous for its lions and, sure enough, on the first evening they came across a beautiful young black-maned lion with a lioness. It seemed the lions were also on honeymoon, and Gerry was able to explain how a lion, in these circumstances, was liable to make love to his bride every fifteen minutes. That was the last game drive Gerry did with the Hordens. He couldn't get them out of their room after that; Ed Horden was evidently trying to emulate the lion. It saved us a fortune in diesel!

* * *

Gerry was, as mentioned, a very keen hunter of big game and retained his love of the hunt well into middle age, unlike a lot of people who are bloodthirsty when young but grow out of it. A small story about Gerry will illustrate that it was the hunt he enjoyed and not necessarily the killing of the animal.

Every year he would book, and pay quite a lot of money for, a hunting block in the Zambezi Valley. This would be for two weeks' duration, and a list of the game that could be shot on licence would be supplied. Gerry collected trophies and had a good selection on his farm veranda, but he lacked a really good buffalo head, so on the particular hunt I am telling you about such a trophy was high on his list. These two-week hunts were expensive, and making biltong out of the meat from any animal shot could offset part of the cost. Biltong is raw meat dried in the sun, having been marinated with a selection of spices, and is a much-prized delicacy in Africa, eaten particularly while watching rugby.

Gerry took a friend on this particular hunt, and arriving at the mighty Zambezi River set up his camp in the early afternoon; then in the cool of the evening he strolled along the banks of the river with a shotgun, hoping to get a guineafowl or francolin for supper. It was not long before a covey of juicy fat francolin rose from a patch of reeds and Gerry dropped one with his first shot. He never saw it fall, as there burst from the reeds the biggest buffalo bull he had ever seen. The enormous, gleaming black horns swung down beside each cheek before curving back in a magnificent parabola. Gerry stood transfixed as the old bull lumbered off into the thick jesse bush, snorting its disapproval at being so rudely disturbed.

Gerry wanted that bull as much as he had wanted anything in his hunting life. Before daybreak next morning he and his tracker were on to the spoor left the night before. They tracked the bull all day, only catching the occasional glimpse of it. Same story the next day. By now they were getting far from camp, so Gerry decided to sleep on the trail, and for the next three nights he did just that, being eaten alive by mosquitoes at night and tsetse fly by day. Then he had to return to camp for more provisions, but after a day's rest was on the trail again. Twice he raised his rifle to fire at the bull, but on each occasion something alerted the old fellow and he crashed off before Gerry could get a clean shot.

Suddenly the two weeks were up and Gerry had not fired a shot (except at that first guineafowl). No biltong to take home and no wonderful trophy either. They were due to leave early next morning, so on that last evening Gerry took a relaxing walk along the river, quietly absorbing the beauty of the valley, listening to the hippos snorting and the fish eagle calling. He was alone, but took his heavy rifle with him as a matter of habit. As the sun was setting over the Zambian escarpment, he paused by an anthill before turning to retrace his steps to camp. As he did so there was a movement in some nearby bushes and he turned to see what it was.

Out of the bush wandered the very bull that he had been hunting for the last two weeks. The sun was behind Gerry, and the gentle breeze was blowing in his face, so the bull had no idea that he was there. The distance was only fifty yards and Gerry slowly raised his rifle and drew a bead on the massive shoulder. The magnificent animal raised its head and seemed to look Gerry in the eye before resuming grazing. Gerry's finger tightened on the trigger and then relaxed. Slowly he lowered his rifle, took off his hat and threw it at the bull shouting, "Thanks for a super two weeks, you old bastard!" With a snort and a swish of the tail the bull disappeared back into the bush, and Gerry wandered back to camp with a smile on his face. Not all hunters are butchers, and it is possibly Gerry's reluctance to shoot that proved his ultimate undoing. In the Zambezi Valley again he was surrounded by a herd of cow elephants with calves. He told the clients with him to get out of it and that he would extricate himself. No shot was fired but he did not return to camp that night. Next morning he was found dead, crushed to death by one of the cows.

* * *

Mike Jackson was a keen golfer, so it was he who took the Moores out, and I joined them for a game of golf on the lovely Ruwa course, as Tom Moore loved his golf. Like all our other clients they also came to Wedza and stayed at 'Scorror' with my in-laws, Rick and Midge Holme. Here we arranged a guineafowl shoot for Tom followed by a big dinner party. Next day Mike took them to Wedza village, and they were able to sit in on a meeting between the District Commissioner, Bob Cunliffe, and a local chief. We really did feel that we were giving our clients a true picture of what Rhodesia was like, and not just the usual tourist bits. This was proved by the fact that many of these clients recommended a safari with us to their friends – there is no better publicity than word of mouth.

We did have one major hiccup though. As most of our clients went to all three countries, we copied each other on all correspondence with that client, so that we all spoke with a common voice. We had one very rich, very grumpy, very demanding old bachelor from New York who wanted to visit South Africa, Rhodesia and Kenya, so we all sent him suggestions as to what he should do and what it would cost. He would reply asking more questions, querying the cost and generally being very picky. Fair enough really, we prided ourselves on catering for this sort of client and trying to fulfil his most pedantic requirements. After weeks of suggestions flying backwards and forwards between New York and us, he finally agreed to a pretty comprehensive safari using our three organizations – Cecil Joss in South Africa, me in Rhodesia and Geoff in Kenya. Unfortunately Cecil, when writing to confirm everything with him, put the wrong letter in the envelope addressed to him. I got the letter meant for him, saying how delighted we all were that he was coming and how much we were looking forward to meeting him, while he got the short note that Cecil meant to send to me, saying,'Thank goodness we have landed the old bastard at last!'

It would have been amusing to have been a fly on the wall in his New York office when he read that, but needless to say he cancelled the whole trip forthwith, and A&K's name in that part of New York took a bit of a battering.

* * *

Nearly all our clients came from America, apart from the Hordens, but we suddenly got an enquiry from a young Englishman. He was arriving anyway in Salisbury and wanted to do a bit of a safari. I met him in Meikle's Hotel and started detailing everything we could offer and what it would all cost. After about twenty minutes he held up his hand and told me to stop.

"Look," he said, "I am not one of your rich American tourists; I do not want all those luxuries and I can't possibly afford that sort of hotel, so perhaps I should just do my own thing."

We had no one else on safari at the time and I had already driven all the way into town, so I was keen to do some sort of deal with him. We chatted and I asked him what sort of money he was prepared to spend. In the end I took him home to 'Chirume' and we went guineafowl shooting with David Hamilton, then I took him over to Headlands, where we stayed with Richard Holme and did more shooting, before going to stay with Micky Buswell on the Inyanga road to shoot a sable. Back in Wedza I took him to try and shoot a reedbuck, many of which were eating Bob Rutherford's wheat. He returned, unsuccessful, in the evening with blood pouring from both elbows and knees. He had spent the day crawling through the African bush in much the same manner as one does on the much softer moors of Scotland after stag. Lastly we sent him up to Kariba to do a bit of tiger fishing. I can't remember what we charged him but it was not a lot.

A month or two after he departed I received a large package in the post. It contained two long articles from *The Field,* the English country sports magazine, obviously written by an expert on the subject about rough shooting and tiger fishing in Rhodesia. They had been written by my client – Max Hastings.

Max returned three times to Rhodesia but on those occasions as a correspondent for the BBC. He always came to stay with us on the farm and invariably brought us some goodies, which were unobtainable in the country at the time, such as Scotch whisky and Marmite. He would then send us copies of what he had written and it was nearly always fair and sound reporting in my opinion. At the height of the bush war he arrived again and telephoned me from his Salisbury hotel.

"Can't come and see you this time," he said, "but you can pick up your goodies from this hotel; I have been deported and am off to the airport."

It seems that PK van der Byl, then Minister of something or other in our government, had been in England recently, was recognized as a rebel Rhodesian minister and chucked out. When Max pitched up representing the BBC, this was PK's revenge. Initially I was angry and sorry for Max, but then a month later I received a package in the post – not from Max, but from my cousin Anthony, saying, 'What have you been doing to your friend Max?'

It was the story Max had written after his deportation. I read it and under-stood why Max had not sent me a copy himself: it was a most virulent, untrue and unjust attack on what the white youth of Rhodesia were like. When he had stayed with us he always said how much he admired our courage, old-fashioned values and general decency. Now he chose to depict us all as overweight, spoilt, useless slobs. To my mind it was a pretty sick sort of revenge for being kicked out. Max of course went on to become famous as the first reporter to enter Stanley at the end of the Falklands War, and then to hold many prestigious posts in the newspaper world, but I never really forgave him for that nasty, biased article.

* * *

I did do my bit of couriering occasionally. Perversely, this was when we were sent some really important clients. This sort of person required the company's top man to take them out personally and the top man was naturally the managing director – me, no less. This totally ignored the fact that I was not a patch on the regular couriers that I had engaged. Thus it was that when Geoff persuaded Philip Pillsbury to pay us a visit, I had to be the courier, whether my mombies were sick, my wife was having a baby or my grandmother dying. Philip Pillsbury will be well known to any Americans reading this. For those who do not know about him, he is the owner of Pillsbury Flour, which provides most of the stuff with which Americans make bread. As this is quite a lot of flour Mr Pillsbury was very rich, and I mean very rich, as only these top American businessmen can be. He also happened to be a very nice man, and I mean very nice. He genuinely adored Africa and had been on safari with A&K in East Africa six times. Each time he had had the same courier, the co-founder of A&K with old Col Kent, Roy Gregory. So when he was persuaded to come to us he insisted that Roy came along as well.

Philip's wife, who always used to accompany him, had just died, so it was a bit of a nostalgic trip, and he first visited some of his old haunts in Kenya before flying down to Beira in Mozambique, as there were no direct flights from Nairobi to Salisbury in those days. I drove down to Beira in the newly acquired Land Cruiser (which had Abercrombie South Safaris painted on the doors – no need for magnetic signs now), met Philip and Roy and drove them to the newly opened, and very smart, Dom Carlos Hotel – Carlos Brito's newest 'trap' for rich Rhodesian tobacco farmers. From there I took them out to dinner at 'Johnny's Place', which in those days served quite possibly the best prawn piri-piri in the world. Philip Pillsbury loved his seafood and was duly appreciative of the excellent fare, so the safari got off to a good start.

We had a fair drive next morning, and I reckoned that a nice picnic lunch on the banks of the Pungwe River, before getting to our destination – Gorongoza – would be a good idea. Seeing how much Philip had enjoyed the prawns, I asked Johnny to prepare a nice, cold prawn salad for us to pick up in the morning. This he did, and we set off in high spirits for the National Park. We crossed the Pungwe River by the old hand-operated ferry and stopped on the far bank for our picnic. Again this was much enjoyed and we arrived at Gorongoza in time to relax before going on an evening game drive. Roy had never been to Mozambique, let alone Gorongoza, so I was very much in charge and keen to show off this lovely park to its best advantage.

About halfway through the drive I started to feel very, very odd. I regret to say I cut the drive short and hurried back to Chitengo camp, had a quick word to Roy and bolted to my room, where I was violently sick. I continued to throw up all night and spent most of the time sitting under a hot shower shivering. I was no better next morning so Roy had to drive

Philip round a park he had never been to before. I had eaten a bad, cold prawn and had the worst form of seafood poisoning. Thank goodness it was I and not Philip. There was absolutely no form of medication or doctor at Gorongoza and we were scheduled to be there for three days with the most important client we had so far entertained. I was a total write-off for those entire three days and poor Roy had to cope. When it was time to drive back to Rhodesia I dragged myself out of the hot shower, filled my underpants with loo paper, gritted my teeth and off we set.

As soon as we reached the border, I telephoned Fran and told her to get me some strong medicine quickly. This she did, and I recovered enough to drive Philip and Roy round Wedza, as they were staying at 'Scorror'. We visited 'Imire Game Park' and then went on to see the Bushman paintings in nearby Markwe cave. To see these, one has to climb up quite a steep, slippery rock. Philip was fairly old and unsteady on his pins, so had some small difficulty managing this, and in doing so banged his camera. He said nothing except how interesting he had found the paintings. Later he told Roy that he had in fact broken his camera, but that Roy was not to tell me, as it would upset me. I said he was a nice man. Later when Rick and Midge did a round the world trip they stopped off in America and stayed with Philip.

After about eighteen months we had organized a number of very successful safaris in Rhodesia, Botswana, Mozambique and, to a lesser extent, in Malawi. We were still relying heavily on Geoff sending us his old clients, but we really needed more to make the whole venture pay. It was then that Geoff said I should go to America myself and do some active promoting. This was totally in line with all his thinking: Get the clients at all costs. As usual he had a cunning plan and by luck this involved polo. Geoff maintained that if Americans were rich enough to play polo in that country, then they could afford one of his safaris. Geoff himself was a very keen polo player in Kenya, and he asked me if I had ever played. Well, I had, and still held a respectable 3 handicap.

"Great," said Geoff, "we will take a Kenyan polo team over there, meet all the right people, I will talk about East Africa and you talk about your area."

Needless to say he already had some polo contacts in America, as his sister Anne had married a polo player from Montana, and they gave him an introduction to the secretary of the US Polo Association. This turned out to be Jorie Butler, the twice-married daughter of Paul Butler from Oakbrook, Chicago, the man who had founded Butler Airlines and other very lucrative business ventures. It could hardly have been a better introduction. Jorie was keen on the idea and arranged a spectacular itinerary for us.

Geoff managed to persuade British Airways that we would generate an enormous amount of business for them between America, Britain and Africa, so they should give him and me free tickets to do this valuable promotion on their behalf. It was hard to resist Geoff in full flow and we were duly given the tickets. We still needed two more players for our team though. The first was quite easy to find. Anton Allen was a professional hunter and was keen to go to the States anyway on a promotion trip of his own. He could play polo a bit, so was included. Now we badly needed someone quite good at polo – I rated 3 goals, Geoff was 4 and Anton 2, so it was not a great looking international side. Kenya's leading player was Don Rooken-Smith and he was good, rating 6 goals, so Geoff talked him into coming along as well. This gave us a total handicap of 15, but we reckoned that the standard of play in America was probably a bit higher than we were used to, so we each dropped one goal, making our team total 11 goals, which was a standard that could probably compete against good amateur sides (who all had plenty of money for ponies).

It was a big decision for me to go. To make it worthwhile I would have to be away at least two months. I planned to go ahead of the team, visit past clients and see what sort of business I could drum up on my own. The polo bit would last for three weeks and I would have a bit more time after that for more business. Fran agreed to hold the fort at home (as well as holding two small children). We opened a small office in Salisbury to help with communications and installed Ivy Littleford in it to deal with routine correspondence.

Geoff told me to come via Kenya to finalise our plan of action, and this very nearly scotched the whole trip. Kenya did not recognize Rhodesia, and no one was allowed to travel from there to Kenya, no matter what passport they carried. I held a British passport at the time and reasoned that if I went to Malawi first, spent a night there and flew on to Kenya on Air Malawi, I would have no problem – I was coming from Malawi wasn't I? The immigration officials at Nairobi airport saw it a bit differently. They knew bloody well I had really come from Rhodesia and would not let me in; they even gave me a bit of paper declaring that I was a prohibited immigrant to Kenya. Luckily my father had come to meet me, and he knew a lot of the officials at the airport, as he frequently met A&K clients off international flights. Some fast talking on his part saved the day and I was allowed in.

I spent a few days in Kenya, seeing my parents and also spending time in Geoff's office. Then I flew, via England, to New York and straight on to Los Angeles. I had only been to America once before, in charge of a horse for BLE, so everything was pretty strange. I spent the first week staying with Johnny Leuthold in Hollywood. Johnny had been on safari with us and had had Norman Travers as his courier. He very kindly gave me a bed. The night I arrived, Sharon Tate, the lovely actress, was murdered in the house bang next door by the perverted Manson Gang. Ghoulishly we peered over the fence, and saw signs like 'Death to the pigs', scrawled in blood on the walls. What sort of place had I come to?

I made some useful contacts in LA then caught a local flight down to San Diego – it cost seven dollars and I got a free glass of Californian wine thrown in. Just outside San Diego I stayed with old clients called the Martyns and played golf with them. I was not a golfer then (most people would say I am not a golfer now) but I was keen to take some exercise to keep in shape for the polo. This was tricky, as you were not allowed to walk round the golf course but had to go in a cart. I solved this by running behind the cart. From San Diego, back up the west coast to Portland, Tacoma, where I had to give a talk to a ladies' garden club, in the hope of persuading them to tour the gardens of Rhodesia (I failed, dismally), San Francisco and finally back to Los Angeles, where I met up with the team.

Geoff was one of the team of course, and I had never seen him in such poor shape. Usually he exuded health and confidence. Now he frankly looked buggered. He was, but not medically. He also had come over early, as he had been invited to attend the annual gathering of an unusual club – the Rancheros. This was a club for wealthy, ageing businessmen, who once a year left their offices and respectable social-climbing wives and went off into the bush for a beano with their mates. Here they really let their hair down, riding and shooting all day, drinking and whoring all night. Membership of the club was by invitation only, but members were allowed to invite one guest. Geoff was one of those guests, tagging along because he reckoned he would meet some pretty influential people. Little did he know that guests had to undergo an initiation ceremony. On the first night his head was clamped in a sort of cattle crush so that he was held still and could not look round. His trousers and underpants were removed. Out of the corner of one eye he could see a blazing fire, and to his horror his host suddenly approached him bearing a red-hot branding iron.

"This won't take a moment, Geoff," he said, "then you will be eligible to become a full member."

Christ, thought Geoff, they are going to brand me. His host went behind him and suddenly Geoff felt a searing sensation on his right buttock and at the same time smelt the aroma of burning flesh. He screamed and fought to turn round but the clamp held him tight.

Everyone was roaring with laughter as his host finally let him go. Geoff immediately clamped his hand to his backside to explore the damage, only to encounter a block of ice. At the same time he saw the branding iron being held on to a large juicy steak! It seems that, if you are expecting something very hot but encounter something very cold instead, it is difficult to tell the difference at first. Geoff spent the rest of that week trying to keep up with this hard-drinking, hard-loving bunch of overgrown schoolboys. He was just shattered, but recovered quickly.

Our first stop for polo was in Hawaii, and it was to these exotic islands that we flew from Los Angeles. I could not have gone further from home – Hawaii is the antipodes of Rhodesia. We were met by Mr and Mrs 'Polo Hawaii' – Fred and Murf Dailey – and booked into their lovely old-fashioned hotel, The Waikikian, which was tucked between two, huge, hideous, concrete monstrosities. It was a charming place in the wonderfully vibrant and colourful city of Honolulu. We were based there for a week.

It appeared that visiting 'international' polo players were treated rather like film stars. The press interviewed us. We had our photographs taken and saw the results splashed across the social (not sporting) pages of the local newspapers. There was a cocktail party every night we were there, and on arrival at these functions flower leis were placed round our necks, which marked us out as guests of honour. It was all immensely flattering and rather fun. During the day we tried out ponies and had a couple of practice games at the Mokuleia Polo Club, which was situated on the other side of the island from Honolulu.

Our hosts also took us on a tour of Pearl Harbour – in the admiral's barge, no less. This was all emotional stuff and the Americans took it very seriously, in that we had to take our hats off and speak in whispers at appropriate moments. It was interesting, though, and also interesting that a mere thirty years after the event the biggest purchasers of real estate in Hawaii were the Japanese.

The day of the big match, Kenya v Hawaii dawned and we drove to the polo ground. Our low-key practice games had all been against or with local amateurs and it was against a selection of these that we expected to be playing. Not a bit of it – the best two amateurs were included but they were strongly reinforced by the top local pro, Ronnie Tong, who played off a very good 6 handicap, and a young New Zealander who had played rugby for the All Blacks! There was a large noisy crowd, a military band, and VIP guests to be introduced to us as we lined up before the game. The match was scheduled for five chukkas, which was an unusual number, as they are usually four or six. We were very well mounted on local ponies and after a shaky start had fought our way to 2-2 after three chukkas. This was half time, which was not the customary five minutes but was stretched to a full half hour, during which time each member of our team was introduced to the assembled multitude over the public address system and was obliged to say a few words. This completely threw us, and the opposition immediately scored three quick goals. We rallied gamely in the last chukka, but still narrowly lost.

Prize giving, speeches and lots of champagne followed, then a full-blown cocktail party in the clubhouse. Hawaii knew how to put on a good show. Sadly, just as the party was really getting going, Geoff and I had to leave, as we had some business to do in Denver, Colorado, where we flew that night. Don and Anton stayed on a bit before we all met up again in Houston, Texas.

I have not told you much about Anton yet, so I had better do so, because his arrival in Houston was a bit tricky. Anton was a professional hunter and, like his father before him, a very good one, but he had one main weakness – women. A lot of the top safari companies in East Africa would not employ him because he had a habit of running off with their clients' wives. This is not an uncommon occurrence with professional hunters, as there seems to be something about the African bush which loosens the inhibitions of pretty American girls, and Anton took full advantage of this. But he was a good hunter, so one of the leading companies did employ him to take out a very wealthy, old, French client. As the French do, the old French client brought along a ravishingly beautiful companion, whom he did not even pretend was his wife. Anton was severely cautioned by the safari company boss.

"Lay off!" he was told. "This is a very important client and we do not want to lose him."

They had a very successful hunt and all was going well until the ageing client had to leave the safari for a couple of days, while Anton and the 'friend' stayed in camp. Disaster! Ageing client returned a day earlier than expected and caught them 'in flagrante delicto' – to put it politely. The whole safari ended in tears and Anton was told he would never be employed again. However, some six months later the boss of the safari company received a letter from the ageing French client saying that he wanted to come back for another hunt, and he particularly wanted Anton as his hunter. He added a PS – 'Please tell Anton – this time I bring two companions, would he please leave one for me?'

Anton did not improve though, and a few months before our polo jaunt he had blatantly 'stolen' the very pretty young wife of a Texas millionaire. This time though he was serious and said he wanted to marry her, and she was actually travelling with us. She was a really sweet girl called Carla. What she had not told us was that her erstwhile husband lived in Houston and was a very keen polo player. We only discovered this in Hawaii, and we suddenly realized that we could be flying into a hornets' nest. Nobody likes their wife being nicked, and we had a feeling that a Texan in particular might do quite a bit about it. We were due to be met by members of the Houston club that were entertaining us, and we were worried about what Carla's husband might have told them to do to Anton. So in case the husband was not there in person and they did not know who Anton was, we all printed little cards which we pinned to our person saying, 'I AM NOT ANTON'.

In the event, the husband never showed his face, and we had another wonderful week of polo played in incredibly hot weather, hosted by Will Farish, who later became American Ambassador in London. On one day we were taken round the NASA space centre at a time when 'Sky Lab' was having problems, and it was fascinating to see, at first-hand, the huge army of technicians working to sort out the problem so many miles away in space.

From Houston to Dallas was another splendid week. I stayed with Norman Brinker, who had married the famous tennis player Maureen Connolly. Had 'Little Mo' not suffered a riding accident and broken her leg, she would probably have been regarded as the greatest female tennis player ever; as it was, she won three Wimbledon titles before she was twenty-one. I asked to be shown where John Kennedy had been shot (I know he was shot in the head but I wanted to see the street). This proved to be an unpopular request, as the people of Dallas were trying to forget that this great tragedy had happened in their fine city. Some hope! I got a taxi driver to drive me down the fateful route, and I looked back at the window through which Lee Harvey Oswald had fired his fatal shot, or shots. The window was marked with a big, black cross, which I thought rather drew attention to it, when it seems this is just what the people of Dallas did not want. It must have been a fine shot, as the window was a long way back. I looked at 'the grassy knoll' and figured that a shot from here would be a lot easier. However the Warren Commission did not ask me for my opinion.

Our polo bit ended in Chicago, where we were based with the Butler family at Oak Brook. Geoff's wife, Andrea, had also been with us throughout the tour so far, and here in Oak Brook she came face to face with a rival. Jorie, despite being some fifteen years older than Geoff, was definitely lining him up as number three and Geoff did not seem to mind a bit. Geoff and Andrea did eventually divorce and Geoff married Jorie. A&K opened large offices in the Butler empire buildings and Geoff spent more and more time in the States. But that was in the future. Meanwhile we were introduced to arena polo.

This is a three-a-side game played with a soft rubber ball in a boarded arena rather like a bullring, and played, as far as I could work out, with similar rules to those applying in a bullring. We were not very good at this, but we did win our last game of proper outdoor polo, and we celebrated by jumping, all of us still in our polo kit, into the club swimming pool, thus making it impossible to put our boots on next morning for the final arena polo battle.

We all went our separate ways after that, but what fun it had been, and never has my minimal polo talent been used to better advantage. From a business point of view, I made a lot of excellent contacts, and over the next year several people that I had met and 'chatted up' came on safari with us. I went on to the East Coast after the polo, ending up in New York, where I stayed with Paul Tracey, Harry's godfather and co-author of the successful musical about Africa called *Wait a Minim*. I visited the Rhodesia National Tourist Board office there, which was run by Renton Cowley. It was like getting into Fort Knox, the security was so tight.

It was while here that I heard of the shooting of two Canadian girls at Victoria Falls back home. This was very bad news for our image, and I tried to apologize or explain it to one potential client, who just said, "What ya getting so steamed up about? We have twice as many shootings here every day." I suppose that did put it into perspective, but it was the start of the rot; the Rhodesian bush war – liberation struggle, whatever you like to call it – had started and a lot of the good I had done on my tour of America was soon cancelled out by reports such as the Falls' shooting.

My parents were still very busy in Kenya doing courier work for Geoff, and my mother made good friends with a female vet from Rhode Island. Dr Chris Sidler loved Africa and, in particular, birds. She did a couple of safaris with my mother, who then persuaded her to do a trip with us. As it was very much a family contact, I felt obliged to take out Chris and her three friends myself. This I did, doing the usual sort of things in Rhodesia, then driving down to Gorongoza before they flew out of Beira.

It was 1974 by now, and the independence struggle in Mozambique was hotting up even more than in Rhodesia. The long time ruler of Portugal – Salazar – had been toppled and the Portuguese troops sent to fight their colonial war were badly trained, badly equipped and totally unmotivated. Samora Machel's Frelimo were clearly winning. The north of the country was by now wholly occupied and under the control of Frelimo, and they had even infiltrated down as far as the Beira/Rhodesia railway line, where they staged sporadic ambushes.

I was sitting at dinner one night in Chitengo lodge, Gorongoza, with the Sidler party when the room was suddenly filled with what appeared to be angry hornets. It was not hornets at all but a Frelimo gang opening up on the lodge with their AKs (AK, in this instance, did not stand for Abercrombie or Kent, but the make of the automatic assault rifle they were using). The gang was beaten off and no one was hurt, but it was a scary experience and not the sort of thing that American tourists appreciate. This effectively spelt the end of our involvement in Mozambique. It was also the beginning of the end for beautiful Gorongoza. Frelimo soon took over the whole area and slaughtered every living thing in that wonderful park to feed their troops. As I write this some thirty-odd years later, some efforts are being made to restock Gorongoza and I am keen to go back there to have a look.

Chris Sidler was made of stern stuff, and when we reopened our safari business after Zimbabwe independence in 1980 she did two more safaris with me in the new Zimbabwe, Botswana and Zambia. But that is another story. As far as Abercrombie South was concerned the writing was well and truly on the wall. Our bookings, so promising after the American polo trip, started to be cancelled, and they finally dried up altogether, no one wanting to come to a country engaged in a terrorist war.

CHAPTER 16

Bush War

OUR SAFARIS MAY HAVE LASTED UNTIL 1974, but as early as 1972 two groups of African Nationalists, who had been trained outside Rhodesia in places like Tanzania, Ethiopia or even East Germany and Russia, decided that it was time to launch the liberation struggle against Ian Smith's regime. Based in Zambia were Joshua Nkomo's ZIPRA forces, while the ZANU forces, under the more disputed leadership of Ndabaningi Sithole, Herbert Chitepo, Josiah Tongogara and Robert Mugabe were based initially in northern Mozambique, and later, when that country attained independence from Portugal in 1975, throughout the whole country.

We in Rhodesia knew perfectly well that there were forces ranged against us, but I do not think that we knew quite how serious this threat was. Whether the government did or not, I do not know, but certainly they did not tell us farmers. It was therefore quite a shock suddenly to hear just before Christmas in 1972 that farmers in the Centenary area had been attacked by terrorists with sophisticated rocket launchers and automatic rifles. Further, the police on rushing to the scene had been blown up by landmines, put there by the same terrorists anticipating just such a reaction.

We, of course, referred to them unquestionably as 'terrorists' or 'terrs', or more officially as 'communist terrorists'. The word 'freedom fighter' was totally unknown.

Most of us farmers had by now joined the Police Reserve, and we attended what were fairly relaxed training days about once a month, when we were taught how to use an FN automatic rifle, amongst other things. We also installed in our houses a type of radio system, where we would communicate with each other as well as with the local police station without resorting to the highly unreliable telephone. This was known as 'the Agric Alert' and from then on it played a very important part in our lives. It meant that we could keep in touch with each other and hear exactly what was going on in any given area or situation. When the bush war ended in 1979 we kept our 'Agric' sets and used them for domestic and social communication.

We were shaken by the events reported from Centenary but thought that it would be an isolated incident and soon dealt with. It wasn't, of course, it was the start of a long, bloody campaign which eventually resulted in Rhodesia becoming Zimbabwe and Robert Mugabe sitting where Ian Smith then was.

However Centenary was a long way from Wedza and life continued much as before – until April Fool's Day 1973 that is, and this was no joke. Fran and I were relaxing after lunch when the Agric suddenly started blaring out. It was Ian Murray, the manager of nearby 'Fair Adventure Farm' and the leader of our local Police Reserve stick. This was an emergency, he was saying, and all members of the Police Reserve should report to 'Fair Adventure' immediately. Strangely, he did not say what the emergency was. Like a good reservist, I immediately changed into my police uniform and, leaving Fran and two small boys alone on the farm, drove the ten miles or so to 'Fair Adventure'.

At 'Fair Adventure' all was chaos. Cars with confused farmers were arriving in a stream, the regular police were rampaging around, rumours flew in all directions and no one seemed to be in charge. Finally, we were all told to assemble in one room of the farmhouse, and the member-in-charge from Wedza's regular police, Tony Glover, addressed us. The news was chilling. Andries Joubert, the young owner of the next door farm, 'Chard', had been shot by a gang of terrorists while investigating a report of strangers near a maize land not far from our own farm boundary.

My first reaction was – Christ! Where are these terrorists now? My wife and two sons are alone on 'Chirume' only a few miles from where the shooting occurred – while the entire complement of the area's menfolk plus all the guns are assembled here. I think this thought occurred to others as well, because the first plan that was made was to collect all women and children in two or three secure houses, so Fran and the boys went to her parents at 'Scorror', together with several other families.

It seemed that Andries had been told about these strangers by his gang of workers and told that they were resting, 'in that kopje'. Naïvely, in hindsight, Andries wandered over to the kopje, parted some bushes and there was a small party of five or six young men, all armed with AK assault rifles, sitting round a fire. As soon as they saw Andries they shot him in the head and ran off. The labour gang, hearing the shot, soon found the body and raised the alarm. All this had happened about two hours before, so somewhere nearby was a gang of armed terrorists quite prepared to shoot on sight. The quicker we found them the better and so, for the time being anyway, that was our job.

Ian Murray was in his element. He had been a sergeant-major during the war and quickly took charge of we police reservists, while the regular police made their own plans. We set up roadblocks on all the roads and drove around questioning any African we met, in the hope that he might have seen some suspicious characters. Meanwhile, help was forthcoming from Marandellas and even Salisbury, in the shape of tracker dogs and PATU sticks.

PATU stood for Police Anti-Terrorist Unit and was comprised of reservists like us, only usually younger and better trained. There were usually five or six in a stick and they stuck together as a unit throughout the bush war, responding to just the sort of situation that had arisen in Wedza.

With all women and children now hopefully safe, we were on duty until the terrorists were found. There were about six of our Police Reserve sticks and we took it in turns to have at least two on duty twenty-four hours a day. On the third night our lot – Ian Murray, Ralph Collins, Paul Edridge, Harry Nel and myself – were driving down the Save West road at about eleven o'clock when, approaching the high level bridge over the river, we saw the light of a small fire burning in one of the Bita kopjes.

This was suspicious, and we reported it by radio to the officer in charge of this operation. Not wanting to alert anyone who might have been sitting by that fire, we decided not to drive back the same way, so went on over the bridge and through the Save North small-scale farming area, eventually crossing back into our area via the low-level bridge on Rudi Erasmus's farm, and not getting back to base until the early hours. A couple of PATU sticks were deployed at first light and they combed the kopjes, eventually flushing out the gang, who had in fact been by that fire. Part of the gang then tried to hide in John Bibby's tobacco barns. One terrorist was shot dead and another wounded and captured. Under interrogation, the terrorist admitted that he had been trained in Russia, some five years ago, and since then had been living in Zambia. The main purpose of his coming back to Rhodesia now was to recruit more young men to their cause. I think Andries was unlucky; if he had not stumbled upon the gang, they would almost certainly not have drawn attention to themselves. As far as I know, the other members of the gang were not caught and after being on the go for some five days we were stood down and all went back to our farms.

This turned out to be an isolated incident in Wedza and there were no more such scares for some time, but it woke us up pretty smartly to the fact that the terrorist threat to the country was very real and had been planned for a considerable time. Until now all our houses had stood in large gardens which were fenced off from the rest of the farm by a conventional four-strand barbed-wire fence. Now the government granted each farmer in isolated areas one thousand Rhodesian dollars (approx GBP1,000) to erect a proper ten-foot-high security fence round his house and part of the garden. Many people objected to doing this, saying they disliked living in a 'concentration camp'. However, as news continued to come in from other areas of lonely farmhouses being attacked, it was not too long before every farmhouse in Wedza was security fenced. Certainly we did it at 'Chirume' and, having got over the unpleasant sensation of being surrounded by a high wire mesh fence, found it incredibly useful. Quite apart from increasing our security, it was wonderful at keeping dogs in and horses out of the garden.

Comparative calm may have returned to Wedza, but in many farming areas bordering Tribal Trust Lands (TTLs), particularly if that TTL stretched as far as the national border with Zambia or Mozambique, there were more and more attacks on farms, along with ambushes and landmines on dirt roads. Any white male leaving school was immediately called up, underwent military training and was committed to serving in some branch of the security forces, more or less indefinitely. Then the younger reservists, whether police or army, started to be called up for tours of duty of anything up to six weeks at a time. Manpower was clearly getting short.

I was thirty-six then, so not in the first flush of youth, but suddenly we were told that our Wedza Police Reserve sticks would also be called up, and initially we would do a seventeen-day stint in some area where more security forces were needed. It was comparatively quiet in Wedza, but the thought of abandoning our farms and families for this length of time was not that great.

As we were to be deployed into areas where terrorists were pretty active, it was felt that we needed to be jolted out of our civilian complacency and generally be sharpened up for active service. To this end, we were sent off to a sort of training camp in the Mazoe Valley. 'We', on this initial deployment, were Ralph Collins as stick leader, Harry and Frikkie Nel, John Bibby and me. After our three days' intensive training we assembled at the police headquarters in Salisbury, together with perhaps three hundred other farmers from all over Mashonaland. We all lined up on 'hard square', early one morning and were addressed by the deputy commissioner of police, Allen. He thanked us for volunteering to do this duty and stressed how important it was. At this stage we were in fact volunteers, but later any able-bodied man under the age of fifty-five would be called up to help.

Everyone was a bit embarrassed at being there and did not quite know how to carry it off. Some joked and talked very loudly, others congregated in small groups with friends from other areas, while some were clearly quite worried over what they were letting themselves in for. I was not particularly happy about the whole thing; I was not frightened, but I disliked being lumped together with a bunch of other guys whom I only knew slightly, and with whom I would have to be very closely involved for the next two weeks in unknown circumstances.

My main mate was John Bibby. I knew him a bit better than the others and so we teamed up together and shared guard duties and generally backed each other up on patrol. John had been at Eton (where I might have gone), and had come out to farm in Rhodesia as a young man. After initially working for the Seager family in Wedza, he had ended up buying his father's farm back from the Land Bank. His father, a delightful old colonel, had been one of the many ex-military gentlemen to go under due to lack of any sort of experience of African farming methods.

We all left 'hard square' in the back of a seven-tonne lorry and drove north, through Bindura to Mount Darwin. There were still white commercial farmers in the Mount Darwin area, but they were even then under a lot of pressure, as they were on the edge of a TTL that stretched directly to the northern Mozambique border and was thus a main entrance route for terrorists to Rhodesia. The night we arrived we had to lay an ambush at a farm store some ten miles from the town. It was cold and damp, so memories of my days (and nights) in the Aberdares ambushing Mau Mau came flooding back. We had, in a way, won that war fifteen years ago – for all the long-term good it did us – but what would be the result of this one? Clearly it was a different type of war. Now, we were fighting terrorists who had received a certain amount of training and who were armed with quite sophisticated weapons, but there would not be so much cloak-and-dagger sort of stuff, and things like oaths were not involved.

Instead Mao's *Little Red Book* was their bible. But the overall aim was just the same, to get us out of what they thought of as their country.

During the Mau Mau we had had the backing of Britain – morally, physically and, perhaps most important, financially. Now, we Rhodesians were outcasts as far as most of the rest of the world was concerned. We did, however, have the support of South Africa, at least morally and physically. Based in Mount Darwin were a number of South Africans, and a pretty rough lot they were too. South Africa would not go so far as to send their army in to help us, so the troops, if that is the right word, were virtually mercenaries, but they were a great help. When John Vorster, the then South African Prime Minister, eventually withdrew this help, following pressure from America's Henry Kissinger, it really spelt the end for Ian Smith and his government. Even with the help of extended call-ups for all able-bodied males up to the age of fifty-five, there was just not enough manpower to cope with the ever-increasing numbers of insurgents.

But there were another six bloody years to go yet before a truce was signed. After our ambush, we boarded another lorry and were driven down the Zambezi escarpment to the border town of Mukumbura, where we were installed in a large tented camp. It seems that the plan was to lay a minefield the full length of the Mozambique/Rhodesian border and to erect a strong wire-mesh fence – an ambitious scheme known as Operation Tampax because of the so-called cordon sanitaire.

When we got to Mukumbura, our stick leader Ralph Collins was called to a meeting with other stick leaders by the officer in charge of the camp. On his return he briefed us on our duties for the ensuing two weeks. Basically, we were to be guards for the men who were laying the landmines. We would go out ahead of them in the mornings to clear any terrs out of the way, and then patrol the bush on either side of the area where they were working for the rest of the day. Like all wars, most of it was deadly boring. It was very hot, very dusty and very uncomfortable back in the camp. Each night a pair of us had to do a two-hour guard stint, which meant sitting behind some sandbags and gazing into the African night in the hope (or not) of spotting an impending raid on the camp. I did my watches with John Bibby, and we never saw anything exciting at all – just lost a lot of sleep.

At the end of the two weeks we were flown back to Salisbury. The first bit, as far as Mount Darwin, we flew very low indeed. This was to prevent any terrorist with a Sam missile from having a go at us. This was a very real threat, as shown only a month later when a commercial airliner was brought down in just this manner flying a scheduled flight from Kariba to Salisbury.

"Well, it will be nice to put our rifles away for a bit," I said to Mike Bartlett, as we were dismissed back at 'hard square'.

"Yes," he agreed, "but when will we be able to put them away for good?" When indeed?

In Salisbury, we were picked up by our wives and driven home. It had been a revealing experience. Things must be much more serious than they had let on to us if the government wanted to put a minefield round the whole country. And they were more serious. This was just the first of many call-ups for us, and in no time we were doing four or five a year, as well as frequently being called out for some problems while at home.

Quite soon it became ridiculous. It was dangerous living on an isolated farm in Wedza, and when I was called up to go and patrol some border we had to employ a 'bright light' to come and look after Fran and the boys. 'Bright lights' were so called because they invariably came from the lights of Salisbury to do protection duty on remote farms. Why could I not just stay at home and look after my own?

It took a long time for this to sink in to the minds of the Defence chiefs and meanwhile I was shipped off all over the place with a variety of companions. The number in each stick was reduced to four, and one learned to get a bit choosy as to who one went with. Definitely not Neville Tapson, he snored far too much. Not Ricardo Belli, Rick Holme's Italian manager, either; he was definitely too excitable to have a rifle in his hands. Harry Nel was still fighting the Boer War, so one was not quite sure where his loyalties lay. Frikkie Nel did not play bridge, so that ruled out a decent four for the many dreary hours when nothing significant was happening. Merv Fagg filled his water bottle with neat vodka and took copious draughts of it throughout the morning, and was inclined to get a bit sleepy in the afternoon. So one had to be careful.

I went to many interesting places that in the normal course of events I would never have visited. Nearly always I had a good other three with me: usually John Bibby, Mike Bartlett, David Hamilton, Ian Murray or 'Cpl' Mike Hill; all played bridge, none snored too badly, they were moderately safe with an FN, and all put neat water in their water bottles. We spent a couple of weeks at Karanda Mission, not far from Mukumbura in the far north of the country. This was quite hairy, as there were terrs all over the place and we had to escort frequent casualties from landmines and ambushes into the mission hospital. At one stage we all had to donate blood, following a particularly nasty ambush nearby. One of the casualties was a young European, so, as the mission hospital was only manned by blacks at night, we had to post a permanent guard over him in case terrs came into the hospital to finish him off. This was odd reasoning, to my mind – all the other casualties were black, local troops enlisted in the RAR (Rhodesian African Rifles). Why would the terrs not want to finish them off, every bit as much as the white man?

There was one pathetic case of a black woman who sat silently all day on the grass outside the entrance to the hospital. Her teeth were bared in a permanent and ghastly parody of a smile. This was because her lips had been hacked off and tongue cut out by terrs, who accused her of being a 'sell-out', one who had given information to the security forces about their whereabouts. It was a great deterrent to anyone wanting to give us information, and I rather wondered why the wretched woman was allowed to sit on the grass where so many would-be informers could see what might happen to them if they did tell us anything.

I think it is fair to say that, even at that comparatively early stage of the war, the security forces were probably in control of any given area during the day, but the nights belonged to the insurgents – and that was when lips were cut off and tongues cut out. To win a terrorist war, one has to win the hearts and minds of the people, and certainly in these remote tribal areas there was not a hope of us doing that. I wondered if we had ever won those hearts and minds during my time fighting the Mau Mau. I worked with seemingly loyal tribal policemen, but what did they really think? What did all the villagers doing forced labour think?

The Rhodesian Government was desperate to portray an aura of normality, despite what was going on all over the place, and they still wanted tourists from South Africa to come and visit the many lovely, cheap holiday destinations dotted all over the country. The terrs knew this and got busy ambushing the main roads into the country. The road from the little border post of Beit Bridge on the Limpopo to the first town of any consequence, Fort Victoria (now Masvingo), is two hundred and eighty kilometres long. In those days the road was not very busy, and it was easy to lie in the long grass and thick bush on the side of the road with an AK rifle or rocket launcher in your hands, and to fire at the first passing tourist. Like the removal of informers' lips, this acted as a very good deterrent to potential tourists.

The government, like Baldrick, hatched a cunning plan. They would provide an escort service for all cars driving up to Rhodesia from South Africa. Suddenly I found myself posted to Beit Bridge, where Ian Murray, Mike Bartlett, the Corporal and myself were issued with a stripped-down Land Rover and an automatic type of Bren gun previously used in aeroplanes in the Second World War. This antique but effective weapon we mounted on the front of the Land Rover, and one of us stood up and pretended we knew how to fire it, another drove, while the last two sat with their FNs pointing out to either side of the road. There were three such vehicles so armed, and at six-thirty each morning we formed up on the main road and waited to see how many motorists wanted to risk the journey to Fort Victoria under our protection.

There were usually about twelve or fifteen, so one armed Land Rover would go in front, one in the middle and one at the back; then off we went, just as fast as the slowest of our convoy could manage. It would take just over three hours to get to Fort Victoria, and once there we would have something to eat, and then reassemble for a return run in the afternoon.

All this added up to a lot of mileage up and down the Beit Bridge road. I cannot remember exactly how many call-ups I did on this convoy duty. It was not always to and from Beit Bridge, nor were we always based there. Sometimes we were based at Fort Vic. and did the shorter run to Birchenough Bridge, sometimes at Rutenga, about halfway to the border. Occasionally we did not do convoy work but undertook foot patrols through the bush on either side of the road. Once we were posted to Bikita and had to escort the veterinary department officials while they patrolled the Fort Victoria/Mutare road shooting any animals they saw. This road was heavily fenced on each side, with the fence meant to be the boundary between the foot-and-mouth infected area in the south and the hopefully clean area to the north.

Despite sanctions, Rhodesia still had a very lucrative beef export market to Europe, and the European vets would, quite rightly, only accept beef from an area free from foot-and-mouth. The area north of the road was deemed to be clean and it was vital to keep it that way. With the general breakdown in the security situation, there was a grave danger that cattle would stray through any breaks in the fence. My cattle on 'Chirume' were nearly all destined to be exported to Europe if possible, as the price we got for these exports was much better than for anything sold locally. I was, therefore, very keen that the clean area should remain clean.

Being based at the little town of Bikita for this exercise, we had to drive some ten miles on a dirt road before reaching the main tar highway. This was very scary, as the dirt road was frequently mined, so we were issued with an extraordinary vehicle known as a 'hyena'. This was basically a Land Rover chassis and engine, but with a back made of inch-thick metal plate and built in the shape of a vee. We sat in this on metal seats and were tightly strapped down. The idea was that if we went over a mine the blast would deflect up either side of the vee and not hurt us (too much), and that being strapped tightly in we would be blown upwards with the vehicle and not thrown out. Believe it or not, it worked, and many lives were saved by this clever invention. To this day one still sees the occasional 'hyena' being driven around by the police. Not because there are any landmines these days, but just because of a gross shortage of transport.

There were several variations on this theme, and some amazing looking vehicles began appearing on the Rhodesian roads. Many farmers had their Land Rovers adapted, and for a long time we had a 'hyena' based at 'Chirume'. I never was blown up by a mine, so am not part of that élite club of people who were. I did see the results, though, on both vehicles and people who had undergone this somewhat unique experience. The vehicles were never quite the same again, and the people frequently had burst eardrums, so I was not too disappointed never to have joined the club. Cpl Hill's son Alan was called up for his National Service and, having completed the initial obligatory two years, was returning from the Zambezi valley for a bit of leave when the lorry he was travelling on hit a landmine. The lorry was big and heavy and protected by sandbags on the floor, but it did not have the vee configuration. Alan was sitting in the very back of the lorry, and it was the rear wheel which detonated the mine. Alan was killed. After Andries, it was the first major casualty suffered by a member of the Wedza community and it affected the whole area tremendously.

Eventually, it dawned on the authorities that it was crazy to send us away from Wedza on call-up duty, as we would have more than enough to do protecting our own area. The war was hotting up, and attacks started happening on Wedza farmers who bordered the TTLs. Every night we sat in the sitting room of 'Chirume' with the 'Agric Alert' ready and my FN to hand. Every night also there was a roll call and a brief 'sitrep' (situation report), to keep us up-to-date as to what was happening in the area. Nine o'clock tended to be a bad time. All too often about this time, the panic button on the 'Agric Alert' would start beeping and a frightened voice would let us all know that they were under attack. This would mean that a group of terrs were outside their security fence, firing into the house with automatic rifles and rocket launchers. If left undisturbed, the terrs could of course easily have cut the fence and quite soon broken into the house, with horrible results. It was therefore essential that some form of reaction stick got there as quickly as possible to prevent this happening.

For every house in the Wedza area there was an allocated stick of four or five men who would react in the event of that house being attacked. Obviously, it was the nearest four or five, and they would have a prearranged plan as to where to meet and go to the farmer's assistance in a mine-protected vehicle. It was thought to be unsafe to drive to the homestead by the normal farm road, as it would almost certainly be mined. So each home had what was called a 'green route' leading there – a normally unused track which, hopefully, the terrs did not know about and so would not have mined.

'Chirume' was situated some fifteen miles from the nearest TTL, which meant that I was quite a long way from the border farms that were most prone to attack, but I was called out often enough. This in itself was risky, as it meant leaving your wife and family alone in the house. Some wives moved into town, while others would spend the night with neighbours. Fran refused to move anywhere and learned how to use a Sten gun.

John Bibby's farm, 'Bita', was situated right on the Save River, which formed the boundary with the Save North TTL, so it was only a matter of time before he was attacked. This was done in some style; the terrs wheeled an ancient cannon on to the kopje behind John and Jill's house, and started blazing away. It was quite an unpleasant experience, but I do not think that John was ever in any immediate danger. The shells certainly did a little damage to his tobacco barns – some two hundred yards from the house – and frightened some cattle in a nearby kraal, but nothing came remotely near the house. By the time we arrived, the terrs had run out of ammo and retired back across the river, leaving some attractive brass shell cases which John had made into lampstands.

Not all attacks on houses ended so easily, and a young policeman staying in a house in 'Dutchman's Corner' was killed when a rocket scored a direct hit on the house. Another nasty trait was beginning to emerge as well. Ambushes were being laid on the roads to catch late travellers. The terrs did not dare draw attention to themselves early in the day, as they knew there would be an immediate reaction, but late afternoon was another story; they could escape under cover of darkness and be well away by the time any security forces arrived on the scene.

Peter Gilpin had been a great help to me with advice on how best to look after cattle in the Wedza area. He had a large farm bordering Charter Estate, but had recently bought another farm near the Wedza Country Club. One afternoon he called in to see us on his way back from this new farm and stayed for a cup of tea. Half an hour later he and his son, Alistair, were ambushed and killed as they turned into the road leading to their home. As a result of this we all tried to be off the road and back behind our security fences by four-thirty at the latest.

The regular police were always called out to these incidents, of course, but there was plenty going on in the Wedza TTL as well, so they were pretty hard-pressed. In those days there was a white member-in-charge and probably two or three other young white officers. All the other ranks would be black, and a very decent bunch they were. For most of the war in Wedza, our member-in-charge was Pete Saunders. He was a nice enough guy and probably a very good ordinary policeman, but these were far from ordinary times and he had had no training in the sort of situation in which he found himself. The result was that senior members of the farming community, some of whom had served in the Second World War, more or less took charge of the security in the farming area. Two prominent leaders in this regard were Norman Travers and Ian Murray.

Our farming was suffering, as we were being called out for some problem or other most days, so we decided to recruit our own little band of mercenaries. In addition, so that we could help the hard-pressed regular police, we detailed in turn one of our number to base himself at Wedza police station for a week at a time and to be on call twenty-four hours a day, to deploy the mercenaries and to call on help from anyone else whenever the need arose. There were perhaps sixty farmers in the Wedza area and we levied a tax on ourselves to pay the mercenaries. First to be recruited was a young British Army captain, who was bored with regular soldiering and wanted a bit of excitement; his name was Mark Colacicchi and he was put in charge of a motley crew of five, one of whom was old Ted Maberly's son, Simmy. They worked for us for about two years – 1978/79 – and, while achieving nothing spectacular, did help to ease the load on the rest of us.

I was appointed stick leader of the bunch of farmers in our part of Wedza and also did weekly turns of duty at Wedza police station. It was a funny sort of chain of command. I, or any of the others based at Wedza, had no real authority over our fellow farmers. On one occasion I needed a stick of four or five to do a job on the Save, but the guys I wanted to do it said they couldn't, as they were going to a funeral. No way could I order them to do anything; it was more a matter of suggesting that this or that might be a good idea and asking if they would do it. Luckily, Wedza was a very friendly, close-knit community and there were incredibly few personality clashes. We were all in it together and determined to see it through.

During one of my stints at the police post in Wedza, Ian Smith decided to come and talk to the people of Wedza about the proposed 'internal settlement'. He brought with him Chief Chirau and Ndabaningi Sithole. Bishop Muzorewa was meant to come as well but didn't, as he wanted to make some petty point or other. The terrs knew perfectly well that they were coming; they did not want the locals to turn up and listen to Smith, and so they decided to mortar Wedza police camp the night before. I was on duty there that night and busy playing poker with Pete Saunders, the member-in-charge, and Ant Fynn (then a district officer) and a couple of others. We all rushed outside and tore around amongst the big gum trees that are a feature of Wedza Township. There is not a lot you can do to stop mortars once they have been fired, and we had no idea where they were going to land anyway. We reckoned that they were targeting the police camp, so that was probably the safest place to be. Eventually we all got into police vehicles and charged off in the direction from which we assumed the mortars were being fired. This seemed to work as the bombardment ceased and we were able to resume our interrupted game of poker.

Ian Smith and his party duly flew into the little Wedza airstrip next morning under tight security and we all stationed ourselves on a small kopje overlooking the market place where the meeting was due to take place. Very few people turned up; the terrs had done their homework well and the little delegation soon flew back to Salisbury and we came down from our kopje.

I think that, even at that stage, the terrs pretty much controlled the Wedza TTL. Cattle theft was becoming rife, with animals driven off our farms almost nightly, and I don't mean just one or two – whole herds were driven off and disappeared without trace into the TTL. On one occasion Pat Hamilton drove us all frantic by charging off after them on her horse, disappearing, alone, into the depths of the terrorist-infested TTL. They must have seen her coming, and why they did not shoot her I will never know – but, then, she is a Hamilton! With the police we did try to arrange some more organized follow-ups to these cattle thefts, but frankly achieved very little more than Pat. Coming back from one of these forays we slowed down for a corner, and then had to stop very quickly – there in the middle of the road were five very dead human bodies. All had been shot some three or four days before and just dumped there – and they were decomposing and stinking. I never really found out why they had been shot; a lot of people were shot in those days. We had to load them on to our vehicles and take them back to Wedza for identification. I did not enjoy my lunch that day.

There was much speculation at about this time over how to solve the whole problem. One school of thought was that we had to talk to the terrorist leaders and see if we could not come to some form of compromise. A leading advocate of this strategy was Alan Savory, a conservationist whom we had got to know when he was the leading light in promoting the 'high density short duration' grazing system for cattle (sometimes called 'The Savory System'). Alan became an MP and strongly advocated dialogue.

"You will have to speak to them some time," he maintained, "so the sooner the better."

This sort of attitude was regarded as little short of treason by the old guard.

"We will never speak to those damned terrorists," they said. "Shoot the buggers, that's the only language they understand." Looking back, it is quite incredible how naïve they were. Of course we had to talk to them eventually.

The result of us all sticking together as a community was that no single farm was abandoned, and at the end of the war Wedza as a farming district was intact. This was a lot more than could be said for many other areas. In these, individual farmers would start living in town, thus creating a gap, which had to be filled by neighbours. The more gaps there were the bigger the burden put on those who remained on their farms, and eventually it was unsustainable and the whole area would collapse.

The nearest we came to this happening was in the Wye Valley area. There was a line of four farms stretching like a peninsula into the Wedza TTL, so the last farm was surrounded on three sides by TTL, and the farmer, Norman Mossop, was under enormous pressure. He finally could take no more and left. We were therefore left with an empty farm in a very vulnerable area, so we advertised for someone to come and live there and farm the place. The government-backed AFC (Agricultural Finance Corporation) agreed to lend money on generous terms to anyone who would take on 'Wye Valley' and it was agreed that at least one of us would live with the new owner at all times to bolster his resolve. We soon got a taker in the form of one Derek Hurlston. Derek was over fifty and had 'been around'. He had been at school in England with David Hamilton, so David championed his cause and we all took it in turns to spend a week with Derek on 'Wye Valley Farm'.

I did two stints there and on one occasion the place got mortared from the hill behind the house. This scared the daylights out of me, but Derek was totally unmoved. "These guys seem to be taking the war seriously," he said, as he topped up his glass. Derek saw the war out on 'Wye Valley' but went broke in the process, in that he spent all the AFC money loaned to him and was unable to repay it. He then came to live at 'Leeds', after we had bought it from John Prentice, and ran 'Bath' store, which he referred to as 'his emporium'. This did not work out financially either, so he married his son's mother-in-law, who happened to be very well off, and retired comfortably to England.

When the war started in the Centenary area in 1972, I had said that if it ever got that bad in Wedza, I would move on and not risk my family in a war we could not win. By 1977 Wedza was in a far more precarious position than Centenary ever was, but there never seemed to have been any one incident to tip the balance and make us move. We never seriously considered it all. Did we really believe we could win this type of war? Ian Smith spoke to us regularly on the radio and was always cautiously optimistic. Every few months there was some fresh initiative from Britain, America, Europe or South Africa. I cannot remember all the very forgettable people who were sent out to try and find a solution – Lord Pearce, David Owen, Ivor Richards, Tiny Rowland – all failed.

My old mate, Max Hastings, then a high-powered correspondent for the BBC, came and stayed with us on 'Chirume' at one stage, before he got deported. I asked him what he would do if he was in my position.

"Stay and fight, exactly as you are doing," he said, "but you will lose. Before long the terrorists you are fighting will be marching down First Street brandishing their AKs. It is an historic inevitability."

He was right, of course. Our cause was just and Smith was a very honest man. Fifty years earlier, even twenty years earlier, he, and we, would have been supported to the hilt by all western powers and helped to expel these criminal communist terrorists. But not in the mid-1970s. The winds of change were howling through Africa and no one was prepared to stop them.

Finally the then American Secretary of State, Henry Kissinger, came – not to Rhodesia, but to South Africa. Here, he told the South African Premier, John Vorster, that if he did not stop supporting Rhodesia there would be sanctions imposed on South Africa. I do not know, of course, exactly what he said, but it was something pretty drastic along those lines, and he succeeded in convincing Vorster to ditch his friend and neighbour Ian Smith.

Why did Kissinger care what was happening in Rhodesia? His country had done exactly the same thing in their time. They had unilaterally declared their independence from Britain. They had then gone on to slaughter so many of the local inhabitants that they, the colonizers, outnumbered the rightful owners of the land and were able to put the few who remained into 'Reservations' and ignore them. This sort of thing was completely unacceptable though in the enlightened era of 1975. The fact that far worse things are happening in the enlightened era of 2006 does not seem to matter anymore, as it is blacks doing it – to black and white – so it is OK. In the 1970s it was whites doing it to blacks, and the white, western world had a guilty conscience because they had been doing it for so long themselves. No way could Rhodesia hold out against this sort of pressure.

I think it is fair to say that neither side would have won our war for a very long time. The whites, in the shape of Smith's Rhodesian Front Party, were still very much in charge, and outwardly at any rate controlled everything. But, particularly after dark, the terrs were in charge of what happened on the ground. There would have been more and more successful terrorist attacks – like the shooting down of commercial airliners and the burning of the Salisbury fuel depot. The strain on the local white people, being called up so frequently, would have had an escalating adverse affect and the death toll would have mounted inexorably on both sides.

The withdrawal of South Africa's support has been detailed by Ian Smith in his book, *The Great Betrayal.* He certainly saw it as such, but it did force him to negotiate. I was, and still am, a great admirer of Ian

Smith. It is fashionable these days to deride him and claim to know that he was bound to lose, but basically he was an honest man and, unlike other leaders, did have the good of the country at heart. He never made any money out of being Prime Minister and continued to live here after independence. It is also interesting to note that he would often walk to work, totally unarmed and accompanied by a single security guard. Compare this with today's convoy of expensive vehicles, motorbike outriders, heavily armed troops and an ambulance that have to support Mugabe whenever he steps outside his fortified house.

My sister-in-law's brother, Rob Wilson, while still at school, was doing an essay on the Rhodesia situation. He was walking past Ian Smith's official residence in Chancellor Avenue, Harare one day and, half as a joke, asked the guard at the gate if he could have a word with the Prime Minister.

"Hang on, I'll ask," was the reply and the guard got on the blower to the house.

A few minutes later he got back to Rob, gave him a pass and sent him in to see Smithy, who was having a cup of tea at the time. Imagine that sort of thing happening today with Mugabe.

The internal settlement, with the diminutive Bishop Muzorewa trying to rule the country, was a farce. One of his ministers, Francis Zindoga, bought Frikkie Nel's farm just down the road from us – bought, mind you, and not just took, as happens these days. But he was a bit of a joke and had no real authority.

The result was the Lancaster House Conference, the return of Rhodesia to British rule, complete with a Governor – Lord Soames – and finally 'free and fair' elections, contested by all the main parties.

Robert Mugabe was by now leader of the main Mashona lot and they, for the sake of supposed unity, had joined up with Joshua Nkomo and his Matabeles to form the Patriotic Front. This was all very well when they were all against the whites, but in reality, the Mashonas and Matabeles hated each other and no way were they going to stand together in an election between blacks. As a result Mugabe went on his own, calling his party ZANU (PF), and Nkomo went his way with ZAPU. We, the whites, wanted Muzorewa's UANC to win, as he had at least co-operated with us and seemed amenable, if ineffective. We thought and hoped that the split in the Patriotic Front ranks would give him an excellent chance of winning. Little did we know. Little did anybody know. It is amazing how bad and totally wrong all intelligence was. Intimidation was rife everywhere and of the 80 seats up for grabs, Muzorewa won precisely three. Nkomo got all twenty available in Matabeleland and Mugabe got the rest. Ian Smith's Rhodesian Front was allowed twenty specially reserved seats.

The lead-up to the elections had been interesting, as all the terrs out in the bush had to be informed that the war was now over, and that they should all congregate at designated assembly points and hand in their weapons. It was not easy to do this with the gangs so scattered and not easy to persuade all of them that it was not just a trick. Contingents of security forces from all over the world converged on Rhodesia and were deployed to the many assembly points in the bush. Having coffee in a small café in the middle of Salisbury, I was amazed to find myself sitting next to a bunch of Fijian soldiers on one side and Australian soldiers on the other. Not all the terrs knew where these assembly points were, but they did know that the war was meant to be over and they could come out of the bush quite safely.

I was driving back from 'Kuatora Farm', which I was leasing from Frikkie Kotze, when, near the turn-off to 'Skipton', Ralph Collins's farm, I ran slap bang into the middle of a gang of some hundred and fifty heavily armed terrs who were just walking up the road.

"SHIT," I thought. "I just hope someone has told them the war's over."

It was a very tense moment. I was on my own and had an FN rifle across my knees. I did not stop, but kept driving very slowly while they, equally slowly, parted to let me through. I waved my hand and tried to smile, but my lips stuck to my teeth. Eventually, I was through them and tried very hard not to accelerate away too fast, but once round a corner went like hell! It had been a nasty few minutes.

We all went to vote on election day and were amused to find an unarmed London bobby wandering around outside the polling booth, just to see that all was well. It was a nice touch. And we did manage to pinch his helmet, which later held a place of honour in Wedza Club. We took our labour along to vote as well, and wondered where they would put their cross – for Bishop Muzorewa's UANC party or Mugabe's ZANU (PF). There was certainly no overt intimidation at that election and it all went pretty smoothly.

We whites had been told that, if Mugabe won, we had better take whatever we could with us and drive for the border – fast. We urged our labour to vote for Muzorewa, but I do not think they did. The much-vaunted government intelligence could not have got it more wrong – they predicted a win for Muzorewa, but in fact he got only three seats and Mugabe won in a landslide.

CHAPTER 17

'Chirume' During the War

MEANWHILE, WHAT WAS HAPPENING BACK ON THE ranch? Farming activities all over the country had been severely disrupted for the last five years. First, farmers were obliged to leave their farms to do call-ups, then they were busily engaged in protecting their own area, and finally in several instances they were driven off the land altogether.

As I have said, Wedza succeeded in avoiding this last scenario, but it had taken quite a knock, mainly through hundreds of head of cattle having been stolen. We were cattle farmers but got off incredibly lightly as far as theft was concerned. The main reason for this was that 'Chirume' was situated far from the border of any TTL, so any potential rustler had to drive the cattle some fifteen miles through commercial farming land before reaching the comparative safety of the TTL. People like Natalie Seager, Ralph Collins and Rudi Erasmus, who lived nearer a TTL, suffered huge losses.

We in fact were able to cash in on other people's misfortunes, and despite my being away so much (or perhaps because of it) our farming venture actually prospered like never before. We were able to lease nearby farms and stock them with cattle bought with borrowed money. Cattle were cheap, as many people were getting rid of them before they were stolen, and auctioneers like H Shapiro (Cattle Co-op), Binks Holland and a young Englishman, Tim Wotton, were only too glad to find a buyer willing to take the risk of increasing his herd. And it was a risk, but I had little to lose.

In those five or six years I bought 'Raleigh Farm', which was just next door, from Ian and Jenny MacIlwaine, with money lent by the Agricultural Finance Corporation (AFC). I leased the lovely nine thousand acre 'Collace', situated on our southern boundary, from Bruce Campbell, leased 'Leeds' from John Prentice, and also at various times leased 'Kuatora' from Frikkie Kotze, 'Laurel' and 'Mount Arthur' from Jane Matthews and 'Eldoret' from the AFC. At the height of the war I was running over two thousand head of cattle.

I did not have many breeding cows but concentrated on fattening steers and heifers off the spring grass. Wedza is a very good cattle area with huge, wet vleis and usually gets early rain. If one burned the vleis in October and then got a bit of rain cattle were eating lovely protein-rich grass by early November. I would feed them up to four kilograms of low protein/high carbohydrate cubes per day and they would be pig fat by late January. Prices were high in January, as other areas found it difficult to get their cattle fat so early in the season. April/May was the usual time to slaughter cattle off the grass and consequently prices dipped sharply then. In late January 1977 I was sending off a truckload of thirty-five fat steers virtually every day. Marandellas, thirty-two miles down the road, had a brand-new and very sophisticated export abattoir and the CSC paid for the transport to get cattle there. For the first time in my life I was making quite a lot of money.

To run and feed this amount of cattle, I had to have quite a large labour force. The nucleus of this was on 'Chirume', where there were perhaps five men solely involved with cattle; then on each farm I leased I had another three, and their only job was to herd the cattle, feed them daily using an oxcart and check the fences. On 'Raleigh', the terrs did try to swipe my cattle and drive them off to the nearby Chimbwanda small-scale farming area, so I built a huge stockade all round the house; the cattle slept there, with Stanlec, the guy in charge, sleeping in the house and with a telephone line direct to me. There were plenty of outhouses full of stockfeed, dip, cattle medicines etc. outside the stockade, and the terrs started raiding these as well. Mick Malzer was in the army then and something of an expert on explosives, so he came over and booby-trapped all these buildings with grenades attached to a string, which pulled out the pin when you opened the door. Crude, but effective. Stanlec had to remember to go in by a secret back door.

A lot of my labour were from Malawi, having come down to work on farms in the Federation days. I found them better than the local Shona, perhaps because they had no ancestral home to go to in the country and therefore valued their job more highly. Their home was on the farm where they worked, and if they got sacked they had nowhere to go unless they got another job. When the farm invasions crippled the commercial farms in early 2000, these Malawians had as hard a time as anyone.

One of my best men was called Enoch Malunga, and he came from Mozambique. Whenever I leased a new farm I sent him there first to set up a modus operandi, and in the twenty years that I employed him he never really let me down. He and two others would be in charge of perhaps three hundred and fifty valuable cattle and I would only visit him once or twice a week. He had to dip them regularly, feed them every day and attend to any minor veterinary problems. It was a lot of responsibility at a time when there was a war on. The local police were pretty overstretched at that time, but on one occasion they saw fit to arrest Enoch. They took him to the cells in Wedza, leaving the cattle unattended, and rang me up. I hurried round to Wedza to find that Enoch had been arrested for stealing a cupful of salt. I always fed salt to my cattle and Enoch had helped himself to a cupful to aid his own cooking. Hardly a jailable offence or worth the policeman's time when there was so much else going on.

Rabe Jambo was my right hand man on 'Chirume'. He was a young Yao from Malawi and was one of the first people I employed. He and most of my other cattlemen attended a series of excellent week-long cattle management courses, laid on by the nearby Grasslands Research Station. It gave them all a very good basic knowledge of cattle management. Rabe died of AIDS in 1990 at a time when the Government refused to admit that the disease was a problem.

I am no mechanic, so, not wanting to be burdened with a lot of tractors that I did not know how to repair, I relied totally on work oxen to cart my stock feed around, to collect firewood for the house and even to plough the few acres on which I occasionally planted something. It certainly saved in garage bills, and when the oxen got too old we just fattened them up and sold them for more than one would have got for a beat-up tractor. Some of these oxen were wonderful characters. They all had names – Bosman, Flaxman, Muruweri, to name a few – and, in many cases, would come when called.

Selling so many cattle meant that I had to be continually buying more in, so I would probably attend a cattle sale at least once a week. Cattle Co-op and J S Holland were the two big well-established companies, but trying to break in was Tim Wotton. Tim had done a bit of farming in New Zealand, then worked for a fading auctioneering company in Salisbury called Gilchrist and Cooksey, before launching his own company, Tim Wotton Auctioneers or TWA. The big boys did not take kindly to this young whippersnapper trying to pinch some of their business, but I was keen enough to have him around as it meant another sale to go to; his prices were often a bit lower, as the big buyers did not always bother to attend his smaller sales. The only snag was that Tim could not offer the extended credit that the other two could, so I was always pretty pushed to pay him on time. Tim tried something that the other two outfits would not touch – trying to run a commercial auction in a wholly African farming area. He selected Hampshire small-scale farming area, just short of Enkeldoorn (now Chivu), down the main road from Salisbury. He would pitch up with his wife Felicity and Aaron, his trusty African assistant, and immediately be surrounded by a milling mass of sellers, African buyers with no money, kaffir dogs, goats, the local police force, and the very occasional European buyer such as myself.

The sale would start some forty-five minutes after the advertised time, when one skinny ox would be driven into a makeshift ring. With the arrival of this ox the noise level round the ring would increase several decibels. Tim would scream out requests for bids and we would respond in the conventional manner. Eventually there would be no more offers and Tim would knock the beast down to the highest bidder. This would be the cue for the seller of the ox to jump into the ring and complain about the price offered. Tim would remind him that he had agreed to accept the highest bid and that therefore the ox was sold. Half an hour later the ox would be driven out of the ring with its destination still uncertain. As far as the sellers were concerned, the end of the bidding merely signified the opening of negotiations.

Tim was patience personified, while Felicity calmly dished out tea and sandwiches in the background. I seldom bought very many cattle at these sales – it was just too complicated. But Tim's patience and good humour were rewarded one day when a bunch of heavily armed terrs pitched up in the middle of a sale. I think they were pretty keen on shooting Tim, but the assembled company persuaded them not to, saying that he was an OK murungu. I think Tim was lucky, because being an 'OK murungu' was not necessarily a passport to safety. In many cases it was these very people that the gooks wanted to get rid of, for fear that the locals would support them rather than themselves.

Despite my not buying a lot of his cattle and seldom paying him, Tim became a good friend and when I became chairman of the local cattle producers' association, I supported his bid to run sales in Marondera. These had previously been the exclusive preserve of H Shapiro and the Cattle Co-op, in the shape of Robbie Isaacson. Robbie did not take a bit kindly to the idea of competition on his patch and invited me to his grotty office in Speke Avenue. Here, he made it very clear that if I continued to support Tim's bid, the extended credit facilities that I enjoyed with his company would be considerably curtailed. Tim did run a few sales in Marandellas, using the showground rather than the smart sale pens.

With the breakdown of law and order in the south of the country, the dreaded foot-and-mouth disease spread up into Mashonaland and effectively put an end to our exporting of beef to Europe. This was a blow to us, as we specialized in fattening quality steers for the European market and got a premium price for doing so. However, there was still plenty of demand locally for our meat, as Rhodesian beef had acquired a worldwide reputation for quality and taste. A lot of it was fattened off the grass and this, which was my method, added something that purely pen-fed animals lacked.

On March 29, 1979 we got foot-and-mouth on 'Leeds'. I remember the date well because on that same day Fran gave birth to our third son – or 'another bloody boy!' as she remarked on being handed the squalling, wrinkled, little, pink thing. Jack Patrick had arrived in Marandellas hospital. I was there at his birth and then rushed back to 'Leeds' to meet Stuart Hargreaves, the Government vet. He confirmed the F & M and proceeded to inoculate the entire herd on that farm with the disease. Foot-and-mouth is not that serious a disease in a beef herd in dry conditions and it was better that all the cattle got it at once in order to limit the time span when it was around. It is interesting to note that while the disease was rampant on 'Leeds' it never spread to 'Chirume'.

Jack Patrick soon joined us on the farm, but there was no Sister Ballance this time as she was dead. Jack was meant to be a girl, but he was very definitely a boy and I was delighted to have a third son.

* * *

All through the war years we tried to keep Wedza Club going, despite not driving at night. Tennis was played regularly on Saturday afternoons, as well as squash. On Sundays during the winter months we tried to persuade Salisbury cricket teams to come and play against us. This they were very reluctant to do, and we had to rely on invitation teams; they would come out on the Saturday, spend the night and leave in good time on Sunday to be home before dark. Ian Piercy brought a team from Umvukwes; Robin Thornycroft raised a side in South Africa and came up for a series of games; Dick Whittaker was always willing to bring a side out from Marandellas; somehow we kept cricket alive.

In the days of Tony Seager, Wedza had been a pretty strong side. But, following Tony's tragic death and the ageing of the likes of Nigel Thornycroft, the standard had slipped and we no longer played in the farmers' winter league, the highly competitive Lilthurbridge Cup. However, by 1978 the offspring of the old guard were beginning to make their presence felt. They were not always available, with call-up duties and university taking a heavy toll, but it was obvious that with three young Seagers, three young Travers, Alastair Amm and a selection of Hills, Thornycrofts and Matthews all playing good cricket, Wedza potentially had a very good side. Being older than this lot and younger than the old lot, I found myself captain of the team, and in 1978 we decided to enter for the Lilthurbridge Cup. This was a lot of fun and we soon found ourselves travelling to places like Rusape, Salisbury South, Norton, Sinoia, and Shamva, as well as our neighbours and big rivals, Ruzawi River. Here we met fellow farmers all going through the same problems as ourselves and made many lasting friendships. The standard of country district cricket was quite high and even the national side usually had three or four farmers in its ranks – for example, Eddo Brandes, Heath Streak and, of course, Graeme Hick, whom I played against when he was a very talented young schoolboy playing with his father for Tengwe.

We did OK that first season, and I handed the captaincy over to Kiff Seager in 1979. Kiff was just down from Cambridge, where he had got his 'Blue', making him much better qualified than me. The result was that the young Wedza side won the Lilthurbridge Cup for the first time in its history. The final was played against Horseshoe at Wedza and, ignoring the self-imposed curfew, celebrations went on far into the night. It was during this evening that we hatched the plan of taking a side to play village cricket in England.

The side we took to England was far from our strongest Lilthurbridge Cup-winning Wedza side and was drawn more from the older brigade, who were the ones who could afford it. David Hamilton was largely responsible for working out the itinerary, in conjunction with his cousin David Pritchard, who knew a lot of the Gloucestershire farming community, and I captained the side, with John Kitkat from our big rivals Ruzawi River as vice-captain. While the team that flew over was fairly elderly, we were reinforced by two youngsters at college in England – Richard Seager and Chris Matthews.

It was all a lot of fun and not only did we play some genuine village cricket, as it should be played, but we also made a lot of lasting friends in the farming world. The Gloucestershire farmers in general were largely responsible for hosting us while in Gloucestershire, and when we left we invited them to bring a contingent to visit us in Zimbabwe. This they did. They were not essentially cricketers, but were interested in our farming methods and in generally having a good holiday in a lovely country. Mike and Di Bartlett were very much to the fore in organizing this return visit and people like David Holburn and the Watts brothers became lasting friends and regular visitors. This was reciprocated when our sons went to Cirencester and got holiday jobs on their farms, just further proof of how many doors a bit of sport can open.

Our main game in Gloucestershire was against Cranham village, and for a change it was a lovely day. The ground was a typical village one with a huge slope from the wicket down to deep square leg; so, when the wind helped as well, the merest flick off the leg stump would go for six. We batted first and made a pretty respectable score, as the wind was in the right direction, then had them on the run when they batted. This was until Fred came in. Once upon a time he would have been the blacksmith, but now he was the local garage owner. He rapidly slogged a few fours, but seemed reluctant to run singles. Then our fastest bowler, Graham Hatty, hit him directly on the foot when, in our opinion, it was well in front of his stumps. We all roared an appeal, but this was suddenly stifled when, to our horror, we saw his whole foot lying some distance from his leg. He had a wooden leg and the articulated ankle had been broken by the direct hit on it. Having got over this shock we managed to win the match, but were well beaten at skittles in the pub later that evening.

Having moved on from Cranham to Shropshire, we were based at Shrewsbury School, where Hugh and Juliet Ramsbotham arranged accommodation for us. Hugh had taught for a while at Peterhouse before becoming a housemaster at Shrewsbury and was a keen cricketer and golfer. He arranged a series of matches against local sides, culminating in a game against the Shropshire Gents, organized by Nigel Thornycroft's brother Guy, who then hosted a farewell party for us at his lovely home.

* * *

Apart from playing a bit of cricket at the club, we also started polocrosse on the airstrip. When I had stopped playing polo in 1969 I put my two mares, Dusky and Terry, in foal and so by the mid '70s we had a number of youngsters ready to be ridden. In those days I used to ride every morning before breakfast, which was a very good way of getting the day started and good training for young horses, so with polo out of the question we decided to give polocrosse a go.

Ruzawi River had a very strong polocrosse side, but we were complete beginners. I went and played a little at Ruzawi River and even represented them in one tournament at Glendale. I had thought that, just because I could play polo, I would be able to shape at polocrosse, but this was very far from being the case; it is a totally different game and a very good one.

Squash at the club was another popular sport and four of us – Richard Holme, Ian Hird, Steve Grinham and I – would meet regularly on a Wednesday evening until we stopped driving at night. Richard then built his own squash court on his farm at Headlands.

For the last couple of years of the war, 1978/9, I had been leasing 'Leeds Farm' from John Prentice. When it all ended and independence was imminent, I asked John if he would like to sell, and I made him an offer dependent on my getting a hefty loan from the Land Bank. It agreed to lend me yet more money, and with a few modifications John accepted my offer of Z$80,000 (then equivalent to about GBP40, 000 and now in 2009 Z$500,000,000,000,000,000,000 – or thereabouts!). I was in his sitting room on 'Leeds' when we shook hands on the deal; his wife Pam was there and insisted on keeping a recently installed electric motor which she maintained she had bought with 'her' money. This motor would normally have gone with the farm but I had no objection to her having it. Pam was understandably upset at the farm being sold as she did not really want to move into town. No sale agreement was signed by John or me, although I did tell him that I would like to have one drawn up as soon as I could get to a lawyer.

It seems that I was not the only person looking at 'Leeds' though. Ken Burton, a successful Zambian farmer, was planning on moving to the new Zimbabwe and had had a look at it, and the day after John had accepted my offer he called in at 'Leeds' and offered John considerably more than I had, and in cash. Pam urged John to accept this new and much more attractive offer; after all, nothing had been legally signed. To John's eternal credit he did not even ring me up to try for a better deal. He merely told Ken that he had agreed to sell Leeds to me and that was that. A gentleman's word is his bond and John was certainly a gentleman. Pam did not take it so kindly though and would not speak to me for two years. It took me a long time to discover why, and even then I could not quite fathom out her logic – surely she should have been angry with John?

Having got 'Leeds' I felt I needed someone to live in the house and Derek Hurlston came for a short time. When he left, I put an advertisement in the local farming weekly, *The Farmer*, for a retired couple who would act as caretakers and do a few odd jobs. I had a few replies and went to interview the most likely-sounding candidate, an ageing Welshman called Calvin Bond. We met in his house in Salisbury (it had not yet been renamed Harare) and he seemed very keen to come and I thought him very suitable.

"What about your wife though?" I asked, "does she want to come out into the sticks?"

For the first time Mr Bond (as I always called him) appeared uncertain; he hummed and hawed until finally I asked if she was around and if I could speak to her. Very reluctantly, he got up from his chair, put his head round the door and called, "Offer, come here."

A few seconds later a pretty young black girl came shyly into the room. She spoke perfect English and appeared to be very well-read – which was more than could be said for old Mr Bond. Further probing revealed that she had two small children by old Bond, her first two, but Bond's twelfth and thirteenth. It turned out that she was a Matabele and related to Joshua Nkomo. I employed them and soon they moved into 'Leeds' house.

Old Bondy died within a couple of years, but Offer (or Mrs Bond, as I always called her) remained in my employ first on 'Leeds' and then 'Chirume' until 2002, when she was brutally threatened by Mugabe's thugs at the height of the land grab and returned to Harare.

When the result of the election became known, my labour force was full of smiles. I am sure they had all voted for Mugabe and were delighted that he was their new President. I was not so sure, but was much reassured by the brilliant speech of reconciliation that he made immediately after he had won. Shortly after that I was driving into Salisbury/Harare when, approaching the turning to the airport, I saw a huge Boeing 747 flying low overhead. I looked up and there emblazoned large on the side were the letters 'BA', with the Union Jack painted on the tail. It was an emotional moment and symbolized to me the end of sanctions and the start of a return to the fold and international recognition after the long years of UDI.

CHAPTER 18

After Independence

NOT EVERYBODY COULD STOMACH THE IDEA OF their beloved Rhodesia becoming Zimbabwe with the erstwhile terrorist leader Robert Mugabe as Prime Minister. Mugabe's name spelt in reverse makes a Yorkshire expression – 'E ba gum'. Was this a good omen for me – a born Yorkshireman? We never really considered leaving, but others did. My great friends from Kenya, John and Lorna Clarke, had sold their Mvurwi farm and moved to the USA a couple of years before, and most other areas lost a few farmers. But by and large most people were hugely relieved that the horrible war was over and that they could now get on with some real farming.

Mugabe immediately made a brilliant move as far as we were concerned by appointing Dennis Norman, the president of our Commercial Farmers' Union, to the post of Minister of Agriculture. Other whites were also given Cabinet posts, and we began to believe that what the new President had said in his first speech was meant.

What of Ian Smith though? He had always said that Rhodesia/Zimbabwe was his home and this was where he would always stay. True to his word, as ever, he did stay and we are told that Mugabe even consulted him in matters of state. This happy state of affairs did not last too long though and they soon fell out, with Smith denouncing Mugabe as a terrorist and predicting exactly what has happened today.

It was not only farmers who decided to leave. Quite a lot of professional people who lived in towns also sought pastures new. The result of this was that property values fell sharply. We had already bought 'Leeds Farm' and now we decided to buy a house in the newly named Harare. There was a wide choice and we finally settled on 2, Aboyne Drive in the upmarket Highlands area. We paid Z$37,000, then the equivalent of about GBP6,000. The boys still own 2, Aboyne and in December 2008 it was worth about GBP60,000.

It was a busy time on the farm, or farms, as we were running cattle on eight farms at the time – 'Chirume', 'Collace', 'Leeds', 'Raleigh', 'Kuatora', 'Eldoret', 'Laurel' and 'Mount Arthur'. This did not last, however, as 'Collace' was soon bought by Hamish Lumsden, and 'Laurel' and 'Mount Arthur' were also sold, to people with a renewed interest in farming now that the war was over. We had to dispose of our cattle on these farms and the proceeds went towards 2, Aboyne Drive.

Obviously at this time there was talk of more commercial land, most of which was white-owned, being made available to black farmers. The British Government at the Lancaster House agreement had put money aside for this very purpose. Frikkie Kotze, from whom I leased 'Kuatora', agreed to sell his farm to the Government of the new Zimbabwe for the resettlement of blacks and gave me notice to move off as soon as any new settlers wanted to move on. Frikkie was paid and I waited for the new arrivals – they never came. When I say never, there are a few there now, but it was years before this excellent little (three thousand acres) farm was used by any blacks. I moved off after another couple of years for different reasons and the farm lay empty for years after that. 'Bath Farm' was also sold for the same reason and an outcry went up when it was taken over, not by the 'land hungry masses', but by one of Mugabe's new ministers. In those days the government cared about this sort of outcry and the said minister was asked quietly to stand aside, and in time some black settlers did go there.

There was now a black government ruling the country but certainly in Wedza there was no significant change in the 'status quo'. Race relations, despite the recently ended war, were good and for this Mugabe and his men must take a lot of credit. An amnesty was declared on all war crimes – and plenty had been committed on both sides – so this was really the only sensible thing to do. There were some predictable changes though. Very soon there were no white policemen left in Wedza. The white District Commissioner became a black District Administrator. Even non-governmental institutions like banks were affected. One morning David Hamilton was sitting outside the office of the manager of the Marondera Standard Bank, waiting for yet another painful interview, when the door to the manager's office burst open and an ashen-faced white neighbour emerged, pointing back over his shoulder and exclaiming, "David! David! There's an African in there!"

Positive results were slow in coming, as the rest of the world watched us a bit warily, but things did start to move. We could export our beef freely to Europe now, and the once famous tobacco floors reopened to the public and tobacco was sold on open auction instead of out of the back door. International airlines started coming to Harare. Embassies and High Commissions from a variety of countries started springing up all over town and slowly, very slowly, tourists started to return.

One night I got a telephone call from Geoff Kent of Abercrombie and Kent. It came at two o'clock in the morning from Chicago when I was fast asleep. Geoff was his usual bubbly self and as I struggled to make sense of what he was saying, I slowly realized that he was sending me an air ticket to fly over to Chicago to see him, with a view to starting up A&K again in the new Zimbabwe. I had sort of kept in touch with him all through the bush war, but with so much happening on the farming front I had never really considered getting involved in tourism again. However Geoff is a hard man to refuse, and as it would cost me nothing I thought it would be quite fun to pop over to the States and have a chat to him. So I went.

There had been many changes in A&K since I was last involved. For a start Geoff had divorced Andrea and married Jorie Richardson. This was sad for Andrea, who I had much liked, but good for A&K because Jorie, who was fifteen years older than Geoff, was the daughter of Paul

Butler, founder of Butler Airlines, owner of a huge, prestigious property in Oak Brook – one of the very upmarket suburbs of Chicago – and a very wealthy man. Jorie was a very wealthy woman and made sure that plenty of office space was available on the Butler property for new A&K offices. I also suspect that she injected quite a lot of capital into the company.

When I had last been involved, A&K had been run entirely from Kenya and agents were not employed, because all clients were dealt with directly. This had been an excellent way of running an upmarket, expensive safari business, but it was very time-consuming and limiting in the number of clients that could be handled in this exclusive manner. So when Geoff wanted to expand he had taken the brave step of deciding to use agents. This in effect meant not dealing directly with any clients at all, as the agent would hear of it, get uptight at not getting a commission and stop using A&K. This change in policy had warranted the move of the head office to America, and more specifically to Oak Brook. So it was to these offices that I was driven when I arrived at Chicago's O'Hare airport.

Actually I went straight to Jorie's house (in Jorie Street!) where Geoff was the new husband. He was as charming and enthusiastic as ever, and she, whom I had met before on the Polo tour eight years previously, was very friendly and a typically well-preserved fifty-seven-year-old American. Geoff produced a sheaf of new, very expensive, very glossy brochures and announced, with justifiable pride that A&K had been granted the status of 'official tour operators' for British Airways. Indeed there was their logo all over the glossy brochures. Knowing Geoff, he had probably persuaded them to pay for them as well. Over the next couple of days I was taken on a conducted tour of the offices and met all the staff, including the girl who was going to concentrate on selling tours to Zimbabwe, Zambia and Botswana. This was to be my territory and Geoff asked me if I would open an office in Harare to organize safaris in these three countries. With such an organized marketing setup it was hard to refuse the offer, especially when I thought of the many little companies back in Zim who were trying to get off the ground. As Geoff often said, "Anyone can buy a few tents, call themselves 'Rhino Safaris' or whatever, and wait for clients to flock in – but they won't – marketing is the key."

If I took it on, it would mean moving into town and opening an office, so I would either have to give up a lot of the farms, get a manager or get Fran to run them with me getting back whenever I could. I told Geoff this and said I would give him an answer within a week.

Back home, Fran said she would love the challenge of running the farms, and I was keen on the challenge of opening a proper A&K office in Harare and promoting tourism in what I knew to be a truly wonderful area. So I said yes to Geoff. All our correspondence in those days was done by telex and we thought it the most wonderful, up-to-date way of communicating that there could possibly be. Does anybody use it now?

Luckily we already had a pad in town, so I went there and initially set up office in a couple of rooms owned by my accountant and old Kenyan friend, Clive Barton-Grimley. As secretary I used the services of a Wedza farmer's daughter, called Sheila Ware (née Mcdonald), who ran her own little business in Harare.

We got reams of telexes every day from Oak Brook, and the first thing we had to do was to organize a series of 'FAMs' for travel agents. FAMs are virtually free safaris for agents who are going to market your product and, quite reasonably, want to see for themselves what they are selling to their precious clients. The 'free' bit worried me. As a brand-new little company, we could not afford to host these quite extensive safaris for nothing.

"Easy," said Geoff, "I'll get BA to fly them to you for nothing and you get all the lodges and guides to look after them for nothing, saying that when the clients started to flock in we would use their services exclusively."

Believe it or not, it worked. Everyone in Zim was so keen to promote tourism that they readily agreed to entertain the agents for nothing, and in the first few months of our existence we brought over nearly a hundred

American agents, hiking them round all the best places, not only in Zimbabwe but in Zambia and Botswana as well. It was very hard work but stimulating stuff. Not all the agents produced any clients by any means, but enough did to have made it a thoroughly worthwhile exercise.

I, myself, was out of touch with the best places to go, as a lot of excellent new little camps had sprung up, and I had never been to Zambia at all. After having a good look round we put together what we called 'The African Hinterland Safari', lasting nearly three weeks. While with us they would visit the Okavango and Chobe in Botswana, Victoria Falls (of course), a tented camp at Makalolo in Hwange and Bumi Hills in Zimbabwe, then finally the South Luangwa National Park in Zambia. We also tagged on an optional extra, which was a five-day canoe trip down the Zambezi, a wonderful little adventure that Eddie Rous had just started up. This itinerary was put into one of those smart, glossy brochures with departure dates and costs then dished out to every worthwhile travel agent in the USA and Canada.

To say that we were overwhelmed with bookings would be a slight exaggeration, but people did start coming – and loved it. There is no better publicity than satisfied customers and we soon had to move to a larger office and employ more staff. We moved into three rooms on the third floor of the Monomatapa Hotel, and Jenny Bickle, who had been running her own little company, came to join us, with Moira Robb not far behind. At Vic Falls we had our own permanent girl in the shape (and a very pretty shape it was too) of Lindy Phillips (now married to Rory Hensman). Lindy would meet our clients off the plane and show them all the wonders of the Falls from their comfortable base at the old Victoria Falls Hotel.

I was now almost entirely living in town at 2 Aboyne and spent most of my days in the office. I did try and meet quite a lot of our clients, but unlike in the past they were now just names and we really knew nothing about them. But when an agent came to town I had to jump around. These were our bread and butter. After the original FAMS we got a fairly constant stream of other agents coming through as well.

Meanwhile, Fran was doing a pretty good job on the farms and came into town on the weekends. The obsessive Polo Bug had raised its head again, and with a number of nice young ponies I joined Harare Polo Club and started playing again. Initially I kept three or four ponies with friends in town and walked them to the old North Avenue polo ground for polo on Saturday afternoons and Sunday mornings. This ground shared a fence with the garden of the Prime Minister, so it was not long before the club received notice that it would have to move. Luckily we knew this was likely to happen and had already acquired a lovely bit of land from Neil McLeod at Thornpark on the Mazoe road.

Mugabe was starting to use the old polo ground as his livestock paddock. All visiting chiefs brought him a present and soon we found the ground full of sheep, goats and young cattle – I dare say there were a few pangolins hanging around as well, this being the ultimate present in Shona custom to give to your leader. Traddles, Harry's naughty little Jack Russell Terrier, caused us untold embarrassment by chasing the flock of sheep and goats, causing them to jump the fence on to North (now Tongogara) Avenue. Traddles was put under close arrest and only a Supreme Court appeal prevented her being shot. Today this lovely old field, left to Harare Sports Club by Cecil Rhodes, is surrounded by a concrete wall topped with razor wire, while guards armed with AK rifles patrol the perimeter; anyone would get shot if they so much as stopped to try and look inside. Large notices forbid any photographs being taken and on one side the whole road is closed to traffic between six pm and six am, a far cry from the days when Ian Smith used to walk unescorted from this very residence to his office in town.

Geoff was also into polo in a very big way. Again Jorie was a big help, as Oak Brook boasted its own polo grounds and Jorie was secretary of the US Polo Association. Geoff proceeded to recruit his own team of professionals to play 24-goal polo in the US Open. He was a pretty useful 4-handicap player himself but needed some heavy, professional guns to raise a 24-handicap team. These he found, and he called the team Abercrombie and Kent. They did very well and won the US Open in

1981, playing as Rolex A&K and beating Retama, who had the famous Gracidas, 10-9 in the final.

When we were kicked off the old polo ground next to Mugabe's house, we moved out to Thorn Park, and this became both the home for the Harare Polo Club and the headquarters of the Polo Association of Zimbabwe. The national team at this time was still very strong by any amateur standards, rating a good 24-handicap, with people like the Hensman brothers, a selection of Meikle brothers, a couple of Brown brothers and Byron Dardagan all competing for a place in the top side. Sadly, Basil Kearns, one of the best of them all, had been killed in the bush war. The Meikles were an amazing family who lived only for polo; the 'Old Man', Dave Meikle, farmed at Banket and had been playing polo since he was a boy and had captained the national team in the 1970s. I played against him in Kenya in 1962 when he was up there on a tour. Dave's wife, Nona, was the secretary of the PAZ and between them they had produced five sons and a daughter – but the daughter did not really count, as she did not play polo. One could always spot a Meikle child when a group of children were playing around at a polo tournament, because they would always canter rather than run like normal children, and would always be carrying a cut-down polo stick.

My club, Harare, boasted a top team and competed in the 'A' division against the three other clubs. By most standards it was not a bad side, consisting of the young, and very promising, Johnny Campbell, his father, the irrepressible and outspoken Bruce, Packet Kemple, still a brilliant player, but not at his old best and the ageing Brian Danckwerts. Brian had been kicked out of Zimbabwe during Ian Smith's time for being too anti-government, and had gone to live in Zambia, but now, I think, Zambia had got tired of him too and he was back in the new Smith-free Zimbabwe. Brian was a bit like the Meikles in that polo dominated his life. He was a very good tobacco farmer, so quite well off and incredibly generous in any matters to do with polo. He was quite a good player but apt to have fits of uncontrollable temper, and I can well remember him chasing after the young Duncan Ellis, after being fouled by him, waving his polo stick and shouting, "I'll get you, you cheeky young pup!" while Duncan hightailed it off the field and into the bush. He also once tried to chuck Fran through a plate glass window following one of her more outrageous statements about the way he ran the club.

I never made the 'A' side, but was very happy captaining the 'B' side off a 3-handicap, and one year we went through the season unbeaten. This was particularly satisfying for me as Harry was an integral part of the team, together with Stuey Kearns (Basil's son) and my good mate Peter Macdonald.

When we moved to Thorn Park a smart double-storey pavilion designed by Liz Nicolle was erected, and it was decided that a suitable international fixture should be arranged to mark the opening. With the blessing of the PAZ I contacted Geoff and asked him if he would bring over his American Open winning team, if we could guarantee that they would be decently mounted. This he agreed to do, and although it was not exactly the same side, it was a very strong 25-goal side consisting of Geoff (4), Antonio Herrera (9), the best player in Mexico, and the two Bostwick brothers (both 6). The side chosen to meet them consisted of Gary and Rory Hensman (both 6), Robbie and Andrew Meikle (both 5), making a total of 22. So it was quite a family affair with three sets of brothers playing. Zim won the first one and A&K the second, so honours were pretty even, although Zim claimed victory overall as they had won their game by a greater margin.

Polo in general was going through a golden era and every year some international side would visit. Usually it was strong enough to play our national side, but once Pakistan sent over a 17-goal side, which was really too weak for our best guys, so a Zimbabwe 'A' was chosen to play them and I was in it. We had most of the Pakistan team staying in our house at 2 Aboyne Drive and very pleasant they were too – when they got up, which was never much before 11:30 am. India also sent a side, which I played against, and both countries invited us back to their country. I could have gone, but like a fool I never took up the invitation, and to this day have never been to the sub-continent.

Despite independence, polo was still very much the white man's sport. There were plenty of blacks involved, of course, as all the grooms were black, but there were no black players. The Hensmans tried to remedy this by taking a unit known as the Grey's Scouts under their wing. The Grey's Scouts had been a mounted unit during the bush war and consisted of both black and white soldiers. With independence, most of the whites left the unit, but the horses and some black members remained and were used on things like anti-poaching. The Hensmans tried to teach this lot to play polo. To be fair, they had some success and a low goal team of all blacks did compete in most tournaments for a few years. But polo is essentially an élitist sport and any black participation had to be heavily subsidized. On one occasion Nigeria sent a team to play in an All-Africa tournament. The whole team was black and if you closed your eyes when talking to them you would think that you were chatting to British Army officers. This to a large extent you were, as all had been trained at the Royal Military Academy, Sandhurst and spoke better English than a lot of Zimbabweans. The local players' children were not to know this though, and one piping little voice was heard to ask, "Mummy, why are all those grooms playing?" in an embarrassingly loud voice.

* * *

One year we invited England to send out a schoolboy side to play both Zambia and us. This they did, and four of their best players duly arrived and were well mounted by local players. With the experience that our boys had had playing in good adult club polo, they easily beat our visitors and were invited back for a tour of England.

This was a memorable experience. The team consisted of Chris and Steve Meikle, Douglas Wyrley-Birch and Harry. Fran and I went as well, as did Dave and Nona Meikle and Robin and Alison Wyrley-Birch. Having been thrashed here the English boys felt it necessary to reinforce their sides with a fully-fledged English international senior player, with the result that in our first game at Cowdray Park we were confronted by three of the schoolboys we had played against in Zimbabwe plus the 5-goal Andrew Seaville. We lost, but it did not matter a bit as we were wonderfully mounted and entertained and the boys learned a lot. We went on to play at Kirtlington near Oxford and at Tolson near Wetherby, where we won against adult sides, then over to Waterford in Ireland where we stayed in Hugh Dawnay's lovely house and had two games against his sides. He obviously rated us highly, as he not only played himself but also included a visiting Argentine 6-goaler in his side. This game we also lost, but only just, in very wet conditions. Hugh Dawnay could not have been kinder and this well-regarded coach went out of his way to help our boys.

We then all drove up to Dublin and had a game at Phoenix Park, against the full Irish national side supplemented by the Argentinean 6-goaler. Somewhat unsurprisingly we lost this as well, but only by seven goals to five. Again we were well entertained and had dinner at the clubhouse followed by an Irish singsong in the evening.

We returned to England for the final two matches of the tour, at Windsor Great Park against an England under-21 team. Ronnie Ferguson, who was running the Guards Polo Club at that time, arranged these. He umpired the first match played on the Saturday and this ended in an exciting draw, so we were all keyed up for the final game on the Sunday. However it rained that night. It didn't rain hard, so we were unconcerned, particularly when we arrived at the club and witnessed a game in progress with Ronnie himself playing. Having finished his game, he came up to us and declared that the ground was too wet for our game and he had cancelled it. We had come all the way from Zimbabwe for this game and the English players had driven their horses there from all over England. He lived near the ground and had seen fit to play his game, so why couldn't we? Both David Meikle and I argued with him but he would not be moved. We had planned an end-of-tour presentation after the game to people who had been so kind to us during our visit, so we now asked where and when this could take place, as we had various presents to dish out.

"Oh!" he said, "just dump them on my desk at the office on your way out."

We organized our own little ceremony without the help of this very unpleasant man.

A few weeks after we had returned, I received a newspaper cutting in the post from my father. It consisted of a lengthy report about how Ronnie had just been sacked from the club. Did his nasty behaviour towards us have anything to do with this, I wondered?

My other involvement in polo at this stage was commentating, and I was privileged to be asked to do all the main Test matches. As long as I was kept supplied with a regular intake of gin and tonic, I enjoyed doing this.

With all this polo going on in Harare, we had been lucky enough to buy a forty-five-acre property in nearby Norfolk Road, and here we kept some fifteen polo ponies together with three grooms. It was an ideal property complete with stables, an office and grooms' accommodation, and being so close to Thorn Park it meant that the ponies could be walked there for all games. Later on, I sold the place and the new British Embassy has been built there.

I did some work for A&K as well as playing polo and was actually very busy. The set departure safaris were filling up quite nicely and we were also getting a number of FITs, that is individually planned safaris, rather like we used to do before, only this time it would be the agent telling us what was wanted instead of the client himself. We also got very involved in the start of canoeing safaris down the Zambezi. Eddie Rous had finally got the licence to do these wonderful trips but did not have the finances to market the idea and really get it going. We as A&K, therefore, bought into the fledgling company and marketed it overseas, while Paul Connolly gave up being a lawyer and moved in to share an office with us and do the actual running of the safaris. They proved to be an outstanding success and many companies, both in Zimbabwe and Zambia, run them to this day.

* * *

The newly independent Zimbabwe appeared to be flourishing and was being held up as a model of what an African state could and should be. Mugabe was the hero of the hour and in the eyes of the world could do no wrong. Indeed, I stood up for him as well when we visited places like South Africa and bitter ex-Rhodesians ran him down – I reckoned he was doing a pretty good job. But in reality the first, and one of the worst chapters in Zimbabwe's history of crimes against humanity, was being written. Mugabe had pretended to make friends with the Matabele leader, Joshua Nkomo, to present a united front against we whites in the bush war, but in reality no Shona was ever going to remain friendly with their old enemy, the Matabele. Nkomo's party, ZAPU, had won all twenty of the seats in parliament allocated to Matebeleland but did not really present a threat to Mugabe with his safe majority of fifty-seven seats. However, now safely in power Mugabe determined to 'sort out' his old traditional enemy, the Matabele, once and for all. To this end he recruited some North Korean Army trainers to supplement those already supplied by the British. These Koreans were given one specific regiment to train – the Fifth Brigade – and their methods would not be found in any British training manual or in the manuals of any civilized nation. Once trained, the Fifth Brigade was unleashed on the unsuspecting, innocent Matebele tribesmen, who were accused of being 'dissidents' and of hoarding arms and ammunition in preparation for a coup against the new government.

There is seldom smoke without fire, and I do believe that Nkomo had not handed in quite a lot of the weapons that his party had used to fight the bush war. Indeed a lot were discovered on farms around Bulawayo. Nkomo claimed they had been planted there, and maybe they had, but what was certain was that the average person living in the tribal areas knew nothing about this sort of thing and it was these young men that were singled out by the Fifth Brigade and systematically shot in an exercise that became known as Gukurahundi – a Shona word meaning 'the early rain which washes away the chaff before the spring rains'. It is still not known how many innocent Matabele were killed in this brutal massacre, but figures of well over twenty thousand are usually mentioned as a conservative estimate.

How could this sort of thing happen without the rest of the world condemning it? For a start there was a strict curfew throughout Matabeleland and no journalist of any sort was allowed in. Then the rest of the world was tired of Rhodesia's problems; their thinking was that it was now independent and called Zimbabwe, so let them get on with their own squabbles. Blacks slaughtering blacks is not nearly such exciting news as blacks slaughtering whites, anyway. So no one really knew it was happening. To try and draw attention to the massive problem they had, the Matabele did slaughter a few whites – six international students were kidnapped on the Bulawayo/Victoria Falls road and killed. This received international press coverage, but the government just passed it off as proof of the 'dissident' behaviour being undertaken by the Matabele. One journalist who clandestinely got into Matabeland dressed as a parson and saw what was happening was Peter Godwin. Word got out about this and he had to flee the country to avoid being arrested and probably killed. He has written a damning account of what he found out in his excellent book, *Mukiwa*.

Our safaris were going well and we frequently went to the southern end of Hwange National Park to stay in Alan Elliot's excellent Makololo tented camp. This was very much 'dissident' country, but we knew nothing of the ongoing problems until one day Alan Elliot suddenly disappeared. Alan spoke fluent Sindebele, had lived in Matabeleland all his life and was in fact a 'blood brother' of the Matabele. He had even named his young son Joshua, after Joshua Nkomo. As such, he was suspected of feeding fleeing 'dissident' Matabele youths from his well-stocked camp at Makololo. I suspect he probably was, but doing so was hardly a crime. Absolutely no word was heard of Alan for over a week.

The Butler family, who were partners of Alan and who also owned the *Financial Gazette* at that time, splashed the story of his disappearance across the front pages of their newspaper, and they even asked me to contact Geoff and get him to publicize the news in American papers and to contact the Zim Government, asking them to help trace Alan.

Whether or not any of this helped, I do not know, but Alan suddenly reappeared in Harare, where I met him. He was very shaken and nothing like his usual bubbly self. He was reluctant to talk about exactly what he had gone through, but at one stage he was quite certain that he was going to be shot.

There were plenty of other goings-on at this stage in the early '80s and there is no doubt that disillusioned ex-Rhodesians were involved with the then apartheid South African Government in trying to destabilise the new Zim setup. This was particularly true of young Rhodesian men, who at the time of independence were still actively engaged in fighting the people who now ruled the country. None had been trained quite like the Fifth Brigade, but members of the élite 'Selous Scouts' had certainly been trained to kill and hate their enemy. It was very hard for them now to accept this enemy as their legitimate government; many left and, particularly the ex-Selous Scouts, were offered lucrative contracts by the South African government to continue the fight against their erstwhile enemies.

Mugabe and his men got quite paranoid about this threat and we all thought that he was over-reacting, but he had a point. All his aeroplanes were blown up at Gweru. He accused the white officers who were then working for him, but it was not them. It was all arranged from South Africa. A bomb went off outside the cinema in Avondale shopping centre; the newly erected Independence Arch just outside the airport on the road into the capital was blown up. Another one has since been built.

* * *

Fran was doing well running the farms with very little help from me, but when we got an offer from someone who wanted 'Raleigh', we sold it and were then just left with 'Chirume' and 'Leeds'. Fran had no time to teach young Jack, or 'Spratt' as he became known, so he came into town to live with me during the week; I took him to nursery school every day on my way to the office, picking him up again at lunchtime. This worked OK when I was around, but about twice a year I visited America to help promote our bit of A&K. I used to enjoy this a lot. It was challenging and very interesting and I visited most of the major cities in the USA. Sadly, it was only the cities though, and I got little chance to see any of the countryside.

Towards the end of my time with A&K, I organized a tour of our area for a selection of zoo directors from America. Most zoos in the US have a travel section, and patrons of the zoo are encouraged to travel to the countries from which the animals in the zoo originate. Africa was of course one of the main destinations, and we were keen that any of this lot coming our way should use our services. We got representatives from some twelve different zoos, including San Diego, New York, Chicago, Boston and the California Academy of Science. The safari started in South Luangwa, Zambia, where we met up with Babette Alfieri, who had come over with the group from the A&K head office. Babette was a great lover of our bit of Africa and did a wonderful job promoting our area over better-known East Africa. She was also a great lover of the man who ran the Save the Rhino Trust (SRT) in the Luangwa valley – Phil Berry – so it was a happy reunion for all concerned. Phil came along with us for much of the safari, as he was very knowledgeable about all game and helped contribute to the enormous success of the whole trip. We went from Luangwa to Livingstone, crossed the bridge to Victoria Falls on the Zimbabwe side of the Zambezi and then flew with Penny and Paul Rawson to their camp in the Okavango Delta in Botswana. We had the whole camp just for our group and were royally entertained, teaching these 'city slickers' how to pole a mukora and fish for tiger. They just loved it.

From there we flew to Alan Elliot's 'Touch the Wild' camp in the Makololo area of Hwange. Again we had sole use of the camp, and Alan was his irrepressible self, leaping out of his Land Rover and chasing white rhino on foot, hotly pursued by the younger, more energetic members of our group. Alan did have one problem though; his vehicles were not in great shape and on a couple of occasions we broke down and wasted a lot of time while he tinkered around fixing them. On the last morning I begged him to take us in a decent vehicle and he produced a brand new one that had just been sent to him from Harare. Great, I thought, we will end on a high note. I was travelling with the group of six of the most important members of our party when, not half an hour into our game drive, the new Land Cruiser spluttered, coughed and stopped. Alan gazed under the bonnet then called me aside."Mark," he said, "we've got a problem, I've run out of diesel!" Shit! It took a lot of fast-talking, with Alan saying he had decided to take the agents for a walk instead of the planned drive. Off they set while I legged it back to camp to get some diesel.

We flew from Hwange to Bumi Hills and thence to Harare for a gala farewell dinner. As a result of this nearly all the participants came back the following year at the head of a group of fifteen of their clients – good business.

* * *

A very interesting client that we had at this time was a well-known Afro/American comedian. I regret to say that I had never heard of him, but his was a household name in the USA, particularly amongst the black community. I got a phone call from Geoff himself one day, saying that the comedian was coming and that I must personally look after him for the duration of his visit.

"What about payment?" I asked, as we always insisted on this up front.

"Just do everything he wants and tell me how much he owes – I'll sort it out," he replied.

So I pitched up myself at the old Harare international airport and, using my special pass, was allowed through to meet the clients straight off the plane and help them through immigration and customs. I was not the only person doing this though, and I had to wade through a large group of tough-looking characters with a smartly dressed African lady in the centre – Sally Mugabe, the President's wife. It seemed that she also had come to meet her 'hero', who was said to be coming to Africa to find his roots. The great man descended the steps from the aircraft and was engulfed by the tough characters. This was a help, as it enabled me to identify him, which was something that had been worrying me. He was not alone but accompanied by a very pretty young wife and two even tougher looking characters than Sally Mugabe's lot. I shuffled along behind this mob and eventually broke through its ranks and introduced myself.

"Who?" he said.

"Milbank from Abercrombie and Kent. We are looking after you," I repeated.

"Oh! Well in that case look after my luggage, I'm going with this good lady," he said, and disappeared with Ms Mugabe.

His luggage consisted of five wardrobe-shaped, seven-foot high containers on wheels and an assortment of fifteen other slightly smaller pieces. No way could I fit this lot into the kombi that I had brought with me, so I phoned for the farm pickup and took everything to Meikle's Hotel and deposited them in the two suites that I had booked. No sign of the great man though, or of his hangers-on. They were no doubt supping morning tea with the President and his wife. I had no idea how to get hold of them and wondered if they knew – or cared – where they were meant to be staying, or whether they had been booked into State House and had no intention of using my invaluable services. I reckoned that they would eventually want their kit at the very least, and as I knew Geoff had given them all our contact numbers I returned to my office.

Sure enough, about two hours later the phone rang. "Milbank?" rasped an angry voice,"Where the hell are you? Get your ass round here now."

Assuming that he meant Meikle's Hotel and not State House, I got my 'ass' there as quickly as I could.

I know that very funny men on screen are often miserable buggers off it, but I do believe that most of them smile sometimes. I had this comedian under my wing for about six weeks and during that time he never uttered a civil word to me and I never saw him smile at anyone. He kept the two suites at Meikle's for the duration of his visit and I reported there every morning. I was always met by the two heavies, one of whom turned out to be his manager and the other his personal bodyguard. Both were charming, and without their help I would never have coped. Quite often I got no further than them – their boss was 'sleeping', meaning he had indulged in too liberal an amount of alcohol and heroin – but I had to hang around in case he suddenly decided he wanted to do something.

Once I took him out to Imire Game Farm for the day, where Norman and Gill Travers did their charming best to entertain him. He barely spoke all day and just muttered "What a dump!" on the way home. I sent him up to Lindy at Vic Falls, hoping he would enjoy that and spend a couple of days there, but he was back that same evening. I tried Bumi Hills – same story. Finally I asked him if he really wanted to spend his entire visit in Meikle's or would he like to go somewhere really interesting. He listened to what I suggested and finally agreed to take a special private charter to Xaxaba, a remote lovely camp on an island in the middle of the Okavango Delta in Botswana, brilliantly run by Penny and Paul Rawson. I waved the little party goodbye from Charles Prince airport and hoped I would have a break from them for at least three days.

I was relaxing that evening over my first whisky when the phone rang. "Milbank, get your ass over here quick," said an all too familiar voice. I was ushered straight into his suite. He was standing by the fireplace with a large drink in his hand.

"So! You fucking honkie, you thought you could get rid of me, did you?" was his greeting. (I had learned by then that it is quite acceptable for blacks to racially abuse whites, but not the other way round.)

It was a difficult question to answer. For the past three weeks I had desperately been trying to find something that would amuse him. At about half past nine, as I was leaving, he thrust a large envelope into my hand. I peered inside. It appeared to be a fabulous diamond necklace and a couple of ruby brooches. I did not believe they were fakes.

"My wife's leaving for the States tomorrow," he said, "and I don't want the bitch to have these."

No way was I about to accept responsibility for this jewellery, and I handed it all back to him and left.

His wife, whom I had quite liked, did leave next morning, but on the incoming flight was an even prettier, much younger black girl, who said she was a friend of the comedian and asked if I would take her to him. I continued to report to Meikle's every morning but he never left the hotel again. Finally, I drove him to the airport for a flight to Lusaka, Zambia where he was due to be met by President Kaunda himself and entertained at a State banquet held in his honour.

"Goodbye honkie, thanks," he said and pressed five hundred dollars into my hand.

For half a moment I thought he was even going to smile. I heard later that he never did turn up for the banquet. When a flunkey went to find him, he was lying spaced out in his hotel room, incapable of movement.

I worked out the total cost of that six weeks, added the cost of my time, doubled the lot and sent the bill to Geoff. It was paid in full immediately.

* * *

Shortly after that I joined the staff who ran other A&K offices throughout the world, to do a mega promotion tour throughout the USA. Not only did I have to promote my own area, but I had to do South Africa as well. I knew a bit about that lovely country but not enough about the tourist destinations that I was expected to promote, so I joined an American group sent by A&K that was doing most of the main areas. As a result I had a lovely and free tour of the mines in Johannesburg, the Cape wine-lands, the Garden Route, and the Cango Caves. I went on the Blue Train, visited Oudtshoorn, the old ostrich centre of the Little Karoo, where there are 'feather palaces' abandoned to the desert sands, dusty monuments to a bygone prosperity, travelled to Durban and the Valley of a Thousand Hills, to Mala Mala and finally, to the newly developed Sun City in Bophutatswana, which was in one of apartheid South Africa's so-called independent Homelands. Here such terrible sins as gambling and black prostitutes were permitted – things that would never be countenanced in the pure religious air of white South Africa itself. There were not many international tourists there other than our group, but the place was thick with South Africans of both English and Afrikaner extraction indulging heavily in both the above pastimes.

I was interested to see Mala Mala, which was owned by my old polo-playing friend, Mike Rattray. It was brilliantly run and we saw a lot of game, including a lion kill at night, but I found it all rather artificial, with the guides all armed with walkie-talkies and chatting to each other in Zulu, with the result that when anything exciting was encountered the whole fleet of open Land Rovers arrived at the given place and formed a camera-clicking ring round the wretched animal. One old couple in my group complained vigorously about the lion kill being 'laid on', and said that it was cruel and in bad taste. I don't think they believed me when I said that this was probably the most natural thing they had seen at Mala Mala.

Being now an expert on South Africa, I joined four other A&K guys in America for our grand tour. Between us we had to cover South Africa, Zimbabwe, Botswana, Zambia, Kenya, Tanzania, Egypt, Britain,

Hong Kong, China and Nepal We each had to give a 45-minute talk, accompanied by slides, on the wonders of our particular destinations, to a room full of sceptical American travel agents. It was a bit nerve-racking at first and, to make it worse, each agent had a form on which he or she rated our performance. These forms were handed in at the end of the day and it would then be calculated who was regarded by that day's group as the best salesman. I often came second, which surprised me a lot. I would not wear a suit like the others at these presentations, but a rugged looking bush jacket, which perhaps helped create the right image (no pseudo leopard skin round my hat though). There was always a big dinner, paid for by A&K, at the end of the day, when we could chat to the agents individually. We would then often fly on to our next destination that same night and be ready for a ten o'clock start next day to do the whole thing over again in another city. It was hard but rewarding work, and we got the weekends off, which we spent in whatever city we happened to be in on Friday night. As a result I spent an excellent weekend in San Francisco being shown the Napa Valley by lovely Sandy Leilich from the California Academy of Science. She had been on the zoo directors' tour a few months previously.

I also had weekends in Washington, Dallas and Toronto. Washington was fun, and I visited many of the fascinating places that abound in that amazing city. We spent a lot of time in the Smithsonian Institute. The whole circus ended in Chicago where we had a three-day seminar at the Oak Brook head office, overseen by Geoff's new general manager, Alistair Ballantine. It was an interesting experience and a far cry from farming in Wedza. It also produced a lot of good business.

Every other year Geoff invited the fifty travel agents who had sent A&K the most business over those years on a very select safari in one of his exotic destinations. Previous ones had been at Tiger Tops in India and Maasai Mara in Kenya. In 1985 it was the Zambezi Valley in Zimbabwe and Botswana. I had to organize it and it had to be exclusive. To this end I enlisted the services of Gail Timms from our Jo'burg office as well as pulling Jenny Bickle back into harness. We booked the whole of Bumi

Hills Safari Lodge on Kariba for three nights and Chobe Safari Lodge in Botswana for four nights as well as a couple of nights at Victoria Falls. Each 'guest' received a gift pack on arrival, the pack containing coffee-table books on the Zambezi Valley, Chobe, the Okavango and Kariba. They each got a hand-carved verdite statue of the Zimbabwe Bird and mountains of bumf on the wonders of A&K. The invited group of agents were inducted into what Geoff called the Connoisseurs Club – connoisseurs, of course, because they had chosen A&K for their clients. Geoff had style!

He did not come himself on this jamboree, and the group leader was Alistair Ballantine from the head office in Chicago. British Airways carried them all free to Harare and we ferried them in a selection of vehicles to the best rooms in the Monomatapa hotel. They were allowed to relax and get over their jet lag for the first day, and then there was a banquet in a private dining room at the Monomatapa to welcome them. We needed a guest speaker, and I invited David Hamilton from Wedza. He is a brilliant public speaker. Whenever anyone in Wedza had a special anniversary, got married or died, David was always asked to propose their health; or, if it was too late for that as they were already dead, their eulogy. At the dinner his friendly, knowledgeable, chatty speech about life in Zimbabwe went down extremely well with this hard-bitten bunch of agents and got the whole safari off to an excellent start.

Bumi Hills was then run by the ex-Director of Tourism, Mike Gardener, and he put on a great show for us, culminating in a take-off of *This Is Your Life* for Alistair with the huge, burning initials, 'A&K' suspended over the spectacular drop in front of the swimming pool, with the lake and Starvation Island in the background. Chobe was equally good, and we had a couple of work sessions there debating how best to market this area to Americans. Tourism was big business and as a result of our – and I am sure many other such – promotions, tourists started flocking into the country, bringing much badly needed foreign currency. The Zimbabwe dollar was pretty strong in those days and one only needed seven or eight to buy a US$. Now, twenty years later, one needs several million and no tourists come anyway. Bumi Hills has been shut for years, and if you want to visit Victoria Falls you go to Livingstone in Zambia. A&K, although still very active in other parts of Africa – and the world – no longer operates in Zimbabwe.

I left them in 1985 by mutual agreement. Tim Somerset-Webb, Geoff's troubleshooter, came to see me one day and said that they wanted A&K Zimbabwe to be run much more from the States, which meant them telling me exactly what to do and what to charge. I did not agree with this, so we parted company quite amicably and I got a decent payout. The company continued though, run first by Travs Nettleton and then by Simon Rhodes.

This meant me going back to the farm and was probably the turning point in my turbulent marriage to Fran.

CHAPTER 19

Divorce and Re-Marriage

BACK ON THE FARM THINGS HAD GONE OK under Fran's management and we still had 'Chirume' and 'Leeds' (as well as lots one and two of 'Hull', which we had bought as part of 'Leeds'). I soon added to this by leasing two farms near Ruzawi River Club – 'Mari' and 'Idapi' – from Ann Dryborough. I also applied for a butchery, liquor and general store licence and built what became known as Leeds Butchery and General Store. Mrs Bond was put in charge.

The boys were scattered – Robert was in England doing a year as a squaddy in the army, Harry was about to leave school and go off to Argentina and America before going to university in Australia, and Spratt had just started prep school at Ruzawi, so it was just Fran and me on the farm for most of the time. She had enjoyed running the show while I was doing my A&K thing, but now with me back she had to play second fiddle and did not like it much. She moved into town – thus reversing our roles – and did a good job buying and improving houses. We bought 288 Rhodes Avenue and she split it up into three separate little houses. She lived at 2 Aboyne and during the polo season I would come in from the farm. Sometimes she would come out to the farms and tell me what I was doing wrong. We were not happy.

We had been married for twenty-three years, had three wonderful boys, shared a lot and built up quite a lot together. So why, after so long, did we want to call it a day? There was no one specific thing; neither of us was having an affair with anyone else and we were doing all right financially. But we had not been happy together for a very long time. Fran was a bit of a perfectionist and did not suffer fools gladly – actually she did not suffer fools at all. She had a very quick temper and cruel tongue, and I am convinced that these traits got worse as she got older, caused by the old car accident in her youth when she had severely damaged her head. I was and am a much more laid back character, so as the years went by I irritated her more and more, as it was not in her nature to be tolerant. A friend had recited to her a little homily when we got married, and knowing her fiery temper said she would do well to remember it in her marriage. It went: 'Be to his virtues very kind and to his faults a little blind.' I don't think she took it to heart much.

Fran had originally wanted to divorce me and had instigated proceedings through her lawyer, but when she started to realize quite what was involved, she tried to back out of it. I had also consulted a lawyer and spoken to a lot of my close family. All advised me to go ahead with the divorce, and when I did I think it infuriated Fran.

* * *

Our neighbour, Cpl Mike Hill, had been chairman of the local Farmers' Association for the past six years and done a very good job – now he came over to see me to tell me that, as I was now farming again, I should take over the post. This I did for the next three years. It was a rewarding job; Wedza was a very progressive and committed farming area and a wonderful community who all supported each other. Unlike in a lot of farming areas, our monthly Farmers' Association meetings were very well attended, and as a result we were able to get excellent speakers to come and enliven the proceedings. We had several government ministers, including Dennis Norman, who was then Minister of Transport. He told us that part of his job was controlling the Zimbabwe Navy. Navy? It seemed that there was one motor boat on Kariba which patrolled the border with Zambia and this constituted the 'Navy'. I wondered if the driver of the boat would be entitled to call himself 'Admiral of the Fleet'.

Moven Mahachi, Minister of Labour, came with a large entourage of hangers-on. He was a large, friendly, jovial man, who eventually died in a car crash under mysterious circumstances. Members of our community were at that time highly placed in the national organized agriculture hierarchy, with my friend Bob Rutherford president of the Commercial Farmers' Union and Jeremy Webb-Martin president of the very important Zimbabwe Tobacco Association. Bruce Campbell was chairman of the Cattle Producers' Association. These people always took the trouble to attend our meetings, so we were kept very well informed as to what was going on at national level in the agricultural world.

* * *

I do not like to dwell on the personal problems that I was having at this time but they do have to be mentioned, as the two and a half years from mid-1988 to early 1991 were probably the unhappiest of my life. Divorce at the best of times is an awful thing, but it can be accomplished in a moderately civilized fashion with both parties remaining friends. Marriage, after all, is a hell of a gamble. How can one possibly know how a pretty young girl will react to the vicissitudes of life or a handsome young man cope with the stress of financial problems, or how each one will react to the other's attitude as middle and older age creeps on? Our divorce, I regret to say, was about as acrimonious as it is possible to be.

Our marriage had always been turbulent – certainly there were highs but also many lows. It is natural to think that you are in the right and everything is the other partner's fault, but it is seldom as one-sided as that and both should share the blame. The thing that I wanted most, when divorce became our only option, was to get it all over as quickly and cleanly as possible and if possible remain friends. However our affairs were complicated in that we shared a lot of things at that time – two farms and four properties in town just for starters. Perhaps we were lucky to have that much to share, but it led to endless complications and countless hours in lawyers' offices. My lawyer was Mervyn Immerman, and he was an enormous help to me, being compassionate, understanding and knowledgeable – also his fees were remarkably reasonable. He had a picture hanging in his office of a cow. Pulling at its head was a furious looking woman. Pulling the tail was an equally angry man. Sitting beside the cow and quietly milking it was a lawyer. How apt!

My other main worry was for the children. Robert and Harry were both out of the country by now and had probably seen it all coming for some time; also they were adults by now. But little Spratt was at the most vulnerable age of ten. He had a hell of a time – we had to move him from Ruzawi to Springvale School, and I will be eternally grateful to Ken Anderson and John Calderwood, the headmaster of Springvale, for their help and understanding at this time.

Ironically, the fact that neither of us was involved with anyone else at the time possibly made matters worse, as neither of us was clearly at fault, which would have been the case if either of us had been involved in an affair.

I had wonderful support from family; Penel came up from South Africa and Sue and Tony came out from England. Both my sisters have a great sense of humour, and even in the trying circumstances which prevailed at the time we were able to laugh a lot and see the funny side of things, which in my depressed state would have seemed much more serious. Fran's brother, Richard, had always been a very close friend and I was (and still am) very fond of his wife, Gay, and their five super children. Richard was very supportive and certainly helped me as well as doing his best for his sister.

It was through Richard and Gay that my life took a turn for the better. In 1990 it was my turn to have the children for Christmas. Robert was still away, but Harry was back on holiday from Australia and of course Spratt was around, so Richard and Gay asked us to spend the time with them at their farm, 'Nyahuvu', near Headlands. We arrived at the little Headlands church on the evening of Christmas Eve for a carol service that was to be taken by our old friend Ken Anderson. Ken and his wife, Polly, were also going to be spending Christmas at 'Nyahuvu', together with a friend from England who they had staying with them. After the service she was introduced to me; her name was Nikki Sclater and I had actually met her son, James, a year or two before when he was staying with Richard in his gap year. Nikki had been divorced for some eight years from James's father and lived in Sussex. She was on her second visit to Zimbabwe, being a very close friend of Ken and Polly.

That Christmas – like many at 'Nyahuvu' – was a lot of fun. Nikki and I got on well and I invited her to come and ride in our annual paper chase, as it soon turned out that she was a very keen rider. This was also fun; she even claimed to have enjoyed riding Roulette, one of my more erratic polo ponies, and was one of the first to catch 'the hare', who was Harry. Shortly afterwards she returned to England, but I visited her there when I went over to see my very sick mother in July. We still got on well.

I spent most of that time up in Yorkshire staying with my father and visiting my mother in hospital, where she was clearly dying of cancer. We managed to have some very happy hours together and I did not come back to England for her funeral when she died a few weeks later. I was just glad to have seen her before she died, instead of only rushing over for the funeral.

I invited Nikki to come out in September to join me on the Zambezi for a few days. She would of course be based with Ken and Polly and we even took a chaperone up to the Zambezi with us – Richard Holme. We were very proper and old-fashioned, that is until Nikki accepted my invitation to come and stay in Zim on a more permanent basis and recklessly gave up her job, packed up her belongings and came to live with me on 'Chirume' together with her little Terrier, 'Baggins'. This however was not until I had visited her again in England and she had thrown a party near her home in Sussex, at which I was introduced not only to her ex-husband, John, but also to her recently discarded beau 'Tig' Mayhew. At one stage of the party she was interested to witness John, Tig and me in earnest and deep conversation. What were we talking about? It was all very refreshing to me. As I have said, divorces can be amicable (as it seemed could be the discarding of beaux) and the fact that we could all chat together in a very civilized fashion was in stark contrast to my own still unresolved situation in Zimbabwe.

The wretched business of the divorce dragged on and on, with court order following court order, and the situation was not helped by the arrival of Nikki. For me of course this was an enormous boost, and when the whole matter did finally come to court in January 1993 and our divorce was ratified, I proposed to Nikki on the steps of the High Court. Nikki's permit to stay in Zim was fast running out, so to solve this problem we had to get married quickly. We wanted a proper church wedding and did in fact have one later, but there was no time to organize this before the permit expired, so we were quietly married at the Marondera magistrate's court. The only witnesses were Ken Anderson and my father, who was over from England staying with us. We told only our children what had happened. As well as James, Nikki had a very beautiful, very talented twenty-one-year-old daughter, called Emma.

Just before this, Emma had come out to stay, and I had taken her to a lunch party at Vicky Rutherford's home on 'Igava' while Nikki drove into town to meet James. At the lunch was Vicky's mother, the redoubtable Patience, whom I had long known and respected. Patience knew of my involvement with Nikki and when she came up to chat to me Emma happened to be by my side.

"Patience," I said, "I want to introduce you to..." I got no further. I suddenly realized what Patience must be thinking as she gazed at this stunningly beautiful twenty-one-year-old girl standing next to a grotty fifty-five-year-old.

Now that she was married to me, Nikki could extend her resident's permit, and we then set about planning our 'proper' wedding. Proper wedding it was too. We were both divorced people, but we managed to get special dispensation from the Bishop to be married in church. James and Emma flew out from England for the weekend and James gave Nikki away; Harry flew over from Australia and was my best man, and both of us had plenty of other relations who flew in, as well as a host of local friends. Ken took the service at the sweet little Wedza St Cross church and the reception was at the club. All our overseas relations stayed with us at 'Chirume' and we had a brand new party the next day.

Despite this wonderful little interlude though, my problems were far from over. The judge who had presided over our divorce was called Smith (nothing to do with all the Smiths that used to be in the Rhodesian Cabinet, but a senior judge). He well knew how acrimonious our relationship was, yet he made the most ridiculous, thoughtless, stupid ruling imaginable about the division of our assets. The crowning piece of unbelievable stupidity was to award 'Leeds Farm' to Fran with the stipulation that I should run it. This was blatantly so impractical that we both agreed it could never work. It was the first thing we had agreed about for years. Poor Harry got roped in and achieved a manageable solution.

It was a huge relief to be able to start a new life. Spratt was still a bit of a worry as I had to share his time with Fran, and when I did have him I tended to overindulge him while hoping that he would get on with Nikki. This must be one of the trickiest of all relationships at his age. Nikki is very difficult not to like and so is Spratt, but they both stepped round each other with hackles raised for the first year or two.

CHAPTER 20

Better Times and Tragedy

THE EARLY 1990S WERE A GOOD TIME, both for Zimbabwe and me. The economy was booming, commercial farmers were producing vast amounts of food for the nation and flowers and tobacco for export, the tourist industry had never been so busy, and the government under Mugabe was firmly in power with no discernible threat to it. There was still a free press and we farmers just got on with doing what we did best – producing the goods.

As far as I was concerned, it was a very happy time. Nikki and I were enjoying being married and she loved 'Chirume'. I did have two setbacks which effectively ended my polo career. Firstly was a fairly major kidney operation, followed under a year later by another big operation, this one on my right knee, which necessitated the whole leg being in plaster for eight weeks – the worst part of this, with plaster right up to the bum, was that it was impossible to sit on the loo. This made my morning sessions in the bathroom painful, experimental occasions, where previously they had been periods of great relaxation and in-depth reading. Fortunately both operations were a success, but as I had been unable to play polo for two years and both the ponies and I were getting no younger I passed on the better ones to various sons and just kept a few to ride round the farm.

Prominent amongst these were Wonder Girl and Rama. Wonder Girl was a real patent safety and anyone who came to 'Chirume' and wanted to ride was put on to her. I think we have photographs of twenty different people riding her, ranging in age from nine to ninety. Rama was my special delight, as he had the slowest, most comfortable canter of any horse I have ever ridden.

Nikki of course was mad about riding and every day rode one of the old polo ponies, delighting in the lovely countryside that she had to ride in – all of which we owned. However she was a bit rude about my 'funny little ponies', as she called them, and vowed to buy herself a decent-sized horse, similar to that which she had been used to in England. She wanted to take up eventing, which she had done successfully in England and which was also a popular sport in Zim. A near neighbour from 'Dutchman's Corner', Dries Smith, advertised a selection of young horses that he wanted to get rid of and we drove down to have a look. They were not up to much, all being small and under-nourished, but there was one perky little three-year-old that took Nikki's eye.

"What about that one, Dries?" she asked, looking at the smallest.

"No, I want to keep that for my kids, and anyway Doug Stanley wants it for a polo pony," he replied. However Nikki rode it, and she then told Dries that she was not interested in any of the others but would like to take this little filly to ride around the farm. Dries then reckoned that the little pony was too small for Doug to play polo on and finally agreed to let Nikki have it, as he desperately wanted to get rid of something. The cost was Z$1,000 or about GBP65.

I immediately pulled Nikki's leg about buying something even smaller than my polo ponies, but she assured me that the little filly was just a stopgap and something of her own to play around with, pending the purchase of the 'proper' horse. We called the filly 'Disco' after the Land Rover Discovery that she had just imported from England.

Later Nikki did buy several 'proper' horses, and some of them were quite good. She competed in three-phase events on most of them, but none quite measured up and were invariably sold on. Disco however remained and to cut a very long story short (although we will hear more about Disco later), she became National Eventing Champion of Zimbabwe at different levels six times; she even competed in the South African Open Championships in Johannesburg on two occasions, finishing in fourth place in 2002, which was the highest placing for a Zimbabwe horse or rider for some thirty years. Not bad for a 14.3hh little Wedza bush pony.

* * *

In July 1993 we went to England to see various relations – my father was over eighty by now but still living on his own in Yorkshire, while Nikki's mum was just over the Pennines in Cumbria, also living on her own but on the lovely family estate of 'Tolson' which was run, together with the paper mill, by brother James. Then of course there were James and Emma in London, as well as a selection of other brothers, sisters, cousins, nephews, nieces, godchildren, etc, etc. It was our first visit to all this lot as a married couple, so we did the rounds and were royally entertained.

At 'Tolson' we were having dinner with James and Sue – grouse (surely the best of all game birds), despite it being only July, washed down by an excellent bottle of red wine. We were all very relaxed and enjoying the evening. Suddenly the telephone rang in the kitchen and James jumped up to answer it. He returned very quickly and said, "Nikki, it is John (her ex-husband); he wants to speak to you." With some reluctance, Nikki went to the telephone while James added to me, "I think you had better go as well – Emma has just been killed in a car crash in France."

It is impossible to digest this sort of statement immediately and in a daze I stumbled out to the kitchen in time to hear Nikki saying, "Something has happened to one of the children, hasn't it?"

I put my arm round her shoulder and just held her tight while John told her the terrible news. Nikki did not want to believe it and kept thinking that any minute Emma would ring up to say it was not true. But, of course, it was. Dear Philippa, Nikki's mother, had to be told too, something she understood only too well, having lost a son in similar circumstances, but, even more importantly, James had to be contacted. He was currently backpacking round India, so almost impossible to get hold of. I remember getting up at two o'clock in the morning and ringing the British Embassy in Bombay and asking them to try and trace him.

There followed days of endless telephone calls, including one to Ken Anderson in Zimbabwe, who insisted on coming over to take the funeral. James eventually rang his father two days later to wish him a Happy Birthday and got the awful news that way. Emma's body was still in France, and it was finally decided that we should all go there to arrange for its return to England. 'We' consisted of John and his wife Catherine, James, recently returned from India, Nikki and me. We flew to Marseilles and were met by some of Emma's new friends from the university she had been attending in Aix-en-Provence. They drove us to Aix – an enchanting small town – where we were installed in a central hotel. We walked round to the local police station, where we met Emma's latest boy friend, Christof Lamy. John spoke a bit of French, Christof a very little English, and the woman police officer in charge spoke no English, but gradually we pieced together the story and finally drove out to the site of the fatal crash – a normal stretch of road where a momentary loss of concentration and sheer bad luck had cost a beautiful, talented, young girl her life. Not much was said; we all had our own thoughts. I remember James picking some flowers that looked like yellow daisies and laying them on the crash site. We drove on to Christof's house, where we met Emma's great friend, Rima. Emma had only been at the university for twelve days, yet at a memorial service in the beautiful Aix Cathedral numerous new friends of hers filed up to the altar steps to lay flowers and say a few words in tribute. Nikki and I flew back to Sussex soon after and installed ourselves in the house belonging to John Sclater's parents, who were away in Norway. Here we waited while the formalities were completed for the return of Emma's body, pending her funeral at Newick church. I barely knew any of Nikki's family or friends at this time, but they were all unfailingly friendly to me and together we did as much as we could for Nikki, and indeed for John and James. It was not easy – whatever one does or says, at the end of the day there is still that aching loss, and poor Nikki regularly cried herself to sleep. Ken took a very moving and inspiring funeral service and little Newick church was filled to overflowing. At the end I walked arm in arm with Nikki down the aisle for the second time in a few short months – but what a very different occasion this was.

Emma was buried in the churchyard and the grave was covered with a mountain of flowers. Shortly after, Nikki and I flew back to Zimbabwe. I remember boarding the plane and being told that we had been upgraded to Club class – thanks to niece Fiona who had done our bookings – one of many thoughtful touches that had been such a feature of the whole tragic business.

James visited us in Zimbabwe soon afterwards, and we all went on a cruise in a houseboat on Kariba with Bobby and Arlene Fernandes. On 'Chirume' we built a pretty little thatched hut near the swimming pool and christened it 'Emma's Hut'. We used it a lot, as there was a bar in it, and it was the site of many parties. It is still there today – I think – but the thatch will be rotten and the timbers eaten by white ants. However, the marble stone bearing the inscription – 'Space, Light, Water' – will have survived even the depredations of Mugabe's thugs and one day we might go and get it. Until then it remains there as a tribute to Emma.

* * *

In the next two or three years we received an almost continual stream of mostly young visitors from Great Britain and Australia. Three of our boys were at university or agricultural college; all of them had made a lot of friends and had invited them to visit Zimbabwe, using us on 'Chirume' as a base. In addition, many young school-leavers were coming to Zim for their gap year, on a variety of holidays, jobs or projects. Prominent among the organizations involved in projects was one called Schools Partnership Worldwide (SPW), which recruited the élite of school-leavers and sent them off to various Commonwealth countries, partly to 'live a bit' themselves but also to work with less privileged communities, before embarking on university degrees. Ken Anderson was very involved in this exercise and every year some thirty or forty, eighteen and nineteen-year-old students of both sexes would arrive in Zim, ready to be deployed for nine months to various local schools scattered throughout the remote rural areas.

Their job would be to teach at these schools and generally get involved with the whole community. It was a great concept, both the young 'Poms' and the local Africans benefiting enormously from the project. The locals were exposed to fresh, young minds with a much wider horizon than that of their own local, insular teachers; the SPWs saw how the other half lived in no uncertain fashion, as most schools did not even have running water and were miles from any sort of shop, on very basic dirt roads that would become impassable when it rained.

It was Ken's job to identify which school each would go to and arrange to get them there. On arrival he parked the whole group on Richard Holme's farm, 'Nyahuvu,' and from there he recruited the likes of us to deliver to their allotted school one boy and one girl. This was fun but needed a lot of organizing. Ken insisted on some small payment for his time and energy and asked that each SPW bring him a decent bottle of Scotch whisky, a commodity in very short supply in Zim at that time. I remember him ushering me into his bedroom once and gloatingly indicating some forty one-litre bottles of single malt whisky lined up against the wall. The job was very rewarding.

Nikki and I both had cousins who came out on these projects – Camilla Vaux from Yorkshire and Joss Sclater from Sussex. As was common with most of these SPWs, their parents came to visit them during their stay. Joss was stationed at a school in the Wedza area quite near us, so we saw quite a bit of him. He finished up as acting headmaster of the school when both the proper head and deputy were arrested for embezzlement of the school fees.

We much enjoyed having relations and the friends of our children to stay, despite the mounds of dirty clothes and the considerable thirst of most of them. We did balk a bit when we started getting friends of friends of friends arriving in groups of three or four and staying for up to a week.

On these occasions we had to revert to some none too subtle hints about our going into Marondera and being able to give them a lift to get to their next destination. They all signed our visitors' book, and once they had gone we pencilled a 'rating' beside their names. This was a ten for a really good guy or girl down to zero for an absolute shocker. I don't think we ever got lower than four and certainly there were a number of tens. It was, perhaps, a sign of the times that even young single girls would travel for miles on the local bus from their school back to civilization and think nothing of it.

* * *

Tourism in general was booming at this time, with lovely little lodges springing up in all the best tourist areas to supplement the existing larger lodges and hotels. Canoeing down the Zambezi had taken off in a big way and both Nikki and I did several trips with relations from England. It was, and still is, a marvellous experience, although these days it is done much more from the Zambian side of the river.

A lot of farmers were following Norman Travers's lead and starting up their own little game farms, running game with their cattle in a large, game-fenced area. Many went further than that and built lodges in which to entertain guests or clients. In the Wedza area both Mike Bartlett and Richard Bedford soon had their own lovely little game parks, and sales of game between the many parks springing up all over the country became quite a feature of this new industry. 'Chirume' by its very nature appeared to fit the bill perfectly for game. It was a large broken farm with no interfering crops, plenty of natural water, and a certain amount of game already there, mainly kudu and the smaller antelope such as duiker, steinbuck and oribi. We therefore decided to make our own game park – not initially with any commercial plans, but just to build up a selection of game that would thrive in the area. To this end we game-fenced some fifteen hundred acres with a twelve-foot fence and removed all existing cattle fences within this area. We then built a 'boma', about half an acre in size, fifteen feet high, with a strand of steel wire every foot and a thick dropper every yard. The whole area of this fence was then padded on the inside with some nine inches of thatching grass. We built a small ramp from which we could unload animals from a lorry and installed a small water trough at ground level. There were some lovely big Msasa trees in the boma for shade and nothing inside could see out – which was the plan. Then we started looking round for some animals.

First to come were thirty impala from Central Estates near Mvuma, twenty-six females and four males, which cost Z\$500 each (about GBP30). These we installed in the boma and left there for some two months, feeding them on specially formulated game cubes and green maize suckers. They were pretty wild at first, but they gradually calmed down, and finally we just opened a gate at the bottom of the boma to let them out. They took a couple of days to emerge, and when they finally did we held our breath in the hope that they would not jump straight out of the game park and head back to Mvuma. Luckily they did not, but they always remained fairly wild and did not breed for at least a year.

Richard Bedford then approached us and asked if we would take some of his surplus sable and eland cows, on the condition that, in the years to come, he could bring hunting clients to shoot any bulls that were bred. We were delighted with this plan, and over the next few months had sable cows and the young eland heifers in the boma. Richard also supplied an expensive sable bull to mate with the cows. The plan with the sable worked and soon we had a lovely little herd of fairly tame sable starting to breed. The first lot of eland were not quite so successful, in that when we released them from the boma they jumped straight out of the game park and headed back to Richard. This would have been a cunning ploy on his part if he had been selling them, but as no money was changing hands it did not really matter and he soon supplied some more, which did settle down; they also started breeding.

We then purchased a further selection of animals – zebra for Z\$5,500 (GBP220) each, blesbok and bushbuck for much the same. All did well except the blesbok, which, having produced a couple of babies, all died over a period of about two years. The zebra did particularly well and became very tame, so much so that when riding with the dogs we had to avoid them, as the old stallion would launch a vicious attack on any dog he spotted. The lovely little bushbuck were always very shy and it was a red-letter day if we ever saw one, but they are renowned survivors and they did breed.

Apart from the animals we introduced, we encouraged the resident game and were rewarded by almost guaranteed sightings of magnificent kudu bulls as well as small herds of their cows and calves. These are my favourite antelope and it gave us both enormous pleasure to get quite close to these magnificent animals whenever we rode in the game park. The cows and their offspring were more or less permanent residents, but the big bulls came and went as it pleased them. They could not quite clear the twelve-foot high fence cleanly but would usually crash through the top two or three strands of wire. As well as the kudu there were resident duiker, steinbuck, oribi, reedbuck, serval cats, baboons, vervet monkeys, bush pig, warthog, jackal, and plenty of mongooses, squirrels and snakes. Hyenas were occasional visitors and a caracal was once sighted. Bird life was also prolific, with a selection of different habitats and a wide selection of different species. Nikki soon became an avid spotter. What a joy it was. We never really considered trying to cash in on it, but did have a few friends come to shoot the odd male impala when their numbers grew too large. Richard Bedford also brought some German clients a couple of times and shot one or two decent sable bulls, but mainly we selfishly kept the place to ourselves, only sharing it with visiting guests.

* * *

In 1996 I took Nikki on honeymoon. Three years late, but better then than never. We drove up to Kenya. We went on our own in the Land Rover Discovery, and quite an adventure it was. We did the same trip again in 2005, but this time had friends in a separate vehicle with us all the way. This first time, on our own, the roads in Tanzania (except the one main road which runs from the Zambian border to Arusha, the capital) were terrible and sometimes we would find ourselves about a kilometre from the real road as we searched for a surface suitable to drive on. It could have been a nightmare but in fact was enormous fun, with plenty of hairy moments when we did not know exactly where we were going.

Nikki had been born and brought up in England at a lovely home in the Lake District. She was very much a country girl; riding was her main hobby, but all country activities were familiar to her. She married very young and moved to another estate in Sussex with her husband, John Sclater, after spending a year in America, where he was finishing a course at Harvard University. Back in Sussex, she soon had two children but was always involved with riding and the outdoor life. She did not come to Africa until after she was divorced from John and her children virtually grown up.

She loved it from the very start: the wide-open spaces, the freedom, the lack of crowds, the game and the birds – perhaps particularly the birds. While there is a lot of wild game in Africa one does not see it all the time; there are times when you can travel for half an hour in a game park and see no animals, but there will always be a bird. If there are a hundred different species of mammal in Africa there will be five hundred species of bird, so the challenge to identify them all is enormous. While Nikki loved the animals she very soon became fascinated by the birds. On 'Chirume' alone, within walking distance of the house, we had three different habitats for birds and Nikki's brother James, on one visit to us, identified forty-two different species before breakfast. Nikki would ride her horses round the farm every day. We had five thousand acres of open, hilly land with very little cultivation. Fifteen hundred of this area was a fenced-off game park containing a variety of mammals and lots of birds. The rest of the farm had cattle but few roads and no people. She revelled in the peace and beauty of Africa every day, and how better to appreciate it than on a horse. I rode with her on occasions and we would take the dogs and wander slowly through the game park chatting companionably, hoping to see a new-born eland or zebra or to spot the rare racket-tailed roller at a place in the kopjes that we had named 'Racket-tailed Roller Pass'.

I looked forward to showing her some of the wonderful game parks of East Africa, places that I had marvelled at as a boy and which were now internationally famous. Top of the list here was the Serengeti in northern Tanzania. After spending a couple of nights in Arusha with Adam and Elizabeth Hill, we braved the appalling road to Ngorongoro crater and on into the Serengeti itself. It did not disappoint. The vast flat plain that constitutes the southern part of the park was alive with game, as the annual migration of wildebeest and zebra had just arrived there. There were many other species of game as well and we had some wonderful sightings of lion and cheetah. We were one of the very few visitors to the park who were 'doing their own thing'. Nearly everybody else was attached to an organized tour-operating group, and they tended to adhere to a fairly set pattern of locations covered. We went everywhere they did not, saw just as much game as them and were never part of a circle of camera-clicking tourists surrounding a single, wretched, sleepy old lion. I was amused to see several smart vehicles bearing the A&K logo; it was obvious that they were pretty active in the area.

We left the Serengeti via the seldom visited western corridor and immediately ran into some unseasonable wet weather, then along the shores of Lake Victoria and into Kenya before turning east again and paying a brief visit to a wet Maasai Mara. The road out of the Mara through the Kidong valley and Narok was appalling. It was barely useable, and at one stage we lost it completely as we spent most of the journey driving in the grass beside it. Finally we reached civilization again, in the shape of the main Nakuru/Nairobi road, and drove on to Muthaiga Club. Muthaiga was still a bastion of white colonial privilege and we revelled in being there. I would peer into the bar, expecting to see people I knew, but they all seemed so young – though still white!

Tony and Susie Church held a lunch party for us at their 'castle' near Langata, where we met a number of my old school friends – boring for Nikki, but fun for me as I had not seen some of them for forty years.

On another day we took a picnic and drove down to the old family farm, 'Momandu'. It was in surprisingly good order. Our farm and several of our neighbours' farms had been lumped together, and this increased acreage was run as one unit and owned by a co-operative. This was much the most sensible thing to do in such a dry area, and the herd of Boran cattle that we saw on 'Momandu' looked excellent. Our house was used as the offices for the whole scheme and also looked in good repair. As I write this in 2009 I cannot help but compare this experience with revisiting any of the old commercial farms round Wedza, including 'Chirume'. These are all a complete mess; the houses are invariably used as beer halls – if still fit for use at all – the fences have been stolen, a very few pathetic stalks of maize produce nothing and most of the rest of the land is not used for anything, except perhaps firewood.

It was fun showing Nikki my old home. I had told her so much about it and now she could better envisage the sort of life I had led there as a boy. It was very much her sort of country, with the endless rolling plains still dotted with many different types of game. Shooting of all game had been banned in Kenya since soon after their independence, and it was a delight to see so much around.

We then drove on to Muranga (Fort Hall in my day) to try to find my old guard post at Gikui near Kangema, where I had been based during the Mau Mau uprising.

It was an interesting expedition – all the small towns and villages in Kenya have become totally inundated with people. There were huge crowds everywhere, and as soon as you stopped your car they would swarm around you trying to sell something, or just asking for money – it was revolting. Muranga was like that. I looked for 'Filo's Bar', but inevitably that was not there anymore, and we moved on quickly to avoid the black cloud that descended on us as soon as we stopped.

Sleepy old Kangema was much the same, except for far more people than in my day. I did manage to locate my old office and even spotted a lone post designed to hold a tennis net, down where the tennis court used to be. Such things as tennis courts are not regarded as a priority by the current black rulers of this country, whereas during the Emergency it seemed that a tennis court was a very necessary prop for the security forces. I certainly had played there before going up to George Grimmett's house for a few Tusker lagers.

We hurried on to find Gikui. Gikui as a village no longer existed, but we did (I think) find where my guard post had been. There was no commemorative plaque or anything like that; in fact the whole place had been flattened out, perhaps because the locals had no wish to remember my 'rule' there. It was still lovely, fertile country though, and we drove on through very healthy-looking tea and coffee 'shambas' to a brand new fly-fishing lodge on the Northern Mathioya River. This was a successor to the original one at Tuso and the temporary one that I had supervised the building of at Kangema in 1957. We stayed just one night and were the only guests, but were well looked after by the resident employee. Next day we took a drive as far as we could on the old road up the mountain, a road that used to lead to the two 'forts' up in the forest. The road quickly became impassable, as it had been washed away. We started walking and were soon joined by an old man, very ready to chat to us about the days of the 'mergency', as he called it, and about the activities of the KAR (King's African Rifles). I did not let on to him my role in the area during that time.

We drove on to Nyeri and then back to the main road, reaching Nanyuki in time for lunch. Nanyuki was then, and I think still is, a bastion for retired whites in the area, and certainly we met a few old faces at the Cape Chestnut before driving on to the home and farm of Eddie and Bisto Fernandes. One of their claims to fame is that they are the first whites to have bought land back from a black owner in independent Kenya. Surely this should not be such a big deal? Both Eddie and Bisto were born in Kenya and have spent their life farming in the country, so why should they be prevented from owning land just because they are white? Well, they do own land now – and very productive it is too, with a huge complex of sheds, producing veggies for Europe. The Fernandes's farm is right on the Equator, and during dinner we argued about which way water would spin when going down a plughole. It is said that in the northern hemisphere it goes round one way and in the southern hemisphere the other – I can't remember which is which – but what does it do slap on the Equator? It goes absolutely straight down of course, as we proved in the kitchen after dinner.

Then it was on from the Fernandes's past 'Kisima' – still owned by the Powys family – and down that wonderful escarpment from rich, wet agricultural land to the arid wastes of the Northern Frontier District (NFD). We stopped first at 'Lewa Downs', owned by David Craig but partly leased at that time to Halvor Astrup, a cousin of Nikki's ex-husband. 'Lewa' was being developed as a game ranch and sanctuary for the few remaining black rhino in Kenya.

We then drove to a new lodge in Shava National Park, which was not there in my day. It was very smart and comfortable, so it was a good base from which to drive round that park, as well as the neighbouring Samburu National Park. In these two parks we were lucky enough to see most of the NFD specialities – Grèvy's zebra, reticulated giraffe, gerenuk, Beisa oryx and the vulturine guineafowl. Buffalo Springs was a disappointment; there were nasty little concrete walls all round it and it was not the natural 'bomb hole' that I had swum in with my friends Viv and Sarah thirty-five years before.

From the NFD we drove via Meru and Embu to Kitui. Here I made enquires as to how we could reach the Athi-Tiva grazing scheme. The old road was still there and I got very excited and nostalgic when we crossed the dry, sandy Tiva River and into the area where I had spent such a happy and eventful few months in the early sixties. Sadly, my excitement rapidly turned to disillusionment. We drove the whole length of the old grazing area, but to my horror the place was full of huts and little shambas all surrounded by tatty euphorbia hedges. Scrawny chickens scratched around where there used to be coveys of francolin, a few goats nibbled at bushes that used to feed the rhino and small, native cattle wandered around where the buffalo used to be. I nearly cried. We did find my old campsite, but there was no sign of the spray race that I had built.

We finally emerged at Ikutha without having seen one single wild animal or game bird. I suppose the whole idea of the scheme had been to open the area up for Kamba settlement and we had pioneered the way, but thank goodness I had seen it as God made it.

Next we drove to the coast via Tsavo East National Park. Tsavo East is often regarded as the 'poor relation' of the better known Tsavo West, but it is a fascinating, wild bit of country bordered by the Galana River. This river is so constricted between rocks at the Lugard Falls that one can jump across it. We did see a bit of game, including a lovely herd of buffalo and a roan antelope calf running with an eland mother. We hit the coast at Malindi and drove on to Watamu and Ocean Sports. This used to be the place to stay at the coast in the late fifties, when Ian Pritchard, the guy given a lot of credit for catching Dedan Kimathi, opened it. It was still OK, but it had gone downhill a lot and black 'tarts' in the bar would certainly not have been tolerated in Ian's day.

We drove on the short distance to Kilifi, where we stayed with Richard and Anne Wilson, ex Kilima Kiu and now dairy farming at the coast. They gave a dinner party for us, attended by a number of ex-farmers whom I had known and who were now retired and living at the coast. Nikki was amused to see that all the male guests arrived wearing a kikoi, or skirt as she tended to call them, which is standard 'going out to dinner' dress in that very hot, sticky climate. The Wilsons' farm was still very productive, with 850 cows being milked every day; this provided most of the milk for the inhabitants of Mombasa.

Leaving the Wilsons, we stuck to the coast and drove through Mombasa and south to Nomads – a lovely little lodge, right on the beach, where we indulged ourselves in some delicious fresh seafood. From there the long trek home started, past Shimoni, where I had learned to hunt elephants with old Commander Blunt in the fifties, when he was on elephant control work for the game department and I was just a boy. We crossed into Tanzania at Lunga Lunga and spent that night at Morogoro. This left us a long drive on the morrow, as we wanted to go back via Malawi, but we reckoned that we could just reach the 'luxury'

Livingstonia Beach hotel by dark. We had looked up Livingstonia on the map, so we knew just how far it was. We crossed into Malawi at Horo Horo (I suppose all these obscure border crossings have to double up their name, or no one would ever remember them) and made good progress along the shores of Lake Malawi. We were looking forward to a good dinner and early bed after the long drive as we drew near to Livingstonia, just as it was getting dark. We were a bit surprised to see no big signs advertising this much vaunted luxury hotel, so we stopped at a roadblock and asked the policeman to direct us there. His face went blank. There were no hotels anywhere near here, he told us. What an idiot, we thought, and drove on to a little dorp nearby. Same answer here. But where was Livingstonia? It turned out to be a little mission station up in the hills and not a town at all. Livingstonia Beach Hotel was another 300 miles south on the edge of the lake in Malawi's main tourist area! We were now in a bit of a fix. It was dark, we were tired, we were hungry and we had nowhere to go. Eventually we were directed to a 'tourist lodge', which we found with some difficulty some ten miles back along the road we had just come on. The manager welcomed us, but added discouragingly that he had not had a guest for well over a month. There were no lights, no food and certainly no hot water. But there was a bed. He killed a chicken and cooked it for our supper, having squeezed it first to produce the egg that we shared for breakfast. We drank a couple of warm beers and collapsed into a reasonable bed.

Next morning we had a lovely drive through the Nyika plateau before reaching Lilongwe, the new capital of Malawi, at lunchtime. Here we knew we had to get a visa to go through Mozambique the next day, so we went to the embassy to get one. It was closed. Further investigation revealed that visas for Mozambique were only issued between 8am and noon, and for some unfathomable reason took twenty-four hours to 'process'. This meant we would have to spend two nights in Lilongwe and then have an impossibly long drive home in one day. I was not amused. At the end of a really good long holiday I just wanted to get home. We were only going to be in Mozambique for a couple of hours, passing through on a main road, and for the privilege of doing this our whole trip was to be delayed three days. This sort of thing is the reason why a lot of experienced travellers cross Africa off their visiting list. Certainly there are some fascinating countries to visit but the totally unnecessary red tape, inefficiency and corruption involved make it just not worth the trouble.

In the end Nikki took me to have a good lunch, to cool down and make a plan, something Zimbabweans are renowned for. Nikki is good at doing that sort of thing. We spent one night in Lilongwe, then made a dash for Blantyre next morning; we had to arrive there before noon, so that we could get the precious visa by noon the following day and be able to make it home the same day. We had left our passports at the embassy in Lilongwe, so we could not collect them until they opened at eight o'clock. This meant a two hundred and fifteen mile drive along a pretty grotty road in well under four hours to reach Blantyre in time. Nikki drove – she rather likes this sort of challenge and – scattering goats and chickens, overtaking overloaded buses, and trying to avoid the worst potholes – we made it by five minutes. We still had to wait twenty-four hours to get the ruddy visa, so we made our way to the very upmarket Kuchawe Inn, high in the clouds of the Zomba plateau, where we spent a very pleasant afternoon and evening – sharing the pub with most of the current Malawi Cabinet. I like to think that they were also waiting for their visas.

Next morning we finally got the visas and immediately drove to the border. Here, despite the visa, we still had to pay 'immigration tax' even though we were just passing through, car insurance even though our vehicle was already fully insured, and, finally, more money to cross the Zambezi at Tete. We slunk thankfully back into Zimbabwe and were home just before dark. The whole trip amounted to just over six thousand miles and was a memorable and fascinating experience.

Now we were glad to be back in Zimbabwe. In those days everything still functioned far better than in any of the countries to the north that we had visited. There were a few cracks beginning to appear though, and there was a feeling amongst a lot of we whites that we should perhaps take a more active role in things like local administration, rural councils, schools, etc. With this in mind, I was persuaded to stand for the vacant position of councillor in the Watershed West area of the Wedza Rural District Council constituency. This was the area that included 'Chirume', 'Leeds', 'Collace' and most of the farms on the banks of the Save River.

* * *

Having put my name forward as a candidate, I was immediately approached by the local ZANU (PF) official and asked if I would like to represent his party, it of course being the ruling party. He added with a smile, "Then, of course, you will win!" I declined gracefully and said that I preferred to stand as an independent. So ZANU (PF) fielded their own man against me – one Elliot Chigwedere, a genuine war veteran in the area and brother of the current Wedza MP, Aeneas Chigwedere. He was also the brother of Fanuel Chigwedere, who was to give us all a lot of trouble in the years to come.

I did very little campaigning as I hardly speak any Shona. I visited a few of the larger farm compounds in the area, and I took my two foremen, Never and Tichaona, with me to tell the assembled masses what a jolly good chap I was and that they should elect me as their representative on the local Rural Council. All this was in the days when elections really were free and fair, and it was a very interesting exercise.

Polling took place at two different sites and I had to provide two people who would remain with the voting boxes from the time they were closed and sealed with wax until they were opened the following day in the presence of me and my opponent. I took along Tichaona and the groom, Daniel. They and the ZANU (PF) representatives did indeed stay with the boxes, sleeping beside them that night and still being there, bleary-eyed, next morning when we all arrived for the counting.

Counting took place in the Fair Adventure school and both boxes were opened and the ballot papers tipped on to a large table, whereupon some ten people started separating the papers into two piles – one for me and one for Mr Chigwedere. He and I stood quietly by and watched our respective piles grow. It quite soon became apparent that my pile was growing at a considerably faster pace than his, and by eleven o'clock I was declared the winner with some two thirds of the vote. I went up to Chigwedere and shook hands in a very British fashion. It was all conducted in a most professional, friendly way with no sort of recriminations whatsoever. What a contrast to what happens at elections today. Four years later, in 2001, when there was another Rural Council election, I as the sitting member was not even asked if I was willing to stand again. Indeed there was no election and a ZANU (PF) war vet from 'Bath Farm', called Nyati, was just told that he was the councillor.

Back to 1997. After a few days I was solemnly sworn in as Rural District Councillor for Watershed West, in the Wedza area. I took my seat in the filthy 'boardroom'. I knew a few of my fellow councillors from cattle- and maize-buying deals, and they were all friendly enough, although giving themselves airs far above their status. They referred to the boardroom as 'the House', and made long rambling statements about trivial matters, standing and clutching the lapels of a tattered old tweed jacket while the others nodded wisely at their eloquence. Most of the talk at these meetings would take place in Shona, so I understood very little of what was happening. However, the minutes of the meeting summarized these marathon six-hour sessions in a few short pages, and these were written in English, so I did have a vague idea of what was going on.

The main preoccupation of most meetings was money and where it was coming from. It soon became pretty obvious that the Rural Council was broke, and this was of great concern, mainly to the permanent office staff worried about where their salaries would come from. It also concerned the elected councillors like me, as we were paid mileage and an attendance fee for each meeting we went to – hence a trip to Wedza from remote tribal homes was not only paid for but there was a bit of spending money as well.

Broadly speaking, money was allocated to Rural Councils by government, and they, having precious little themselves, would only dish it out on receipt of meticulously prepared budgets stating why it was required, and perhaps more importantly what sort of money the council was raising itself. Taxes paid by the local commercial farmers featured high on this list, and one of my first jobs was to try and persuade late payers to cough up. Payment of council tax was in fact compulsory, but many farmers were reluctant to pay, as their roads were all in a shocking state and their maintenance was one of the few benefits they got from paying the tax.

The production of the annual budget used to interest me, as it soon became clear that a lot of items listed as potential income for the council had not the remotest chance of producing anything. Gold had been mined on Wedza Mountain in small quantities some thirty years previously and the miners paid a fee to the council to get a licence to dig for it. No one had bought such a licence for at least thirty years, yet a large estimate for funds to be forthcoming from mining fees was religiously entered into the budget every year. Later on, after 2000, when land was dished out freely to anyone who might be persuaded to vote for ZANU (PF), it was decided that these new settlers should pay tax to the council just as their predecessors, the commercial farmers, had done, and a substantial figure was entered into the predicted income column of the budget to reflect this. To my knowledge not one single cent was ever paid by these people to the council.

A lot of the income of Rural Councils came via the government, in the form of aid or grants from such countries as Sweden and the old colonial power, Britain. When the land grab started in 2000 these grants were stopped, and I used to have some fun asking why these donations had been stopped. I got some interesting answers.

* * *

335

Farming was still quite profitable in general and a lot of development was being undertaken in the field of horticulture, with huge rose and other flower ventures springing up under acres of plastic. Paprika was also a new and paying crop, and this was one of the main crops that Harry grew when he eventually took over 'Leeds Farm' from Fran, who moved into town. Harry had by now been back from Australia for a couple of years, after a very distinguished four years at the University of New England in Armidale. He had shocked us all by becoming the university's top student, winning various awards and getting a year's scholarship, which meant that I had to pay nothing for his last year. Milbanks don't usually do that sort of thing and it was a very pleasant surprise. He was offered any amount of excellent jobs in Australia immediately after he left, but all he wanted to do was to return to Zim and farm here, and, after a stint with a crop trading company and more time with Barclays Bank, realized his childhood dream and went farming on his own.

Just before moving on to the farm, he rang me up one Monday and asked if we were doing anything on Saturday. I thought for a bit and finally said, "No."

"Good," he replied, "because I want you to come to our wedding."

He and Flip Shaxon had been living together for some time so it was no real surprise – just a little sudden. The wedding was to be held in the little Anglican Church in Arcturus, with the reception on the nearby farm belonging to Ian and April Piercy. Flip had previously been engaged to their son, Simon, whom Ian employed to work for him in his very successful hunting company, Zambezi Hunters. Simon arranged for his bachelor party to be held on the Zambezi River at one of his father's camps, and the party duly took place. But as can so easily happen when high spirits are fuelled by drink, tragedy struck. No one quite knows exactly what happened to Simon, but he fell into the river and was drowned – not being found for several days.

It was therefore a very brave and generous gesture on the part of April and Ian to offer to host the reception for my son's marriage to Flip; Flip was to them virtually an adopted daughter. It was a lovely occasion, and after the wedding we were delighted to have them living just next door on 'Leeds'.

Our eldest son, Rob, had by now disappeared from the Wedza scene. He, like all my sons, had left Zimbabwe when they finished their 'A' level exams at Peterhouse, to see something of the world. He started off in Florida working as a groom for Geoff Kent, who was then very involved in high-goal polo at West Palm Beach. He then joined the British Army as a 'squaddy' and did a year before attempting to get into Sandhurst. Sadly while training for this he injured his knee very badly, left the army and went to Cirencester Agricultural College instead. I don't think that 'Skel' was ever cut out for the army but he thoroughly enjoyed Cirencester, made a lot of friends, drank a lot of beer and even learned a bit. He did a stint in Australia before returning to Zim and working for Robin Wyrley-Birch at Guruve – always an enlightening and interesting experience. It was not long before he was courting Robin and Felicity von der Heyde's daughter, Amanda, and this culminated in one of those glorious Zimbabwe farm weddings on their beautiful farm, 'Vigila'. There can be few better sites for a wedding reception, and this was a wonderful occasion with all the family there, and several of Rob's Cirencester friends making the effort to attend. Having married the boss's daughter, Rob moved on to 'Vigila' and took over the running of the farm, until Mugabe's purge of white farmers in 2000.

Jack, or 'Spratt' as he was generally known, having survived the traumas of our divorce and an eventful last year at Peterhouse, also took off round the world. As with Rob and Harry polo provided a useful introduction to interesting, influential people and, after a brief stay with old friends John and Lorna Clarke in Florida, he got involved in the American polo scene, before going on to Australia and university at Gatton College, which is the agricultural department of the University of Queensland. Again, like Rob and Harry, he had worked a bit and lived a bit after leaving school and before going to 'uni'. I am sure this is a very good thing, having a break from schooling, and learning what the world is all about on your own, before settling into more studies.

When Rob and Harry were at college in England and Australia, I had been allowed to remit funds from my Zimbabwe bank account to pay the fees, but in Spratt's case Zim was already running out of foreign exchange and I had to use hard-earned savings in England. Polo once again came to the rescue here and to Spratt's eternal credit he paid his own living expenses by working for rich local polo players in his holidays. Thus I only had to find the tuition fees. Australia is very good at encouraging even overseas students to work and get paid. Spratt always intended to return to Zim when he had finished university, but by then Mugabe had made quite sure that no more talent would ever come to Zimbabwe while he was in power; he could make much better use of the agricultural land by dishing it out to his cronies on condition that they went on voting for him. So Spratt stayed in Aussie where he remains.

* * *

At the end of the 1990s there was no pressure at all on land. Any farmer of whatever colour or nationality could buy as many farms as he could afford, provided he got a document called a 'Certificate of No Interest' from the government. This meant exactly what the title said, that the government had no wish to purchase that bit of land and that the person applying to do so could go ahead and buy it with their blessing. Everybody was conscious though that the white commercial farmers did own a disproportionately large chunk of the best agricultural land in Zimbabwe. Most were making very good use of it but some certainly had more land than they could usefully manage. It was therefore agreed that funds should be made available by the international community to purchase land that was offered for sale, to settle deserving indigenous black farmers. This same idea had been put into practice straight after independence in 1980, and there was still some money in that pot which had not yet been used. Likewise, there were several farms purchased under that scheme and still unutilized by indigenous farmers.

A donor conference was set up in Harare in 1998 and many countries agreed to pay money into the fund, which would be used to buy out farmers who wanted to sell, on a 'willing buyer, willing seller' basis. This would usually mean white farmers selling to black farmers. This exercise would cost the government of Zimbabwe nothing – the white farmer would be paid a fair market value for his land and the black farmer would get a decent farm for virtually nothing. There were of course certain conditions that had to be adhered to. I do not know them all, but broadly speaking the whole deal had to be transparent and above board and the recipient of the farm had to prove that he knew how to use it, i.e. that he knew something about farming and would live and work on his new property.

It was all a very good idea and all parties were happy. I am jumping the gun a bit now in this tale when I say that none of these funds have yet been used. Thousands of excellent farmers have lost their farms and homes without one cent of payment, while in their place are either ignorant peasants or 'fat cats', influential cronies of Mugabe like generals and high court judges. They were given the land as a bribe, on condition they continued to support an otherwise unsupportable government. They have been given the very best farms, but few of them live on them– they continue to live in Harare and employ unqualified managers to see that a beast is slaughtered and that the water is hot at the weekend, when they occasionally deign to visit their farm, with a bunch of friends from town who want to have a good time in nice surroundings.

But that was still in the future, and as the 20th century ended we farmers were still optimistic about the way ahead, despite widening cracks in the whole infrastructure. As we produced most of the country's food, brought in huge amounts of foreign currency and provided work for hundreds of thousands of rural people we thought that we at least were something of a sacred cow and would not be disturbed by political upheavals. Little did we know.

CHAPTER 21

Two Thousand

THE WEDZA AND RUZAWI RIVER FARMING COMMUNITIES celebrated the new millennium in some style. A mammoth party was planned to take place on the banks of the area's largest dam, which was situated on 'Scorror Farm', the property of Jenny Whaley and run by her son-in-law, Ian Duvenage. Marquees were hired, a band brought out from Harare, tables, chairs and cutlery lent by both clubs and mountains of food and gallons of drink laid on.

Virtually everybody turned up and most planned to spend the night, bringing some form of camping equipment. Nikki and I drove over from 'Chirume' and joined up with the Bartletts, Burgoynes and Whitfields for the evening. The magnificent dam had originally been built by Rick Holme, my father-in-law, in the early '70s, but had been considerably enlarged by the present owners. As dusk fell on the evening of December 31, 1999, it was a colourful scene, with multi-coloured tents all along the shoreline, smart, new 4x4 vehicles parked close by and many sailing and motor boats on the dam itself.

The mood was cheerful and cautiously optimistic for continued prosperity and security in a booming community. There had been a few dark clouds on the horizon for sure. A few farms had been 'listed' sometime ago but nothing had happened. Mugabe was universally unpopular, as the economy was suffering mainly due to corruption and mismanagement, and he was openly referred to in the streets of Harare as 'Tim', which stood for 'That Idiot Mugabe'.

But farming was booming and most of the people present at that party were making plenty of money. Many had expensive motorboats on the dam, all had two or three newish cars, others had new holiday bungalows on the recently opened up Mozambique coast. Sons of older farmers had come back to help run, or even take over the family farm, having completed university or agricultural college overseas. The older farmers were contemplating a relaxed semi-retirement on their farms, probably concentrating on running the cattle while the youngsters took over the more demanding side, doing tobacco, maize, paprika or horticulture.

Tim Bartlett had recently married his English girlfriend, Becks, and was heavily involved in expanding the rose business on the family farm, 'Rapako'. Peter Bibby, also recently married, was back transforming 'Bita'. David England, having taken over 'Lifton' from his father, Jack, was fast becoming one of the best tobacco growers in the whole country. Amongst others, Clive Webb-Martin, Paul Grinham and John Travers were all firmly in the saddle, running the family farms much more progressively than their fathers. And of course Harry, now married to Flip, was getting stuck into 'Leeds' in no uncertain fashion.

Rob had taken over the running of his in-laws' farm, 'Vigila', at Mvurwi and Jack, just finishing his university degree at Gatton College in Queensland, was keen to come home and possibly take over 'Chirume'.

I think it is true to say that no one was considering any kind of move either away from agriculture or out of the country. The opposite was true, as a lot of the money being made was being ploughed back into the land. Centre-pivot irrigation was an expensive new tool for producing even better crops; huge plastic greenhouses were home to an ever-increasing volume of flowers for export to Holland and then all over the world, and the very dam where we were was proof of the long-term commitment to agriculture in the Wedza area.

There was rain the night of that party and many of the 4x4s were glad of the 4-wheel drive bit to enable them to drive home after a memorable party. The rain was seen as a good omen for the year and indeed for the millennium to come.

* * *

Farmers' meetings at Wedza had always been well attended and there was no exception to this early in 2000. There was much talk at these meetings about the approaching referendum concerning a new constitution, which, if passed, would virtually have guaranteed the incumbent President – Mugabe – lifetime tenure. Clearly this would be undesirable however good the incumbent, and in Zimbabwe's case it would be a disaster. Our Farmers Association chairman, Scott von Memerty, got speakers out from Harare to explain the whole scenario to us and we were urged to explain to our labour what was going on. A new, independent newspaper called the *Daily News* had just hit the streets, to give its readers a truer insight into what was actually going on in the country as opposed to the government's version as detailed in *The Herald.* We were urged to subscribe to this and distribute copies to our labour.

We also learnt about a new, fledgling political party with the Trades Union leader, Morgan Tsvangirai, at its head; this was challenging the government over the proposed new constitution and gaining a lot of support in the urban areas. The party was called the Movement for Democratic Change or MDC, and it promised a clean-up of the corruption that was now clearly widespread in the current government. This sort of scenario is not uncommon in Africa or in a lot of Third World countries. A long-term ruling party runs out of energy and ideas, so it reverts to corruption to keep its top brass happy and in funds. Any change can only be for the good if one party has been in power for over twenty years. The MDC was a very new party and it is easy to make fanciful promises, but there was a general feeling amongst blacks and whites that we were well overdue for a change. We were urged to donate funds to this party, as it was the first really viable opposition to Mugabe's reign as leader of ZANU (PF) and a general election was due early that year.

I well remember queuing up with most of the other people at one meeting and donating money towards this new party. They had promotional T-shirts printed and made available locally. It became quite common to see bands of youths walking around the area wearing these MDC shirts and waving their hands in the open palm salute, which MDC had adopted as their trademark.

A big meeting was arranged at Bromley Club to co-ordinate the views and feelings of all Farmers Associations in Mashonaland East, and the president of the Commercial Farmers Union (CFU), Tim Henwood, addressed it. He stressed the vital importance of getting a 'NO' vote at the forthcoming referendum and then supporting the MDC in the general election, which would follow soon after. I confess that I had never paid a lot of attention to national politics – Mugabe was President and no one had really challenged him; it had not seemed our responsibility to help bring about his demise. But now we were told that the country really was slipping downhill quite fast and it was essential for a change at the top, and we whites must help bring it about.

I had been, and still was, quite prepared to do my bit in our local community and was still the councillor for Watershed West on the Wedza Rural District Council, but while supporting a change in government I was not going to do a hell of a lot about it. I did distribute the *Daily News* to our labour but never bought them MDC T-shirts or preached the need for change. I am not sure quite what they really thought at that time but I suspect much the same as me. In a way the local black community in our immediate area had demonstrated their disenchantment with the government by voting me in as their councillor instead of the ZANU (PF) candidate, whom I had easily defeated the previous year.

In mid-February the much-anticipated referendum was held and to everybody's amazement a resounding 'NO' vote was recorded. The streets of Harare were thronged with a jubilant population celebrating the first defeat that Mugabe had suffered in twenty years. It was now that we got the first taste of things to come. Riot police brutally broke up the celebrations and many innocent people who just happened to be on the streets got beaten up. Mugabe appeared on national television to say that he would accept the will of the people, but this was just the first of a string of blatant lies which he deliberately told to lull people into believing that he would always act democratically. Nothing could have been further from the truth.

It did not take long for the reaction to the referendum result to make itself felt in the commercial farming areas. We in Wedza were no exception. Within days a group of squatters had moved on to Paul Grinham's 'Shaka Farm' just outside Wedza. They put up tatty little grass shacks near the barns and refused to move. At first they were not aggressive but just a minor nuisance. Paul approached the police and asked for them to be removed from his property. It was immediately clear that the police had received instructions not to remove them. They did not say as much to the farmer but embarked on a series of weak excuses and just did nothing. The most frequent excuse was, "We have no transport", a refrain that was to become a catchphrase in the months and years to come.

Soon after this, gangs of youths, usually led by one or two older men who claimed to be war veterans, started pitching up at farms and rattling the security gates, blowing whistles, singing, shouting and demanding to see the resident farmer. If the farmer appeared, he was usually harangued, insulted and told that they had come to take over his farm and that he should leave. Often they would stay all night making a filthy din and generally making life extremely unpleasant for the farmer and his family – it was scary! They were nearly always well fuelled with drink and drugs, so there was no telling what they might do, and there was no one in authority who was prepared to come to your assistance. Friends and neighbours certainly did whenever possible.

Due to the complete non-co-operation of the police it was obvious that we had to help ourselves. We already had a Wedza Farm Security group, most ably run by Richard Tilley and Sgt-Major Moses, but their resources were very stretched, and so it was decided that the Wedza area would have what became known as 'the talk team'. This consisted of three local farmers who all possessed good negotiating skills, and it was they who went to the assistance of farmers being hassled by bunches of thugs – thugs who, as it soon turned out, were being paid to make our lives a misery. The three were Harry Orphanides, a past chairman of the Wedza Farmers Association and current owner of the large agricultural supply store, 'Farm-A-Rama', in Marondera. Harry was of Greek extraction, a good businessman and formidable debater. Then there was Derek Hinde, who was a leading farmer in the area, ex-captain of the Rhodesian hockey team, ex-dairyman of the year and currently a very prominent exporter of flowers to Europe. Derek had a very cool, calm temperament and acted as a foil to the more excitable Harry. The third member of the group was Ben Fourie, leader of the Afrikaner community from 'Dutchman's Corner'. Ben was another very calm character and had the vital attributes of speaking fluent Shona and being a strong Christian.

I do not think that the debt the whole area owed to these three was ever properly acknowledged. When a gang of thugs arrived at your security gate – all full of Dutch courage in the form of booze and drugs – you were advised to lock every door and gate possible, enter into no sort of dialogue, get on the agric-alert and call the talk team. Harry, Ben and Derek would then drop everything they were doing and come immediately to your assistance.

They would sometimes have details from the Wedza Farm Security to back them up, but virtually never a regular policeman, whose duty it was to protect people against public violence. They would drive up to the gang and try to persuade them to disperse quietly, and to bring up any demands or grievances they had through the proper channels. As the thugs did not have the faintest idea what the proper channels were and as far as they were concerned were carrying out orders to the letter, this was not an easy task. But it is to the talk team's eternal credit that they did manage to defuse countless nasty situations that could easily have got a lot nastier. Perhaps even more importantly to the farmer, locked in his house, was the knowledge that there was somebody outside whom he could talk to on the radio and knew was trying to help him, because sure as hell no-one else was.

On Wednesday, April 19, 2000 I was attending a meeting of the Rural District Council when I was called away to the telephone. It was Nikki saying that the Hills, just next door, were locked in their house with a gang of thugs outside and she thought that I should return. I thought so too and told her to get off the farm and go to Marondera, which she was sort of planning to do anyway. When I got back, the whole place was eerily quiet and the house and garden staff were nowhere to be seen. I locked the security gate and got myself some lunch.

At half past one there was suddenly a lot of shouting, the bell that we had attached to the security gate was repeatedly rung, and I heard my name being shouted out. Acting on what we had been told to do in these circumstances, I ignored demands for me to appear and got on the agric-alert to the talk team. As luck would have it they were already heavily involved in another 'scene' some distance away and were unable to come to 'Chirume'. I peered through the sitting-room curtains which I had drawn, and could just see a large mob by the main security gate; they were rattling it and shouting for me. I felt frightened and alone, wondering what I would do if they broke the gate down and came inside. 'Chirume' house had no burglar bars on any of the windows and anyone could get inside with no trouble at all. I returned to the agric-alert and gave the talk team an update on what was happening. They told me to keep talking to them, and if matters did get worse they would try and come to help – but they were a long way away.

The afternoon wore on with a lot of singing, beating of drums and general noise, then quite suddenly at about four-thirty all went quiet. At first I was suspicious, thinking that perhaps they had broken down the gate and were creeping up on me – but no, they had all gone. Even so, it was quite a long time before I ventured out. Eventually I plucked up courage and went in search of my labour and my foreman, Never. He appeared from his compound with a sickly smile on his face and looking suitably embarrassed.

I quizzed him on how he had been involved. His story was probably true. The mob that had been at Mike Hill's was led by a so-called war vet named Choto, who was about Robert's age and would have been in nappies during the war. Choto was backed up by others from Wedza Township, namely Magumesi, Chibaya and Zinyoro, all of whom held minor government jobs and all of whom I knew slightly because of my involvement with the Rural Council. The vast bulk of the mob consisted of Mike Hill's labour force, which had been press-ganged into coming along to create the illusion of a spontaneous demonstration against the wicked white farmer who had stolen all their land. The singing had had nothing to do with land though; it was entirely about the wonders of the ZANU (PF) government.

Had I been frightened while all this was going on? Yes, certainly. One just did not know where these staged demonstrations would end up. I think I would have been a lot more frightened if I had known what would happen to friends of mine in similar circumstances in the very near future. Barely two weeks later, Ian Kay, who farmed in the Ruzawi River area, was lucky to escape with his life when a gang set upon him with the clear intention of killing him, and he only escaped because of the intervention of his son, David. Soon after that David Stevens, from nearby Macheke, was murdered in the most brutal manner. Then Alan Dunn, who had farmed just next door on 'Fair Adventure' and who had celebrated his twenty-first birthday in our house, was murdered on the farm he now owned in the Norton area. It happened on a Sunday afternoon in broad daylight, with his wife and children inside the house.

Alan's murder shook me. He had recently defeated the ZANU (PF) candidate in the local Rural Council election, and the loser, a very prominent war vet leader, had vowed revenge. I had defeated the brother of our local war vet leader, Fanuel Chigwedere, in our local election. There is little doubt that there was a government approved 'hit list' and it crossed my mind that I could be on it.

In fact I knew Fanuel Chigwedere very well. For the past few years I had been buying his maize, and he still owed me money for some seed potatoes I had sold him. He was a genuine war vet and had been elected at this time to mastermind and lead the gangs involved in the farm invasions. As far as the government and he were concerned, he did a very good job. Over the next couple of years his would become a household name throughout the area. He had a loud blustering manner, wore an appalling old battered hat, seldom shaved and usually smelt of booze. He listened to no reason at all – as far as he was concerned we whites could and should all go back to England. The fact that the farmers in Wedza, like those in most other areas, came from a variety of different countries like Greece, Germany, Holland and, particularly, South Africa, was irrelevant. More to the point, many had been born and bred in Zimbabwe as had their parents and often grandparents, before them.

We had a very odd relationship with Chigwedere. We all knew him and might bump into him at the post office in Wedza, and have quite a civilized chat. I frequently sat next to him at Rural Council meetings, as he was often co-opted in because of his new exalted status, yet that same night he could be at the head of a gang of thugs, demanding that you vacate your farm or threatening to kill you.

This sort of relationship epitomized what was going on. It was hard positively to identify your enemy. I had fought against the Mau Mau and there the battle lines were clear. It was the colonial government, backed by the full resources of a civilized administration, against a bunch of bandits. In the 'bush war' in Rhodesia during the seventies much the same had been true. We were employed by the government of the time to fight terrorists, insurgents, or freedom fighters – whatever you like to call them. If you had a problem, organized and legal help was readily at hand. Now though, you were fighting your own government and it was impossible to know what 'weapons' to use.

We did not know whom to turn to. The police clearly were not going to help. David Stevens had been shot while being held in Mrewa police station, and no police officer made any move to prevent it let alone arrest anyone for murder. The Government branded us as enemies of the state, and any government official, like the District Administrator, was totally unapproachable. In theory we could have all banded together and fought the illegal invaders of our property, but any sign of violence on our part would have had us arrested immediately – indeed, the strongest advice given to us by our leaders in the Commercial Farmers Union was not to react in any way. This was excellent advice, although sometimes difficult to act upon. The mobs wanted us to react so that the police could arrest us, not them, for breaching the peace or on some other trumped-up charge.

Harry once reacted to trouble on the Amms' farm, Bolton, just next door to him. The Amms' manager, Mike Moran, and his wife and family were locked in their house with a howling mob outside, and Harry persuaded his own labour to come with him just to show some sort of support and a presence, as the talk team was unavailable. The mob reacted violently to Harry and his guys being there at all; then the police miraculously appeared and arrested Harry for disturbing the peace. There followed the first of many of Harry's appearances in court on similar such trumped-up charges. A lawyer came out from Harare to defend him and a large number of local farmers congregated near the courthouse to give moral support. The case was 'remanded' by a nervous magistrate, who clearly did not know what he should do. There was clearly no case against Harry but he did not dare say as much.

It was a very difficult time and one constantly had an ear to the agric-alert to hear what was going on in the area – and there was nearly always a lot going on in the months of March to June in 2000.

Richard Tilley and his Wedza Farm Security had an unenviable task. When the little company had been formed it had the blessing of the police, but now they were definitely frowned upon by them, because they reacted to calls for help that should have been dealt with by the police themselves. However the police would not now react because they had received orders from higher up to do nothing. Every evening Richard did a roll call on the agric-alert of everyone in the area and then followed this with a sitrep (situation report) of what had been going on in the area that day. This was often followed by another sitrep (often read by Mandy Keith from Marondera North) detailing what had been happening in the rest of the country – this could take a very long time. It was apparent that there was plenty going on countrywide.

About this time a member of the new political party, the MDC, arranged a meeting for our area, which was held at the nearby Lustleigh Farm School. He wanted to explain what his party was all about and to try to persuade us and, more importantly, our farm labour, to vote for them in the forthcoming election. Most of us went to that meeting and took with us as many of our labourers as possible. The result was a huge gathering at the school and the MDC guy got a very good reception. I think we were all very heartened that there was what appeared to be a well-organized opposition, which we could vote for and hopefully get a change of government.

Russell Tapson, who farmed with his father, Neville, on 'Dean Farm' just south of us, was thrilled by the idea of ZANU (PF) getting a bloody nose, so on his way home when passing a bunch of ZANU thugs camped on Doug Stanley's 'Fair Adventure Farm', he waved two fingers at them and generally shouted abuse to the effect that their days were numbered. This action nearly cost him his life. Within hours he had received death threats, his house was trashed, his father's house burned, the farm labour force beaten up and the entire tobacco crop, which had been graded, baled and was just waiting to be sent to market, was set on fire (I suppose tobacco gets burned eventually, anyway, but this was a bit premature). Russell had to leave the area immediately and go into hiding in Harare. He never returned.

It was immediately apparent that ZANU (PF) did not take kindly to opposition meetings in our area. It was the first and only such meeting ever to be held in the Wedza farming area, and from then on the very use of the words 'MDC' was likely to get you into trouble.

Around Easter time for the past few years our old friend Ken Anderson had visited us. He was now working at Durham University in England. Ken still had many friends in Zimbabwe, and he usually timed his visits to coincide with a local wedding or christening, at which functions he was in great demand to officiate. The year 2000 was no exception and he came to stay with us on 'Chirume' for the Easter weekend; he agreed to take the Easter church service at the little church near the club where he had married us. With him were his twin brother, Mikey, and a friend from Italy called Jenny Greenleaves, professor of African History at Florence University. We had planned a lunch party at the farm to follow church and had invited a lot of Ken's friends from the area. Everybody looked forward to Ken's visits, as we were very short of decent priests and his presence would guarantee a full house at church.

This Easter Sunday though was different. From early in the morning the agric-alert was blaring with a series of crises all over the area. We were still on the mid-band channel at the time, while most people were on high band, and so we only got a bit of a second-hand version of what was going on, and I had not been able to respond to many of the pleas for help from neighbours having problems. The talk team was fully occupied trying to help Bill Maltzer, who was barricaded in his house with a screaming mob outside demanding to know why he owned more than one farm. Doug Stanley, just down the road from us, was trying to prevent thugs from driving off with his tractors, and Neville Tapson's tobacco barns on 'Dean Farm' had been set on fire.

When we arrived at the church with Ken I think I was about the only other man present – all the rest were busy elsewhere. There were a lot of the area's womenfolk there, and a few men drifted in towards the end of the service, but it was far from the happy family occasion that we had all hoped for. When we arrived back at 'Chirume' I was stopped at our security gate by a small gang of thugs headed by Zinyoro, a 'war vet' from Wedza and some twenty-odd years old. He wanted to know why I was selling 'the people's' wood to a dealer from Harare and he had the driver of the lorry transporting the wood under arrest. He said that he wanted to take me to Wedza for questioning. I had written permission from the correct authorities to sell this wood. Zinyoro was a private citizen and had absolutely no right to question me on the subject, and even less to arrest a poor man just doing his job. It was one of our first direct experiences of the complete breakdown of law and order in the country.

It all made for a bizarre scene. As our guests arrived for lunch they had to wade through a gesticulating knot of thugs, with Zinyoro and me

351

arguing the toss in the centre and the wretched driver asking for help from anyone who would listen. No one was remotely interested in his problem though, and all pushed on towards the house, where Nikki was waiting to fortify them with Bloody Marys. I managed to escape and joined them, while more guests drifted in throughout the afternoon with hair-raising stories of what was going on in the area. I am sure Ken wished he were safely back in Durham.

On the Easter Monday we decided to drive over to Ruzawi River Club for a game of golf with Ken, Mikey and Harry. On the way we drove through numerous gum plantations and in each case the road through these plantations was strewn with leaves stripped from gum branches. We wondered what the reason was for this, and were told by Harry that thugs were breaking off branches and stripping the leaves, before using the resultant sticks to beat farm labourers whom they suspected of being MDC supporters. These labour beatings were a nightly occurrence. David England's workers had been so badly beaten that none could work next day. David asked Harry to close the bottle store, which he ran in conjunction with 'Leeds Butchery', as David maintained that the thugs, most of whom lived on nearby 'Bath Farm', stopped in at the bottle store and filled themselves up with booze to lend impetus to their beating mission. They were being paid to do the beatings but clearly it still worried a few of the more thinking souls amongst them, and a hefty intake of vodka did much to dispel any queasy inhibitions.

Our golf at Ruzawi Club was interesting. No one else was playing and the club was closed, having been trashed the night before. Initially no one was around, but eventually a few caddies appeared and we set off on our round. We were just finishing the first nine when we heard a huge din coming from the direction of the nearby 'Igava Farm' headquarters, and soon we could discern a gang of youths, waving sticks, approaching the club. I was keen to beat it to the vehicles but we would not have got there before the gang arrived at the club and Harry maintained that he wanted to finish the round anyway. The caddies had no such wish and immediately took off into the bush. Rather like a cat being attracted to anything running away, this drew the attention of the gang, who immediately took off in hot pursuit and ignored us. Amazingly we were left alone and completed our round, albeit carrying our own clubs.

Another meeting was called, which was to be attended by all commercial farmers in the area plus their labour, but this time it was a ZANU (PF) meeting. The venue was again Lustleigh School. On arrival we were greeted by teenage ZANU (PF) thugs carrying whips, who acted as ushers and indicated where we should sit – commercial farmers in one area and the labour somewhere else. It was a bizarre scene. Harry, Tim Bartlett and other youngsters started giggling and taking the mickey out of the young thugs; this did not go down well and I remember telling Harry to shut up. The meeting was addressed by leading ZANU (PF) bigwigs from Harare, supported by the local hierarchy, with Chigwedere and the Wedza District Administrator, Munuwe, well to the fore.

Also on the podium, as it were, was John Parkin, a commercial farmer from Macheke. John had once worked on 'Scorror' for Rick Holme and I knew him well. It seems he was a bit of a progressive thinker and had taken the lead in his area, Macheke, in trying to defuse the mounting tension between the government and commercial farmers, by getting the farmers to adopt a different outlook to the whole land issue. When his turn came to speak he urged us to be more liberal in our thinking, drop our old prejudices and, above all, show more respect to the local indigenous population. I am sure he was well-meaning, but as was proved later he had entirely missed the point. There was only one agenda for this whole circus – to win the election – and the best way to do this was to terrify the population into not voting for the MDC.

When the bigwigs from Harare had had their say, this is pretty much what they proceeded to do. They spoke mainly in Shona and told our labour that they would be in deep trouble if they voted for anyone but ZANU (PF). They made it perfectly clear that they had ways and means of knowing how everyone had voted – despite what should be a secret ballot. The meeting ended and we were escorted back to our vehicles by the whip-bearing thugs. This was by no means the last such meeting to be held in the Wedza area, and our labour were frequently being summoned to rabidly pro-government meetings, accompanied by dire threats of what would happen if they did not go.

Most of the local troublemakers were recruited from 'Bath Farm' just down the road from 'Leeds'. 'Bath' had until quite recently been a commercial farm owned by Peter Hudson and then Gerry von Memerty; however it was bought by the government during one of the early resettlement programmes with money supplied by Britain. Bought, mind you and paid for. Initially the farm was given to one of Mugabe's ministers; given to one man instead of being parcelled out to the land-hungry masses. In those days there was a moderately free press, and such an outcry was made that the minister had to give the farm back. It was then settled by a new bunch of indigenous, small-scale farmers. It was the youths and dependants of these farmers who had little income and so were recruited and paid to be the basis of the gangs used to terrorise the white farmers in our immediate area.

The farm labour from 'Bolton', 'Leeds', 'Corby', 'Lifton', 'Collace', 'Fair Adventure' and 'Chirume' were frequently told to report to 'Bath' and would be kept there all night, either being marched up and down the road singing party political songs, or subjected to lectures on the glory of ZANU.(PF), frequently accompanied by beatings to reinforce the message. It was intimidation of the most basic and brutal kind. The police knew all about it, but as in other such matters had been told not to interfere. Our own member-in-charge at Wedza was called Nyamatamba. He was probably originally a perfectly good honest policeman of the old school; he did sometimes make some attempt to carry out the duties that he had sworn to, but it was never more than a gesture, and he would usually fall back on the timeworn excuse of 'no transport' if some of the more blatant human rights abuses were carried out.

Our workers on 'Chirume' were in a permanent state of nervous tension, never knowing when they would be summoned to yet another session on 'Bath'. I tried talking to them about the whole problem, but they were too terrified to say much. Occasionally, if I had Never or Tichaona in the front of the car with me and no one else within earshot, they would convey their deep concern and ask me what was really going on. I could not be much help to them, I am afraid – none of us knew what was going on either.

A question that we frequently asked, both of our own labour and at farmers' meetings or in private conversation with friends was, "Why don't all the farm labour gang up together and beat up the thugs?"

In truth there were only relatively few thugs and far more farm labourers, and if only a few farms had joined forces they could easily have routed the thugs. This however was exactly what the government wanted to happen. If the labour had reacted in this way, the police would miraculously have found some transport and descended on the farm in no time at all, arresting not only the labour for disturbing the peace, but the white farmer as well for 'inciting violence'. We were told in no uncertain terms by our leaders to prevent this sort of thing happening at all costs.

* * *

My old friend John Bibby now had his son Peter working for him on 'Bita Farm', which bordered the Save North African farming area. Peter was a very progressive farmer and had realized some time ago that to succeed in farming in today's Zimbabwe it was necessary to get on with and be helpful to one's African neighbours. To this end he had gone out of his way to help the small-scale African farmers across the river from 'Bita'. He gave them advice, sold them seedlings, transported goods for them and even did a lot of their ploughing. The result was that he had excellent relations with his neighbours, and the last thing they wanted was for Peter and John to be chucked off the farm. This certainly did not suit the government's plan, as they were painting all white farmers as racist pigs who only used the locals to enrich themselves. The last thing they wanted was to have a white farmer liked, respected and wanted by his black neighbours. So they hatched a plan.

Peter was away on holiday when one Saturday afternoon they sent a truckload of thugs from 'Markwe Farm' to 'Bita'. In the truck was the dead body of a youth who had been killed in a fracas the day before. They dumped this body in the 'Bita' compound and set about beating up the labour. The labour put up some resistance and John phoned the police in Wedza. This time they arrived in double quick time; not to arrest the gang of thugs who had started the trouble, but the farm labour for fighting and John Bibby himself for murder. John was whisked off to Wedza police station, where he was charged with inciting his labour to murder the youth whose body had been dumped in his compound. Several of his labourers were also charged with the murder.

John was to remain locked up in a crowded cell in Marondera prison for two weeks before being brought to trial in Marondera. His thick, grey hair had all been shaved off and he appeared in the dock in dirty green prison shorts. His lawyer managed to get the case remanded and John released on bail. John went into hiding in a house in Harare and never lived on 'Bita' again. The case was eventually dropped because the government had achieved their objective in getting the Bibbys off their farm. Peter had returned from his leave as soon as he heard what was going on and was prepared to take his elderly father's place in prison. There was a warrant out for his arrest to face similar charges anyway, so there was little point in them both being locked up and Peter just made himself scarce.

The farm next to 'Chirume' was the lovely 'Collace Farm', which I had leased from Bruce Campbell for a number of years during the war. Bruce had since sold it to Hamish Lumsden. Hamish died, and his widow Betty took over the running of the farm aided by Bill Malzer. Betty did not live on 'Collace', as she had two other farms near Marondera, but employed a series of managers. None appeared to last very long, and we had barely got to know them before they suddenly disappeared under some sort of a cloud. The latest was one Ednam Dudley, an impoverished aristocratic Englishman aged 65-plus. Ednam and his older wife, Joan, had fallen on hard times and were glad of the job on 'Collace'. Betty kept them on a pretty tight rein, and they were given very little fuel for their ancient Mercedes car and so seldom got off the farm.

We had had to rescue them once when they were being threatened by a large mob of thugs who wanted them off 'Collace', claiming that Betty already had two other farms and did not deserve to have 'Collace' as well. They came and stayed with us for a week until the situation calmed down a bit before moving back. Then just before the elections we got another frantic call from them on the Agric saying that they were being threatened at knifepoint to get out of their house immediately. We got hold of Richard Tilley, and he alerted other farmers in the area and a posse of us drove over to 'Collace' house to see what we could do to help.

We got a very hostile reception. The old Dudleys were locked in a room while a bunch of women rattled tins and kept up an appalling racket, singing Chimurenga songs while the men, spearheaded by the local deputy war vet leader, Choto, were busy chucking furniture out of the house. Richard acted as our spokesman and succeeded in persuading the thugs to let us remove all the Dudleys' possessions and load them on to a lorry supplied by Dries Smith. This we proceeded to do. We got zero help from the thugs, who stood insolently watching us while Mike Bartlett, myself, the Smith brothers and one or two others loaded everything on to the lorry. At one stage Choto took me on one side, grabbed me by the shirt front and hissed at me, "OK, where are the guns?"

As far as I knew there were no guns, and Ednam confirmed this, but Choto took a lot of convincing. If we had found any, there is no doubt that we would not have been allowed to put those on the lorry – Mr Choto would have taken them for himself.

Having finally loaded the lorry, Dries drove it off to his place for safekeeping, and I helped Joan and Ednam to their car, telling them to follow me back to 'Chirume'. Joan's main concern was for her sewing basket, and I had to go back and rummage through the contents of the lorry until I could locate it. Once she had it safely in her hands she visibly relaxed. They stayed with us at 'Chirume' for about ten days before finally departing to an old folk's home in England, which Mike Whitfield had gone to some trouble to locate for them.

Mike and Fiona Whitfield were having plenty of troubles of their own at that time. Their son, Ed, recently married to Katherine, was back on their farm, 'Plymtree', doing most of the active farming, while Mike swanned off to Pietersburg in South Africa to buy spares. Ed was a bit like Harry and did not take kindly to being asked to leave the farm that he had just taken over. The result was that he was somewhat confrontational and therefore targeted for a lot of trouble. One day Mike was in Pietersburg and Ed and Katherine in Harare when we got a desperate call for help from Mike's old mother, Judy, who lived in a cottage at the bottom of their garden. Nikki and I rushed over there, to find a gang of thugs chasing all the farm labour out of their houses and also making off with some of Mike and Ed's tractors. Chaos reigned, and poor Judy was in the middle of all this, not knowing what was going to happen next. We loaded her and her precious little Jack Russell into our Land Rover Discovery and took her back to 'Chirume'.

That was just one more nail in that particular farm's coffin and it was not long before Judy was relocated into Borodaile Trust, Mike and Fiona moved to their house in Harare and Ed and Katherine returned to England.

* * *

The build-up to the general election was hotting up, and the farm labour came under increasing pressure. Almost nightly they had to attend some sort of meeting, and this was often followed by their being marched up and down the tar road opposite 'Leeds Butchery' and forced to sing pro-government songs while damning the MDC opposition. The result was that we were getting very little work done on the farm. The flip side of this antagonism towards the labour was that deputations arrived from the administration in Wedza with instructions to parcel out bits of my farm and give it to the labour. At one stage I was asked which bit I wanted to give them. This was just the start of the totally chaotic allocation of land to anyone. On one such occasion, an old cattle buyer happened to be sitting around waiting to see me when one of these delegations arrived, and to his amazement he was allocated a bit of my farm as well!

The day of the election dawned and we were all determined to vote. There were a number of polling stations in our immediate area – at 'Lustleigh', at 'Fair Adventure School' and near the Save River. I had intended taking a truckload of our labour to the nearby 'Fair Adventure', but I was warned on the Agric that this had long queues and voting could take a long time, so I decided to drive a bit further and go to the Save River one. Opposite Ralph Collins's old farm, 'Skipton', I encountered a log across the road, and when forced to stop was immediately surrounded by a gang of young thugs, some of whom I knew. They were quite open in their questions; they said that if any of us had anything to do with the MDC we could go no further. I talked my way through that one only to be confronted with exactly the same thing a few miles further on. There was nothing remotely official about these roadblocks – just bunches of thugs. When I eventually got home I rang the police to tell them that people were being actively prevented from exercising their constitutional right to vote for whoever they wanted. I might as well have been speaking to a brick wall for all the response I got.

I have no idea who my labour actually did vote for but I suspect ZANU (PF), as they were pretty well cowed by that stage. At any rate the ZANU (PF) candidate for Wedza, Aeneas Chigwedere, Fanuel's brother, got in quite easily. The result of this election has been well documented and it is now history that the ruling party just squeaked in. I have not the slightest doubt that they lost. I heard too many authentic stories of the sort of rigging that took place. Close to home in Marondera, the counting of votes was being monitored by a selected bunch of officials. One of these was the Rev Sam Ndoma, Ken Anderson's successor as the Rector of Marondera. The vote count was going seriously against the incumbent ZANU (PF) candidate, Minister Sydney Sekeremai. Sam was asked to leave the room, and you can guess who finally won.

So ZANU (PF) had their majority – just – and the thirty seats that the President was allowed to add by nominating his own MPs then boosted this; it was something that I never really understood. However, with over forty seats the MDC were a real opposition, and we are told that as they took their seats at the opening of parliament, there was a real sense of optimism. There were five whites in this group.

We in Wedza were very disappointed, but we hoped that the pressure on us would now ease, as the government had got what they desperately needed. It is true to say that most farmers were still on their farms at this stage. Many had had a 'Section 5' notice, which was published in the *Herald* newspaper and came out every Friday. This was a sort of preliminary warning that your farm was about to be 'acquired' by the State, and you were invited to appeal, saying why you thought this was a bad idea. Endless meetings with lawyers ensued, papers were submitted to the relevant authorities and that was usually the last anyone ever heard of it. Later on, 'Section 8s' were issued, which informed you that, although they had given no answers at all to your appeals, they were about to take your farm, home, livelihood and most of your possessions anyway. But this was in the future and we still naïvely believed that, while a few people might lose their farms, most of us with a legitimate claim to remain farming would be allowed to do so.

On 'Chirume' we had not received a 'Section 5' by the end of 2000, and we did not get one until December 14, 2001. I can remember giving a lift to Fanuel Chigwedere one day when I was in Wedza. He was as talkative as ever and continued his favourite refrain of telling me to rein in Harry, who caused him a lot of trouble. He went on to say that 'they' – meaning, I presume, the lands committee or some other local bunch of thugs – had at one stage planned to leave a few whites farming in Wedza, and that I would be one of them as I was useful, in that I sold cattle to the locals and bought their maize.

"But now," he continued, "they have decided to take all the white-owned farms in Wedza."

I did not believe him. I thought that it was just his way of being aggressive with a lot of big talk – but he was right.

I suppose that pressure did let up a bit, but it was only temporary, and every Friday the *Herald* continued to list the different farms that were going to be stolen. Not just new farms, many were listed again and again. If you happened to get a court order saying you should not have your farm taken, it did not make the slightest difference. You were kept in a state of continual confusion. The 'talk team' continued to do a great job in that, apart from helping any farmer with problems on the ground, they tirelessly lobbied anyone who might be able to help us stay on our farms – the local DA (who was usually drunk or high on drugs), the Mashonaland East Governor, the Lands Committee, the Minister of Agriculture, right up to the Vice-President, Msika. Most gave them some hope that at least some of us would be able to continue farming, and we attended endless meetings – usually called at short notice – at Wedza Club to hear about the latest 'lifeline'.

I have often wondered if there was ever any intention of allowing any of us to remain on our farms. Was it all bluff and just stringing us along? I am inclined to think that it was just incredible inefficiency, with no one in any form of authority liaising with other heads, each department just doing its own thing, often contradicting what others were doing. It was an expensive, frightening, chaotic shambles – and our very livelihoods were at stake – but full marks to Harry Orphanides, Derek Hinde, Ben Fourie and, later, Ian Burgoyne for trying so hard on our behalf.

* * *

We continued to farm after a fashion, and bought and sold heifers as well as maize. Selling heifers for cash to the locals, though, led to a very nasty experience. One day we took about Z$150,000 (then about GBP1,000) and put it as usual in the safe, ready to take to the bank next day. Unknown to us, a bunch of 'war vets' had witnessed this sale and knew that we had a lot of money in the house. At seven o'clock, while Nikki was preparing supper in the kitchen and I was sitting down to my first drink of the evening, the dogs suddenly started barking at the door leading from the sitting room to the garden. Naïvely, I got up and opened the door to see what they were barking at. I was immediately confronted by a thug with a 'badza' raised high above his head. As he started to bring it down to smash my head, another thug rushed past me and into the house. I grabbed the wrist of the badza guy and screamed a warning to Nikki. I was 64 at the time and found myself in a wrestling match with a young, strong thug, though admittedly smaller than me. It turned out to be a stalemate. We rolled around on the sitting room floor for what seemed like an eternity but was probably only a few minutes. I managed to push the badza into his face, and it inflicted a good big cut, which squirted blood all over me – Aids infected? – but he had me face down on the carpet and I could not get away. My main worry of course was what was happening to Nikki, as I had seen nothing of the other thug after he had burst past me. It turned out that Nikki had heard my shouts and came running out of the kitchen, only to be confronted by the thug, who hit her over the head with an iron bar then nearly broke her wrist as she tried to reach the agric-alert. She had to take refuge under my office desk and, pouring blood, asked him what he wanted: money. Luckily she knew where the safe keys were and got them for him. On opening the safe he discovered not only the cash but all my guns as well – a 12-bore shotgun, .410 shotgun and a .22 rifle. He came staggering back into the sitting room carrying all this lot and the ammunition.

The youth I was wrestling with released me and joined the other, each holding a firearm. Nikki was shocked and bleeding, and there was no way we could take on these two guys, although we knew the guns were unloaded. It turned out that they knew little about firearms and asked me which ammunition went into which gun. I said, "Give it to me, and I'll show you." He very nearly did! They threatened to tie us up, but they were getting a bit jumpy, as they presumably knew that we had a guard outside. Before leaving one of them went and smashed our agric-alert set.

Luckily we had two agrics – a mid-band set, which we hardly used, and a high band, which the whole area used. The thug only smashed the mid-band set, so as soon as they had left with their booty Nikki ran to

the high band set and put out a 'May Day' call. The result was incredible – 'Chirume' house is a good ten minutes off the main road down a
rough dirt road and everyone was beyond that, yet within fifteen minutes
at least twenty farmers had arrived from all over the place. The first to
arrive was Harry from 'Leeds' – quite how he managed to get there in ten
minutes I will never know. There was not a lot they could do of course.
Richard Tilly and his guard force attempted a follow-up, Claire Milne, a
trained nurse, attended to Nikki and finally Mike Whitfield drove us both
to Borodaile Hospital in Marondera, where we spent the night.

Nikki was quite battered and had to have stitches in her head and
arm. Next morning we made a full report to the CID in Marondera and
gave them the details of the guns stolen. For a couple of weeks two young
CID guys came to the farm, but they had no transport, so I had to lend
them my driver, Never, and the farm truck to ferry them around. I am
convinced they had no intention of finding the guns; it really should not
have been difficult, but the guns have never turned up. I was particularly
sad to lose my Westley Richards 12-bore. I had bought it in England in
1960 and had had it specially fitted.

We returned to the farm that day and set about clearing up the mess
round the safe. Shortly after that we had an electric fence put round the
garden but that would not necessarily have saved us – where had the
guard been? If he had been anywhere near he must have heard the noise,
even if he had failed to spot the intruders. Our labour had thought we
were having a party when so many vehicles suddenly started pitching up
at the house, and Flip was interested to know if my kikoi had come off
during my wrestling match – it didn't.

*　*　*

The chaotic and unpredictable situation continued into 2001, with
every few weeks some new crisis or hoped-for solution requiring yet
another emergency meeting at Wedza Club. I have often wondered what
the government was thinking at this time. They had crooked their way

back into power, but already the economy was taking a nosedive. Most farmers were still utilizing at least one farm, but virtually no long-term or even medium-term development was going on. Cattle prices were not good and we were struggling on 'Chirume'.

In June 2001 there was an eclipse of the sun over a large part of Zimbabwe and a certain number of tourists came to view this phenomenon. We were told that the main area of the total eclipse would be over the Zambezi Valley, so with great foresight we booked a couple of lodges at Tashinga on the shores of Kariba, quite near Bumi Hills. Here we thought we would get a wonderful view of the eclipse from a lovely base in Matusadona National Park. We invited friends and relations out from England and went to enormous trouble, carting up drums of diesel, borrowing another vehicle and laying on food for twelve people for a four-day stay at the lodges, which had minimal catering facilities. What we had failed to appreciate was that we were in the wrong place. There is a vast difference between a total eclipse of the sun and even as much as 97%. The eclipse was over the Zambezi Valley, but the total bit was actually over the Mana Pools area, some one hundred miles from where we were. We only got 97% – or thereabouts – and our ardent eclipse watchers, who had come all the way out from England for this once-in-a-lifetime sighting, had to hide their disappointment.

Instead we hired a game scout to take us to look for some lions on foot. He was armed with an ancient .303 rifle – which he might have known how to use – and we naïvely attempted to follow the spoor of one of the local prides. There were a dozen of us on this walk, which is far too many for safety, and the game scout had no control over us at all. There were plenty of lions about and we kept hearing them, and Nikki and I both saw a swishing tail on at least one occasion but, thank goodness, the guard also realized how close we were. Far from trying to find lions for us he tried to avoid them at all costs, as he had no idea how to cope with the situation. The whole trip was fun as an experience in the African bush for our English visitors, but I do not rate it one of our more successful safaris.

Top: Spratt's christening in Chirume garden
Above: Fathers and Sons cricket – Wedza

Top: Spratt receives cricket prize from David Hamilton. Wedza
Above: British Pony Club polo team which toured Zimbabwe, in red.   Harry far right

Top: Copper Cup at Umboe Polo Club. Harry, Reddy Watt from England, MRM, Nick O'Connor
Above: Nikki feeding young rhino at Imire Game Park, Wedza

Left: MRM at Mana Pools with friend
Below: My favorite picture of Nikki and Disco - SA Champs 2001

Top: 24th April 1993 – Harry, MRM, Nikki, James, Emma
Bottom: Lamplighters win a golf prize – all smiles from Peter Bradshaw, Roy
*   MacIlwaine, Nikki and MRM*

Top: Last Xmas at Vigila, Mvurwi
Bottom: The Mafia? No, Spratt's wedding assistants

*Top: Lucy Milbank's christening. L – R Harriet Piercy, April Piercy with Lucy,
Packet Kemple, Flip, Harry and Caspar*
*Above: Farm weddings were happy occasions! Strath Brown, Robin Wyrley-
Birch, Richard Holme and Anthony Swire-Thompson at Pel and Atherton's
wedding on Nyahuvu*

Top: Harry relaxes on the banks of the Zambezi
Above: Our boys – Harry, Spratt, Skel and James

Top: Jacinta in a field of tobacco on Vigila
Above: MRM and Nikki on the Old Course, St Andrew's

Iyi ndiyo nzira yekuvhota nayo.
Le yiyo indlela yokuvota.
Directions for the guidance of the voter in voting.

Name of candidate	Name of party	Symbol	Marking space
Chigwedere Ellen Tichawra	ZANU PF		X
Milbank Mark Richard	INDEPENDENT		

SHONA
KANA UCHIDA KUVHOTERA ZANU PF ISA X SEPANUFANANIDZO UYU.

NDEBELE
NXA UFUNA UKUVOTELA IZANU PF BHALA u X NJENGALOKHO OKUTSHENGISIWEYO.

ENGLISH
IF YOU WANT TO VOTE FOR ZANU PF PLACE AN X AS SHOWN.

Name of candidate	Name of party	Symbol	Marking space
Chigwedere Ellen Tichawra	ZANU PF		
Milbank Mark Richard	INDEPENDENT		X

SHONA
KANA UCHIDA KUVHOTERA VAMILBANK MARK RICHARD VAKAZVIMIRIRA VEGA ISA X SEPANUFANANIDZO UYU.

NDEBELE
NXA UFUNA UKUVOTELA uMILBANK MARK RICHARD OZIMELE YEDWA BHALA u X NJENGALOKHO OKUTSHENGISIWEYO.

ENGLISH
IF YOU WANT TO VOTE FOR MILBANK MARK RICHARD PLACE AN X AS SHOWN.

Above: Harry's seed beds after being trashed by farm invaders

Left: MRM elected Rural District Councillor for Watershed West

Top: Picnic in the Serengeti
Above: Best 4x4 by far – pulled out of the mud by an Imire elephant

Top: Emma's hut in Chirume garden
Above: Nikki's blood outside the safe on Chirume after being attacked and robbed by 'war vet'

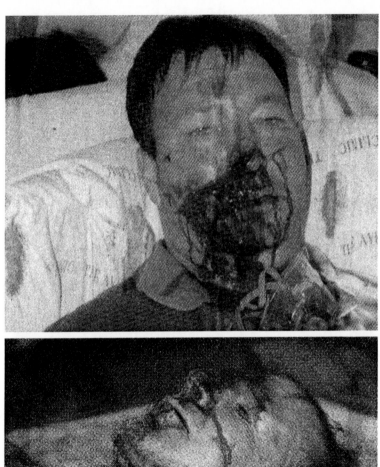

Farmers who disputed the government's right to steal their farms and homes
Top: Marshall Roper
Above: Ian Kay

Top: Our prize Sable bull – slaughtered by poachers
Above: Chirume dam

*Left: Four
generations of
Milbanks at
Barningham
2002
Below: Rob &
Amanda*

Sunset over the Zambezi

CHAPTER 22

Final Days on 'Chirume'

BY THE END OF 2001 I THINK we all realized in our heart of hearts that our farming days were numbered. There was another election due in March, this time for a new president, and of course Mugabe was standing, and his opponent would be the MDC leader, Morgan Tsvangirai. There was a very real chance, if the election was even remotely free and fair, that Tsvangirai would get in. Quite how this would have worked I do not know – how could an MDC President rule with a ZANU (PF) majority in the House of Assembly? Why not have parliamentary and presidential elections at the same time? They do now.

Having had one bad scare, Mugabe was not going to risk losing this election, and immediately there was a ratcheting-up of pressure on us farmers. One day a lorryload of thugs – euphemistically called 'new settlers' – arrived on the farm, closely followed by officials from the Lands Department and last of all by Fanuel Chigwedere himself. I was summoned and went reluctantly to the security gate, but I kept it locked and glared through at Chigwedere as he advanced towards me, wearing his battered old hat.

"Good morning, Mr Milbank," he said, "these are your new settlers, and until they have time to build their own houses they will live in your compound."

"What about my own labour?" I asked.

"They will have to move."

Chigwedere then introduced me to the 'Headman', who would from now on be in charge of 'Chirume' and responsible for the wellbeing of all the new settlers. He turned out to be a nasty, rat-faced little man called Mvavwa. I knew him slightly from previous cattle deals, but he wasted little time in getting the message across that it was he who was now in charge of 'Chirume', and not me.

Most of my labour had been with me for about thirty years, and many of them originated in Malawi and so had no 'musha' or tribal home in Zimbabwe. 'Chirume' was their home – they had nowhere else to go. I talk as if I had a large labour force. I did not. I had a very small one compared to the tobacco and crop farmers in the area, but for every male that I employed there were probably six or eight dependants – wives, old parents, children, brothers and sisters, and just friends who had somehow overstayed their welcome. I estimated that we had about one hundred souls on 'Chirume', all dependent on the wages that I paid to the one wage-earner of each family. If I, a small cattle farmer, had a hundred how many did the big crop farmers have?

It was the start of the criminally wicked purge of farm workers. As these people worked for the white man, they were perceived to be MDC supporters; they must be scattered away from this evil influence and placed somewhere that they could be properly indoctrinated into the wonders of ZANU (PF) in general and Robert Mugabe in particular. In fact they were not 'placed' anywhere, and it was a common sight to see hundreds of them, with their pathetically few possessions, huddled on the side of roads, hoping to be picked up and taken somewhere. But where? There was precious little we could do to help them except to continue employing them. There was precious little we could do to help ourselves. So long as we were able to remain in our homes, trying to continue farming, we needed these workers to do the jobs for which they were paid.

Then a new twist was added. We were told that as we no longer wanted our labour we had to pay them off. For a start this was a downright lie – we did want our labour and had no wish to lose them. However they were told that we were obliged to pay them a form of gratuity based on the length of time that they had worked for us. In the case of someone who had been employed for some thirty years this came to a huge amount, and many farmers were totally unable to pay it. It had the effect of turning the labour against the farmer, which of course was all part of the plan.

It was not long before my own workers, who were by now camping in the bush on 'Collace', the farm next door, formed up one morning and demanded their gratuity (SI6 payment, as it was officially called). It was no good my pointing out to them that legally (a stupid word to use, as there was no law) I owed them nothing, as I was not sacking them. I had liked to think that I had always had a very good relationship with my labour, but now some of them showed their true colours. One of them, a cattle herder called Tongesai, donned a pair of dark glasses and proceeded to accuse me of a string of abuses that he had suffered while employed by me, how I had insulted him, withheld pay, denied him land for his own use, racially abused him, etc. He stood very close to me and shouted, and a fine spray of spittle soon covered my face. It was no use saying or denying anything, as it would have just provoked him further. Our housemaid, Constance, then joined in, and even old Enoch, whom I had long since pensioned off but was still paying something every month, took part. I just stood there – unhappy and disillusioned.

Eventually I said I would take them all to the labour officer in Marondera, give him the details of their past employment, current wages, dates when they started working for me etc., and let him decide what they were 'legally' due. This I did. I sat down with each employee and the labour officer and made him calculate what they were all due on this newly introduced scheme. The labour officer had been well briefed and eventually worked out a figure for each employee, and I insisted that each of them sign saying that they would be satisfied with this payment. It came to a huge amount of money that I did not have. I told them this and said it would take time to find the money. I then rang the 'talk team', Harry and other neighbours and asked them what they were doing. I got a different answer from each one. The 'talk team' said, "Keep negotiating, buy time."

Harry said, "Don't give the bastards a cent; it's all a con and legally you owe them nothing."

Other farmers said, "Just pay, you will have to in the end and it will save a lot of unpleasantness."

There was a lot of unpleasantness too. Most labour forces were aware that their bosses would be extremely hard pressed to pay them the full amounts that they reckoned they were due. If and when they saw their employers packing up their belongings and leaving, they suspected that they were doing a bunk and that they would renege on paying them. This led to many farmers being locked in their own houses, surrounded by a screaming mob of employees, ex-employees and anyone who could dream up some excuse to claim some money. They seemed to think that the farmer could magically produce vast sums while locked in his house miles from a bank. This sometimes led to the very unpleasant situation where the farmer was ordered to go and get money while his wife and children were held hostage against his return. It goes without saying that it was a complete waste of time contacting the police and requesting them to prevent this totally illegal behaviour. They had one of two replies if you did get hold of them. Either they would trot out the old excuse of having no transport or they would say they were on their way but do nothing about it, having no intention of coming.

Telling outright blatant lies became a very common tactic by government officials. You could go to the District Administrator (DA), for example and outline to him some important and legitimate problem that only he could and should deal with. He would listen with apparent attention and when you had finished would say, "OK, I quite understand, leave it to me and I will fix it." There is not much you can add to that sort of response, except maybe to ask when, to which the reply would be, "Straight away." So you leave his office naïvely believing that something will be done. Nothing is done and the DA had never intended doing anything. Making a promise and just not keeping it was a very handy way of getting the irritating farmer out of his office.

My immediate neighbours started paying off their labour, so the pressure mounted on me, and eventually I did too. I did not have the money, so I paid them in kind in the shape of cattle. This turned out to be vastly to their advantage. Inflation was beginning to manifest itself in a big way and any money paid out to these guys was soon spent or worthless, while cattle retained their value.

If you are confused and are wondering what was going on and how we were still on the farm at all, you are not alone. We were totally confused. Every farming area had a slightly different scenario, rather depending upon the resident ZANU (PF) hierarchy, but there was one constant. Every Friday the government-controlled daily newspaper, the *Herald*, published a long list of farms which were to receive a variety of 'section' notices ranging from five to eight. Section 7 was actually the worst – it meant 'get off now'.

As time went by, practically every farm was listed and very often several times, as the totally chaotic 'land reform programme' got under-way. The government tried to kid everybody that this process was both well-planned and legal. Hence the endless false alarms, false hopes, new plans, negotiations with so-called sympathetic ministers, and plans put forward by farming bodies or individual farming associations. These last two were legion. Wedza had a plan, Macheke had a plan, Mvurwi had a plan, all slightly different but all with the same theme – a desperate attempt to retain farmers on the land, with at least a viable portion of their own land.

One of the biggest and most publicized plans was known as the Zimbabwe Joint Resettlement Initiative (ZJRI) and the Zimbabwe government at a big meeting in Abuja, Nigeria, apparently accepted it. Broadly speaking, the plan was to give deserving new black farmers land in the commercial farming area taken from white farmers who had more than one farm, and to pay for that land with funds allocated at the 1998 donor conference. It was a good and fair idea and the agreement was signed on September 9, 2001. What happened in New York on September 11 is well known, and Zimbabwe disappeared from the world stage. The pending Commonwealth conference, at which Zimbabwe was high on the agenda, was cancelled and the Zimbabwe government conveniently forgot everything they had agreed to in Abuja. George Turner, our brilliant but eccentric doctor in Marondera, told me what Abuja really stood for – "Another Bloody Useless Jungle Agreement" he said and roared with laughter.

As the current District Councillor for the area, I attended one of the ceremonies at which a farm was handed over to new black farmers as part of the ZJRI plan. Harry Nel had several farms and was willing to give up one so long as he could retain one for himself. We all met on the farm offered, and a high-ranking official from the Commercial Farmers Union (CFU) got up and made a speech to the assembled crowd of some two hundred, explaining the whole ZJRI plan and how we must all work together for a better and fairer Zimbabwe. He ended by naming the people who would be getting the land – people chosen by a committee because they had demonstrated a reasonable knowledge of farming – and by presenting some maize seed and fertilizer to these lucky chosen few. Polite but muted applause followed. Chigwedere then rose to reply. He had probably had a few drinks, as his battered, trademark hat was at an acute angle; he proceeded to tear into the whole ZJRI plan as a colonial façade for the white man to keep land belonging to the people of Zimbabwe. Who were these people chosen to have this land? He, Chigwedere, would decide that and the CFU could keep their ruddy maize seed and fertilizer. He sat down to deafening applause and we whites all hurried away. It had perhaps been a good try. Was there ever any intention of the government honouring any sort of reasonable agreement? I very much doubt it.

Wedza's 'talk team' of Harry Orphanides, Derek Hinde and Bennie Fourie, now supplemented by Ian Burgoyne, left no stone unturned in their efforts to keep the community to some degree intact. On many occasions we were all summoned, via the agric-alert, to urgent meetings at the club, where yet another possible lifeline was explained, and we all filled in more forms, drew more diagrams of what part of the farm we were prepared to give away and hoped that something realistic might come out of it.

The presidential election was now upon us, with Tsvangirai due to stand against Mugabe. The election was to be keenly contested, and polling stations were set up all over the country, including of course Wedza. As in all elections, each candidate was required to provide observers, whose job it was to stay with the ballot boxes from the time they were sealed until they were opened, thus preventing either party stuffing the box with fictitious votes. ZANU (PF) had no trouble at all in providing such observers and used government vehicles to cart them to and from the polling stations. MDC, though, had a mammoth problem. They were short of funds, and if any of their representatives were seen anywhere near a polling station they were chased and, if caught, severely beaten. This made it very difficult for them to perform their allotted task. Any appeal to the police for protection and assistance in doing their legal job fell, needless to say, on deaf ears.

We in Wedza therefore determined to try and help these brave volunteers. Scott von Memerty, incumbent chairman of our Farmers Association, asked us who would be willing to help ferry the MDC observers to and from the polling stations. We would not be properly accredited observers, but to give us some credibility he had printed large stickers for our vehicles bearing the legend 'Zimbabwe Citizen Support Group'.

Harry was one of the first to volunteer and he raked me in as his assistant. Talk about a 'cloak and dagger' exercise! We left before light on the morning of the election and, still in the dark, delivered three men, whom Harry had picked up in Harare the day before, to three of the polling stations in the communal area. As well as the stickers on the car we also had a neatly printed bit of paper saying we were just there to help, were completely apolitical, and were just exercising our constitutional right to see an election carried out freely and fairly. As we were also carrying MDC observers we fooled nobody as to where our support lay.

We passed through a couple of police roadblocks with no problem before arriving at the first polling station. By law we, as non-voters, were not allowed within two hundred metres of the polling station, so we dropped our observer in the bush, wished him luck and said we would bring him some food and check on him that evening. We did the same at the next two and started heading back. We were carrying a radio and could hear how others in the area were getting on, doing the same thing as us. The Wedza area alone had fifty polling stations. This was because Wedza was perceived as being a ZANU (PF) stronghold, so they wanted to milk every possible vote they could. Cities like Harare, which was where the MDC were strong, had pitifully few polling stations – only one hundred and sixty-three for the whole area, which was a hundred fewer than at the general election – and despite queuing all day many people were unable to cast their vote.

On our radio we soon picked up the news that Fanuel Chigwedere and his men had learned of what we were doing and had unilaterally taken over the roadblocks that had been manned by the police earlier, and that he was after our blood. Harry and I took a different route home. I had wanted to vote myself, and as far as I knew I was on the voters' roll. Some years previously I had officially renounced my British citizenship and become a Zimbabwe citizen. I reasoned that if you wanted to own land in a country you should become a citizen of that country and so now I held a Zimbabwean passport. However, when I reached the polling station at 'Fair Adventure' and produced my voter's card, I was told that my name was not on the voters' roll and so I could not vote. Why? No one knew, they just shrugged.

In the afternoon Harry and I went back over the morning's route, detouring round Chigwedere's roadblocks, and trying to locate our observers. At the first stop we could not see anyone, so we parked on the side of the road in sight of the polling station but some three hundred metres from it. It was not long before we were approached by a policewoman.

"What did we want?" she asked.

"Nothing," said Harry, "just waiting to see someone."

She walked away but was soon back, saying we were acting illegally and spying on the polling station and would one of us accompany her. Harry went and was away for nearly half an hour. I was getting worried but eventually he did reappear, striding grimfaced and purposefully. Suddenly he stopped, well before reaching the car, and drew a line with his toe in the sandy road. He turned round and shouted back towards the polling station, "This is two hundred metres, so we are well within our rights."

This it seemed did not matter and the police still wanted to arrest us, so we just got in the car and drove away without having even seen our observer.

At the next venue we did much the same thing, and soon a very dishevelled, frightened observer crept out of the bush and jumped into the car. He told us that he had been identified as an MDC observer and immediately chased by a bunch of ZANU (PF) thugs – in full view of the police – and had spent a nerve-racking, uncomfortable day hiding in the bush. We drove on to the next place, but before getting there were confronted by a bunch of thugs standing in the middle of the road waving sticks at us. We had no option but to turn tail and drive away again, with no sign of the observer.

We got home late and depressed, having achieved little except put ourselves squarely in the limelight. What crimes had we committed? Absolutely none, but we soon got confirmation that both the Wedza police and Chigwedere's men were after us. We were not the only ones of course, and we soon hatched a plan whereby we would disappear for a bit. Harry and Flip came over to 'Chirume' and we kept the gate at the bottom of the garden unlocked, telling Nikki and Flip that if anyone came looking for us we would disappear into the bush, and they were to say that we had gone to town. No one appeared, but we spent a pretty nervous day watching the road up to the house. Shortly after this we went to Mozambique for a week, and Harry and Flip also made themselves scarce. Farmers from other areas, who had done the same as Harry and myself, were arrested on trumped-up charges and spent some very unpleasant days in police custody. We got away with it.

Mugabe duly 'won' the election, and reprisals were not long in following. Anyone who had overtly supported MDC was in for it. A gardener who worked for a friend of ours in Marondera had been stripped naked by ZANU (PF) thugs and had the initials MDC branded on his back with a hot iron. I saw this poor man when he was giving evidence to a foreign observer and he was in a terrible state. What would the foreign observer do? He would include it in his report no doubt, and someone might eventually say the election was not free and fair, but nothing would actually happen and Mugabe, ZANU (PF), Chigwedere and Co. would continue to do exactly as they pleased.

Hans Christian, another friend from Marondera, lent some petrol to an MDC candidate. He was arrested and accused of supplying petrol for the manufacture of petrol bombs. He was locked up in the local police station for over a week without being charged, and had the soles of his feet beaten in an effort to make him confess to this ridiculous charge.

Roy Bennett, the very brave and popular MDC MP for the Chimanimani constituency in the Eastern Highlands, was alone on his farm when two lorryloads of police arrived to arrest him for allegedly supplying soap to his labour, the crime being that this soap would wash off the indelible ink in which voters had to dip their fingers to prove that they had voted. By removing this ink, it was claimed, Roy's people could and did vote many times. Roy Bennett was later provoked in Parliament into pushing a ZANU (PF) minister who had grossly insulted him and his family. For this Roy was sentenced to a year's hard labour. This of course was a far more serious offence than branding someone with a hot iron.

Our near neighbour, Gary Stein, was absent from his farm for a few days immediately after the election, and thugs broke into his compound, trashed the homestead, burned his pick-up truck and stole two tractors.

When Gary rushed back and saw what had happened, he phoned his wife, Clare, and said philosophically, "Things are not too bad." What on earth is 'too bad', then? Predictably, Clare's first question was one that many of us would have asked – "Are the dogs all right?" They were.

Jon-Jon Worsley-Worswick from Marondera North was summoned to the local ZANU.(PF) youth camp together with his security guard, accused of helping the MDC over the election. Both were held face down on the floor and beaten with pick handles. The guard passed out but they continued to beat Jon-Jon until someone said that the guard was 'serious'. He was. The thugs panicked and took both of them to Marondera Hospital, where they dumped them. Jon-Jon was admitted and later recovered but the guard died. Was anyone ever arrested for this brutal murder? Of course not.

These were just some of the things that happened in our immediate neighbourhood to people we knew. The same sort of story was being repeated all over the country; many such assaults perpetrated on innocent tribesmen in the more remote rural areas were never heard about.

* * *

Early in 2002 another tragedy struck. I am sure it was related to the ongoing lawlessness in the country, although not directly connected to the election or farm invasions. Having left 'Leeds', Fran had bought a small plot of land near a lake just outside Banket, and she was living there in a rented house while she built her own. One morning Harry rang me up from 'Leeds' and said that his mother was 'missing', and that he was off to Banket to find out what was going on. She was missing, and after an intensive search, which lasted a couple of days, her body was found. She had been murdered and pushed down a Blair toilet. I was horrified. We were still on very bad terms after the divorce, but I had hoped that time would heal and that eventually we could at least become friends again. After all we did share three of the most precious things anyone can have – our boys Robert, Harry and Jack. Now that would never happen.

Spratt flew back from Australia for the memorial service, which was held in the Anglican Church in Avondale. An old friend and now lay preacher, John Hoskyns-Davis, took the service and David Hamilton gave an excellent eulogy. I sat quietly at the back of the church, which was filled to overflowing with friends. Afterwards a wake was held in the house of friends and I was able to chat to a lot of them. Out of respect for Fran's feelings Nikki had not come to the church, but at the request of the boys she did attend the wake.

* * *

With the elections now over we hoped that perhaps things would calm down a bit, like they had after the previous election. But this was far from the case. Having previously softened us up, as it were, the 'war veterans' – new settlers, young thugs, Mugabe's cronies, call them what you like, except farmers – moved in for the kill and started kicking farmers out of their homes physically. Everybody had objected to having their home and farm stolen from them and most had court cases pending. Some had won the right to have their farm de-listed. Others had agreed to sacrifice additional farms or surplus land that they owned on condition that they could keep their most productive piece and remain in their home. Let it be quite clear that the official government policy, as stated by Mugabe on many occasions, was that every farmer would be allowed to keep one farm. One assumed that even white farmers would be included in 'every farmer'. Neither this official policy nor any court order made the slightest difference to the thugs on the ground. They just moved in, and the police once again turned a blind eye. The only phrase to describe what was happening is 'ethnic cleansing'.

Guy and Ros Cartwright were very progressive farmers and ran a lovely set-up not far from Marondera. Their two sons, both recently married, had joined them on the farm following time at agricultural colleges. The farm boasted its own school, which had been built and paid for by Guy. His workers' children, plus those of neighbouring farmers, attended this very well-run school. There was a large communal hall at which beer could be purchased and television watched. Guy also sponsored a football team raised from among his own workers, which played in a league against other farms. Wages were paid on the dot every month with the addition of a decent bonus at the end of each year. In short it was a happy well-run set-up with everyone benefiting.

As with most other farmers, they had received a Section 5 notice some three months previously, stating that the government wished to make a compulsory purchase of their farm. Again, like all of us, Guy had lodged his objection and heard nothing more.

One Sunday Guy and Ros were out walking when they got a message on their mobile radio to return to the house, because there was a problem. When they arrived they were met by an army brigadier, who said that the house –and farm – was now his and that he was moving in now. There was a lorry outside and some of the Cartwrights' belongings were being thrown on to it, china was being chucked out of the windows and smashed on the ground, while anything else was just being trashed. Meanwhile the brigadier's men were busy moving his furniture in through the front door. While this was all happening the two sons were being given two hours' notice to clear out of their homes.

Just think for a moment what this meant. Guy and Ros had been in that house and on that farm all their married lives. They brought up their children there, surrounded themselves with friends, and had gathered a lot of very nice possessions, but even this is not really the point; it was their home and there was no possible justification for removing them with no warning at all. They never lived there again. They left under duress for South Africa the following day. Maybe you live in Sussex or on a farm in Australia or in the Cape. Can you imagine this happening to you? This is just one story of an eviction from one's own home with no warning; we were involved in several others, and there were hundreds more throughout the country that we never heard of.

Shortly after the Cartwright episode, we were relaxing on 'Chirume' one Saturday lunchtime when the agric-alert suddenly came to life. There was nothing new in this; almost daily some drama was being transmitted from somewhere in the area. Today it was our golfing friend, Roy MacIlwaine, saying that our old Kenyan friends, the Buswells, who lived next door to him, were in the process of being kicked out of their home and asking if anyone could come and help rescue some of their belongings. Micky and Myrtle were both over seventy and had lived in that house for some twenty years – we had had lunch with them the previous Sunday, and they said then that they were under no immediate threat, as far as they knew.

Nikki and I radioed back to say that we were on our way, to be of what help we could. Nikki hitched up the horse trailer to her Discovery and I went in the farm truck. We had our hand-held radio with us, and we tried to contact the Buswells to say we were coming, but the battery went flat and we arrived at the end of the drive leading to their house with no idea of what was going on inside. I opted to go in with the truck, as it would be easier for me to turn round and escape if our reception was too hostile. Nikki waited outside with the horse trailer.

In fact there was a lorry already there, lent by another neighbour, and Micky was busy heaving furniture on to it, while Myrtle was inside packing crockery. It turned out that Micky had managed to speak to the thug who was stealing his house, and he had persuaded this thief to give him six hours to get his stuff out – jolly decent of him! We phoned the police, and amazingly they turned up. Micky and I went to talk to them as they lolled in their car. Unfortunately there was nothing they could do, they maintained, as no crime had actually been committed. Mr Buswell was merely loading his own furniture on to a lorry. It was no use pointing out that in a similar situation at the Cartwrights a few days earlier, a crime had clearly been committed, in that someone's personal possessions had been trashed and the police had done nothing then either. "Ah!" they said, "but that was political." It was painfully obvious that they had received instructions to offer no help whatsoever to any white farmer who was being robbed of his house and possessions.

Clearly there was no sense in waiting for the inevitable crime to be committed, and the Buswells wanted to remove as much as they could before it all got smashed, as the Cartwrights' possessions had. We spent the rest of that afternoon loading the lorry, and as it drove off Micky got on the phone to try and find somewhere to spend the night. We stood together on the now empty veranda of his home. Micky's little Jack Russell dog, 'Digger', who had fathered two litters of puppies with my bitch, 'Turbo', pushed his wet nose against Micky's leg as if to ask what the hell was going on. Micky looked down at him and his face tightened. He turned to me and asked, "Can you take him, Mark? I don't know where I am going, but I am sure dogs won't be welcome."

It was an impossible decision; we had three dogs of our own and we had no idea what our future was. We did take Digger that night but he never made it to New Zealand where Micky and Myrtle finally ended up. Just one more little victim of the ongoing tyranny.

Derek Hinde farmed just down the road from us and was one of the first in our area to export roses to Europe. He had a large acreage under plastic and employed a lot of people. Early in April 2002 a gang of twenty-year-old 'war vets' moved into his compound and drove out the entire labour force, plus all their families and anything they could carry. These people were left stranded on the side of the road, most with nowhere to go and no means of getting there anyway. These same 'war vets' then stole five tractors, one lorry, one pick-up truck, all belonging to Derek, and drove off three hundred and twenty-five head of his cattle. While this was happening to Derek, much the same was happening to Dave England and Mike Whitfield, who farmed between Derek and us.

The main road all round the Wedza turn-off was crowded with the workers from these three farms – hundreds of them. Derek could do nothing to help as he was barricaded in his house, so some of us drove up there to see what we could do to help. Harry took his video camera and started filming the chaotic scene. This was not well received, and he was promptly set upon by a gang of thugs, who stole his camera and cell phone as well as giving him some nasty bruises and cutting his leg so badly that it required several stitches. Three policemen were standing nearby and did nothing to stop this blatant assault. When I asked them why the hell they were doing nothing they meekly replied that Harry had no right to be there. Why on earth not? It was a public road.

Harry had to go on to Marondera to have his leg stitched, but I took a number of the older men, women and children, who were desperately wondering where they were going to spend the night (and the rest of their lives?), back to 'Chirume' and gave them what food I could gather up. Next day a gang of thugs arrived on my doorstep and said that if I continued to look after these people the whole of my labour force would be beaten up.

These are just a few incidents in which I was personally involved. Similar ones and many far worse were happening throughout the country. Near Chinhoyi, a big commercial farming area a hundred kilometres north-west of Harare, some twenty white farmers had gone to the house of a neighbour who was having problems and all had been arrested for disturbing the peace. They were all locked up in the local police cells, and other people (whites) who had nothing to do with them were also locked up when they arrived at the police station on totally different business. These people remained locked up for some weeks without being charged, had their heads shaved and were treated like criminals. I don't know if this was the start of the rather unattractive custom of shaving off all one's hair but a lot of farmers did just this in sympathy with their incarcerated colleagues.

* * *

Meanwhile the war vets in the Chinhoyi/Mangura area went on the rampage, completely trashing some twenty-five farms and doing an untold amount of totally pointless damage. All this with the blessing of Minister Chombo who had told them that everything on a white-owned farm belonged to the people. If they really believed that, why were they trashing it all? With all this sort of thing going on we decided to take a few precautions and started packing up our more valuable and/or break-able possessions and taking them into Harare to leave in the care of good friends.

We could no longer use the Wedza Club for our farmers' meetings, because it would certainly be invaded by a bunch of thugs and we would be accused of holding an MDC meeting. So when yet another emergency meeting was called, it had to be held in the boardroom of the big agricul-tural co-operative, Farm-A-Rama, in Marondera. The talk team had been meeting representatives from other farming areas and it was pretty obvious that we were all in a desperate situation, so maybe some sort of co-ordinated approach was needed by us all towards our very hostile government. It was decided that we should all adopt one of the following five attitudes:

1) Eat humble pie, apologize for our perceived wrongs, denounce MDC and accept that the ZANU (PF) government had won a free and fair election.

2) Stand back and do nothing. i.e. just let it all happen.

3) Stand on principle and take the consequences, that is be as obstructive as possible.

4) Deal individually – i.e. make private deals, possibly involving bribes.

5) Try for the maximum land we could retain – first prize one farm, second prize four hundred hectares.

Debate on which of these policies to adopt raged for two hours, while the talk team said nothing. No one liked the first, and the second and fourth did not get much support. Harry, who had just become a father for a second time with the birth of Lucy, was the most outspoken. Needless to say he advocated the third option. Finally the talk team told us that the hierarchy of the Commercial Farmers Union thought the only option for any of us to remain farming was to eat humble pie and take the first option. The message from Mugabe was loud and clear; he did not want us white farmers. He perceived us (correctly) as a threat to the continued dominance of ZANU (PF) in that we actively supported and funded MDC and persuaded our workers to do the same. The gangs of thugs currently moving through our area not only had his full approval but were actually paid to be as nasty as possible to us; further, we were blamed (incorrectly) for getting the sanctions put in place by the British, American and EU governments against him and his immediate cronies – sanctions that exist to this day, in 2009, and are still blamed by him for the total chaos, poverty, starvation and inflation which is Zimbabwe today. If we could not be seen to be actively backing his government, we would be out.

I sympathized with Harry. He could have got any top job he wanted in Australia, but had opted to come home and farm in Zimbabwe. He had already proved that he was a very good farmer, he had a lovely wife and two small children, and all he wanted to do was farm on his own farm in Zimbabwe. Now he saw that his lifetime's dream might be snatched from him when he had only just achieved it. He was prepared to do almost anything to hang on to his farm, so that in years to come he would have a clear conscience and be able to say to himself, "At least I fought for it and did not give up easily."

Actually we had nothing to fight with. The government wanted us to be confrontational. If we had been at all aggressive we would immediately have been locked up – many people were for the most trivial of reasons. You cannot stand up for your rights and win in the short term if there is no law and order to back you.

There was continued debate at our meeting, and inevitably at the end we adopted a compromise resolution based on option one. We could not take the 'humble pie' bit, so we said that we sincerely wished to continue farming for the good of the country and would remain apolitical and work with the 'de facto' government of the day. I had suggested the 'de facto' bit. ZANU (PF) were in fact the government but that did not mean that we recognized they were legitimate.

I do not think it would have mattered what we decided to do – the die was already cast, and all but a very few of us were already doomed.

In East Mashonaland alone there were already a hundred and ten farmers off their farms and many more hanging on by their eyelids. Yet none of us really believed then that this was the end of our farming days.

Making any sort of a living was now becoming a major problem. For a start your whole mental approach and energy was directed towards just continuing to live on your farm. Then innumerable obstacles were put in your way. I was a cattle farmer and existed by trading in cattle as well as breeding and fattening. Now we were told that all cattle belonged to the State and we could not move any off our farms without permission from the local DA. This decree about the State now owning all our cattle was accepted by some authorities but not by others. The usual total confusion reigned but all government departments, war vets and thugs agreed on one thing, and that was that we could not move any cattle. This caused a curious predicament in May 2002. The government, in the shape of an organization called the Livestock Development Trust (LDT), was trying to buy cattle for its own purposes and was even offering a reasonable price. Rather than have all one's cattle 'stolen', a lot of farmers in the Wedza area were taking advantage of this offer. I certainly was and had already had some weighed and was just waiting for payment to be confirmed before sending them off. Rob Edgar, who had finally been kicked off his farm and to make a few bucks had set up as a cattle-buying agent, then complicated the whole situation. He arrived in the area with a high-powered army colonel who claimed that he was buying cattle on behalf of the government and that we should deal directly with him and not with the LDT. He said he would pay a better price and pay more promptly. It was clearly some sort of a fiddle but one was at least able to talk with Rob and emphasise that nothing would leave the farm until any cheques had been cleared into the seller's account.

Rob brought Col Blessing Hove to 'Chirume' and I offered him a lot of heifers – some of my own, some of Harry's and some of John Bibby's – as I was looking after a lot of his young stock following the problems on his farm, 'Bita'. The colonel checked them over fairly perfunctorily, did not bother to weigh any, and offered a price slightly higher than that which I had been offered by the LDT. I accepted. I told Col Hove about the problems we were having moving any cattle, so he asked to come into the house and use the telephone (which still worked in those days). He made his call and said there would be no more problem moving cattle. I then offered him a cup of tea, which he accepted and while waiting for it to come he wandered round the house.

"What a lovely house and garden," he said. Oh! Oh! think I, other army colonels have admired other lovely houses recently and in quite a short time ended up stealing them.

The colonel left me (and I hoped the house, for good) and continued round the area buying up virtually everything that was available. We all telephoned each other and Rob, asking when and how we would be paid. A couple of days passed then Rob rang us all up and said we should assemble at Sable Lodge, Imire Game Park's tourist lodge and restaurant, that evening and we would be paid. Needless to say we were all there pretty smartish and were met by an extraordinary spectacle. The colonel was there to greet us personally, by name – he remembered us all.

"Good evening, Mr Milbank, how good of you to come, do help yourself to a drink, the bar is over there." Indeed it was, and a very well stocked bar it was too. There were several different types of imported beer, single malt whisky, brandy, vodka, gin and all the right mixers. Standing by this bar with a large drink in one hand and a broad grin on his face was John Harris from Ruzawi River, who, when I had last heard, was barricaded in his house by a howling mob of ZANU (PF) youths.

"Evening, John," I said, "what are you looking so cheerful about? I thought you were having mega problems."

"No, no," he said, "no more problems, I have just joined the 'club'. I no longer have a farm."

There was a large gathering from both Wedza and Ruzawi River, and in a side room sat Jane de Witt, a friend of Rob Edgar, writing out cheques on Time Bank, one of the new, emerging, locally run banks. All had just one signature – not that of Col Blessing Hove but that of his partner, said to be the current head of Combined Operations and top guy in the air force. Most cheques ran into large sums of money. Would they all be honoured? That was the question on everybody's lips.

Meanwhile a four-piece band from Harare was belting out '60s' music and dinner was announced. Dinner was a huge braai consisting of prime beef, pork, lamb, sausages and the inevitable boerewors, complete with huge bowls of salads. To follow was a selection of puddings and a magnificent cheeseboard full of imported cheeses.

The colonel moved among his guests with a handshake here, an arm round a shoulder there and many an indulgent chuckle. This was an obvious arm of the very government that was bent on totally ruining our lives. It was bizarre in the extreme. At about ten o'clock I was ready to go home, so I approached the colonel who was standing at the bar, to say my thank you's.

"You can't go yet, Mark; have another drink and why aren't you dancing? I want to see the farmers happy and dancing!"

Some people were dancing and I did have another drink and stayed to chat to him and ask what he thought the prospect was for my pen-feeding steers – a ninety-day exercise. He became a bit evasive in his reply to that one. Eventually I drove home and early next morning drove into Marondera and presented my cheque – it was honoured within hours.

Meanwhile the total confusion continued. Some people definitely were off their farms; others had a Section 8 and were now told that if they were not off their farm and out of their home (with no promise of any compensation) by August 9, they would be put in gaol. As far as I knew I did not have a Section 8 and so did not fall into that category, though Chigwedere and the local thugs said that I did and that we would have to go. Things had got too hot for Harry and he, Flip and the two little children were now based with Ian and April Piercy in Ruwa, with Harry paying regular visits to 'Leeds' to try and protect what he had left there. He had sent a lot of his equipment over to us to prevent it from being stolen or vandalized. One day Chigwedere saw Harry's tractor parked inside my security fence.

"Ask Harry if we can hire his tractor to do some ploughing, as he is not using it," he said to me. Harry at this time had no income at all so, with my tongue well in my cheek, I asked him. I got the sort of reply I had expected.

"No fucking way! I'm not helping those bastards who are chucking me off my farm; I'd rather they burned the tractor." Soon after, they did just that.

On June 11, we were all summoned to yet another meeting, this time at Peterhouse School. The plan was for all farmers in Mashonaland East to congregate there and listen to what the ranchers in Matabeleland were doing. The leader of them was one Mac Crawford; basically he maintained that our current Commercial Farmers Union (CFU) leaders – Colin Cloete as president, William Hughes and Doug Taylor-Freeme – were not doing enough to help, and the Matabeleland farmers wanted to go on their own. Crawford and another farmer, Dave Pretorious, talked a lot in platitudes and tore the CFU top brass to ribbons; they emphasized the need to 'hang in there' but came up with very few practical ideas. To my mind it was the classic situation of divide and rule as far as Mugabe and Co. were concerned. He was trying to get us fighting amongst ourselves, which was the last thing we should be doing. Kerry Kay, who is a tough and brave lady if ever there was one, maintained that land was not really the issue anyway and no reasonable plan would work. The issue was a corrupt, illegal government intent on committing genocide on its own people to remain in power. Kerry does not mince her words and there was a lot of truth in what she said. A lot more talk but yet again I drove home with a spinning head, none the wiser.

* * *

I worried a lot about Rob, Amanda and little Sabrina on their farm, 'Vigila', near Mvurwi. I had good reason to, because they were having a torrid time. A favourite tactic by the young thugs at this time was what became known as a 'jambanje' or 'pungwe'. This entailed thirty or forty youths (even over a hundred on some occasions), high on drugs and booze, coming to an isolated farm and surrounding the house with the farmer and his family locked inside. They would then keep up a filthy racket all night. They would throw rocks on the roof; rattle the windows and light fires in the garden. Not only was it impossible to sleep through all this but it was very frightening as well. Sometimes they did actually break into the house and then they would force the farmer to 'dance' with them, shout ZANU (PF) slogans, deride the MDC and generally humiliate him. This was about as nasty as it could get. They were high on drugs and thoroughly enjoying the unusual experience of treating a white man in this derogatory fashion. They were also being paid by the government to do so.

It was obviously useless to call the police when it became apparent that such a mob was about to visit you, as they would 'have no transport', but you could usually get word out to a neighbour and if that neighbour was a very good friend he would come and share the ordeal with you. It was an enormous help to the beleaguered farmer to have at least one mate by his side during this revolting, degrading experience. While Harry was always one of the first to volunteer for nasty and dangerous jobs in Wedza, Rob was getting quite a name for himself in Mvurwi by doing exactly the same thing. He was a bit of a marked man, as he had overtly embraced the MDC cause and had been seen distributing MDC shirts in the area.

Rob and Amanda were at the Mvurwi Polo Club one Saturday when they got a frantic call from Amanda's parents, who were back on the farm living in the lovely old house. Felicity, speaking on the farm radio, just said, "Rob they are here!" – no more explanation was necessary. He rushed back to find the whole gang of thugs actually in the house. A next-door neighbour, Paddy Kramburger, was there as well, doing what he could to help, but there was really precious little that could be done when faced by such a mob. Robin was being very badly treated and Felicity, in aiming a kick at one of her assailants, had a minor heart attack. She claims this was brought on by the anger of missing with her kick. Whatever the reason, she had to be rushed to hospital, but the 'pungwe' went on. An ox had to be slaughtered to appease the mob, and next morning Tobs Strong answered another of their demands by bringing round some bread for them. For his pains he had to undergo a severe beating.

Why give in to them, you may ask? Why give them meat and bread when they are behaving so appallingly? Just think for a moment. There are three or four of you and sixty or eighty of them. They are all high on booze and drugs and highly excited. Other farmers had been killed in similar situations. What would you do? Say, "No, you naughty boys, I won't give you anything," or do as they say?

I got through to Rob on the telephone early next morning when he was still in the house with the thugs. Far from sounding distressed, his only comment was, "I'll be late for polo if they don't bugger off soon!" He always did get his priorities right.

Rob and Amanda had their own turn soon after, when a gang of about a hundred drug-crazed thugs broke into their house and chased Rob from room to room, eventually trying to flood him out. Fortunately Amanda and Sabrina were out at the time. Three brave neighbours came and managed to rescue him at eight o'clock that night, but the house was severely damaged. They did go back to live there, but it was the beginning of the end for them and they had to move out soon after. It was certainly no easier in Mvurwi than in Wedza or indeed any of the country's farming areas.

It was a measure of the type of coward that we were dealing with, when it is noted that if any of them wanted to say anything to you they would always arrive with at least ten other thugs as back-up, often to speak to just one elderly white man. On 'Chirume' the nasty little Mvavwa had assumed the title of 'headman' and almost daily wanted to tell me something. Standing immediately behind him was always a huge young idiot called Costa, and a little further back a gang of six or eight other thugs. If ever I objected to anything that Mvavwa said, which

I usually did, Costa would ostentatiously move forward and clench his fists. He never did become violent but the message was clear.

*   *   *

We heard on the news that the World Bank reckoned Mugabe could only survive in power for another fifteen to eighteen months, by juggling the very small amount of foreign exchange that he got and feeding less and less people, until presumably only he got three meals a day and everybody else starved to death. I believed he was prepared to do this, but I maintained at the time that there would be revolution before that happened. The World Bank and I were both very wrong. As I write in 2009 there are a lot more very hungry people, Mugabe is still in power and inflation is 200,000,000%! It's the highest in the world.

On the advice of my old friend Bobby Fernandes, I had 'Chirume' officially valued by his company Valcor/Agric Africa. His valuator did a very thorough job and came up with a figure of US$235,000. In those days this was the equivalent of Z$77 million. This official valuation will I hope form the basis of any compensation that I may or may not get. I am writing this in 2009 and haven't had a sniff of anything yet.

*   *   *

In July 2002 my father was due to turn ninety, and I was determined to be there. When you are ninety, you probably do not have very long to go. No way was my father going to travel from England to see me before he died, so we went to see him. Penel also came over from South Africa, and Sue, who had borne the brunt of looking after the old man over the years, was of course there too. So for the first time in many years his three children were together with him. Another big bonus was that Harry and Flip also came over, with Caspar and tiny little Lucy. This meant that when we all foregathered at Barningham on his birthday, there were four generations of male Milbanks present – my father Denis, me, Harry and three-year-old Caspar. Cousins Ant and Bea laid on a lovely lunch in the old family home where father was born, and it was a very happy, nostalgic occasion, which I think and hope Father enjoyed. He died only five months later after breaking his hip in a fall and going into hospital. I believe that he never wanted to leave that hospital, knowing that he would have to move into some sort of home and thus lose his independence. I did not go to his funeral, held in the little church at Barningham, but sent a farewell message that Sue read out at the service.

While in England – or rather Scotland – I achieved one of my very few ambitions at golf. I played on the Old Course at St Andrews, the very home of golf. It was a wonderful occasion, shared perhaps with not the best golfers available, but certainly the best company – Nikki, Harry and Ant. The weather was fine and none of us disgraced ourselves, although we were all pretty nervous standing on the first tee being photographed by a lot of Nip tourists hoping to see Greg Norman or Nick Faldo. I managed to par one hole which I later witnessed Tiger Woods bogey when playing in the Open, and for one fleeting second in time I felt myself a better golfer than Tiger. Harry's big moment was when he parred the notorious Road Hole – the seventeenth – which most pros would give their eyeteeth to par when playing in the final round of any tournament. The cost, at GBP90 each for the eighteen holes, seemed pretty steep, but as a one-off worth every penny.

* * *

All good things come to an end, and all too soon we had to return to Zim and face the music again – and pretty loud it was too. While we had been away, a deadline of June 25 had passed without too much fuss. This was the date given for all farmers with a Section 8 to have stopped active farming and started to get out of their homes and off their farms, meekly handing over a lifetime's work. By August 9, they all had to be gone. Not unreasonably, very few farmers made any effort to move. The country was already feeling the pinch foodwise, and there was a big drive to produce more wheat. Packet and Mike Kemple, who farmed near Chakari, had just completed a huge dam and were capable of producing 600 hectares of badly needed wheat, but as soon as they started preparing the land they were kicked off the farm. All that grew on their land in that season and in the years to come was weeds. Fifteen sugar farmers from the lowveld started watering their sugar cane when the rains ended in April and were promptly arrested and locked up. Meanwhile there was no sugar to buy in the shops.

Harry had planted seedbeds for his new paprika crop, and Mike Moran on 'Bolton' just next door, had as usual put in his tobacco seedbeds. One night both lots of seedbeds were irretrievably trashed. I tried to take a photo of the devastation that was once Harry's super, neat seedbeds, but I was spotted doing so by some thugs and I had to run to my car. Why are they so sensitive about having their crimes recorded? The answer is simple – because they know they are crimes.

I was still in a real quandary, as I had definitely not had a Section 8 at this time, but some authorities/thugs said I had, while others said I should have had one and others admitted that I did not. The result was that I spent a lot of time and energy going round to see people like the DA (who was usually drunk), the police (who claimed it was nothing to do with them), Agritex (who just lied) or the Lands Department (who told me a different story each time I saw them). I will never know if this sort of total confusion and inefficiency was intentional or a complete lack of any planning. I suspect a bit of both.

Nikki continued to ride her two horses, Disco and Kelpie, round the farm every day and was often able to report problems, the most common of which was the leaving open of gates and the destruction of fences on purpose by the now resident squatters. She encountered few security problems though, until one evening approaching the house she suddenly ran into a gang of about a hundred men, all converging on the house. They stopped and looked at her, and, as I happened to be near the security gate at the time, I shouted to her, "Just keep walking." To her credit she did just that, and looking straight ahead walked Kelpie straight through them. I think that her dressage judges might have termed it 'an extended walk' though. In fact this gang turned out to be harmless, as they were some religious sect just passing through, but it had been a very tense few moments.

Amazingly, Nikki was still competing in 3-phase events on both horses. A lot of the lovely cross-country courses in the farming areas, like 'Igava' and 'Pilmuir', had been forced to close down, but there were still some round Harare. Little Disco was at her peak and had been national eventing champion for a couple of years, but the competition was not great nor the courses particularly demanding, so Nikki was determined to test herself and Disco at the highest level possible. This was to be the South African Open Championships, very generously sponsored by Sappi and held each year on a lovely site near Johannesburg. We had been down two or three years before and Disco had competed with some success at the lesser levels. Now as national champion she was accepted in the very prestigious Open class. Open it was, with competitors from all over South Africa, Botswana and Swaziland, plus of course little Disco.

Training for this gruelling event was difficult, and marauding war vets were often amazed to see Nikki galloping down the verges of the main road only to come tearing back again a few minutes later. What they thought she was up to I have no idea, but they never dared to try and stop her – she was quicker than them anyway!

Arriving in South Africa for the big event we were confronted by fifteen huge thoroughbred horses in the Open class, and Disco was nearly chucked out at the initial vet testing, as people thought she was a kid's pony, only there to collect the jump judges' sheets. Dressage was never Disco's strongpoint, and she was well down the field after that discipline. However, thereafter only she and the eventual winner had clear rounds in both the very demanding cross-country and the show-jumping phases. On the last day Disco jumped fifty-five fences without hitting one and ended up fourth overall. It was an amazing performance and gave our flagging morale a big boost.

CHAPTER 23

Kicked Off

THE DEADLINE OF AUGUST 9, 2002, BY which time all farmers who had a Section 8 notice had to be out of their homes and off their land, was fast approaching. We were still uncertain whether or not this included us, but it certainly did include practically all of the rest of Wedza, including Harry. Harry as usual was trying every trick in the book to remain. His initial Section 8 had been in the name of Fran, so Harry replied by saying that you could not serve one on a dead person and it was therefore illegal. It was a good point, but as everything was illegal anyway it did not make a lot of difference.

About this time the resident squatters devised a new ploy to annoy us and extract money. They had planted small areas of maize spasmodically all over the place with seed and fertilizer provided by the State. They had not used the fertilizer, reckoning it was more profitable to sell it to people who had not invaded farms and therefore could not get any. However they did plant the seed, and to no one's surprise a very poor-looking crop resulted, so poor in most cases that it was obvious to the meanest intelligence that they were going to reap nothing. So this is when their cunning plan kicked in. They would cut whatever fences were necessary and drive a herd of the white farmer's cattle into the pathetic plot and herd them there while they tramped about and ate some of the miserable little maize plants.

Next morning there would be a delegation at the farmer's house led by the wretched guy whose lovely crop of maize had been destroyed by the wicked white man's cattle, backed up by a number of wailing women who maintained that now they would starve for the rest of the year, while behind this lot would stand a menacing band of young thugs all armed with sticks. The farmer would be 'invited' to come and take a look for himself at the terrible damage wrought by his uncontrollable cattle. It was a farce, of course, but initially farmers did go and tried to reason that:

a) What had been destroyed would have yielded nothing anyway and
b) That the fence had clearly been cut and the cattle, which were quite happy where they were, had been driven there.

This sort of reasoning would produce a dramatic increase in the wailing of the women and a significant move forward of the stick-wielding thugs. These guys were very brave when there were fifty or sixty of them against one old unarmed white farmer standing in a field far from any assistance or means of communication with any form of help.

It would not be long now before some considerable 'compensation' would be demanded. There would be the pantomime of counting each eaten plant and multiplying that number by the value of a prime cob of dried maize and some staggering figure would be mentioned. Meanwhile the offending cattle would have been impounded and would not be released until this compensation was paid. But this was outright extortion, you could say – go to the police. You would be quite right, and people did call the police. If they came at all, and it was a very big 'if', they would just say it was a civil matter and nothing to do with them.

Some people tried to call in an independent assessor to work out a realistic value of what, if any, damage had been done. Genuinely independent assessors were very reluctant to get involved and government ones, like Agritex, always agreed with the squatters, so that was not much help either.

Inevitably the farmer would be forced to pay something, and he would sometimes say, "OK, I'll go and get some money." Not that easy. Some of the thugs would immediately jump into his vehicle, saying that they would go with him to collect it. It was a horrible situation. It happened to Harry, who being Harry refused pointblank to pay anything. The result of this was that he, Flip and the children were barricaded in their house for two days with their water shut off, while most of his cattle were driven off the farm, some never to be seen again. He never did pay anything, but at what cost?

It happened to me on several occasions – not just in 2002 but also in the following years. Once I did go to the police, and I was arrested for 'causing malicious damage to property'. At 'Chirume' a herd of my cattle was driven from near my dip for approximately three kilometres and through three fences on to the next-door farm, 'Collace', which was by now completely taken over by squatters, and into some fields of stunted maize and tobacco. The inevitable mob arrived on my doorstep and I wondered what to do. Neither of us wanted to be barricaded in, so I decided to try and get a few guys on my side before going through the farce of inspecting the damage. To this end I told my foreman, Never, to take the old farm truck and collect my cattlemen and go to the site of the crime, while I followed with a truckload of the aggrieved maize growers and the inevitable thugs. However I did not go straight there but deviated via a police post near Wedza Club and persuaded a policeman to come with me. This did not go down particularly well with the other occupants of the vehicle.

It all made very little difference. When we got there, I was immediately surrounded by a screaming mob and dragged off to inspect the pathetic, somewhat battered plants, while my men and the policeman stood in the shade under a tree at a very safe distance and said or did nothing. I attempted to speak to the mob, saying we were now neighbours and must work together and help each other. Broken boundary fences were the responsibility of both of us – not just me – I had done all in my power to look after my cattle correctly, and they had never strayed this far before. It was stirring stuff but did stuff-all good. Eventually I loaded a bunch of thugs into both my truck and the one Never had brought, and drove back to the house, where I gave them six bags of maize to share and a packet of cigarettes for the guy who claimed I had ruined his tobacco crop. My cattle were released and we were not barricaded in the house, but I had capitulated and paid them something that they were blatantly not due. Was I right? Everyone had to make their own decisions at this time and I was not particularly proud of mine.

At the beginning of August I went to Wedza and did a round of all the so-called authorities, to try and find out if I was expected to get off 'Chirume' on August 9. I was finally directed to Agritex and went to see the top man there, one Mupinda, with whom I had had many dealings before. I asked him straight if he had found out about my so-called Section 8 from other sources, as he had promised to do. Needless to say he had done nothing. This is the conversation that followed.

"What must I do on August 9 then?" I asked.

To which he replied, "As far as this office is concerned you do have a Section 8, which means the government has acquired your farm, and as from August 9 you will have no right to be there."

"What about my house – my home?"

"That will be owned by the government."

"Where will I live? I have no other house."

"You can be allocated ten hectares like everybody else."

"What about compensation for stealing everything that I own?"

"That is not my department."

End of conversation. I just looked at him and left. It really did not help at all, but it is not a nice feeling being told that you no longer own your home.

There were more meetings at Ian Burgoyne's farm in a last desperate attempt to try and make some sense out of the whole catastrophic situation, and the local press was full of speculation as to what affected farmers would do. All labour on these farms had been told that they were not to turn up for work on the ninth or thereafter.

Our house girl at that time was a sweet girl called Juliet; she was Daniel, the groom's wife. Her first job every morning was to bring tea to us in bed, so it was with some anxiety that I waited for her knock on the bedroom door early in the morning of Friday, August 9, 2002. Would she be there or would she obey the thugs who had decreed that no one should turn up for work on that day? Six-thirty arrived and there was a knock on the door, and first Turbo ran in for her early morning cuddle followed by a smiling Juliet with my tea. First hurdle over, but I wondered who would be at my gate when I got up.

Just my own labour was there, and no one else. The day actually passed very quietly, but it was the lull before the storm. We later heard that police in every farming district had been told to arrest at least five farmers and lock them up over the weekend. On the Saturday they started to do this. They came for Harry first, but although he was still trying to farm at 'Leeds' he had already moved to Ruwa. They did get our next-door neighbour, Tony Olivey, plus Jenny Whaley from 'Scorror' and John Bibby (again). The idea of this happening just before a weekend was that no lawyers would be available to come and help bail people out. But we had got lawyers standing by for this very reason, so no one from Wedza spent the weekend in gaol. Not so in other areas though, and many wretched farmers spent a very uncomfortable weekend.

On Monday there was a warrant out for Harry's arrest. The police came to see me at 'Chirume' and asked where he was. I told them that I did not know but would try and get a message to him if I found out. This seemed to satisfy them but then they said, "Why are you still on the farm anyway?"

"Because I do not have a Section 8," I replied. This floored them, and they departed muttering that they would 'see about that'.

I phoned Harry, and told him what was going on, but he said that, due to some small oversight, his Section 8 actually expired on August 16 and not the ninth, so there was nothing the police could do – until then. This was sort of symbolic of all our thinking at the time. We could not really believe that we were all going to lose everything. Buy another week and something good must happen. We live in the 21st century; this is meant to be a civilized country; we were part of the British Commonwealth (we were then), and this sort of thing just could not happen. So Harry had 'bought' another week, and the other Harry – Harry Orphanides with his talk team – was still in touch with Vice-President Msika, who had told him that all our applications were even then with the Politburo. He came on the Agric-Alert on the evening of August 9, telling us all to sit tight as there was still hope. At the end of his message he asked if we had all received the message OK. A few of us said we had, then a mocking African voice came over the air saying that he had also received the message loud and clear. We well knew that our radio system had long been compromised but we were not doing anything illegal or trying to hide anything, so it did not really matter who heard what we were talking about.

Harry would not pay his labour any of the retrenchment packages, maintaining that this was admitting that the government was right. This caused the war vets to put a lot of pressure on his labour, and one day they all arrived at 'Chirume' having been kicked out of their houses, because they had not persuaded their boss to pay them.

I admired Harry enormously for his stand, but I told him I thought he was beating his head against a wall; however he would not give an inch and went as far as to say he didn't mind if they trashed his house and burned his tractors. That would put them clearly in the wrong and he would sue them. He reckoned that he would get little or no compensation anyway and he wanted to be able to look back on this period of his life with pride, knowing he had done all that he legally and morally could to keep his farm.

His predictions were pretty accurate. They did trash his house and burn his tractors. He did sue them, but so far he has got nothing. Later he also tried to sue the police for helping to steal his cattle, and this nearly got him into a lot of trouble. We will hear more of this later. Harry was by no means unique in taking this attitude; many others did the same, but I do not think that any of them gained anything by doing so except to salve their own consciences. Others went the other way completely and actively collaborated with the thugs in an attempt to keep part of their land and/or their house. This was generally frowned on, but it was very difficult to draw a definitive line. Harry was young, fit and very well qualified. He could get another job anywhere. But what about an unwell sixty-year-old with no qualifications and no savings? His only asset would be the farm on which he had lived all his life and made an honest living out of. If he refused to co-operate in any way with the thugs he would walk away with nothing, every cent of his capital tied up in his farm. Can you honestly blame him for trying to make some sort of a deal?

We were so involved with our own problems in Wedza that we saw little of Rob and Amanda up at Mvurwi. I got through occasionally on the phone and it seemed that they were having exactly the same sort of problems as us, and it also seemed that Rob had exactly the same approach to the problem as Harry. He would give the thugs nothing. I have some obstinate sons.

Some people tried to be clever and go into a form of business partnership with the thugs. This invariably turned sour, and many came badly unstuck. I suppose we were sort of taking a middle road. I was certainly over sixty and had no other qualifications but I was pretty fit and did have a few savings. However losing my home, my farm and my entire business was not exactly what I had hoped for as I approached retirement age.

A week after the eviction deadline we were still on the farm and were still selling a few of our remaining cattle. I decided to see how many of our immediate neighbours were still around. The answer was chilling – there were none. Harry and Flip were in Ruwa with the Piercys, the Corporal and Jean Hill, our neighbours, were in a flat in Harare, as were Tony and Gill Olivey. Bev and Peter Becker from 'Bolton' were living in Marondera, Ednam and Joan Dudley from 'Collace' were in England, Jim and Elizabeth Paliuras from 'Hele' were in Greece, Chris and Marylin Duirs from 'Raleigh' were in New Zealand and their parents, Bill and Joan, in Harare. There was a barrier across our exit road put there and manned by the thugs now resident on the Hills' farm, to prevent Tony Olivey from removing his own irrigation equipment. Why? Because they wanted it. Chris Duirs had removed some fittings from his house on 'Raleigh' to try and raise a little cash to pay for his ticket to New Zealand. He was immediately arrested and accused of stealing 'government property'. How much had the government paid for this property? Nothing, they had stolen it from Chris who had paid good money for it.

About this time our good friend and golfing companion Peter Bradshaw and his wife Janice from near Marondera were kicked off their farm. The man who did this was a youngish African who already had one farm of his own, and who, although considerably younger, had been at the same school as Peter – St George's in Harare. He was therefore a fairly civilized and well-educated man. Peter confronted him and asked him straight if he really thought that what he was doing was right.

"Oh no!" was the reply, "but everyone else is doing it and I do not want to lose out."

Peter's daughter-in-law Karen got hold of the international news network CNN (which were still allowed in the country then, though now banned) and asked them to come out and film Peter removing his belongings and moving out of his home. This they did, with the result that the whole Bradshaw family was then kicked out of the small cottage that they had moved into on a neighbouring farm. Clearly Peter's school 'mate' wanted no record of what he was doing. Why not? Surely he should be proud of his part in the liberation of the land from the wicked colonial whites and would want the world to see what he was doing? Perhaps the fact that he was a fat, prosperous looking guy in a new suit and with a brand new 4x4 in the background was not quite the image that was required – that of the land being given to the landless blacks.

Nikki's son, James, had a new and 'serious' girlfriend and he wanted to bring her out to see 'Chirume' and us while we were still there. It was a brave and thoughtful decision, which we guardedly encouraged – we did not get many visitors in those last few months on the farm. They duly arrived, and after a couple of days on 'Chirume' we were invited by Mike Bartlett to go with him to his house on the Mozambique coast just south of Inhassoro. This seemed like a good idea, as sitting in a deserted and rather tense Wedza was not a lot of fun for anyone. We had a very pleasant week there and even caught a few fish. But coming back was not such fun.

We spoke to Harry on the cell phone as soon as we got back into Zimbabwe, to see if he knew what had been happening in Wedza while we were away. He did know and it was not good news. He told us to call in on the police when we got to Wedza. This we did, and we were told that our house on 'Chirume' had been broken into and ransacked. Also our electric pump, which we relied on to pump water from the stream below the house, had been stolen and our labour had been told to stop working for us and that all the cattle currently on the farm had to go and stop grazing 'their' land. 'They' were the current squatters on the place.

The house was a mess. All my clothes and shoes had gone, so had a lot of Nikki's, also the obvious things like TV, video, radio plus a lot of crockery, cutlery, blankets, food etc. It took us some days to realize quite how much had been taken. What had the guard been doing? Not a happy homecoming! It was nearly dark when we arrived, and there was no food or water in the house and very few blankets. At least James and Suse got a first-hand taste of what life in Zimbabwe was like in those days.

Next day was not much better. All the squatters plus the nasty little 'headman' were at the gate early, plus a woman claiming that my cattle had eaten all her vegetables and a gang of thugs saying more cattle had trampled on some unbaked bricks that they were getting ready to bake. I palmed the woman off with the promise of getting an assessor out to evaluate the damage done to her precious cabbages but had to go with the thugs to view their destroyed bricks. There were some bricks lying in the open in a paddock which the 'headman' had very graciously said that I could use for my cattle. Some of these cattle had passed through, and possibly they had damaged a very few of the completely unguarded bricks. Again I took the easy option and paid. Admittedly it was not very much and certainly the easiest way out, but as I had now paid twice I suspected that they would go on using this source of easy income.

James and Suse left to fly back to London and we were feeling very lonely and isolated. Were we crazy to be hanging on when it was pretty evident that we were only delaying the inevitable?

Meanwhile Mugabe was in Johannesburg at the Earth Summit, and in a rousing speech he declared that the land redistribution in his country was going very smoothly and that everybody would be allowed to keep one farm. When interviewed later he reiterated that no white farmer would lose his farm if it was the only one he had. This statement was widely publicized and I presume a lot of people outside Zimbabwe believed it. In Zimbabwe at least two thousand people who only owned one farm had already been kicked off their land and out of their homes on the express instructions of Mugabe himself. This telling of absolutely blatant lies was a tactic that he would continue to use in the years ahead. The world, it seemed, could not believe that a previously respected head of state could stoop so low.

Our own labour continued to badger me for more money despite the fact that I had already given them cattle. I suppose that in their situation I would have done the same. They all knew very well that they would get nothing from the government. They also knew that my days were numbered, and that when I went they would have no job, no house and no future, so their only hope was to extract what they possibly could from me while I was still around. Some farmers had just abandoned their farms without paying off the labour, and had gone to live in town. These were often tracked down and subjected to severe pressure, not only by their labour, but also by gangs of thugs in town who took a percentage of any money that they did manage to extract.

In the end we came to some sort of compromise, and I agreed to pay some of my guys something more, as recommended by the labour officer, but only after I had sold some cattle. Until then they would get nothing, as I had nothing to give them. They finally all agreed to this.

On the way back from Marondera that day I picked up our post, and in it was a large package from Spratt in Australia. When I got home I opened it. Inside was a brochure on Bundaberg, the town in Queensland where he was planning to settle, having left university; there were also photos of his rugger teams, and a business card with the proud letters B.App.Sc. after his name and a framed picture of himself in his graduation cap and gown, holding his degree and wearing a huge smile. I put it on the now empty shelf in my dressing room and suddenly burst into tears. I had been so close to Spratt and now he was so far away and we were in such an unhappy situation. He should have been coming home now to take over 'Chirume', but under the current conditions this would never happen.

This symbolized one of the major tragedies of the whole scene – the complete break-up of the family unit. Wedza was certainly not unique, but it was special in that it was a very close-knit community. You didn't go through Wedza to get to anywhere – it was the end of the line of commercial farms. They say that a son should never work for his father on a farm, yet in Wedza practically every farm had the young generation working happily on the same farm as the previous generation, families such as England, Olivey, Smith, Bibby, Travers, White, Seager, Whaley, Thornicroft, Malzer, Whitfield, Raynor, Milne and Bartlett. All the sons had been to agricultural college, and when they returned the parents gladly handed over the running of the farm, in recognition of the advanced technology they had learnt. It worked well. And there were plenty of inter-Wedza marriages as well. We had been a very happy community, and now we were suddenly scattered all over the world. No more farmers' meetings, no more WADS groups, no more cricket matches, no more Father Christmas at Mike Hill's Evening, no more church services at the little church on the hill where we had been married. Quite apart from the obvious crippling financial losses that most families were suffering, this personal tragedy was almost worse.

The morning after my meeting with the labour officer, all my workers, plus a large selection of thugs, the 'headman' and some caterwauling women, were all waiting outside the gate, again – not what I needed before even having a cup of coffee. The labour, egged on by the thugs, wanted all their money immediately, despite what they had all agreed to the previous day. The thugs and the 'headman' wanted me to remove all my cattle from 'their' farm immediately; the caterwauling women said that my horses had eaten all the grass off the houses they had just built in the paddock. They all clustered round me in a tight, shouting mob. I was frightened. By luck at that very moment a neighbour, Hank Botha, arrived in his truck with a policeman, on some other mission. I did not know Hank that well but asked him just to hang around for a bit while I tried to accommodate my 'friends'.

I told my labour to wait. I argued that all my cattle were for sale and that I was providing an invaluable service to the community by selling quality heifers at a very reasonable price – true. I told the women that if I could not graze my horses anywhere, I would have to shoot them – also true. There was a lot of discussion about this last statement, but finally they said, "Do not mock us." I was not mocking them; I had about twelve horses at the time – Nikki's two special ones and the others, equally special in their own way but now old and retired, polo ponies like Rama and Wonder Girl. We could and would keep Disco and Kelpie, but the others would indeed have to be shot. Most eventually were.

All through this time I was keeping a pretty detailed diary, and now as I write this in 2009 I am reading what I then wrote, to refresh my memory. I am staggered that, with what we were going through and with all our neighbours gone, we were even contemplating remaining on the farm. It just shows how one's mind can become numbed and refuse to accept what, to any sane thinking person, is perfectly obvious. We did not have a hope of remaining on 'Chirume'. We were only lucky not to have experienced as much physical violence and abuse as a lot of our friends.

By mid-September 2002 though, the message was finally getting through – we would have to move sooner rather than later, so we started actively looking for somewhere to go. Neither of us could quite swallow the idea of moving to a little flat in town or anywhere in Harare like some of our friends, so we concentrated on cottages round Marondera and Ruwa. There was not a lot available, because so many other farmers were doing the same thing. Every time we went to town we took furniture and personal belongings, which we dumped with Bobby Fernandes or David Cruttenden, kind friends who looked after these things for us. 'Chirume' house was getting very naked and sad.

We looked at a house just outside Marondera, Tim Wotton's cottage in Harare and a couple of cottages near Ruwa, but none was quite suitable. One stumbling block was the necessity of having the two horses somewhere near as well. I never let on to the squatters that we were planning to go, but kept negotiating with the 'headman' to keep what few cattle I had left for as long as possible, so as not to have to make a forced sale on a very depressed market. I did not have a lot of cards to play but harped on about never having had a Section 8 notice and that therefore he had no right to be there at all. It was pretty thin, as he said quite openly that he didn't give a damn what the lawyers or courts said. He took his orders from Chigwedere and Chigwedere said I had to go.

Our search for somewhere to go finally ended when we were offered the former manager's cottage on Ruwa golf course. In addition there were some stables, and grazing on a nearby plot, where we could put the horses. It was as good a solution as we could have hoped for. The cottage was tiny and no way could we move the bulk of our possessions there, but it was safe and there was lots of lovely space all around.

Meanwhile a large number of farmers, most of whom were by now off their farms, were summoned to yet another meeting, this time in the big hall on the Agricultural Research Trust (ART) farm. Apparently a firm of Indian lawyers had a solution to our problems, and yet again we were enjoined to draw diagrams of what land we wanted to keep, what we would give away, how we would manage it, etc., and all this had to be with the Indian company by the end of the week. I did do all this and went to see the Indian lawyer in charge, but I am afraid that by now we all were really grasping at non-existent straws.

We learned at this meeting of an incident in Odzi, just up the road from Marondera, where a farmer called Chris Bezuidenhout had accidentally run over a drunken squatter who jumped in front of his car as Chris was trying to escape from a threatening mob on his farm. In a remarkably short space of time, considering how crowded the courts were at that time, Chris had been convicted of murder and sentenced to fifteen years in prison. It just went to prove how careful one had to be and how the government would seize on any opportunity to blame and convict a white man while completely ignoring blatant crimes committed by their own supporters.

On Thursday, October 3, 2002, Nikki and I woke up on 'Chirume' for the last time. We both took a swig of 'Rescue Remedy' to try and keep calm on what was going to be a very trying day. We were moving out. 'Chirume' had been my home for the past thirty-five years. It was the first place I had bought on my own and the base for all my business for all those years. It had not all been easy by any means and I am the first to admit that I was not a particularly brilliant farmer, especially when compared to some of my neighbours. However 'Chirume' had provided a wonderful home, enabling my family to live a good life, indulge in some expensive hobbies like polo and skiing, with regular trips out of the country. Above all it had given all three sons a private education up to 'A' level, followed by university for two and agricultural college for the third. Not too bad really for a bit of rocky Africa. And now we were leaving it – not because we wanted to and certainly not because we were being paid a lot of money to do so. We had not had to put up with some of the more blatant abuse meted out to some of our neighbours, and we had never been locked into our house and 'jambanja'ed', but we now had no water, nowhere to graze our horses and no neighbours. In addition we were hassled every day by the new squatters, were losing money hand over fist and living a miserable life into the bargain – it was time to go. We have still not received one cent in compensation.

Nikki went first in the Isuzu, towing the horse trailer, loaded to the gunwales with last minute furniture like our double bed, the stove and the kitchen sink! She took Never and Daniel with her to help unload. Nikki had lived on 'Chirume' for just over ten years and I believe she had really loved it. She rode her horses virtually every day so had probably ridden round the farm some three and a half thousand times, loving the beauty and the solitude, the game, cattle, birds and trees – everything about it in fact. As she drove out she told herself, "Don't look left." Looking left meant looking over the river and the 'Chirume' hills towards the game park – the place of so many happy rides and memories. She looked straight ahead through misty eyes.

My day started badly. Outside the gate inevitably were all the squatters, arguing with my workers about why I was supplying them with maize meal but not the squatters. I really did not want to get involved and stayed inside. The squatters then put their padlock on the gate, so now I could go nowhere. I rang Harry, who I knew was planning to come out from Ruwa to Leeds that morning, and asked him to contact the police (who might help, as I was planning to leave the farm), and stand by to help get me out if necessary. Two hours passed and eventually they unlocked the gate and dispersed. I wandered back into the now virtually empty house to make sure I had forgotten nothing. I went into my dressing room where there was still a bed and bare mattress. Curled up on it and shivering was little Turbo. A sensitive little dog, and the vibes had got to her – what was happening to her home?

The staff were very silent and downcast. I am not bragging or being egotistical when I say that I had been at the centre of their lives for thirty-five years. I had housed them, fed them, looked after many of their ailments, helped solve family problems, given them land to grow crops on, transported them to hospital, and above all paid them a fair monthly salary every month on the nail despite any financial problems I might have been going through at the time. Now I was going – they knew that – and I think they suddenly realized that from now on they would be on their own and at a bad time. They had been labelled as white man's lackeys and as such MDC supporters. They faced a very uncertain future. Was I sorry for them? Yes, I was. They had been fairly unpleasant and insistent on their entrenchment package but, let's face it, it had been their last chance of getting any sort of capital to start a new life. I was not totally abandoning all of them by any means. I still had a few cattle which needed looking after and I offered my two foremen, Never and

Tichaona, jobs at Ruwa. Then of course Daniel was still employed as Nikki's groom. We wanted to take Juliet as well, as our house girl, but she opted to stay and dig the bit of unfertile land that she and Daniel had been 'given' on 'Collace'.

I finally bundled Tandy and Turbo into the front of my truck and drove to the little cottage at Ruwa Golf Club which would be our home for the next year.

CHAPTER 24

Ruwa

OUR INITIAL FEELINGS HAVING LEFT 'CHIRUME' CAN be summed up in one word – relief! Relief that we now had some near neighbours, relief that we had some water and power in the cottage but, most of all, relief that there was no longer a continual mob of people waiting at the gate to trot out a string of unreasonable demands.

Next we gave a bit of thought to our immediate future. Would we ever get back to the farm? Would we ever get any compensation? What sort of action should we now take, such as pursuing the matter through the courts? We had still not.received any definite proof of having been issued a Section 8 notice, and this made a difference as to how we would approach any court case. In my heart I did not think we would ever return to 'Chirume', but I believed that eventually there would be some sort of compensation for this monstrous theft. As I write this, in 2009, there is still nothing remotely on the horizon. I do, however, understand that no one will pay anything while Mugabe is still in power.

We had filled in countless forms and answered all relevant questions and given all these papers to the two excellent organizations which, over the years, had continued to do battle on our behalf – Agric Africa, headed by Bobby Fernandes, and Justice for Agriculture (JAG) headed by John Worsley-Worswick. These two organizations have a slightly different approach and do not quite see eye to eye. It would be to everybody's advantage if they joined forces, as it is essential that we Zimbabwean ex-farmers speak with one voice.

We still had cattle on the farm, and I went back perhaps once a week to check on these. Never and Ephraim remained there and were in charge of the cattle, and an old night-watchman called Electa was meant to keep an eye on the house, as we still had a few bits and pieces left. There was precious little he could actually do to prevent anything being stolen, but perhaps he would be able to tell us afterwards who had stolen it. I never advertised when I would be pitching up, so I seldom met any of the squatters or the bloody little headman. However it soon became obvious that all the cattle would have to go, sooner rather than later. The count was never correct and on at least two occasions I was shown the recently butchered carcass of one of my animals.

On one occasion, when the cattle had been rounded up near the house, I saw several animals with bad cuts all over them. These had clearly been made by thugs slashing them with pangas. As I was wondering what to do about these injured animals, one of the local war vet leaders, Nyati from 'Bath Farm', pitched up with a gang of friends. Nyati had actually taken my place on the Rural District Council. There had not been any sort of election, I had just been told I was no longer required and Nyati had been appointed in my place by Chigwedere. Now I wondered why he was snooping round my farm, and I decided to take the initiative. I rounded on him and, pointing at the slashed cattle, asked what sort of farmers his friends the new farmers were, when they treated cattle like that. He was a bit taken aback by my shouting at him; I think he had planned to shout at me for being on the farm at all.

A short time later Nyati gave me a letter saying that he was moving into my house on 'Chirume'. I took this letter to my lawyer and asked him to try and get a court order banning Nyati from taking my house. This he did and the court found in my favour. I showed the court order to Nyati and he did not like it a bit. Not so much being banned from moving into my house (he already had a perfectly good one of his own), but the fact that his name was now officially recorded as trying to do an illegal thing. This was common to a lot of the thugs who were blatantly committing crimes at the time. The fact that they did not want any record of their actions proved that they knew they were doing wrong.

The other thing that was really suffering was the game park. All our lovely game was being slaughtered wholesale. The place was full of snares and Never reported hearing gunshots on most nights. Very few Africans have any sort of affection for wild animals and have no idea of the priceless heritage they are destroying. (Mind you, nor did the early settlers in South Africa. Whatever happened to the Quagga?) They view wild game purely as a source of food. Most do not even know the different names of individual species and refer to them all just as 'nyama' – the word which means meat and is used pretty much throughout Africa. I hired a professional hunter called Neil Curry, who also ran a skin-tanning business near Bromley, and said that he could shoot as many of the zebra as he could. He could keep all the meat and I would pay him to tan the hides, which would be mine. He did go out to the farm twice and managed to shoot seven, before he got severely warned off by the resident thugs. These seven hides were all I ever got back from my investment in game. Shooting our prized game like that might sound callous, but better professionally shot than snared and speared or hunted by dogs.

It was now virtually impossible to go on keeping the cattle on 'Chirume'; apart from the slashings, they were being stolen fairly steadily and were allowed very little grazing, so I cut my losses and sold them all at a Marondera sale. In many ways it was a big relief, and with them gone there was no reason to go back to the farm at all, so we set about rebuilding our lives at Ruwa.

I joined the Mashonaland Senior Golfers Association and once a month went to play on the lovely Royal Harare course, just next door to the old polo ground. I immediately discovered that the vast majority of my fellow 'oldies' were businessmen from Harare and not involved in farming at all. I did not know many of them, as most of my friends were farmers. Setting off down the first fairway we would get chatting and they would ask me where I came from and what I did, etc. I would tell them that I now lived in Ruwa having previously farmed in Wedza.

427

"Oh!" they would say, "so you have sold up and retired?"

No! I had no wish to retire or sell up. I was quite staggered to discover how little they knew of what had been going on in the farming areas. We had been so caught up in it for the past two years that we assumed everybody knew what had been going on. When I started telling them what had happened they were uninterested and just dropped the subject. Sitting in the bar after one game, my opponent got chatting to someone else and was complaining about how his business was suffering due to the country's financial problems. He added that small indigenous companies were suffering even worse, and that he was 'thankful that the government seemed to realize the importance of being nice to the whites, as they were so vital to the economy of the country!' Really? I had not noticed this benevolence.

Were we bitter about what had happened to us? Yes, perhaps a little bit, but there was no point in dwelling on it. We had had a wonderful life on the farm and now that chapter was closed. Other people did not find it quite so easy to move on. Rob and Amanda were – and to a certain extent still are – convinced that they will return to their farm. Harry was still fighting like a tiger, but must have realized by now that he would not live on 'Leeds' again for a very long time, if ever. I think that it was the sheer stupidity and monumental waste that galled people most. The whole land redistribution exercise had perhaps 5% to do with Africans wanting land and 95% to do with Mugabe wanting to remain in power. There was plenty of land available and money to pay for it. I am not writing a history of Mugabe's land grab but just about how it affected us and our family. There have been several books written by other ex-farmers, all with heart-rending stories about the land that they had built up from virgin Africa into highly productive, foreign currency-earning enterprises, that had been snatched from them and were now producing nothing.

For many, apart from the actual farms, there was real heartache about the theft of their homes; a home and garden that had been cherished for decades; flowers planted; plantations established and love and care lavished on the whole place. I fear we have seen the last of some of these lovely farm homes in Africa. No one in their right senses will ever again pour money into improving a farm for their children's inheritance – knowing that they risk having it removed at the whim of a government.

When Mugabe was about to take over Zimbabwe it is said that he had a chat with President Samora Machel of Mozambique – he wanted a few pointers on how he should approach the problem of taking over a colony. One of Samora Machel's much-quoted bits of advice was, 'Don't get rid of your whites.' What is not so often quoted is what he said immediately after this statement, which was, 'Let them build the country up first and then get rid of them.' I have a nasty feeling that the governments of Zambia, Nigeria, Malawi, Mozambique and Kenya, to mention a few, could well have had this in mind when they invited the highly skilled ex-Zimbabwean farmers to come and work in their countries. Many have gone to these countries, but you can be sure they are not going to build any fancy houses.

Those who went to farm in other African countries included a lot of our friends. Others went to Australia, New Zealand, England, Canada and a variety of other countries. We were frequently being invited to leaving parties in Harare, and sad nostalgic occasions most of them were too.

*   *   *

We ourselves were very undecided as to where we wanted to spend the rest of our lives. We made a short list – England, South Africa, Australia or stay put. We both knew England pretty well. I knew South Africa very well and Nikki had by now seen a good bit of it. The unknown was Australia. Nikki had been there once, briefly, years ago but I had never been. However, we suddenly had the perfect excuse to go there – Spratt was to marry his long-time lovely girlfriend, Jacinta Swain, whose parents farmed in northern New South Wales.

It was a wonderful occasion, made even better by the fact that Rob, Amanda and Sabrina, Harry and Flip all went as well, plus numerous

Warrens from New Zealand and our old Kenya/Zim friends John and Lorna Clarke. All we Milbanks stayed in Jack and Jacinta's recently bought house in Bagara, then moved to a large guesthouse near Tamworth, on the shores of Lake Keepit, for the wedding itself. The marriage service took place in the Roman Catholic Church in Tamworth with the reception back at Lake Keepit. Jack and Jacinta's friends had flown in from all over Australia and Jack's best man, Roy Ormerod, had come from Zimbabwe. All spent the night 'on site' and the following day the celebrations started all over again! All Milbanks and Warrens then joined the happy couple on their honeymoon. These days, with couples living together, sometimes for years, before getting married, honeymoons are rather different occasions from what they were years ago. All of us had travelled thousands of miles to attend the wedding and obviously we wanted to see as much as possible of the people we had come to visit, Jack and Jacinta.

The result was a marvellous trip to Barrington Tops National Park and the Hunter Valley wine estates. Harry, Nikki and I played a lot of golf, and every evening there was a huge dinner party culminating in games of 'wink murder' and liar dice. I had seldom been so happy – all my family around me, a wonderful occasion, an exciting new country – and not a war vet or squatter in sight.

All this contributed to giving me an excellent impression of Australia – I loved the place. This view was reinforced in 2007 when we again visited Spratt and Jacinta and the new addition to the family, Alexina (Lexi). We stayed with them on their recently acquired farm near Gympie and travelled to the Great Barrier Reef and a short way into the Outback. Nikki was not quite so taken with the place as I was and we both decided, reluctantly on my part, that we could not really afford to live there and Australia probably didn't want us anyway. So Australia was crossed off the short list.

We also crossed off the easy option of going to South Africa. We felt it would be a question of jumping from the fire into the frying pan, if I can put it that way round. I do not believe that South Africa will ever go quite the same way as Zim, but it is certainly going to have its problems.

That left staying put or going to England. We would both easily be able to get into England and we both had a lot of relatives there – particularly Nikki. We had been offered help in finding cheap accommodation and we both knew, and liked, England well enough– but! I think Nikki could handle it but I was not so sure that I could. I have lived in Africa virtually all my life and have become accustomed to the sun, the freedom, the opportunities and general lifestyle that we would never be able to afford in England. So England was, if not crossed off the list, at least put on hold, and we opted to stay put.

We settled back into our little cottage and started getting to know our new neighbours. Ian and April Piercy were just down the road and we saw a lot of them, partly because Harry and Flip were living in their cottage. The Piercys were still farming. They had had Section 5 and 8 notices, as Ian put it, "falling on this place like confetti". But they were still there despite regular visits by the leading local thug, who despite owning a large house in nearby Goromonzi had designs on Ian and April's lovely house and garden – not to mention the valuable gum plantations. Ian had genuine friends who were well placed in the ZANU (PF) hierarchy and he used these shamelessly when threats of eviction became too serious. Did they help? Yes, I think they did and I saw no harm in using them.

* * *

My ex brother-in-law, Richard, and his wife Gay had by now been living in England for some time and had no intention of returning to Zim. They had made their decision and were making the most of it. However their farm, 'Nyahuvu', near Headlands had been leased out. Not the whole farm, but four hundred acres, which was a deal that, they and some other Headlands farmers had managed to make with the new settlers. This provided a bit of income if it could be smuggled out to England. Still on 'Nyahuvu' was a fair amount of Escorro orange wine. This had been invented by old Rick when he owned 'Scorror Estate' in Wedza in the 1960s and could not sell all his oranges. Richard had moved the winery to Headlands when he moved there and up to the time he left had been doing a good trade selling this excellent tipple to the locals. Since then gallons of this wine had been sitting untouched in huge fibreglass vats locked up in a barn. With time on my hands I offered to try and sell it.

I managed to get rid of most of it – partly by drinking a lot myself and partly by selling lots to the Ruwa Golf Club caddies, who still ask me for it whenever I go to play there. However just as I was coming to the end a local thug pitched up one day and said that the farm was now his. I had no wish to get involved in this argument. As far as I knew the place was leased to Graham Chadwick, and his brother-in-law Brian Anderson was living in the manager's cottage and running the place. I told the man this and went to see Graham. Graham was not surprised and said it had been brewing for some time, and that the best I could do would be to try and get off what I could as quickly as possible. The main house still contained a lot of the Holmes' furniture as well as some valuable farm tools, computers and, locked in a special room with no key, a selection of firearms.

The house was looked after by their faithful old servant, Aaron, and guarded by a couple of guards still paid for by Richard. This did not prevent the place being broken into (or was it why the place was broken into?). Doors were knocked down, windows smashed and the whole house well and truly looted. I had said I did not want to get involved, but inevitably I was. The main house was nothing to do with Graham and I felt that I had to try and save some of Richard and Gay's things or else the thug would just take everything. Despite every effort, no one had yet managed to get into the locked room, which had a huge steel bar, slotted into the wall across the door. Of course I could not get in either. None of the house keys fitted and there was no clue how to open the door. I rang Richard up.

"Just unscrew the cover of the light switch outside the door," he said, "you will find a lever there, pull it and the door will open."

It did! Richard always had a devious mind and he must have had a lot of fun devising this.

Firearms were bad news in those touchy days, so I located the valid certificates and went straight to Headlands police and handed them in. From there I managed to sell them at a price, which was a fraction of what they were worth. Next I hired a lorry and Nikki and I accompanied it out to the farm with some of our own guys. We spent most of the day sorting out the better stuff and loading it on to the lorry. As the lorry started pulling away from the house there was a general commotion in the direction of the barns, and suddenly a horde of running, gesticulating Africans waved the lorry down and started trying to pull the frightened driver out of his cab.

This mob turned out to be all Richard's old labour – currently employed by Graham. They knew all about the retrenchment payments and despite the fact that Richard had paid them right up to the date when he stopped employing them, they now reckoned that he owed them back pay depending on how long each one had worked for him. They had thought that with the house still fully furnished Richard would be return-ing and they would get their money then, but now we were removing everything, so clearly he was not coming back and they were about to lose out.

Richard was certainly not to blame, as this particular bit of legisla-tion had not even been invented when he had last been here, but in the convoluted ways that the law was then supposed to work the labour did have a point. Graham was certainly not going to give them any back pay – they had only been working for him for a year or so – and Richard was miles away in England, so they beamed in on me and Nikki. I was not amused – I thought that I had finished with this sort of nonsense.

I addressed the somewhat threatening mob and pointed out that, although we were taking Richard and Gay's personal possessions, mainly because they were being stolen (by them?), we were leaving behind all the much more valuable farm equipment consisting of tractors, ploughs, trailers, carts, irrigation equipment etc, and surely their late boss was not going to desert the farm when he still had all this equipment? This weighty statement was received in silence. So I quickly followed up my advantage by saying that I would take a delegation of them to the labour officer in Marondera and that if any back pay were due to them I would see they got it. Meantime would they please release the driver and let him proceed. A lot of mumbling followed but slowly they stood back and the lorry driver leapt into his cab and tore off. He tore off at such a rate that he failed to notice a low, overhanging branch and completely smashed the lovely old Welsh dresser which was standing tall at the front of the lorry above all the other furniture.

We then had to extricate ourselves, and we only succeeded in doing this with a promise to return next day and take the said delegation to Marondera. This I did, and most of them did get a bit more, which I funded out of wine sales. It was not nearly as much as they had wanted and future visits to 'Nyahuvu' were a bit of a problem, because when they saw me they would start trying to squeeze a bit more.

However, when the 'Nyahuvu' saga ended we had the Welsh dresser repaired, and bought it and some other bits and pieces, which now grace our new house.

* * *

Harry, although now well and truly off the farm and living in Ruwa, still had cattle on 'Leeds' and these were being systematically stolen, hand over fist. Harry reckoned that he had some pretty accurate information that the Wedza police, far from protecting his cattle, were involved in stealing them. Harry was not prepared to let this go unchallenged and sought help from higher-up brass in the police force. Some of the police appeared to be helpful and Harry pressed his advantage, going as far as going to pick up some 'details' from Wedza police station and going with them to investigate the site of some possible thefts. There was an awful lot of dithering around and absolutely no positive action was taken. At that time Harry always carried a small pistol just in case things got too hairy. I never thought that this was a very good idea, as the days of shooting oneself out of trouble were well and truly over. However the police knew he had this correctly licensed pistol on him, and at the start of this particular exercise said they would rather he did not carry it and asked him to give it to them, which he did immediately.

Nothing came of that search into his missing cattle but Harry continued to probe into the matter. Some three days after the abortive search I was playing golf with him at Marondera. His cell phone rang just as I was about to putt on the eleventh hole. It was the Wedza police saying that he should report to the police station immediately as he was under arrest. When enquiring why, he was told that there were three charges against him:

1) For breaching the new Public Order and Security Act (POSA).

2) For carrying an unlicensed firearm.

3) For threatening a policeman with a firearm.

All were so patently untrue that it would be laughable if not so serious. I particularly disliked the third one.

Harry managed to talk his way out of going to the police station immediately, continued with his game of golf and actually won the tournament. However he agreed to go to Wedza early the next morning and I went with him. When I picked him up he was dressed in his warm old rugger jersey and carried some insect repellent. I asked him why. "They want to lock me up," he replied, "and I'm told it's very cold in those cells and they are full of mozzies." He was right. He spent an hour and a half giving his statement in answer to these charges to the very constable who had been with him at that abortive search for cattle. The constable maintained that Harry had said he would lose his job after the next election when MDC won and that that statement breached POSA.

The unlicensed firearm bit was quickly squashed when Harry produced the valid certificate, but the threatening bit looked bad. I was sitting in on all this and asked the constable why, if he had been threatened, he had not arrested Harry straight away, rather than wait for three days? However he insisted that Harry had a case to answer and said he should appear in court the next day in Marondera. There was no alternative but to accept this and we were just about to leave when the Wedza member-in-charge, who was the guy whom Harry suspected of stealing the cattle, arrived.

He called Harry into his office. I tried to follow but was stopped. I waited outside for a very nervous forty minutes during which time I heard raised voices coming from inside. Eventually Harry reappeared with a sheepish grin on his face and, ominously, crossed his wrists in front of him indicating that he was about to be handcuffed and chucked into the filthy cells, pending his appearance in court. I am probably flattering myself when I say that possibly my presence tipped the balance, but they suddenly changed their mind and said that we could both go home, but to be sure to be on time in court next day. Phew!

It is never pleasant being involved with the police but when dealing with them in a case which is clearly a setup, it is positively scary. We went straight to Marondera to see the very good local lawyer, Richard Mufuka, and asked him to come to court with Harry. Inevitably next day the case was remanded. This was then, and still is, a very common thing in Zimbabwean courts and can drag on for ages. This is not too bad if you are remanded out of custody, but it is a nightmare for the wretched people who have to remain locked up for the entire time that it takes to prepare their case. Harry had to pay a deposit and surrender his passport.

To cut a long story short, he made six further appearances in court with each one being remanded. By then he wanted to leave Zim and take up a job in Tanzania. They gave him his passport back but insisted that he return to Zim for yet another hearing. He flew down especially for this hearing and we were both supremely relieved when he was told that the case had been dropped, as the police had still not prepared their case. I have often wondered why they dropped it. Perhaps because Harry was now out of the country and no longer bothering them. I do not know, but what I do know is that Harry has not dropped his case against them.

So Harry, Flip and the grandchildren were gone. They spent a year or so near Arusha in Tanzania, where we visited them once, and then moved on to Kenya. A sad loss to me particularly, but also to Nikki, who had become very fond of them. We had been through a lot together and now Zimbabwe had lost another talented, well-trained, young farmer, who like many others could have contributed immeasurably to the future wellbeing of the country. A phrase often used at this time was that from being the breadbasket of Africa, Zimbabwe was now the basket case. How true! Exports of any agricultural produce except a small amount of tobacco and some flowers had ceased, and when the government wanted more money they just printed it, thus starting an astonishing spiral of inflation which is still with us today.

In mid-2003 we took a gamble. We had chosen to stay in Zim, for the time being at any rate, but did not want to go on camping in the little golf club cottage, happy as we had been there. We liked the Ruwa area and so started looking around for something to buy, and it was not long before we were shown a very nice house with excellent outbuildings standing on about fifty acres of very rocky land. It was really bigger than we had in mind but the owners were sick and wanting to leave the country in a hurry, so we made a fairly modest offer, which was accepted. What had we done?

"Crazy," said some people.

"Good buy," said others.

Worth the risk, we thought, as we would only be paying over the next four years. It was worth the risk and in 2009 we are still here, having now fully paid for the place.

The last few years have been far from easy, but we have managed to keep ourselves busy. We built some stables and Nikki has never had less than two horses here and still competes in dressage, showjumping and very limited cross-country events. Ian and April Piercy were looking after the few cows that Harry managed to rescue from 'Leeds' just up the road from us, and when Harry left I took them over, on the understanding that when he returned I would give him back the same weight of beef that he had given me. Meanwhile I would keep any progeny. It was a good deal and gave me some mombies to look after again. Ian most generously let us have free grazing at 'Chaddesley' so long as the mombies did not damage his precious newly planted gum trees. The herders that I employed were not always in total agreement with this and the telephone line between 'Chaddesley' and 'Merrywood' sometimes became very hot.

Then there was the inevitable occasion when the cattle were driven off Ian's farm and into the stunted maize of a nearby new settler. This resulted in me being arrested and charged with causing malicious damage to property. Malicious? I thought that implied that it was pre-planned and intentional. Nothing came of it, and this time I paid nothing except the considerable legal fees of Richard Mufuka. But it was symptomatic of the ongoing attitude that new settlers could get away with anything, particularly if they were trying to fleece the white man.

Generally speaking though, our black neighbours were very pleasant. Nikki rode round the area virtually every day and always got a cheery greeting and a wave. There was certainly no racial tension at all. I had offered jobs to Never and Tichaona on our new plot, but having accepted they then reneged on the agreement; they went back to 'Chirume' to look after the land they had been 'given', for fear of it being taken away from them because they still worked for a white man. Instead we took on the resident worker who had been with the previous owners for some time. This proved to be an excellent alternative. Gift has turned out to be quite one of the best and pleasantest Africans that I have ever employed. He is a committed Christian and goes to church every Sunday (which is more than we do these days), speaks excellent English and, unlike me, is very good with his hands.

Life in our new pad soon settled down into quite a pleasant way of life. We had some very nice neighbours, some of them ex-farmers like ourselves while others had been in the area for some time. Nikki rode and competed and became very involved in building some of the few remaining cross-country courses. We both played more golf, both at Ruwa and also regularly at Marondera, plus a few sorties into town. We spent more money, rightly or wrongly, in developing our plot by putting in more fencing, improving the staff housing, and building rainwater storage tanks and a wood-burning 'Rhodesian' boiler.

Frankly, we were not nearly so aware of the ongoing chaos and rapidly deteriorating situation in the country as we had been on the farm. Having some foreign currency, we were able to bring in funds as and when we needed them at the unofficial rate, which more or less kept up with inflation. This meant that it increased rapidly. The official rate to currencies like the US dollar and British pound was kept ridiculously low by the government. The 'fat cats' in the ZANU (PF) hierarchy were able to cash in on this in a big way. They had access to the limited amount of hard currency that was available and promptly changed it into Zim dollars at the unofficial rate, thus making a huge profit. There were and still are some seriously rich people in and on the fringe of government. It is little wonder that they want to hang on to power at all costs. The current rate of exchange became a regular talking point as the Zim dollar became more and more worthless. In August 2006 the Governor of the Reserve Bank redesigned the currency, lopped off three noughts and declared that by doing so all inflation problems were over. Soon afterwards the government stopped publishing the official inflation figures, as they were too embarrassing. To give you some idea of what the British pound was worth I will quote a few recent examples (and remember, these figures are after the three noughts came off):

Month	Year	Z$ to £1	Previously
August	2006	1,500,000	
September	2006	1,500	1,500,000
November	2006	3,800	
Febuary	2007	8,250	
April	2007	40,000	
June	2007	320,000	
September	2007	700,000	
November	2007	3,000,000	
March	2008	125,000,000	
May	2008	1,000,000,000	
Early June	2008	6,000,000,000	
Mid June	2008	8,000,000,000	

One comparison worth noting is that in 1973, at the height of international sanctions against the Smith regime, one Rhodesian dollar (the same unit as the Zim dollar) was worth one British pound.

I don't really understand how inflation works, but one reason for sure was because the government, with no access to hard currency, just printed money. If they suddenly really had to pay off interest on a World Bank loan, they would just print trillions of Zim dollars and buy US dollars on the black market. Similarly, when the army and police force 'other ranks' became restless because their salaries were going nowhere, they would again print more money and increase their pay tenfold, to buy their loyalty. Prices of everything naturally went up in sympathy with this rate, as by now Zimbabwe was producing very little and most things had to be imported. We tended to shop on a Friday, as everything would be much more expensive by Monday.

* * *

Then in February 2005 a major tragedy struck our family. Rob, Amanda and Sabrina were by now off their farm and living on the huge Austrian-owned estate, 'Forrester', near Mvurwi. They had got a certain amount of their own equipment off their farm 'Vigila' and had been lent land by the owner of 'Forrester', Heinrich von Pezold, to grow a crop of garlic. One evening while Rob was quietly having a beer he suddenly collapsed and passed out. Amanda had to rush him the one hundred kilometres into Harare and contact the excellent neurosurgeon, Auchterlonie. It turned out that a small vein at the back of his brain had burst, causing a lot of bleeding around and within this part of the brain.

Apparently the vein was congenitally weak, and anything could have caused it suddenly to burst. Why this had not happened earlier, when he had fallen off his horse and banged his head, which had happened on several occasions, I have no idea. One theory was that stress could have triggered it, and Rob had certainly been under a lot of stress. I am not going to go into a lot of medical speculation; the fact was that poor, dear, brave Skel was very, very sick. I went to St Anne's Hospital in Harare as soon as I heard the following morning. Amanda was there, of course, plus half of the white population of Mvurwi. They had all come to town to see what help they could be, to offer advice and support, and generally to be around to do what they could. There was not a lot anyone could do. Rob was in the care of Dr Auchterlonie and there were few better hands in the whole of Africa to be in than his. So that was a minor comfort. We all had a conference with him and, although he was quite capable of operating to relieve the pressure on Rob's brain himself, we reckoned that the vital after-care would not be up to scratch in the deteriorating Zimbabwe environment. So he would have to be flown to Johannesburg, and quickly. Luckily Heinrich had shares in a medical air rescue plane and he had already taken the precaution of having this on immediate standby. So with no more ado he was flown to South Africa and admitted to Milpark Hospital in Johannesburg, where a Dr Snykers operated on him.

To say it was a worrying time would be a massive understatement. Amanda went down to be near Rob and was helped by friends from home like Nina Firks, Vee Marffy, Margy Badcock and Flip, who stayed with her and gave her moral support. I rang up twice a day and all up-to-date news on Rob's progress was relayed to me. Shortly after Nikki and I drove down ourselves and spent a couple of weeks in Jo'burg, visiting him twice a day. Later, when he was transferred to Cape Town to convalesce, we flew down there as well. But it was Amanda who was with him nearly all the time, only dashing back to 'Forrester' occasionally to check on her home and animals.

Then of course there was little Sabrina. She had to be introduced to a new dad – not the fun-loving, active dad who used to take her everywhere with him but someone who could not walk without a stick and who had great difficulty speaking. If it was very tough on Rob, it was certainly tough on Amanda and Sabrina as well. Both coped magnificently. Magnificent, too, was the support and help that the family got from their Mvurwi friends. Hard times shared forge lasting friendships, and the people who Rob had helped and been helped by during the worst part of the farm invasions certainly stood by him now.

Money to pay massive medical bills was obviously a big worry, and here again old friends turned up trumps, with Caroline Calascione, Nick and Sally Gambier's daughter, organizing a sponsored bike ride in England between Oxford and Cambridge. Nick, Ed and Ant Holme organised a sponsored walk by the whole Holme family in the Brecon Beacons. Tobs Strong organized a huge lunch party at Thorn Park polo grounds, which was well attended by a lot more of Rob's friends. Spratt organised a sponsored run at Noosa in Australia. If anything good came out of this whole horrid business it was the massive demonstration of support and helping one another that always was and still is such a feature of the Zimbabwe farming community. Rob eventually came home to 'Forrester' and is still there, making slow but steady progress.

* * *

About this time there was another election in Zimbabwe, which was pretty much a repeat of the previous ones. Intimidation, doctoring of the voters' roll and straight cheating were again there for all to see. Only monitors from countries friendly to Mugabe's regime were invited to see what was going on, and even some of these admitted that it was not a free and fair election. The 'international community', that somewhat nebulous body, condemned it. Thabo Mbeki, that apology of a President of South Africa to succeed the great Nelson Mandela, indulged in some 'Quiet Diplomacy' to try and get some sort of rule of law back to Zimbabwe, but nothing actually changed for the better at all – in fact it got much worse, with Mugabe realizing that he could get away with practically anything. He just started ruling by decree, with one thing only on his mind – to stay in power at all costs; costs to his own people, not to himself.

A lot of the rural Africans were slowly starving to death despite being given all our farms, and many had moved into Harare and other smaller towns to try and get some sort of job. As a result a lot of scruffy shanty towns had sprung up all round the main centres. It is rumoured that Mugabe consulted one of his foreign 'guests' as to what to do about this. The said guest was none other than the ex-Ethiopian dictator, Mengistu Haile Mariam, who had been granted asylum in Zimbabwe after having been kicked out of his own country for slaughtering a large proportion of the population. This last qualification made him admirably qualified to give advice. He advised that the government should get rid of all these new urban dwellers and send them back to their rural areas. If they stayed around the towns they would be able to read the independent press and could cause trouble or, even worse, be persuaded to vote for the opposition. In the rural areas it would be a lot easier to starve them and beat them into submission if they showed signs of voting the wrong way in the future.

The government thought this was an excellent idea and promptly brought in bulldozers to flatten all the little shacks surrounding Harare and other towns throughout the country. The fact that it was June, the coldest month of the year, and that the wretched people had nowhere else to go did not worry them one bit. In addition, all the little stallholders who scraped out a meagre living selling a few vegetables on the side of the road were banned from doing so. This Operation Murambatsvina, known in English as 'Clean out the Filth', caused unbelievable hardship and promoted worldwide condemnation – but nothing was actually done about it.

Nikki and I continued going to Marondera every Wednesday to play golf with our friends there. Thirty-five to forty players took part in the competition each week; perhaps 20%were black and all very pleasant – it was a lot of fun. This happy little club did not go unnoticed by the Marondera ZANU (PF) thugs and on two separate occasions they shut down and trashed the place. The first was at the time of President Kabila's assassination in the DRC (the Democratic Republic of the Congo – a misnomer if ever there was one). When we heard of the assassination one of the older white members of the club, Eric Ross, raised his glass in the bar and said, "Here's to Kabila." That is all he said. I heard him. This comparatively harmless, but perhaps ill-timed, remark caused the club to be trashed by the local thugs, all the drink and money in the till stolen and Eric to be deported. It took the best part of a month and a lot of talking to get the club reopened. The club is situated about five hundred metres from the large Marondera police station, but despite calls for help they did not even bother to pitch up.

On another occasion the club was only operating on skeleton staff during one of the opposition-organized work 'stayaways' in protest against the deteriorating situation. The thugs chose this moment to go to the club and demand food – not that they were entitled to do so, being non-members. There was no food, so again they trashed the place. Nikki and I happened to arrive to play golf in the middle of this. The front gate was closed, so not knowing what was going on we drove round the back to find out. Here we found the greenkeeper, Frikkie Kloppers, surrounded by a bunch of young guys who we thought were the caddies. We drove up to them and discovered that they were not caddies, but the ZANU (PF) thugs, and they were giving poor Frikkie a very hard time. As we stopped we were surrounded, and one thug put his hand in through the driver's window and tried to grab the ignition keys. Luckily Nikki had the presence of mind to put the automatic window up thus trapping his arm and making him let go of the keys. I was driving and reversed out in a hurry.

We then had to make a plan to help Frikkie, and it is interesting to remember that we did not even consider going to the police – it did not cross our minds. We managed to get him on his cell phone and asked him what we could do to help, and he suggested Richard Mufuka, the lawyer. We alerted Richard, but even so Frikkie was dragged off to the ZANU (PF) headquarters and spent a very unpleasant few hours there. What had he done to deserve this? You may well ask. Again, the club was closed for a couple of weeks while expensive repairs were carried out to the place. Needless to say no one was ever charged with this theft and malicious damage to property (obviously my cattle eating a few sticks of dead maize was a far more serious offence).

I recite these incidents to give a picture of what was going on in Zimbabwe during early 2000. To a large extent Nikki and I, living in Ruwa, were protected from the worst atrocities. Sure, we got involved in the occasional incident like the one recounted but overall we were able to live a fairly happy life. Zimbabwe has a wonderful climate and even Mugabe cannot spoil that. We had friendly, good staff and plenty of friends still around. We were also able to travel a bit, and we visited some of the lovely local areas, which were that much better because very often we were the only people there. Places like Kariba, Mana Pools, Nyanga and Matopos used to be heaving with tourists, but they were now virtually empty, and many of the lovely little lodges in these areas had closed down. We went to many of the ones that were still open, usually with a few friends, and very often had the area to ourselves.

Members of our immediate family got married and we attended some marvellous weddings, in Australia for Jack and Jacinta, in Sussex for James and Suse, in Cape Town for Ant and Emma Holme and in Dorset for Kate Holme when she married Nick Robinson. Weddings are great occasions and a wonderful opportunity to meet a lot of old friends when they are all in a happy frame of mind. With our family now so scattered we valued these times greatly.

We occasionally drove down to South Africa to see Penel and Huffie on the South Coast of Natal, and on the way would stop off at some of the many places of interest in lovely South Africa. I had always been interested in the Zulu and Boer Wars, so we visited such historic places as Spion Kop, Rorke's Drift, Blood River and Isandhlwana. I had never been to these sites when I had lived in South Africa, but all are excellently preserved and fun to go to, and they try to relive those desperate days. People are still being killed in wars all over the place but no one has romanticized them quite to the same extent that the Victorians managed to do. The end result is the same though – you are dead – no matter if you are killed by a Zulu spear or an Afghan suicide bomber. Not a lot of progress has been made over the last hundred and fifty years in this respect.

We also went to some Game Parks in South Africa, such as the Kruger Park, which we found very well done, but far too commercial to our rather spoilt way of thinking. Another was the Mountain Zebra National Park in the Eastern Cape, which was small but interesting, and most attractive.

To the north of us we did another memorable drive up to the Serengeti in Tanzania. This time we did not do it on our own but joined up with our good friends Tim and Felicity Wotton; we drove in convoy through Zambia and into Tanzania. The drive up was interesting in that eight years before there had been virtually no development at all for the northern six hundred kilometres of Zambia, but now the whole place was coming alive. Certainly the arrival of a number of ex-Zimbabwean farmers round Mkushi had given that part of the country a big boost, but it was more than that: Zambia, it seemed had at last realized that they could no longer rely just on copper but had to develop the whole country as well. We crossed into Tanzania at the incredibly crowded and shambolic Tunduma border post, before driving on to a small guesthouse on a farm near Iringa. This was run by the long-time owner of the farm, who was now back on it after years of not living there.

At independence in the 1960s, the new President Julius Nyerere had virtually 'done a Mugabe' in that he had kicked all the white commercial farmers off their land. It had not been anything like as violent as in Zimbabwe, and in most cases the white farmer was allowed to keep his house. However there was not much future in living in a nice house in the middle of nowhere with nothing to do, so most had left. Partly as a result of this policy Tanzania had gone through an incredibly difficult time and ended up virtually broke, so now it was inviting white farmers back, and indeed our hostess, Nikki Cox, was buying up more land. Could the same sort of thing happen to us in Zimbabwe, we thought.

From Iringa we drove down to the enchanting Ruaha National Park where we spent a wonderful five days living in little bandas on the banks of the Great Ruaha River and exploring this huge but little known park. Then it was on to Arusha to see Harry and Flip, where we also met up with Nikki's brother Phillip and his wife Tussie, plus James and Suse, who had all flown out from England to join us. Here old Kenyan friends, Adam and Elizabeth Hill, royally entertained us. We drove on to Ngorongoro Crater and then to the northern part of the Serengeti, which we had not visited on our last trip. Here we stayed at Lobo lodge and, by an incredible stroke of luck, had the whole area to ourselves at the height of the migration. It seemed that tour operators from Kenya had had a row over costs at the Tanzania lodges and so were temporarily boycotting them. As no one else was prepared to drive themselves to this wonderful destination, we had it to ourselves. We revelled in it and saw a huge amount of game of all sorts under perfect conditions. We drove back via the Tanzania coast, having decanted Philip and Tussie at Arusha to fly home, then later James and Suse, before driving back to Zimbabwe by the same route through Malawi that we had taken some years before.

We also flew up to Kenya to see Harry, Flip and family, when they moved up there from Tanzania. They were producing vast amounts of vegetables for export to England and living on the shores of Lake Naivasha. Other companies were producing quantities of flowers to go to the world's largest flower market in Amsterdam. This was and still is big business. Environmentalists claim they are draining the lake but this is rubbish; one good rainy season and it is quickly back to normal. The vast acreage of plastic under which all these things are grown is a real blot on the landscape, but go a mere couple of kilometres away from the lake and you are on 'Longonot Ranch', which, with the hunting ban that has been in place in Kenya for many years now, is full of all types of lovely game. Flip took us riding there one day on ponies borrowed from Tony Church, who sadly was not there himself. We rode to the foothills of 'Longonot' volcano and saw herds of gazelles, eland, zebra and giraffe – all fairly tame. It was a real joy.

Harry had become involved in the excellent plan to build a game-proof fence separating the Aberdare National Park from the farming area, and to this end he had recently taken part in a fund-raising car rally called the 'Rhino Charge'. Hair-raising would perhaps be a better description from what he told me about it. However, it did and still does raise a lot of money for the excellent cause, which is already proving a big success in keeping game in the National Park and out of the farming areas. As a participant in this event, he was entitled to hire the little lodge, high in the Aberdares, called 'Rhino Retreat' and while we were staying he took us all up there for three nights.

Quite apart from being in a delightful little lodge with game coming in for salt and water at dusk every evening, the whole trip was interesting to me, as we visited the exact same areas in which I had chased Mau Mau up and down that mountain just fifty years ago. How it had all changed! No roads in my day, just the old 'Wanderers Track' which sort of connected Nyeri and Fort Hall (Muranga) on the one side to Naivasha on the other. Now there was an excellent dirt road along which we sped, seeing quantities of buffalo, elephants, lovely bushbuck and the occasional giant forest hog, but sadly no bongo. We were told that there are still quite a lot of bongo left in the Aberdares, but they have always been incredibly shy.

Also during this visit to Kenya, we met up with John and Lorna Clarke and Simon and Jane Fletcher (all old Kenyan friends now living elsewhere) and visited Zanzibar. I had been there once before on my way back from Argentina in 1959. It was full of Arabs then, but they had all been slaughtered shortly after independence in the early sixties in payback time for their part in organizing the slave trade. Not an Arab was in sight this time and not much effort was being made to preserve the island as a tourist destination. It was filthy. The reef, which we walked out to, was barren of any form of life, and some of the lovely old buildings, like the Sultan's Palace, were in ruins, with rain dripping in through unrepaired roofs. I thought it was a disgrace that the idle locals could not be bothered to look after the lovely things they had inherited and yet still try to pretend to tourists that the place was worth visiting. It is not. It's a tip.

* * *

In 2007 I reached my allotted span of three score years and ten, so to celebrate we decided to do something special. The Senior Golfers Association of Zimbabwe was asked to send a team to the world championships to be held in San Diego, California, USA. I put my name down to go. It would be nice to say that, after fierce competition for places, I won the right to represent my country by defeating many others in tight finishes. But the truth is that I was the only one who was prepared to travel that far, and so I was a one-man team! You cannot go much further from Zim than the west coast of America without going the other way round – via Hawaii, perhaps – but it was a long way. We had both wanted to visit the US again at some point, as I had much enjoyed the country during the times I went there in my A&K days, and Nikki had lived there for a year shortly after her first marriage.

We flew via London to Florida, where we spent a few days with John and Lorna Clarke. John is my old friend from Kenya and Zim, in which places we shared many of the same interests. In Florida he still loves nothing better than a walk after birds with a dog and shotgun, and he is still the charming, quietly spoken guy that I have always got on with so well. But under this façade he is an incredibly successful businessman and has achieved an enviable reputation in the Sarasota area for being responsible for the building of a new model town. In conjunction with a bunch of venture capitalists, who put up the money but did little of the work, he has created the luxury very upmarket 'Lakewood Ranch'. He and Lorna live nearby and they showed us round. It was most impressive; not least the two Arnold Palmer-designed golf courses and extensive polo grounds. John has now retired but I was immensely impressed by the amount of forelock tugging indulged in by all the staff at the one golf course that we played on. It is clear that he is a highly respected member of the community and has, as Lorna says, 'Lived the American dream'. To the full. While I do believe that John is unusual he is certainly not the only ex-Zimbabwean farmer to have done really well in an entirely new field in another country.

We flew on to San Diego, hired a car and drove the twenty miles out to 'Rancho Bernardo'. We were based at this very comfortable inn for the next eight days, and with the ninety other competitors from all over the world we played golf for seven days running. I started nervously and badly, playing off an 18 handicap, and only got slightly better. However on the last day I was part of a team of four which won that particular competition and so was called up at the final banquet to receive my prize – a clock (which does not work) mounted on some shiny wood and made in Taiwan. I have had the names of my team engraved on an attached plaque in memory of a thoroughly enjoyable week. Nikki competed in the Ladies section and also won a prize in a team event. Not wanting to take my own clubs all that way, I had arranged to hire clubs from the local pro's shop. These were very smart, brand new and quite expensive to hire, but when I handed them in at the end and asked what I owed the resident pro just said, "No charge".

It was a charming gesture that epitomized the camaraderie of the whole event.

From San Diego we went to Boston, where Nikki had lived when in the States. Here we stayed with John and Judy Fox. John had just retired from an important job with Harvard University and having always lived nearby knew the whole area extremely well; he proved the perfect courier for showing us some of the more cultural side of that lovely area.

It was back to England and down to Dorset for my seventieth birthday. Sue and Tony had hatched a great plan and had rounded up other 'old farts' of the same age in the shape of Tony himself, Richard Holme, John Byng-Hall and Ian Ross, whom I had last seen at school in Kenya. The party was filled out by a large selection of relatives and we all gorged ourselves off a delicious lunch served in the garden on a (mercifully) beautiful, sunny day. I was stunned by the number of really nice and useful presents that I got. I had thought that once one got that old presents were a thing of the past!

We ended our great trip by spending a weekend with James, Suse and little Saskia at their cottage on James' father's estate in Sussex, where I was lucky enough to be included in the season's first duck shoot, courtesy of John Sclater, Nikki's ex-husband.

* * *

We slunk back to Zim and almost immediately noticed how much things had deteriorated in the month we had been away. The exchange rate had doubled to Z$700,000 to the British pound, there was very little to buy in the shops and we got a power cut, or load shedding as they called it, virtually every day. In June I had applied for an agricultural loan to buy some heifers to run on 'Watershed Farm'. My application was for Z$1 billion, which would have bought a hundred heifers. Now this loan had finally been approved and I would only be paying 25% interest on the money. You might think that 'only' is not the right word to use when talking about such interest rates, but the official bank rate was 2,000%! The agricultural bank, in their wisdom, had upped the amount of money they would lend me to Z$30 billion, but unfortunately even this amount would only buy six heifers. In June 2008, when I repaid the loan, it cost me all of GBP3 to do so!

The few white farmers still on the land were being steadily whittled away as top brass from the army retired and wanted to cash in on a bit of land grab while the going was good. In Wedza the only farm still in white hands was 'Imire', owned by the Travers family. They were only allowed to stay there because they also ran a game park, which at the time of the main land-stealing exercise was declared a National Park and so owned by the government, the Travers being allowed to farm it. They took care of the now state-owned animals but could keep any profit derived from visiting guests. The main attraction as far as the animals were concerned revolved round 'Imire's' black rhino breeding exercise. They had been doing this for some twenty years and had returned several youngsters to the wild to bolster the ever-dwindling numbers that still existed on the shores of Lake Kariba.

The owner of the next farm to 'Imire' was a retired army brigadier. He did little or no farming and had a pack of uncontrollable dogs that were wont to hunt on 'Imire' and disturb the game. One day one of these dogs was shot by guards on 'Imire'. A few days later, three black rhino breeding cows were shot by a gang armed with AK assault rifles. Arrests were made for this brutal act but the culprits received only token prison sentences and are now back on the farm next door to 'Imire'.

We were putting up with more and more problems at home, and we reasoned that if we were to go on living in this chaotic country we must enjoy some of the better things that were still on offer. One of the best is a visit to Mana Pools on the Zambezi River at the end of the dry season. National Parks have some lovely little self-catering cottages on the banks of that mighty river and they were always in great demand. In November we applied for one and got a booking with no trouble at all. Normally such a booking had been subject to a ballot, so many would have been the applications. We drove up there with Mike and Fiona Whitfield and spent three nights.

The little cottage was in very bad repair, but the staff were all very friendly and helpful – there was just no money, they said, to maintain the place. The park itself was dry and barren in the November heat, but there was game everywhere and we were even privileged to witness a pack of the increasingly rare wild dogs catching an impala. Lions walked past our veranda, hippos snorted in the river just in front of the cottage, elephants wandered around everywhere looking for the last of the Acacia Albida seed pods and baboons broke into our kitchen and ate most of our remaining food. Luckily it was the last day. It was heaven and we hardly saw another vehicle.

The year 2007 ended with another election pending early the following year. This would be a crucial one. For the first time votes would be cast for four different appointments: parliamentary seats (MPs from over two hundred constituencies), the Senate, Rural District Councillors, and the all-important one for President. Robert Gabriel Mugabe would be standing, and there was a general feeling that if he did manage to get in again the whole country would be pretty much a lost cause. I use the words 'get in' and not 'win', with good reason.

CHAPTER 25

2008 Elections

THE YEAR 2008 STARTED WITH NEWS OF terrible post-election violence in Kenya. We were naturally very worried about Harry and family, as a lot of the trouble was centred round Naivasha. However, he assured us that they were OK, being some ten kilometres out of town. In the town itself there was indeed a lot of bloodshed, as the resident Kikuyu tribe chased out the visiting Luos in a payback for what was happening to them in Western Kenya.

It was all about the opposition leader Odinga accusing the incumbent ruling party leader Kibaki of rigging the election in his favour. What's new? Is there ever a genuinely free and fair election in Africa these days? We were watching with interest – not just because of our family there, but because we were due to have an election ourselves, where it was more than probable that the same sort of thing would happen. How would Kenya sort things out without the whole country descending into civil war? Well, with the help of ex-Secretary-General of the United Nations Kofi Annan they did sort it out, and there was a fragile truce in Kenya with a cobbled together power-sharing agreement in force, which went a long way towards restoring Kenya's fortunes. This was two very different tribes having a go at each other. In Zimbabwe it would be two different political parties, each drawn mainly from the same tribe – the Shona. But their hate for each other appeared to be even deeper than Kenya's tribal one.

The situation in Zimbabwe was pretty grim by now – inflation was over 100,000%, the black market exchange rate to the British pound was about Z$20 million and rising weekly, unemployment was running at 80%, cash was almost impossible to get hold of, and the highest denomination note was only Z$750,000 or about four British pence. The last thing you wanted was cash sitting in the bank, because after a very few days it would be worth a fraction of what it was when you put it there. Basic foodstuffs like bread, sugar, maize meal, cooking oil and flour could only be bought on the black market. When shopping, you did not go into the supermarket but to a certain tree on the edge of the car park, where you would meet a selection of 'traders' who would offer you these scarce commodities at an inflated price. No one really knew what the proper price was, but government in a futile effort to control this runaway inflation fixed a maximum price for all essential foodstuffs. This price was so unrealistic that shops just did not stock them – hence the 'traders' under the trees.

There were a few exceptions – 'Fat Cats' in the government often owned a supermarket and, with limitless access to what foreign currency was available, were able to stock their shops with the most exotic of goods imported from South Africa. One of these supermarkets was at Borrowdale Brook – an upmarket residential golf estate – and there were plenty of buyers for this exotic fare, buyers such as government officials and the diplomatic corps. Mere mortals like us could barely afford to shop there and spent many hours bargaining in car parks for our own provisions, and to try and get something reasonable for our staff.

We still had Harry's cattle at Watershed College, but there were problems with the herders and security guards milking the cows at night and selling the milk. The result was very thin calves and unhappy mothers, which eventually broke out of their night boma and, inevitably, ate some of the stunted maize grown by one of the indigenous teachers. Not a new situation for me but one that I was getting very tired of. The usual pantomime was acted out with the aggrieved plot holder making outrageous demands while his wife howled on cue in the background and a mob of onlookers stood around sucking their teeth. If I did not pay up, the police would be informed, the ZANU (PF) youth would be called, the governor of Mashonaland East would take action against me and the press would be called to witness this terrible tragedy and publish a story about the wicked white man ruining a wretched black man's livelihood. I let him rant on for a bit before finally saying, "How much?" We agreed on a figure about ten times more than the cost of the damage but not too painful on my pocket. We sacked the herders and guard, for all the good that would do; their successors would probably do exactly the same. I was glad that I was not farming in the true sense of the word, as these scenes were getting boring in the extreme.

Nikki and I needed another break, so we drove down to South Africa to stay with my sister Penel and her husband, Huffie, on the south coast of Kwa Zulu Natal. On the way we spent a very pleasant few days in the foothills of the Drakensberg Mountains, then on the way back attended a cross-country building seminar near Howick, run by the people who were building the Olympic cross-country course in Hong Kong later that year. I doubt that the very few eventers left in Zimbabwe will want anything quite like that in the near future, but it was all very interesting and constructive nonetheless.

We also took the opportunity of doing a lot of shopping, and we arrived at Beit Bridge with quite a carload of groceries, paint, veterinary medicines and other things unobtainable in Zimbabwe. Going through customs on this sort of occasion is always a nightmare, but this time we had been advised to employ someone to 'assist' us. The going rate was two hundred rand (about GBP15) and we had this ready when approached by a 'helper' immediately after we stopped on the Zimbabwe side of the border. The result was that we sailed through in about ten minutes with no one showing the slightest interest in anything we had bought. The blatant queue-jumping and official stampings organized by our helper were all done in full view of the police and other officials. I had never previously bribed anyone quite so obviously but this was the way things had become.

Our old friends Mike and Di Bartlett had somehow managed to hang on to their house and ten acres of land on their farm 'Rapako' in Wedza. Their son Tim was about to give up his farming job near us in Ruwa and return to the farm, to grow passion fruit in the area round the house where previously they had grown export roses. It was all a bit of a gamble, but the local Wedza authorities did not seem to mind. They probably wanted a white farmer back in the area so that they could borrow things off him and get him to do their ploughing. Anyway, Mike and Di were spending some time on 'Rapako' getting the passion fruit planted, pending Tim's move there, so we went out to spend a night with them.

It was not really my scene or Nikki's. They had the use of their house, in which they virtually camped, and they had the use of the old rose-growing area. However all around on their once lovely farm there were nasty little patches of maize and small mud huts, providing basic subsistence farming for a few indigenous settlers – this on a farm that had once been hugely productive and bringing in massive amounts of foreign currency.

The morning we left we drove back via 'Chirume'. We had not been there for about two years but now we drove down 'Harry's' road and almost up to the house. It was eerily quiet and we did not stop. There seemed to be no one about and nothing going on. At the end of the road, as we emerged on to the tar, there were an old man and his wife wanting a lift. I decided to stop and chat to them to see if they knew anything about what was happening on 'Chirume'. It turned out to be Mvava, the 'headman' who had been such a pain in the neck when we were being kicked off – not my favourite person. However, we chatted to him, and he told us that my old foreman, Never, had died. I asked him why nothing was happening on my farm – no crops, no cattle, not even any people. What was he doing with all the land that he and his thugs had stolen off me?

"Oh!" he said, "we cannot do anything because of sanctions."

This has been Mugabe's excuse for years, but the only sanctions that have anything to do with Zimbabwe are what they call 'smart sanctions', targeting Mugabe himself, his family and about a hundred and twenty high-ranking ZANU.(PF) officials.

The sanctions prevent these people from travelling to places like Britain, Europe and the United States, and also attempt to stop their wives spending Zimbabwe's hard-earned foreign currency in shops like Harrods and Saks in Fifth Avenue. Far from there being any other type of sanctions, quite the opposite is true. Britain and America are major donors of foodstuffs to help keep the people of Zimbabwe alive. Perhaps the squatters on 'Chirume' knew this, and being supporters of the government which dished out the aid, found it easier to accept this free gift than to do any work. To my mind, it is scandalous to go on giving aid to corrupt governments, as they just use it to spruce up their own image. It is used as a bribe to make people vote for them, and those who really need it seldom get anything.

Campaigns for the elections due on March 29 were hotting up by now, and the government was using its old tactic of dividing the rural areas up into very small areas with a voting booth in each area. By doing this they would know precisely which small area had voted against them, and they wasted no time in letting the voters in these areas know that retribution would be swift if they voted 'the wrong way'. This worried our friend Johnny Campbell. Johnny was still running a very large farming enterprise just outside Marondera where he produced tobacco, maize, potatoes, cattle and polo ponies for export to South Africa, so he employed a very large labour force. A polling station was placed on the next-door farm to him, which only catered for his immediate area; thus if all the votes at this polling station were for MDC it would be pretty obvious who were not supporting the government. When the results were announced and it was seen that many of these areas had voted against the government, retribution was swift and brutal to the extent of being sub-human.

Neither Nikki nor I could vote, but our labour could, and I had long chats with Gift over what they would all do. Gift is a committed Christian, attends church every Sunday and just did not want to get involved in politics in any form whatsoever. However feelings were running high that this could at last be a chance of getting rid of this current president, so he decided to vote.

Apart from Mugabe running for a sixth term in office and Tsvangirai representing the MDC, there was another candidate, Simba Makoni, an ex-finance minister in Mugabe's government. We worried how this might split the anti-Mugabe vote. Arap Moi in Kenya had survived for years with only about 30% of the vote, simply because there were so many splintered opposition parties. Would the same sort of thing happen here where the MDC was already split into two factions? As well as voting for a new president, voters also had to choose their next MP, as well as a Senator for the Upper House and a Rural District councillor.

The MDC pressed for the presence of a wide ranging selection of international monitors, to try and make the election as free and fair as possible, but the government would only let in monitors from countries friendly to themselves, and these did not arrive until just before the election, well after a lot of the groundwork to rig the voting had already been done. To my mind one of the biggest stumbling blocks to a fair result was the voters' roll. This had been in the hands of the government for years now, and there were all sorts of strange names on it of people who no longer existed. It also goes without saying that no one in the diaspora had the right to vote. Most of the four million or so middle-class locals now living mainly in England or South Africa would undoubtedly have voted for a change in government, so that they could come home.

Meanwhile there were posters being stuck up everywhere with pictures of Mugabe – very appropriately – waving his fist in the air. This did indeed symbolize all he had to offer – a fist in the face or much worse, for anyone daring not to vote for him. The picture of a quietly smiling Tsvangirai was in stark contrast. Predictably all army and police personnel got a hefty wage increase, paid for with a rash of newly printed money, which pushed the exchange rate up to about Z$75,000,000 to the GBP.

MDC were able to campaign reasonably freely, and when I was playing golf in Marondera one Wednesday there was a big MDC rally at Dombotombo Stadium. When the rally ended we were very heartened to see lorryloads of supporters driving past, all with big smiles on their faces and waving the open-handed salute. Again such a nice contrast to the lorry loads of ZANU (PF) youths, who only scowl and wave their fists at you.

Most political commentators reckoned that Mugabe and ZANU (PF) could only win the election by massive vote rigging, so we apprehensively awaited the big day, March 29.

It was also Spratt's birthday and I got through to him in Australia with no trouble and had a good chat. It is often easier to phone places like Australia and Mongolia (not that I often phone Mongolia) than it is to get hold of the Piercys next door.

Not much work was done here, as all our labour went off to vote. Voting throughout the country went off fairly smoothly; as a result the monitors, all drawn from African states friendly to Mugabe, said that the whole election was free and fair, while totally ignoring the build-up and the voters' roll manipulation. From the evening of that day on we kept a very close eye on the television to see what sort of results were coming in. We did not watch the local station, ZBC, but concentrated on the excellent coverage given to the event by BBC, Sky and even Al Jazeera. Both BBC and Sky are banned in Zimbabwe but had very brave, clandestine reporters operating in the country. Al Jazeera was officially allowed in and had good reporters speaking openly, both from Harare and from polling stations throughout the country.

Saturday's voting closed at 7pm, and by Sunday evening speculation was rife that MDC had won a substantial victory. This was based on the fact that, for the first time in recent elections, it had been agreed that results from each individual polling station would be counted on the spot and posted outside that polling station, and not, as in the past, only from the central office in Harare after having been transported there.

The Zimbabwe Election Council (ZEC) were very slow and apparently reluctant to announce any results but they started trickling through on the Monday after Saturday's election. By evening we only had six results – three seats won by MDC and three by ZANU (PF). Tuesday, April 1 (a most suitable date to announce Zimbabwe election results) saw more results coming through, but carefully staged so that the tally was always about even. By the end of that day it was sixty-two to MDC, sixty-four to ZANU and five to others. By Wednesday there had still been no word at all about the vital Presidential election, although MDC claimed that Tvsangirai had won an overall majority. There was a lot of speculation on the BBC and other news channels that Mugabe was about to concede defeat and stand down. Many rumours claimed that he was in fact about to do this, but his army and police chiefs persuaded him to fight on. They had a vested interest in doing so. Mugabe himself might be able to negotiate a deal guaranteeing no prosecution of himself for crimes against humanity but his chiefs of staff might not be so lucky.

Nikki and I were glued to every news broadcast and our moods fluctuated like mad at each new announcement. By Wednesday evening it was clear that ZANU (PF) could not have a majority of seats in the House. They only had ninety-three as against MDC's ninety-six, with nine seats won by other parties out of the total of two-hundred and ten seats. On Thursday morning it was confirmed that MDC had won a majority in parliament. I went to town that morning and there was a carnival atmosphere everywhere. Street vendors came up to me waving the MDC open palm salute and saying, "This is the new Zimbabwe – now you will get your farm back."

It was all very stimulating, but by Friday it had already started to turn sour. Many MDC leaders went into hiding, Tsvangirai and Tendai Biti left the country, police broke into MDC offices and some foreign reporters were arrested. Mugabe called an emergency Politburo meeting and that evening it was announced that he would fight on (operative word here is 'fight'). There was still absolutely no word about the Presidential election result although it was clearly known by ZEC. If no candidate had won an overall majority, the rules of the election stated that a run-off must be held within twenty-one days. Already seven days had passed and no one was being told what the result was.

By the following Monday world pressure was mounting on the government (ZEC, actually, but clearly under strict orders from the government) to announce the results and MDC took the matter to the High Court, demanding that the results be released.

Gift had gone to his home in Bindura over the weekend and I had a long chat with him on his return. He was very upbeat and said that in the previously very ZANU (PF) orientated area, chiefs and headmen were now openly supporting MDC and had Tvsangirai's picture hanging on their walls instead of Mugabe's. Within another month doing that sort of thing would virtually guarantee a death sentence.

By mid-week the independent press was claiming that there had been a de facto military coup and that the country was now being run by the army, with Mugabe just a figurehead. The SADC countries called an emergency meeting in Lusaka to discuss the 'Zimbabwe crisis'. There should have been no crisis – but an election had been held and the results had still not been announced. The Zambian President, Levy Mwanawasa, chaired the meeting, and both Tsvangirai and Mugabe were invited to attend. Mugabe refused to go, so Thabo Mbeki, who was given the brief of sorting out this mess years ago, called in via Harare and spoke to Mugabe. My guess is that all he said to him was, "Hang in there, old boy, you are doing a great job!"

By the end of April, a full month after the election, Tsvangirai was still out of the country trying to drum up support. No official result had been announced but it was generally agreed that the result would say that Tsvangirai had won, though not with a sufficient majority, so there would have to be a run-off. MDC claimed that Tsvangirai had won outright and that therefore no re-run was necessary. Therefore if a re-run were called for he would not compete. Later the official figures confirmed this speculation, when it was announced that Tsvangirai had won 49.25% of the poll, Mugabe 42.5% and Simba Makoni 8.25%. My initial reaction was – what a disaster it was that Makoni had stood at all. If only a small fraction of the people who had voted for him had voted for Tsvangirai, then it would have put him squarely over the 50% required.

Meanwhile a reign of terror was being unleashed in the rural areas. Due to electoral results being published on polling booths in each area, it was clearly known what areas had voted MDC. In these areas anyone known to be an MDC supporter was grabbed by Mugabe's youth militia and beaten within an inch of his life, and some even beyond that. Houses were burned and many terrified people fled to the towns. Police and army were deployed in these areas and knew full well what was going on, but far from trying to prevent this bloodshed they encouraged it or arrested MDC leaders on the pretext that they had started it.

Our friend and near neighbour from Wedza, Ian Kay, who had stood for and won the Marondera constituency, was arrested and imprisoned for 'inciting violence on the farms'. Ian had heard that there was a warrant out for his arrest, so he willingly went to Marondera police station and handed himself in. It is said that the police there said, "We know you have done nothing, but we have to lock you up." They did, and he was transported far away to a cell in Mtoko prison so as to make it harder for his family to bring him food.

On the home front Nikki reached a milestone and turned sixty. We planned a big party in our garden and were thrilled when James said that he would fly out especially for it. It was a very sensitive time, with the government paranoid about anyone holding meetings or even celebrating MDC's success. We had planned a party for sixty people, all white, who would clearly be celebrating a happy occasion. We were very nervous as to how this might go down if any ZANU (PF) authorities found out about it. Friends of ours cancelled similar parties but, in the event, our party was a huge success. The only negative side was that James was delayed here for forty-eight hours because Mugabe and his family had flown off to Malaysia for a few days and had taken Air Zimbabwe's only long-haul plane.

Throughout the rest of May and into June the situation in the country got rapidly worse, and every day we heard horrendous stories about what was happening to people in the rural areas perceived to be MDC support-ers. Pictures started appearing in the independent press of men and girls with their buttocks flayed to a bloody pulp. People known to have voted

MDC had their hands chopped off so they could not do it again. MDC officials were abducted, and some were never seen again until their mutilated bodies were found days later, decomposing in some remote stream.

A run-off date was announced for June 27. Morgan Tsvangirai eventually returned to the country to start campaigning for this election. He had reluctantly agreed to take part, reasoning that if he did not he would just be handing the Presidency over to Mugabe. Mugabe's regime would never accept that Tsvangirai had won the initial vote, especially as it had now been 'officially' announced that his majority was insufficient. Tsvangirai initially delayed his return following assassination threats but eventually returned, much to the relief of his followers. His deputy, Tendai Biti, also returned, but he was promptly arrested at the airport, locked up in leg irons and accused of treason, for daring to announce that Tsvangirai had won the Presidency before it had officially been announced. All Biti had done, as far as I could see, was to count the officially published figures displayed on every polling station and announce what they added up to. If found guilty of doing this terrible thing he would face the death penalty.

The US Ambassador to Zimbabwe, a black American called James McGee, determined to go and see for himself if all the stories about state-sponsored violence were true. He recruited some other embassy officials, including the British, and set off to visit a hospital in Bindura. When presenting his credentials to Mugabe on taking up his post a few months previously, he had been assured that he and his staff could travel anywhere in the country quite freely. Now, however, his small convoy was stopped at a police roadblock just short of Bindura and he was told he could go no further and must report to the local police station. McGee refused to do this and insisted on being allowed to visit the hospital. At this juncture a lorry with no number plates arrived, full of young thugs, who immediately surrounded the convoy of three cars and tried to drag the occupants out. The British car and one other drove off at speed, puncturing all their tyres on the spikes placed across the road. The driver of the American car was dragged out and severely beaten and the thugs threatened to do the same to the Ambassador. He eventually escaped, but it was an unbelievable thing to have happened to a top diplomatic convoy. Did the thugs know quite how serious this was? I doubt it. The incident provoked outrage throughout the civilized world.

Mugabe happened to be in Rome at this time, attending – of all things – a summit on the world food crisis. Why on earth he was there at all, I do not know. Firstly he was, and still is, banned from travelling to Europe, but as this was a United Nations meeting, they weakly let him attend. Secondly, quite what he could contribute to any discussion on producing more food was highly debatable. He had presided over a country that used to export food all over Africa and the world; now it relied heavily on international aid to feed a starving population, with the only people having access to this aid being his own supporters.

Mugabe was told at this meeting how badly his men back home had behaved. Bush, Brown, Ban Ki-Moon and many others all made statements deploring this behaviour, but to date nothing concrete has been done about it.

What exactly could they do? This was a question that we often asked each other and it was a frequent topic of conversation. In truth it was not an easy question to answer. Mugabe was, and is, totally immune to conventional diplomatic pressure – he just does not care what the rest of the world thinks. So what could foreign countries do to a supposedly legally elected head of state in another country, to make him comply with diplomatic or humanitarian norms of behaviour? Saddam Hussein was a case in point. America took fairly drastic action in the case of Iraq and has been criticized ever since. OK, there have been unforeseen problems since, but would all these critics really rather have Saddam still in power, while they wring their hands and say, "Why doesn't somebody do something about him?" Well, Bush did 'do something about him'. Saddam got his just desserts and I will always respect Bush for taking positive action and removing a psychopathic and murderous dictator.

Someone who could, and should, have done something about Mugabe was Thabo Mbeki of South Africa. I imagine that history will in time reveal what sort of hold Mugabe had on Mbeki, but it must have been considerable, because despite the most blatant human rights' abuses he really did nothing at all. Yes, he flew up to Harare occasionally and chatted to Mugabe, but he always came away saying that it was an internal dispute and up to the two disputing parties to come to some sort of agreement. This had been a good idea eight years previously, but in all that time absolutely no progress was made, because ZANU (PF) regularly did not even pitch up for these planned talks. Clearly this solution was not working, and some outside honest broker had to be called in.

If Mbeki had really wanted a solution, all he had to do was close the border and/or switch off the power that South Africa was providing to Zimbabwe (and not being paid for). There was a precedent for this. It was the apartheid government of John Vorster that finally brought Ian Smith to the negotiating table, when South Africa was finally forced to give up supporting him. Zimbabwe is a landlocked country and relies heavily on export routes to the sea to maintain its survival. Cut those off and it cannot last for long.

South Africa was due to hold the Soccer World Cup in 2010. Meaningful threats to remove this prestigious event from them, unless a solution to the Zimbabwe crisis was found quickly, would have put enormous pressure on Mbeki to do something about it. Again, there was a precedent. The world cut off sporting links to South Africa towards the end of the apartheid era, and this had an enormous influence on the sport-mad South African public in agreeing to bring an end to that régime. Soccer is a much-loved sport in Zim and the national team competes regularly with its neighbours and has a huge following from the rank and file. If any of the neighbours really wanted to make a point, they could cut off all sporting ties, and this would get the message through to the man in the street pretty quickly that this country is not recognized by her neighbours.

How long do you allow a dictator to go on murdering his own people? Idi Amin did quite a lot of this in the seventies in Uganda. It took an invasion, sponsored by Tanzania, finally to get rid of him. In 1994 thousands of people were killed in Rwanda. This was one tribe slaughtering another that they had hated for generations. This in no way excuses it but gives slightly more reason for it happening. The equivalent of the African Union at that time vowed that they would never let that sort of thing happen again in Africa. Even then, in the early 1980s, Mugabe had already perpetrated the slaughtering of another tribe when he authorized the massacre of some twenty thousand Matabeles, but in 2008 he was doing it to his own tribe, the Mashona, and the AU just talk and talk but actually do nothing.

Why is a known murderer allowed to attend and address international meetings in places like Rome and New York? Italy and America are respected members of the United Nations and they have seen fit to ban him from visiting their countries. So why on earth do they let him come to these meetings? He contributes nothing, instead using them as a forum to slang his hosts and make political speeches, while his wife and aides spend a large percentage of Zimbabwe's negligible foreign currency in the best shops and restaurants.

Throughout the 2008 elections the only real point Mugabe and ZANU (PF) made as a reason for keeping themselves in power was that Tsvangirai and MDC were puppets of Britain, which wanted to effect a régime change in revenge for the white farmers being kicked off their land in 2000/2002. If MDC won, they maintained, the land redistribution process would be reversed and Zimbabwe would effectively become a colony again. This refrain was repeated so often that many of the less educated rural people started believing it – repeat a lie often enough and it will be believed.

Tsvangirai was repeatedly stopped from attending his own rallies. The method would usually be to stop his motorcade at a 'routine' roadblock just short of his destination. His vehicles would be searched and all personal documents of everybody scrutinized. Inevitably the police would find something that they thought was wrong, so they would ask everybody to report to the local police station, where they would be held for three or four hours, thus rendering it impossible to get to the rally. Eventually Tsvangirai had a special bus made, planning to drive around the country broadcasting from it. It was a good idea, but the police quickly 'discovered' that the bus was 'incorrectly licensed' and impounded it. For the Sunday immediately before the election, the High Court of Zimbabwe had overturned a ban on MDC holding a huge rally in Harare and ordered that it could go ahead. Tsvangirai could walk to the stadium if necessary, so there was a lot of anticipation that the rally would take place.

However, as the mass of MDC supporters started arriving they were confronted by two problems. Outside the stadium were gangs of Mugabe's youth brigade all armed with sticks, and inside the stadium, if anyone did manage to get through, all the seats were taken by members of Mugabe's army. Riot police were also very much in evidence, and as soon as any scuffle broke out they fired teargas and aimed water cannons at the MDC supporters. Total chaos reigned and it was impossible to hold any sort of rally at all.

It was this final straw that prompted Tsvangirai to announce that there was absolutely no point in him trying to stay in the run-off elections. His supporters were being kidnapped, tortured, raped and slaughtered. His elected MPs were being arrested and locked up, while he himself was not even allowed to campaign. He said he was pulling out of the race, hopefully to stop any further violence. Threats were made on his life immediately following this announcement and he was forced to take refuge in the Dutch Embassy in Harare.

Nikki and I were playing golf that Sunday in Marondera while all this was going on, but we were kept in the picture via a continuous stream of text messages on cell phones belonging to Alan Burl and John Harris. Finally a message came through that there was a ZANU (PF) meeting in Bromley, and that this had deteriorated into youths chucking stones at passing vehicles. Bromley was on our way home, so we left Marondera in convoy with the Wrights, who were also heading back to Ruwa. When we got there the meeting was still in progress at the old club but we managed to get through without intercepting any projectiles.

I think that the withdrawal of Tsvangirai from the run-off annoyed Mugabe. He wanted to win and prove that he was still the people's choice and he reckoned that he and his thugs had done enough groundwork to achieve this. However, there was another solution – hold the election anyway with himself as the only candidate. Holding the run-off some ninety days after the original election was illegal anyway, as the constitution stated clearly that any re-run had to take place within twenty-one days. However, small matters like bending their own rules were not going to interfere, but a change of strategy was necessary. When they feared that Tsvangirai could win the run-off, thugs in the rural areas went to some lengths to ensure that potential MDC supporters were denied the possibility of voting, but now that it was impossible for Tsvangirai to win they wanted as many voters as possible to turn out, so as to give the run-off an aura of respectability.

There was a lot of very mixed feeling about Tsvangirai's withdrawal. Gift told us that a lot of the rural people, currently taking refuge in towns, had braced themselves to go back to their homes on the day to vote and so get rid of this tyrant Mugabe once and for all. Now they were to be denied this opportunity. Personally, I think Tsvangirai did the right thing. It certainly stopped some of the violence and served to highlight the whole farcical pantomime. More importantly, there was a very real chance that Mugabe could have won, such was the massive vote rigging that had already taken place. Now, the inevitable 'victory' would be very hollow at best.

In the week immediately before the run-off, our area was inundated with bands of thugs moving up and down 'James Farm' and Gardiner Roads, forcing everybody to attend meetings. It was terrifying to recall what power these youngsters had. They were teenagers, or slightly older, and were completely immune from any form of prosecution. If anyone tried to resist them, they were picked up, taken to a torture camp and severely beaten. Most of these gangs were made up of youths picked up at random and moved to a different area to do their dirty work. Indeed, I discovered one day that Nikki's groom's son had been recruited. I asked

Christopher how this had happened and asked if he approved of what his son was doing. Christopher claimed that his son was really an MDC supporter, but that he had to go along with it to save being beaten himself. This was quite possibly true, as each gang would have two or three really hardened leaders, who had gone through special intensive training in the art of brutality, and the likes of Christopher's son were just needed to bolster the numbers.

We encouraged our own workers just to do as they were told, with the result that they frequently disappeared to a meeting at short notice. In theory Nikki and I should have gone along as well, as many of our white neighbours were forced to do, but we managed to get away with it. It was a very tense time for everybody and we just stayed at home most of the time.

Election day dawned and the youth gangs were soon out and about, 'encouraging' people to turn out and vote. When you had cast your vote, your little finger was dipped into indelible red ink, which could not be washed off. This was proof that you had voted, and there were threats that, if you did not have this tell-tale identification when the thugs did their rounds that night, you would be severely beaten. It was no idle threat.

After the March 29 election it had taken a full forty days to learn what the result was. This time results were to hand within thirty-six hours. Contrary to what the state-sponsored media claimed and in spite of the attentions of the youth gangs, there had only been a very low turnout, but with a great fanfare of patriotic fervour it was announced that the people had spoken and yet again Mugabe would be the country's president. He wasted no time in having himself sworn in, but unlike on previous occasions there was not a single representative of any foreign state present.

We tuned in to the Zimbabwe Broadcasting Corporation on our TV and were in time to witness Mugabe, standing beside the country's chief justice, with a Bible in one hand, swearing to uphold the constitution, and so on. I felt sick and left the room.

Nikki and I both had a bad dose of 'flu at the time and this did not help our depression one bit. We were not the only ones to be totally shattered by how much this man could get away with. Immediately after being sworn in, Mugabe departed for an African Union meeting in Egypt. I am glad to say that he was not very warmly received. Some countries like Kenya and Botswana were overtly hostile, though others – particularly South Africa – could not bring themselves to be too critical of their one-time liberation hero, despite the outrageous brutality that had dominated his election. In the end the AU passed a resolution recommending that a government of national unity be formed. Quite how this would come about was not detailed and, with both ZANU (PF) and MDC poles apart and each demanding all sorts of pre-conditions before even entering into any talks, the likelihood of it happening in the near future appeared bleak indeed.

Meanwhile on the ground in Zim and as usual particularly in the rural areas, the violence continued unabated. Seventy-four-year-old Mike Campbell, his wife Angela and son-in-law Ben Freeth had instigated a legal appeal to the SADC (Southern African Development Community) court in Windhoek against being evicted from their farm. It was the first case that this recently formed court had been asked to pass judgment on, and they were proceeding with some caution, but they had ruled that the Campbell family should not be evicted or troubled pending their decision, which was due on July 19. However on the very day that Mugabe was sworn in, the Campbells were abducted by a gang of some fifty thugs, taken to a torture camp, atrociously beaten and forced to sign a document saying they would drop their case. When the police were made to investigate this brutal act, they reported that it was just the work of 'common criminals'.

Throughout the rural areas voting patterns in the recent run-off election were scrutinized and the number of people voting for Tsvangirai recorded. In our small area forty-three people had been brave enough to vote for MDC, and so immediately the notorious youth brigade was out in force trying to discover who these forty-three people were.

John Travers, who was still living on and running 'Imire Game Park' in the Wedza area, was receiving death threats daily and being told to move off the farm, and his cattle and game were being systematically slaughtered. My old foreman from 'Chirume', Tichaona, suddenly pitched up one day wanting to know if we could help him cash a cheque that he had received for tobacco he had sold. I had not seen him for about four years and did not recognize him at first. There was no way we could help with the cheque; it was dated two weeks previously, so was already worth only a fraction of the stated amount and it was made out in his name. He told us that our brief visit to 'Chirume' just before the first election had really put the cat among the pigeons, in that the bloody little 'headman', Mvava, had reported it to the local war vets and said that it meant we were expecting to get back to the farm when MDC won. The local thugs had then taken it out on any that they could find of our ex-labour, including Tichaona.

Money was becoming a real problem – you could not get hold of cash and very few shops would now accept a cheque. The maximum you were allowed to withdraw from your own bank account at any one time was Z$100 billion. It sounds a tremendous amount doesn't it? But in early July 2008 it was worth just one British pound.

Nikki and I were due to go up to Kenya to see something of Harry, Flip and the grandchildren, and then on to England to meet a new grandchild and attend a family wedding. We had very mixed feelings about going. Yes, we were keen to get away, but with the situation so volatile and uncertain we felt we would worry unduly about our animals and what was happening at home. Then, what would we get back to? For perhaps the first time ever we began to think seriously about whether we wanted to continue living in Zimbabwe. We would look at England in a new light – would I spend the rest of my days where I had started them or could I yet survive the winds of change?

CHAPTER 26

What Now, Zimbabwe?

NIKKI AND I ENJOYED OUR VISIT TO Kenya which has a remarkable ability to overcome political problems and still present a smiling face to its many tourists. Even so, the election dramas in January had certainly scared away a lot of potential visitors, and when we visited the coast a lot of hotels were still closed. But bookings were picking up again, everyone seemed happy and busy and there was plenty to buy in all the shops.

On the surface at least the power sharing deal was working. All Harry's labour were back at work and he was expanding the vegetable export business he was involved in. We stayed on the farm with him and his family just outside Naivasha and Nikki got involved in a Pony Club camp which my two grandchildren took part in. It took me back all of sixty years. Not a lot had changed in this department. Young children wearing maroon, blue and white ties were being led around on fat little ponies by African grooms, while anxious mothers shouted advice and instructions from the sidelines.

"Sit up straight, Caroline."

"Don't hang on to your pony's mouth all the time, Neil."

"Toes up, chest out."

The grooms plodded on round in a circle with a resigned look on their faces. A very colonial scene!

We also attended the seventieth birthday party of my old friend, Tony Church. Another very colonial occasion, made more so as guests were encouraged to wear 'Out of Africa' kit. I met old school friends whom I had not seen for fifty-five years. They had all remained in Kenya and prospered. I had left but need not have done so. We compared our lives and agreed that both had had interesting and fulfilling lives in Africa, albeit in different parts of our huge, diverse continent.

We also had lunch with Tony and Sarah Seth-Smith at their lovely lakeside home, and I reminded him of the elephant that he had missed out on in my Athi/Tiva days. He then told me that it had been his father who had settled the dispute between my Great Uncle F O'B Wilson and Frank Joyce, when they had a row over milk stealing in the 1920s. As already recorded in this book, the two of them jointly owned a huge farm in the Machakos area. When the row broke out Tony's father was asked to help settle it. He decreed that one partner should divide the property and the other partner choose which half he wanted for himself – one divide, the other choose! Nothing could be much fairer. Perhaps Mugabe and Tsvangirai should adopt the same plan to end the current deadlock over which party gets what ministries.

We nearly missed our flight driving to the airport – it took us three hours to cover the short distance from the centre of Nairobi to Jomo Kenyatta airport. The two lane highway swelled to five lanes as every conceivable variety of transport took every opportunity to barge the queue, push in, drive on the grass verge and generally do anything they could to beat the ever increasing traffic jam, which we were told is a daily hazard on that particular bit of road between four and eight pm. Inevitably there was an accident and the multiple lanes suddenly became a virtually stationary single lane. Kenya is still a very lovely country, as long as you keep away from the towns – which are 'tips'.

England also was lovely, and it was while we were there that we got the news that Mbeki had brokered a deal for a power-sharing government of national unity between Mugabe and Tsvangirai. The papers were full of it and very optimistic. People came up to Nikki and me with big smiles, saying how wonderful it all was and weren't we delighted that, at last, our problems would be sorted out. I am afraid that we did not share their optimism.

My sister Sue and husband Tony gave a small lunch party at their home in Dorset, and here I met George Campbell-Johnston and his wife. George started, and still masterminds, the Zimbabwe Farmers Trust. This organization does an immense amount of good, raising money for destitute ex-Zimbabwe farmers who have come to England, often with no money at all, having lost everything when kicked off their farms over the last few years. Not only have these people lost their homes, businesses and in many cases most of their moveable assets, but with inflation running at the rate it does in Zimbabwe they have also lost any savings that they may have made. The ones who were fortunate enough to have a choice over coming to England came because they were able to hand back their Zimbabwe passports and get British ones; this gave them the right to live in England and claim the basic state benefits. Many others who would appear to have every right to a British passport have been unable to get one, for a multitude of obscure reasons. I have a very clear philosophy on this. If a Hereford bull is born in China it is still a Hereford bull – not a Chinese bull. Similarly, if a Pekinese dog is born in France it is still a Pekinese dog and not a French poodle. So why cannot a white Caucasian of British descent, however remote, still be labelled British, even though he or she was not actually born there?

* * *

I returned to Zimbabwe before Nikki, as she stayed on in London to help with a new grand-daughter. It was an interesting time to arrive back. The Governor of the Reserve Bank, Gideon Gono, had cunningly worked out a way to end inflation. At that time you required Z$1.5 trillion to purchase one British pound, so Gono just knocked ten noughts off the currency. Suddenly you only needed Z$150 to buy one pound. Gono also printed a lot of new notes while simultaneously decreeing that the old notes would still be valid – minus 10 noughts – at their face value, and the old coins that had not been used for years were now suddenly worth what was inscribed on them. This last involved a lot of scrabbling around in various drawers to find the few old coins that had not already had holes punched in them for use as washers.

I went into Harare the Sunday after I arrived back and tried to buy a newspaper from a vendor on the side of the road. The newspaper cost Z$500 billion in old money, so I produced a selection of filthy old notes and a few grimy coins. After fifteen minutes of trying to add this lot up, the vendor said that he did not think I had given him quite enough. As I had no more, and anyway had read all the headlines in the paper, the deal fell through.

Apart from battling to get money and then trying to understand what you had got, there was intense speculation as to what the outcome of the much-vaunted talks would be. Mbeki came here, and Mugabe and Tsvangirai went to Johannesburg, but nothing concrete ever emerged. Finally Mbeki spent a whole week here in Harare and announced on Thursday, September 11, that the two main parties – ZANU (PF) and MDC, plus the small, breakaway faction of the MDC, led by Arthur Mutambara – had agreed a power-sharing deal. He ended by saying that the deal would be officially signed at a ceremony to be held on Monday, September 15, and that it would be attended by various heads of state from the SADC region. What he did not tell us was who was typing up the official documents which each party would sign at the ceremony. Later, this was to prove a very significant point.

On the Monday we duly tuned in to the BBC, and they relayed full coverage of the whole ceremony. I was pleased about this, but wondered a bit quite why Zimbabwe warranted this amount of blanket coverage. I suppose that it has been such a protracted saga that there was a lot of interest in seeing how it would all end.

Mbeki opened proceedings, and then other heads of state like the Swazi king had their say; Mutambara shouted a bit and then Tsvangirai spoke. He started by quoting Mugabe's own words, spoken in 1980 in his first speech broadcast to the nation when he became Prime Minister of the new Zimbabwe. It had been a brilliant speech then, focusing on forgetting the past and turning guns into ploughshares. To a large extent this had happened in 1980 – before it all went horribly wrong. Could it happen again? Tsvangirai was determined that it should and dedicated himself and his party to the task of rebuilding the country.

Then came Mugabe. I am afraid that I had to walk out before the end of his rambling, incoherent tirade. He spoke very slowly and dwelt entirely on the past, first detailing the bush war which ended twenty-nine years ago; then he had his traditional crack at Britain and America, blaming them for all Zimbabwe's ills caused by the illegal sanctions on the country. Naturally he did not explain that the only sanctions in existence were against himself, his immediate family and about a hundred of his close cronies who had systematically been bleeding the country dry for years. Nor did he add that Britain and America and other Western countries had been providing most of the food to keep millions of rural Zimbabweans alive. Mugabe's government has been unable to produce anything like enough food to feed the country, despite the theft of all the best farming land. Not once did he mention anything about the agreement and how it could solve all the above problems. At one stage the cameras panned across to Tvsangirai and a picture of him slumped in his chair, drawing a tired hand over his eyes, said it all. You could almost hear him saying, "Oh God! Here we go again."

Having had my breath of fresh air, I returned to watch the actual signing of the agreement. On such occasions a leather folder is put in front of each of the participants who are due to sign – in this case three people. You sign the document in front of you and pass it on for the others to sign. You do not read through the document – that is totally impractical. You have previously gone through the document, which contains all the conditions that you have agreed upon, carefully and in detail. But that was all three days ago. What if it has subsequently been changed? There is now said to be ample evidence that the signed documents were not the same as the ones originally agreed upon. The most important part of the agreement was that Tvsangirai would become the new Prime Minister of Zimbabwe, while Mugabe – despite the totally unacceptable Presidential election – would remain as President, but with reduced powers. I am quite certain that Mugabe never had any intention of abiding by the 'reduced powers' bit.

Anyway an historic agreement had been signed and we all eagerly awaited the formation of the new government. After a day or two when nothing happened, we were told that agreement could not be reached on which party would have which ministries. MDC (T) had been awarded fifteen, MDC (M) three, and ZANU (PF) sixteen, but it had not been specified which ones. This, to my mind was incomprehensible, as ministries like Defence (the army), Foreign Affairs, Finance and Home Affairs (the police) were far more important than ministries such as Posts or Higher Education, for example. Mugabe insisted on having all of the four important ones. Tsvangirai had himself been beaten up by the police as had many of his supporters who were tortured, or killed by the army and police. So, he was quite rightly totally unwilling to cede control of these forces back to Mugabe. He had won the parliamentary election by a wide margin, despite the attentions of the army and police. The vast majority of ordinary Zimbabweans wanted this power removed from the ZANU (PF) bullies, and it would be a criminal betrayal of their vote not to do so. Quite why these vital details were not contained in the original agreement I had no idea. Perhaps they were included, only to have been deleted by someone before the signing of the agreement.

What on earth had they all been talking about for all those months if the allocation of ministries had not been included? Mbeki, whose standing as a respected African leader had been very much in decline due to his inability to solve the Zimbabwe crisis, suddenly got a lot of kudos for having, apparently, sorted it all out. But it seemed his own party, the ANC, thought so little of him that they told him to stand down as President. This meant that he had lost a lot of his clout when called back to have another go at ending the dispute. At the same time, Mugabe, despite the chaos reigning in his own country, swanned off to

New York with a huge entourage to attend a United Nations meeting. Who on earth invited him? He certainly no longer spoke for the people of Zimbabwe.

Shortly after his return from New York, and with absolutely nothing settled, he unilaterally appointed ministers to the key posts that he wanted to keep and also appointed governors to all the country's provinces. Most of these should have gone to the MDC, and both actions were totally contrary even to the agreement that had been signed.

Mbeki was roped in again and spent a week here. I suspected he was pretty fed up with the whole thing. He had just lost his job and was in the process of helping to form a breakaway party to contest Jacob Zuma's bunch that had sacked him. I could not believe that his mind was totally on Zimbabwe and the ridiculous, ongoing intransigence of his friend. Anyway, yet again he totally failed.

Next, the troika currently running SADC – Swaziland, Angola and Mozambique – invited the parties down to Mbabane in Swaziland to see if their representatives could sort the problem out. There was another problem though. Tsvangirai could not go as he did not have a passport. The Passport Office, presumably on the government's instructions, had refused to issue him with a new one, as they did not like him visiting other countries and drumming up support for his cause. Can you imagine the prime minister of a country being denied a passport to attend a vital meeting to determine the very future of the country? Surely that can only happen in Africa. As that did not work, they all came up here several days later, together with the new South African President, Kgalema Motlanthe. There was more talk, talk, talk, as the country slipped further and further into chaos, but again Mugabe would not budge on who would have the Home Affairs Ministry. Tsvangirai had agreed to let him keep Security, which allowed him to control the army. That was bad enough in my opinion, but no way could he be allowed to have control of the police as well. Some rumours (and there were plenty of them) maintained that they would share the police portfolio by controlling it for six months each. Can you imagine what would happen then? Tsvangirai would arrest all Mugabe's thugs and put them inside, only for Mugabe to let them all out when the six months was up and then put all Tsvangirai supporters inside for his six months. Gilbert and Sullivan would have loved it!

Meanwhile the noughts chopped off the currency by the Reserve Bank Governor as recently as August were all back again. In mid-September I asked my bank for a loan, on the reckoning that it was much better to use someone else's money, when it was devaluing so quickly, rather than my own. Despite it being impossible to get cash, my bank had no hesitation in lending me Z$400,000, which was then worth about GBP4,000. They had our house as collateral and charged 2,000% interest. I used some of that money straight away to buy some stockfeed and invested the balance, some Z$275,000, on the local stock exchange. With inflation running at some astronomical figure, I was reluctant to sell my shares when I needed more money in mid-October, so I asked the bank to lend me some more – this time Z$6 billion (but worth perhaps GBP500), just a month after the original loan. I invested most of this on the stock market, so by mid-October I had invested some Z$6billion of borrowed money on the market. Three weeks later my share holding was worth Z$5 quintillion – and I had sold a few shares along the way. With it rapidly becoming worth some sextillions I could repay my entire loan by selling one share!

Before you start kidnapping my family and demanding huge ransoms, please remember that this huge sum of Zim dollars was almost certainly worth considerably less than the equivalent in hard currency when I first took out the loan. No one would accept a cheque in those days and the most cash you could withdraw from the bank at any one time was Z$20,000. So I couldn't use my quintillions. Everything was quoted in US$ or SA Rand. It was illegal to use those currencies unless you had a special licence, which cost US$20,000, so only a few people could afford this. One of Mugabe's big rallying calls throughout a number of elections was, "Zimbabwe will never be a colony again!" And he would go on to slang Bush, Blair, and then Brown, and blame them for all Zimbabwe's ills. So we could not even use our own currency, but had to use Bush's. That, to my mind, was worse than being a colony.

* * *

With any money so difficult to get hold of, many people had resorted to a barter system, by offering something that a seller might want, in place of money. To pay my internet account I used fuel coupons; golf club subs were paid with a bag or two of fertilizer, and garage repairs to vehicles with imported parts, such as filters. Our local stockfeed merchant would no longer accept local currency, but people desperately needed feed for their cattle. Once he was offered a thousand samoosas for a bag of feed.

October is a very hot month in Zimbabwe. It is very dry, and thunderclouds gather in preparation for the rainy season, which bursts upon us in dramatic fashion in November. Farmers call October the suicide month, as cattle get thin, dams dry up and early-planted crops wither. But, in many ways it is a lovely month, and if you can stand the heat it is a wonderful time to visit the Zambezi Valley or other game areas. The reason is obvious – there is little water or feed, and consequently a lot of game is concentrated in areas where this can be found. Also, with little vegetation, the viewing is very easy. We always tried to get up to the Zambezi at this time of year and stayed at Mana Pools on the banks of the river, where the game concentrates most. We did so in 2009, but first visited one of my favourite stamping grounds from years gone by – Gorongoza in Mozambique.

I was last there in 1974 with a bunch of American clients and we had to evacuate pretty quickly when coming under fire during dinner from the Frelimo 'freedom fighters' who were about to take over Mozambique from their Portuguese colonial masters. They made their headquarters in Gorongoza National Park – almost certainly because there was a ready supply of meat there. At that time there were the following species of large game in the park:

Elephant	2200
Buffalo	14000
Lion	500
Sable	700
Wildebeest	5500

By 1994, well after independence in Mozambique and with Frelimo firmly in control as the ruling party, there were the following numbers in what was left of the park:

Elephant	108
Buffalo	0
Lion	0
Sable	0
Wildebeest	0

What an indication of what game means to emerging Africa.

After that, however, a big effort was made to re-introduce game to the park. An American organisation called 'The Carr Foundation' poured money in and did a lot of work to reorganize the park and to introduce game again from places like the Kruger Park in South Africa. The understanding, I gather, was that every dollar put in by the foundation would be matched by the Mozambique government. The foundation must have put in a lot, but I gather nothing much has been forthcoming from the government, whose current rulers ate all the original animals.

There was game there when we went, and it was said that there were some three hundred elephants, one hundred and eighty-five buffalo, forty lions, three hundred and twenty sable and two hundred wildebeest. Of this lot we saw only one sable, but there was plenty of evidence that the other game was there, and we did see a lot of antelope such as bushbuck, nyala, waterbuck, impala and oribi, warthog by the hundreds, and a wonderful selection of birds. Also, with so little game in the area over the past years, the vegetation and general feed for game was magnificent. So, perhaps this wonderful park can eventually reclaim some of its past glory – it was an interesting visit and proof that with money and goodwill some of Africa's glorious wildlife areas can perhaps be reclaimed and its heritage preserved for future generations.

Finally we went to Mana Pools on the Zambezi. What a contrast! There was lots of game but very little to eat – very little to eat, that is, for both the game and the humans. For the game it was normal for the time of year; most of the animals looked in reasonable condition and rain was due any day to transform the arid, grassless areas under the canopy of trees into wonderful, lush pasture in the annual miracle of transformation. The animals would soon be all right, though the imminent rain would make precious little difference to the starving people of the Zambezi Valley. We saw vast herds of buffalo, there were hippo all over the place, and huge majestic bull elephants wandered into our camp seeking their great delicacy – the pods of the Acacia Albida tree which fall to the ground at this time of year. We sat quietly in our camp chairs and these magnificent animals came almost within touching distance to pick up the pods with their trunks. We all sat there entranced.

The African fish eagle screamed out its challenge, hippos grunted in the river and a lion roared in the distance. Mike Bartlett even caught enough fresh bream from the river to give us supper one night. This was Africa as it always used to be. It can still be a magic place – preferably with no politicians.

* * *

The year 2009 heralded the implementation of the Government of National Unity whereby ZANU (PF) led by Mugabe, MDC (T) led by Tsvangirai and the other very small MDC faction led by Mutambara agreed to try and govern the country together. In October 2009 the unlikely team still ran the show – just. Virtually none of the outstanding issues which were unresolved when the agreement was originally signed had been sorted out and Mugabe still appeared to be totally in control.

One of Tsvangirai's main demands was that the Governor of the Reserve Bank, Gideon Gono, be removed. This had still not happened and in February Mr Gono chopped yet another twelve noughts off the Zimbabwe currency (thus bringing the total to twenty-five). So my ten trillion dollar note was suddenly worth only Z$10 and Mr Gono then told us that two of these were the equivalent of US$1. That was OK for a few hours, but you cannot stop inflation just like that and by the following day I needed at least a hundred of these notes to buy US$1. In fact this really spelled the end of the Zimbabwe currency. The Stock Exchange closed and it was not long before the US$ was officially adopted as the legal currency of the country.

This dramatically increased the cost of living, partly because store-owners were so used to upping the cost of things every day that they continued to do so regularly and, so used were the buying public to seeing these increases, that to begin with they did not query it. This meant that prices went rocketing up with no justification at all. Afterwards they fell back a bit.

* * *

In April I suddenly realized that my gun licence had expired. I still had the little 28-bore shotgun that I had had as a boy, because Harry had been looking after it the night we were robbed of all our guns. I went to our local police station with the old licence to get it renewed. "Ah, to do this we need your fingerprints," I was told. I pointed out that they already had my fingerprints on record, as they had been taken when I originally licensed the firearm.

"But now we need them again."

"OK."

"However we do not have the necessary form, but you can buy one at Mr Tendai's shop in the village."

I was also told that I had to pay a fine for not renewing the permit in time.

I went to Mr Tendai's shop, but he had run out of the forms, so my visit to the village was a totally wasted journey. When next in Harare I managed to buy a copy of the required form, so I went back to the police station in triumph.

"Ah, but we need three copies of the form," I was told (why didn't you tell me this before?). "Mr Tendai will photocopy the form you have got though."

Back to Mr Tendai's shop. His photocopier was broken so it was another wasted journey. Eventually I got the form photocopied in Harare and for a third time approached the local police. Three entirely different policemen from the ones I had been dealing with confronted me; none were in uniform and all were chewing on mealie cobs. They gazed at the three fingerprint forms that I proffered.

"We do not require these if you have already registered the firearm with us before," they said. "Where is this firearm now?"

"At home."

"We need to have it here for safe-keeping before re-issuing your licence."

Why wasn't I told this before? I went back home and got the offending weapon. No one was in the office when I got back to the police station.

After ten minutes, a policewoman (I think, but it was hard to tell as she was not in any kind of uniform) shuffled into the office. What did I want? I indicated my 28-bore lying on top of the desk and told her that I had come to re-license it.

"Ah, you must first pay a fine of $20."

I know. I produced a $50 bill. She disappeared with this only to return after ten minutes to say there was no change available.

Another policeman whom I had never seen before ambled into the office and, having outlined my problem to him, I was told that they, the local police, could not actually give me a permit. All they could do was write a letter saying that they had no objection to my obtaining a permit, but that this had to be collected from the firearms headquarters in Harare. OK, please write this letter. The policewoman sat down behind an ancient manual typewriter and started shuffling some paper, as the letter had to be in triplicate. Unfortunately there was no carbon paper, so she said she would type it three times. OK, I'll wait. Unfortunately the typewriter did not work. Policewoman said in that case she would do the letter by hand – did I have a pen she could borrow? Yes. I waited while she laboriously wrote the same letter three times and then attempted to stamp the copies with the official police stamp. Unfortunately the pad containing the ink was dry and nothing appeared on the sheet of paper when the stamp was pressed on it. Policewoman wandered off in the direction of the charge office and within about quarter of an hour returned with all three sheets correctly stamped.

"You will now require a letter in triplicate from the Agritex office to prove that you need this firearm for crop protection," she said as she handed me the three now stamped sheets. "Then bring them back here so that we can stamp them too."

I managed to achieve this and the Agritex office had carbon paper (and a pen, though no functioning typewriter). Back at the police station there was no one to be seen. It was one o'clock by now and everyone had gone for lunch. My 28-bore lay unattended on the desk. I tried the charge office and a strange man in civilian clothing asked me what I wanted. Having explained, I persuaded him to stamp my newly acquired letter (in triplicate) from Agritex. I was now keen to leave and asked what I should do with my gun, which I had been told to go and get as they needed to keep it safe for me (although I had kept it safe in my own house for the past four years).

"Ah, we need the armourer to lock it up," he said. OK, get him. He disappeared, leaving me as sole occupant of the charge office.

Half an hour later he wandered back, picking his teeth and saying that the armourer had gone to Harare and no one else had the keys to the armoury.

"So what happens with my gun?" I asked.

"Oh, just take it home!"

I tell this story as it is symptomatic of how a lot of government departments function these days. It can be very frustrating! They are badly paid, so they rely on bribes (I never did get change for my $50), have no motivation whatsoever and have lost any pride that they once had in their job. This is incredibly sad, because the BSAP, even when it became the ZRP (Zimbabwe Republic Police), was highly efficient, and much the best police force in Africa. Frighteningly, the last is probably still true. Superficially though, things had improved, mainly due to the fact that we were using a stable currency. Most supermarkets were now pretty well stocked, fuel was readily available for about $1 per litre, and one could get a variety of spares that were not available before. We all opened Foreign Currency Accounts (FCAs) and could even transfer funds from an overseas account directly into them. You did not leave it there very long however a) because it was badly needed and b) because the government might decide that they wanted it as well!

* * *

Various farmers won international court cases concerning the theft of their farms. Twelve Dutch farmers won their case in The Hague and were awarded compensation, which was due to be paid within ninety days. At the SADC Tribunal in Windhoek seventy-two other farmers won their case for the right to remain on their farms. We got excited at both of these results and our hopes were raised that one day we might get something for the loss of our farm, home and business. However the Dutch have certainly not yet been paid a cent, some six months after the ruling, and the only outcome of the Windhoek ruling is that the farmers who were part of it have been subjected to new and ferocious attacks on their farms, while the government here denies that they are bound by a ruling from a SADC court, despite being signatories to the whole SADC agreement.

In fact since September 2009 attacks and eviction orders have increased dramatically throughout the country, and one wonders who is running the country and whether they want investors here to kick-start a recovery.

Ellen Fischer was a bridesmaid at Pel Holme's wedding to Atherton. Shortly after that she married a neighbour called Charlie Lock, against whom I used to play cricket. Charlie took over Ellen's parents' farm, 'Karori', in the Headlands area and has been allowed to farm a part of it for the last few years. Then, inevitably, someone high up in the army was short of a good farm and moved in on Charlie. Charlie fought it through the courts and got a ruling from the highest court in the land that he could at least remove his harvested crops and personal belongings. In late September 2009 he went to do just this. Here is a copy of the report that he sent in to Justice for Agriculture (JAG):

1. Karori Farm – Charles Lock

On Thursday we obtained a High Court order, notwithstanding an appeal, to remove our crops and equipment from Karori farm. The value of this is well over one and half million dollars. We arrived on Friday morning with the messenger of Court and were only given three police officers by the DISPOL. The order specified that the Police were to ensure that the order was enacted. On arriving at the farm the messenger attempted to serve the papers on the soldiers under Brigadier Mujaji; however the soldiers said that they had been instructed by Mujaji to shoot anyone who attempted to take anything off the farm. The two lorries we sent there were returned to Harare.

We returned to the DISPOL in Rusape and the messenger requested more police officers to enforce the order. The DISPOL told the messenger to take his order back to Harare as the police would not support it.

That message was conveyed in my presence to Superintendent Mahle by Ass^t. Commissioner Crime Khumalo at PGHQ. I heard the order as I was in the office of Sup^t. Mahle. We had to return and the messenger filed his return papers citing gross contempt by the soldiers and police. On Sunday Mujaji and his soldiers stole diesel from the farm then using our tractors evicted all the senior staff from the farm and drove off all the workers who were trying to guard the maize and tobacco that we are attempting to deliver. The workers were dumped at Halfway House. Our cattle were driven off the farm. As it stands it is now a looting exercise as Mujaji has stolen over 300 tons maize and 150 tons of tobacco and all my equipment in spite of High Court Orders issued by Judge Patel. I am not even allowed in my home as the soldiers have threatened to shoot me. My domestics have been evicted off the farm by the army so my house will likely be looted tonight.

It is apparent that a military coup has taken place in Zimbabwe as the army are running the show and looting at will in face of the highest courts in the land. The Police are party to this and refuse to help openly. We have had workers shot, starved, evicted, over US$750 000 worth of crops stolen and that amount again in equipment by the Zimbabwe National Army. We are appealing to the GPA to sort this out or do we take the GPA to Court and SADC for this theft by the Army and Police.

And this is not an isolated case. Many of the very few white farmers still actually on the land are under this sort of pressure. So who does run the country? Who cares? I fear that the 'international community' – that nebulous body appointed judge of all things international – has got very bored with the Zimbabwe saga and feels that after ten years it is up to us to sort our own problems out. They are probably right.

* * *

The first 2 editions of this book were published in late 2010. This, the third printing, is being undertaken in the spring of 2011. Nikki and I are no longer living in Zimbabwe. When the book became available to anyone in that country it immediately became apparent that a lot of the ruling hierarchy would not take too kindly to what I had written about them. It is still a criminal offence to insult the [so called] President – let alone call him a murderer!

With this in mind several people advised me to make myself scarce. Journalists were being arrested and locked up at the time so I made a hasty decision and flew up to Harry in Kenya and then on to England. Nikki joined me in Kenya for Christmas but then flew back to Zimbabwe to undertake the horribly difficult task of selling up and, worst of all, disposing of our beloved animals. She did this with bravery and compassion and is now with me in England where we are setting about starting a new life.

I may never know if I over-reacted to the perceived threat. The problems in Zimbabwe are far from over and I hope for the country's sake, that I made the wrong decision and all will turn out well in that beautiful country. However, despite what is currently happening in other parts of Africa where dictators are getting their just deserts, I fear there will still be a lot of violence in Zimbabwe as the criminal old guard desperately try and cling to power.

Perhaps we are better off here – but we do miss our friends.

Where is Everyone?

S ALREADY STATED, OUR FARMING FRIENDS ARE now scattered throughout the world. The following few pages will give you some idea of what some of them are up to and how they are coping with life after being a Zimbabwe farmer. We remain here and hope some might return one day.

At our Sunday golf in Ruwa the other day, Tony Walker, who used to farm north-west of Harare at Tengwe, invited five of his old friends and one-time farming neighbours to join our little group. All had been kicked off their farms at about the same time as Tony and us. All are now living in Harare. They were a cheerful bunch and clearly extremely capable farmers, which soon became evident as they chatted amongst themselves about their farming days. The farms they once ran so efficiently now lie idle with nothing being produced on them at all and I got to wondering what these guys were doing now.

One sells ceiling board and cornices in the industrial sites, another imports fuel, and Tony is a greenkeeper– all pretty menial jobs and not really benefiting the country at all. What a tragic waste! But at least they are still in Zimbabwe. I then thought about all my farming friends and neighbours and where they had got to. The answer was staggering – they are literally all over the world.

South Africa was the obvious first choice for many, followed by other African countries like Zambia, Botswana, Mozambique, Malawi, Tanzania, Kenya, Uganda, the Democratic Republic of Congo and

Nigeria. Many, though, reckoned that 'leave Zimbabwe, leave Africa' was the only way to go, and these people opted mainly for Australia and New Zealand. Europe was quite popular as well, with Britain, France, Spain and Portugal the most sought after. Others ventured further afield to the USA, Canada, Brazil and Argentina.

A very small proportion of these Zimbabwe farmers actually ended up farming. However, one of the very first places that some friends from Wedza went to was Mozambique, where they planned to grow tobacco near Chimoio, an area only some hundred kilometres from the Zimbabwe border at Mutare. The advantages were that it was very easy to get to and that any equipment that they had managed to salvage from their stolen farms could be driven there. Land was comparatively cheap to lease, rainfall quite good and the soil thought to be suitable for tobacco. The disadvantages were that it was in fact not an ideal climate for tobacco and that the bureaucracy involved in buying or leasing land, all of which negotiations were carried out in Portuguese, was hopelessly inefficient. These far outweighed any advantages.

Some of Wedza's very best farmers like Derek Hinde, David England and Scott von Memerty went there, but all gave up the unequal struggle within a very few years. Two families are now back in Harare and not involved in farming. David imports generators, car tyres, wire, batteries and practically anything else you want, from a contact in Dubai. He runs the little business very efficiently and this is a good example of why and how Zimbabwe still operates. It is often the ex-farmer living in town who 'makes a plan'. An efficient, honest businessman provides at a very fair price items that Zimbabweans of all races badly want and need. The government does not encourage or assist in these matters so it is left to private enterprise. But what a waste of real farming talent.

Another popular place was Zambia – particularly the Mkushi area north of Lusaka. This was also comparatively easy to drive to and had other advantages that Mozambique did not. Land could be bought with borrowed money (and this was facilitated and encouraged by the Zambian government, which recognized the ability and expertise of these farmers), the climate and soil were suitable for tobacco, maize and other cash crops, and negotiations were carried out in English. A number of farmers, particularly from the Mvurwi area, went there, and I think it is fair to say that a large number of them have prospered and are still there doing well. At one stage they farmed so well that profit became a disadvantage. They had borrowed money to buy their farms in US$ but were paid for what they produced in Zambian kwachas. Largely thanks to them, the Zambian economy boomed and suddenly the kwacha strengthened to such an extent that it was very expensive to pay off the loans in US dollars.

Nigeria hatched a plan that tempted some. Recognizing the ability of Zimbabwe commercial farmers, they thought that if they could entice a number of them to come and open up a largely unused agricultural area it would greatly benefit their own food production, which in that huge, corrupt country was largely dependent on imported foodstuffs bought with the money from oil sales. To this end they offered a large cash package (some US$2 million) to a group of ex-Zimbabwean farmers who were prepared to go to Nigeria, open up a large tract of virgin land and grow food for the masses. The cash package was a loan with a very low interest rate and only repayable after five years. The thought of such a large, cheap loan tempted some farmers who had the guts and initiative to accept the challenge and about twenty took up this first offer.

It was tough. They had to live in hotels at first and drive miles each day to the allotted areas. The promised money was very slow to come in, decent equipment was hard to find and the attendant bureaucracy knew no bounds. Any wife who went there with her husband quickly returned to live in Harare while he got on with it as best he could, and even he returned to Zimbabwe whenever possible for welcome breaks. Some of the first bunch that went over did reasonably well. I remember speaking to Graham and Judy Hatty, who said they planned to work really hard for about five years, make as much money as they could and come back to retire in Zim, which they hoped by then would be a much better place than when they left. Those five years are now up and Zim is still much the same as it was, and I don't think that Graham has made as much money as he had hoped.

A second group of farmers also went to Nigeria a year or two later and for these people the whole scheme became a fiasco. Some sat over there waiting for the promised funds for over three months and eventually crept back here. Nigel Worthington was one of the first to realize that he was wasting his time and is now back here managing an apple orchard in the Eastern Highlands. My old polo mate, Robin Wyrley-Birch, who used to employ my son Robert and was once a highly successful farmer near Mvurwi, decided to give it a go. Robin is about my age and was bored with sitting in Harare, twiddling his thumbs; he decided to give it a full go, despite his wife Alison saying that she would not go near the bloody place. But it all ended in tears and Robin is now back here.

Of our immediate neighbours, Corporal Hill went into a sheltered accommodation in Harare. Mike had been a very conscientious farmer and had invested his money in various local pension schemes; when he was kicked off his farm at about the same time as we were, he reckoned that he had enough saved to see him and Jean through their old age, if they were careful. Then inflation kicked in and of course their saved money became valueless, they had to move to a cheaper home in Marondera, and they are now largely supported by their children. In June 2010 the old corporal died.

Tony and Jill Olivey (Mike and Jean's daughter and son-in-law) now live in Harare and own a small flower seedling business which supplies urban householders with plants for their gardens. They do this very well but it is a pathetic waste of Tony's farming skills. He used to produce tonnes of very high quality tobacco for export, as well as maize for the internal market, and he had a fine herd of beef cattle. 'Leap Year Farm', which for over fifty years produced all this and paid and fed a workforce and their families of over two hundred and fifty souls, now barely supports a few squatters. All the fences have been stolen and the house burned down. Progress?

Jim Paliuras, from the other half of 'Chirume', returned to his native Greece and died shortly after. The two Duirs' families from next-door 'Raleigh Farm' went to New Zealand. Betty Lumsden, who owned (owns!) the lovely 'Collace Farm', is now in South Africa. Beth Bedford, whose new husband Mick was murdered by poachers a few farms away from us, carried on farming after his death and had a lovely herd of beef cattle which she doted on. These cattle have now been butchered, the farm is empty and Beth is teaching English in Buenos Aires. Richard Moore, who farmed next to her, is in America. My son Harry hung around here for a couple of years after being kicked off 'Leeds Farm'. He attempted to bring charges against the local police force for assisting in the theft of his cattle, but when they finally brought a trumped-up charge against him he gave up the unequal contest and left; he went first to Tanzania and then to Kenya, where he now exports forty tonnes a day of vegetables to England. Harry could easily be doing just that from Zimbabwe.

Ben Fourie and most of the other farmers from 'Dutchman's Corner' predictably went to South Africa. Harry Orphanides moved to Harare and has expanded his agricultural supply business. Ian Burgoyne went to South Africa and has done very well dealing in property in Kwa-Zulu Natal. Of all our friends who have left the country, Ian and Ardre (who is a thirteenth generation white African) are probably the keenest to return here. Indeed Ian has compiled an excellent little booklet detailing what any future Zimbabwe Government needs to do to get the country up and running again. I doubt any future government will pay much attention to it though, as there is no chapter on how to fiddle the books.

Peter Bradshaw, with whom we used to play golf most Wednesdays, moved first to Harare; then went round the world to try and make up his mind where he wanted to spend the rest of his days. He finally opted for England, and he and Janice now live in a tiny little house in the middle of Sherborne, Dorset. We see them sometimes when we visit my sister, who lives just outside the town. I think what Peter misses most is space. All his life he was on a farm, first in Malawi and then in Zimbabwe, where his days would be spent outside under the African sun. Now he lives in cramped circumstances in a small English town. Peter and Janice's son John was an expert at lifting landmines in the Rhodesian bush war – that is until he lifted one only to find another one underneath. He was lucky to escape with his life, but lost most of the fingers on one hand and is still virtually blind. A highly intelligent person, John qualified as a lecturer and taught at the University of the Witwatersrand in Johannesburg before the lure of the land brought him back to Zimbabwe. He joined Peter on the farm just outside Marondera. His reward for doing that was to be evicted together with Peter and Janice. He was left homeless and jobless. Undaunted, he applied for and got the job of headmaster at the local agriculture-based school, Watershed College, teaching an all black student body. Here he did a fantastic job for a number of years; he has now moved on to be headmaster of the prestigious Peterhouse Girls' School.

Roy MacIlwaine, another golfing mate and third generation Zimbabwean, hung on to the family farm, 'Larkhill', for as long as possible, feeling that he owed this much to his grandfather – the redoubtable 'Major Mac' – who had originally built up the farm from virgin Africa in the 1920s. As for most of us, this was a vain attempt, and with virtually no money Roy tried first England and then New Zealand, where he is now a janitor at a school – hardly a worthwhile job for a farmer of Roy's experience. Roy's mother, Pat (née Wyrley-Birch) is also there and still teaching riding while aged well over eighty.

Our old friends Mickey and Myrtle Buswell, whom we helped when local ZANU.(PF) thugs gave them a few hours to get out of their home and off their farm, also ended up in a small town in New Zealand, but have both recently died.

We go to Australia occasionally to see Jack and his family, so often see old farming friends who have thrown in their lot with that great country. Near neighbours of Jack's are Jeremy Brown and his wife Coleen and three daughters. Jeremy is the eldest son of a very large (in all respects!) farming family, who used to own huge tracts of land north of Harare. They produced vast quantities of tobacco, maize, soya beans and coffee, as well as beef. When the land-grab started, Jeremy tried to co-operate and assist one of the more influential local thugs in a kind of partnership arrangement, but, as in many other such cases, he was taken for a ride and lost everything. Leaving the country in disgust, he got a job in a tractor garage in Gympie, Queensland, and is still there. He has recently saved enough money to buy a smallholding just outside the town and is trying to establish a new home for his now grown-up family. We saw him the other day and walked round the whole property in about twenty minutes – a far cry from the thousands of productive acres that Jeremy used to run. The only livestock on the property were five polo ponies. Jeremy, once a six-goal international player in Zimbabwe, still has his priorities right and is a stalwart of the local polo club. Zimbabweans do not easily give up their sport! While this is his new home, he does not rule out going back to Zimbabwe and getting involved in some sort of farming venture again. Jeremy is still very bitter.

His uncle, George Watson, also lives near Gympie. George and his wife Shauna used to be big farmers near Banket, some sixty miles north-west of Harare. Like most tobacco farmers, he employed a large labour force and spent his days in the lands supervising their work. Today George, who is over seventy, drives a tractor himself and cuts the grass on the side of the roads in the Mary Valley while Shauna and son Angus run a small photographic shop in the town.

By far the biggest wheat producers in Zimbabwe used to be the Nicolle brothers – Clive, Vernon and Piers – assisted latterly by a selection of offspring. It used to be said that every loaf of bread one ate in Zim contained some grain in it produced by the Nicolles. I can believe it! As you approached Chinhoyi on the main road from Harare to Zambia and all places north, you could, in the winter months, look to your right and see a vast sea of green flourishing under sprays of water pumped from that wonderful underground supply of water – the aquaflow. In the distance you would also notice some huge grain silos, built by the Nicolles, standing ready to receive the October harvest of the wheat crop. Today that amazing expanse of fertile red soil produces a reasonable crop of weeds and the silos stand empty, while international aid agencies pay to import the wheat that is made into bread for today's Zimbabweans to eat.

I knew Clive the best of this family, as he was long time president of the Zimbabwe Polo Association and a frequent rival on the polo field. Nikki and I had lunch with him and his wife Liz in Mapleton, Queensland, the other day. We were guests of an old Kenyan friend, Dennis Bower, who used to beat me at squash in our school days. Clive is also quite bitter and vows never to set foot in Zimbabwe again. His vast family empire is now completely disbanded and the farms owned (but not lived on) by High Court judges, high-ranking army officers and cabinet ministers. Not one cent has been paid to any Nicolle despite the millions of US dollars invested in the improvements of the land over a couple of generations.

Two of Clive's sons, Philip and 'J.C.' are also in Australia, while Patrick is in New Zealand. Clive appears to be a bit better off than some ex-Zim farmers and lives quite comfortably in Maleny, busying himself assisting his sons, who also seem to be doing OK, but on nothing like the scale of the Zimbabwe enterprise.

Ross Milne married Mike and Di Bartlett's daughter Clare and used to farm just down the road from us in Wedza. Ross was a third generation Zimbabwean and one of the most progressive farmers in our area, producing seed tobacco as well as tobacco, maize, oranges and a fine herd of Sussex cattle. When he was finally chucked off his very productive farm he just wanted to get out of the country. With his export crops and the farm better developed than some, he had managed to get a bit of money out of the country, so he decided to go to Australia. The money he had was not sufficient to guarantee him entry to that country and he had to rely largely on Clare's nursing qualifications to be accepted. They rented a nice house in a Sydney suburb, Clare went to work in the local hospital and Ross invested his savings in a small business with fellow ex-Zimbabwean cousins.

Zimbabwe is a comparatively small country and most whites in the farming community knew, or knew of, each other to a greater or lesser degree. This developed a huge degree of trust amongst the farmers and a lot of deals were concluded by verbal agreement with nothing signed. I am not for one moment suggesting that people in Australia are any more dishonest than in other countries, but it is a much bigger society and very competitive, so some Zimbabweans entering business there could be a trifle naïve. Ross was a farmer through and through and did not make it in Sydney business circles. He now has a job on a farm north of Perth where his considerable skills will be put to better use. Clare has been back to Zim once but Ross vows not to and his farming skills are lost to the country forever.

My one time brother-in-law and great friend, Richard Holme, was a very successful tobacco farmer in the Headlands area. He saw the writing on the wall quite early, leased his farm and went to England, where he gives computer lessons and does house-sitting for people who want their property looked after while away. His wife Gay is quality manager in a bakery in their village, and the world is short of a few million more cigarettes from Zimbabwe; his farm, as recorded earlier, has been taken over by a thug who lives in Mutare and only comes to the farm to chop the timber down.

Quite apart from the number of excellent farmers who were forced off their farms, there were also large numbers of farmers' sons studying at agricultural colleges overseas in preparation for returning to Zimbabwe. They intended to return to Zimbabwe and get some farming experience before taking over their parents' farms. My own youngest son, Jack, is a case in point. He was at Gatton College – the agricultural wing of the University of Queensland – and would certainly have returned to farm in Zim if the theft of white-owned farms had not occurred. When he was due to come back he did not need my advice to stay where he was. Still only thirty, he won a Nuffield scholarship in 2006, owns a fruit farm in Queensland and runs a couple of other export-oriented businesses. Zimbabwe can ill afford to lose such entrepreneurial talent as his. I doubt that Jack will ever return to live here, but there are many other sons of farmers who would love to return and certainly will not while the current régime is in power.

Richard and Gay's three sons have all left after being to university or agricultural college with the intention of farming in Zimbabwe. Nicholas is in Scotland, Edward was in the British Army and now is an international investment advisor, and Ant is in South Africa working for an international wine company. The two daughters are married and in Australia. Kate Holme married an Englishman, Nick Robinson, and they are in Sydney, where he is a currency broker, his company moving money around the world at a considerably cheaper rate than the banks; Zimbabwe is unlikely to see them. Pel, married to David and Mary Lilford's son, Atherton, lives in NSW where her engineer husband, who should be taking over the family farm near Guruve, builds dams for Australians, while David remarried after Mary's death and grows custard apples nearby. He and his new wife Sarah have no assistance on their fruit farm and do all the work themselves. Australians reading this will say, 'So what's the big deal?' The answer is, 'None'. But if you have lived all your life supervising labour on a big scale, it is not that easy, at the age of over sixty, to do the job yourself. I think it is fair to say that most ex-Zimbabwean farmers in this situation have made a point of proving to themselves and others that they are perfectly capable of doing so.

My godson, David Seager, who has just finished studying at the University of Queensland, would, under normal circumstances, be coming home now to where most of his family still live, but I very much doubt he will. Australia's gain will be Zimbabwe's loss. John and Judy Travers's son Bruce is still in Perth, Australia. He would love to come home and help on 'Imire Game Farm', but John continues to receive threats and attempts to evict his family from the only farm still run by whites in the Wedza area. The three MacIlwaine boys – James, Henry and Richard – are all in England, whereas they should be taking over their great-grandfather's farm, 'Larkhill'. Nick Arnold, whose father farmed at Macheke, runs a security company in Dubai.

I have, of course, mentioned only a fraction of the farmers who have left Zimbabwe. The ones I have mentioned are all friends. Some might return if things get a lot better – most won't. The brief pen-pictures that I have painted give a fair idea of the diverse countries, jobs and situations that they have landed up in. Some are doing well, some are struggling, some are happy, some a bit sad, some would like to return, some will avoid the place like the plague, but if there is one thing all have in common it is this. None are moaning. They know that what they once had can never be the same again. They were privileged to have enjoyed what Zimbabwe once was and are now busy making the best of a new life.

We still have a lot of friends here. They tend to be rather old, but then we are rather old too. Most are pretty much reconciled to sitting it out here now and just hoping that justice will eventually prevail. There are still a few people drifting away, but then again one hears of the odd person coming back. It is all a gamble, as is life in general.